THE
Republican
Right
SINCE 1945

David W. Reinhard

THE UNIVERSITY PRESS OF KENTUCKY

Coypright© 1983 by The University Press of Kentucky

Scholarly publisher for the Commonwealth,
serving Bellarmine College, Berea College, Centre
College of Kentucky, Eastern Kentucky University,
The Filson Club, Georgetown College, Kentucky
Historical Society, Kentucky State University,
Morehead State University, Murray State University,
Northern Kentucky University, Transylvania University,
University of Kentucky, University of Louisville,
and Western Kentucky University.

Editorial and Sales Offices: Lexington, Kentucky 40506-0024

Library of Congress Cataloging in Publication Data

Reinhard, David W., 1952-
    The Republican Right since 1945.

    Bibliography: p.
    Includes index.
    1. Republican Party (U.S.)   2. Conservatism—United
States—History—20th century.   3. United States—Politics
and government—1945-   .   I. Title.
JK2356.R28   1983   324.2734   82-40460
ISBN 0-8131-1484-5

Contents

For Mom and Dad

Preface

The Republican Right. Few terms in American political history have conjured up more meanings, more emotions, and more myths than this one. But more historical understanding is needed, now that a Right Wing Republican currently presides in the White House over perhaps the most important restructuring of American society since the New Deal.

This is not to imply that contemporaries failed to analyze or sought to ignore the Republican Right. How could they? In much of the post–New Deal period, hard-line Republicans commanded the Republican party in Congress, often enhancing their power by working with conservative southern Democrats. Also, GOP conservatives drew attention by bucking the trends of the era, and political observers constantly speculated about their motives—benighted obscurantism? ideological or constitutional scruples? economic self- or class-interest? As for historians, much has been written on certain aspects of the Republican Right—"McCarthyism," foreign policy, and the presidential campaigns of 1948 and 1952—and there are several excellent biographies on Right Wing leaders during the period. But an adequate, full-scale treatment of the Republican Right in the post–World War II era has been conspicuously missing. This book attempts to fill that gap in American political history.

The major focus of this work is the period from 1945 through 1965. These twenty years represent a natural and tidy period. The year 1945 was crucial for all Americans. Roosevelt had died and World War II had come to an end. But for Right Wing Republicans that year was especially important. Republican conservatives now faced a national and international world wrought by Roosevelt, but without the intimidating presence of that popular figure. By 1965 Right Wing Republicans had confronted this post-Roosevelt world, the foreign policy demand of fighting the Cold War against the Soviet Union, as well as Eisenhower's "Modern Republicanism." And, finally, they had nominated their own GOP standard-bearer.

Beginning in 1945, the present work investigates the general doctrine of the Republican Right, and the Republican Right's successful and unsuccessful response to major post–World War II domestic and foreign policy issues. It attempts to show how GOP conservatives controlled important party posts and how during the various political battles within the party, such as the nomination struggles of 1948, 1952, and 1964, they tried to retain the old-line conservative faith. It also examines the Right Wing response to Eisenhower's "Modern Republican" administrations, as well as such related subjects as the postwar conservative intellectual movement and the emergence of the Radical Right.

If the current political scene in Washington underscores the importance of an historical understanding of the Republican Right, the existence of many valuable manuscript collections provides the basic material for this first portion of the study. The Robert Taft Papers at the Library of Congress are only the most important of the available collections. The Hoover Papers and related holdings at the Herbert Hoover Presidential Library in West Branch, Iowa, as well as manuscript collections at the Dwight D. Eisenhower Library in Abilene, Kansas, also contain much of value. Besides some rich personal collections, the Olin Library at Cornell University houses the records of the Republican party for part of the period. The papers of important Right Wing figures are found at the Chicago Historical Society, and sections of the Everett Dirksen papers at the Dirksen Center in Pekin, Illinois, were open. These are but a few of the more than thirty-five collections examined during the course of the study. Material found in these collections helped confirm, contradict, and otherwise enhance the accounts and viewpoints found in memoirs, oral history interviews, newspapers, periodicals, government documents, and, of course, works of historical scholarship.

The final two chapters cover the period from 1965 to the inauguration of Ronald Reagan. They differ in content and tone from the preceding ten chapters, which make up the bulk of the book. Although these earlier chapters hardly cover ancient history and may be considered current events by many historians, the contemporary nature of post-1965 America required a slightly different approach. In the last two chapters, therefore, the coverage is less detailed and there is virtually no use of personal papers, which are unavailable for obvious reasons. Moreover, time and perspective are needed to put the events of this most recent period into clearer focus.

Despite the hazards involved in writing contemporary history, it seemed important to bring the history of the Republican Right Wing forward to the beginning of 1981. First, there was the altogether natural desire—a desire I hoped the reader would share—to "complete" the chronological story. Furthermore, the historiographical limitations, though admittedly significant, were not paralyzing. Finally, even if the implications of many post-1965 events remain unclear, these developments can still be considered in the context of the more fully treated period from 1945 through 1965.

Thus, this present work is hardly a definitive treatment of conservative

Republicanism in the thirty-five years after World War II; not all issues are examined, not all questions answered. It is a necessarily selective, old-fashioned political narrative that seeks to explain larger social, economic, and political forces and trends by examining the ideas and activities of some of the major political actors.

A study of almost any movement presents the problem of definition. Who is included? Who is excluded? And why? These problems are compounded when one is examining the world of American politicians. Of course, certain common positions, outlooks, or dispositions characterized the Republican Right Wing throughout the post–World War II period and will become obvious during the course of this book. Generally, conservative Republicans stood in arch opposition to the domestic, foreign, and political changes wrought by Franklin Roosevelt and later the Great Society of Lyndon Johnson. They opposed a strong chief executive like FDR and a powerful federal government that overregulated business and meddled in the affairs of state and local governments. They supported only limited government intervention in America's capitalistic economy. Federal budgets should be kept low (and in balance), along with federal taxes. In foreign affairs, Right Wing Republicans generally favored a strong American defense that relied heavily on air and sea power, and a foreign policy that allowed the United States to "go it alone" in pursuit of its own national interest. Fierce anticommunism was also a hallmark of conservative Republicanism, and this influenced their foreign and domestic programs. Right Wing Republicans consistently argued that the Republican party had to offer a real choice to Democratic domestic liberalism and internationalism.

Yet other Republicans, and indeed other Americans (Democrats included), embraced many of these same conservative positions in the twenty years after World War II. The "Radical Right" of the early 1960s, for example, shared many of these outlooks, yet these ultras are not properly considered Right Wing Republicans, despite the fact that many probably gave their support to Right Wing Republican candidates. In the late 1970s and early 1980s, much the same could be said of the "New Right." Distinctions between American political parties and among party factions or even groups outside political parties are often merely matters of degree or differences of temperament, tone, rhetoric, or style. It is the Radical Right's all-encompassing conspiratorial view of American politics that places it apart from Right Wing Republicans, who may themselves entertain limited conspiratorial notions. Nevertheless, these differences—however subtle they may seem—can be crucial, as this work will demonstrate.

Another difficulty in tracing the history of one element of an American political party is that neither American political parties nor their factions are bastions of ideology. This study examines practical politicians going about their business of trying to get elected and trying to represent their constituencies. In this political world, they represent different regions and interest groups—important factors which serve to waylay anyone hoping to find an orderly movement in American politics. American politics is, at base, local politics, and mainly pragmatic politics. The special needs of local voters, assessments of personality and electability, and subtleties of disposition and style are often far more important than a politician's stand on particular issues, let alone his philosophy. This fact will be demonstrated time and again throughout the course of this study.

How then to define and delimit the Republican Right? There is no tidy way. In this case, reality scrutinized tends to become more confusing than reality unscrutinized. The task is made more confusing by the fact that over the postwar period, Right Wing Republicans, and even other Republicans, were constantly reading certain Republicans in and out of the Republican Right. Despite these difficulties, the present study works from rather broad definitions and contemporary designations. If certain Republicans considered themselves at this time to be Right Wing Republicans, or were considered Right Wing Republicans by other Republicans or national political observers, then Right Wing Republicans they remain, while the confusions of image, record, and categorization are straightened out in the course of the present work. Along this same line, many contemporary terms for Right Wing Republicans are used interchangeably. Some of these tags—Old Guard, Diehards, Hardshells, and others—may seem to be terms of denigration. This is not intended. Such "loaded" phrases are employed chiefly because they had real, though perhaps imprecise, contemporary meaning, and because they also convey much of the feeling and color of a particular period.

In the end, any attempt to give adequate definition to the Republican Right holds all of the lessons of the story of the six blind men who rendered six different descriptions of the same elephant. Trying to comprehend one portion of the Republican elephant as it lumbers over roughly thirty-five years of American history is all the more difficult. But such a task is insurmountable only for those who seek a nutshell understanding of such a complex intraparty political movement as the Republican Right Wing.

Perhaps the most illuminating and certainly the most rewarding find in the course of such a project is the large number of individuals who offered their expertise, their time, and their encouragement. In the course of my writing my doctoral dissertation at the Pennsylvania State University, the people in Pattee Library's Inter-Library Loan Office and the Microforms Room met my many requests with efficiency and good cheer. The staff of the Liberal Arts Data Laboratory answered all kinds of anguished cries for help. I am especially grateful to the College of the Liberal Arts for its Sparks Dissertation Fellowship. The Penn State Department of History has provided aid and comfort throughout my graduate studies, first through graduate assistantships and then through teaching fellowships and its Hill Dissertation Fellowship.

On the road, I was constantly amazed by the willingness of librarians and curators to explain manuscript collections and to lighten the load of the wayworn scholar. James J. Kiepper, editor of the Styles Bridges collection, James J. Kenneally, professor of history at Stonehill College, Edward J. Boone, Jr., acting director of the Douglas MacArthur Memorial Library, and Gary Arnold of the Ohio Historical Society all deserve special thanks. The staffs of the Library of Congress, the Department of Manuscripts and University Archives at Cornell University, the Lilly Library at Indiana University, the Kansas State Historical Society, the William Penn Memorial Museum and Archives, as well as the presidential libraries of Dwight D. Eisenhower and Herbert Hoover also made my research that much easier by their unceasing efforts and kindnesses. Archie Motley of the Chicago Historical Society and Frank Mackaman of the Dirksen Center and their staffs cheerfully contributed everything from guidance through their manuscript collections to a ride to the airport. I thank all these professionals and the many others too numerous to mention.

I am also grateful to the members of my doctoral committee, Gerald Eggert, Charles Ameringer, and Philip Young, for their helpful suggestions and comments in overseeing the dissertation that led to this work. The inadequacy of such acknowledgments becomes painfully obvious in trying to thank my thesis advisor, Robert K. Murray, who, in giving this book the benefit of his keen editorial eye, has given me a lifelong model of a scholar, a writer, and a teacher.

Most happily, I wish to acknowledge the selfless labors of the person most responsible for the completion of this book—my wife, Susan.

1

If Roosevelt Lives
Forever

"Hell," rumbled Kenneth S. Wherry, Senate Republican whip, "the way things are going now it'll take a national catastrophe, revolution or great depression or something before we get Roosevelt out, if he lives."[1]

It was mid-November, 1944, and the Republican party had just lost another election to Franklin Delano Roosevelt. He had defeated four consecutive Republican contenders, and the Grand Old Party had not controlled Congress since 1930. FDR's 1944 showing—25.6 million popular votes (432 electoral votes) against the 22 million (99 electoral votes) for Thomas E. Dewey—surprised even "Mr. Republican," Senator Robert A. Taft of Ohio.[2] In the Senate, the Republicans had gained one seat overall, but three of their veterans had lost. In addition, the Democrats had added over twenty seats in the House of Representatives, giving them a 242-to-190 vote command over the GOP. Also, there were five new Democratic governors as of 1944. With results like these, Kenneth Wherry was probably just the man to consult on the Republican plight; his Senate colleagues, recalling Wherry's prior occupation, had dubbed him "the Merry Mortician."

Definitely dead was the Republican political world that existed before the first election of Franklin Delano Roosevelt in 1932—except for Right Wing or Old Guard Republicans. That pre-Roosevelt day remained alive as an ideal, as a foundation for the Right's continued opposition to liberal Democratic policies and politics, as well as for any statement of Republican first principles. Right Wing Republicans simply rejected the "Roosevelt Revolution"—rejected its economic and diplomatic changes and rejected its political challenge.

Beyond question, however, was the reality that Franklin Roosevelt and his New Deal had altered the course of American society since his inauguration on March 4, 1933. Gone were the remnants of laissez faire philosophy as the federal government attempted to shape the economic affairs of the nation in unprecedented ways. Businessmen, farmers, workers, and the unemployed all had come to count on the government for something—aid or regulation or both. Although New Dealers—especially Roosevelt—had prided themselves on their realism and pragmatism in attempting to handle the problems of the Great Depression, Right Wing Republicans such as Noah Mason of Illinois claimed that the New Deal was a "brand of socialism." His House colleague Wat Arnold of Missouri went further: "It is difficult to distinguish between the New Deal and Communism."[3] Right-wing columnist Westbrook Pegler saw no such order at work. "Actually the New Deal is not a reform but a debauch," he said.[4] In GOP conservative eyes, the New Deal was a disaster that had given the United States "the most extravagant government . . . on the face of the globe."[5]

By 1945 Franklin Roosevelt represented the Right's major institutional enemy—the strong chief executive. The presidency and the entire executive branch had mushroomed in size during the 1930s and 1940s, becoming synonymous with New Deal reforms and later the bureaucratic wartime intrusions. The new agencies of the executive branch, often mandated by Congress, now frequently made policy—hitherto a congressional prerogative, thus destroying many fundamental safeguards through bureaucratic regulations, decrees, and directives served up, said one Right Wing Republican, by a "bunch of professors, theorists, nitwits and nincompoops." Basically, the eradication of the New Deal was still the primary Old Guard hope in 1945. "True a sudden and complete repeal of the New Deal legislation would subject the country to violent shock," conservative Representative Clare Hoffman of Michigan admitted, "but it would . . . not be fatal and a recovery would be comparatively quick and more important complete."[6]

In contrast to New Deal "socialism," Republican Right Wingers offered in 1945 "Americanism," a term that later made it easier for Republicans to use "unAmerican" to malign their political foes. This was not the first use of "Americanism" in America's political battles. In 1920 Pennsylvania Old Guardsman Boies Penrose had declared Americanism to be one of the main issues in that year's presidential campaign. When asked to explain its meaning, Penrose replied, "Damned if I know, but you will find it a damned good issue to get votes in an election." If, in 1945, Americanism was less vote-worthy than in Penrose's day, it was at least more clearly definable.[7]

In opposing the New Deal, the Republican Right used "Americanism" to mean a strict construction of the Constitution, fiscal sobriety, and local control rather than federal regulation. Conservative Republicans staunchly defended local rule and business from encroachments by Washington. The Republican Right was most vociferous in resisting New Deal economic policies. Although the Old Guard normally squawked at the mention of government regulation, pure laissez faire was seldom advocated. For conservatives, government was not the issue, *big* government was. It was a menace to liberty and brought the United States that much closer to socialism. "Liberty" meant the opportunity to freely pursue one's economic welfare, and a federal government that overregulated and overtaxed could quash the individual's incentive to improve his material well-being and jeopardize the pioneer virtues of individualism and self-reliance. All Republicans, of course, espoused fiscal conservatism, but for the Right it was dogma. The Republican Right Wing scorned Keynesian economics. Limited government spending and low taxes—these were the bases of real prosperity, a prosperity assured by a balanced budget. As conservative Nebraska congressman Howard Buffett intoned in May, 1945, "A balanced budget is the all-American goal, and the future of American depends on it."[8]

The Republican Right was no less set against the sweeping changes in American foreign policy under Franklin Roosevelt. Although in his first term Roosevelt generally followed existing public attitudes, he moved away in his second term from one of the prevailing foreign policy ideas of the American people and the Republican party: isolationism. From the time of his quarantine speech in 1937 to the undeclared naval war with Germany in the fall of 1941, FDR labored to involve the United States more deeply in world affairs, particularly in the European conflict. Inevitably, the Japanese bombers that hit Pearl Harbor in late 1941 propelled the United States into global war and left American isolationism gasping. Yet prewar isolationist assumptions persisted as new issues emerged—among them, the administration's culpability in the Pearl Harbor debacle and the troubling trends in American-Russian wartime relations. The Republican Right represented the primary source of such sentiment.

Republican Right foreign and domestic policy went hand in hand, with some observers even contending that the Right used foreign policy issues primarily to discredit Roosevelt and the domestic New Deal.[9] Indeed, the Republican Right believed that the New Deal's "destruction of free enterprise" had enfeebled America in its foreign dealings. Roosevelt's foreign and domestic policy had but one aim—collectivism. Moreover, heavy international commitments inevitably increased federal spending. Some Right Wing Republicans even suspected that traitors in the government encouraged foreign spending in order to bankrupt the United States and sap its military strength.

New international commitments also enhanced presidential power, and GOP conservatives naturally opposed this trend. Congress had a constitutional right to be consulted on foreign policy matters. Robert A. Taft constantly warned against "the unlimited delegation of discretion to the President in all foreign affairs."[10] In addition, FDR's style of diplomacy— personal and secretive—encouraged suspicion and hostility. Often criticized for a myopic view of foreign affairs that denied the relevance of events in Budapest or Istanbul, the Republican Right linked the conduct of foreign affairs with conditions at home.

"I'm no isolationist," conservative Republican Kenneth Wherry insisted in late 1946.[11] Clearly, astute GOP politicians wanted to avoid the isolationist tag after Pearl Harbor, a fact further evidenced by the many isolationists who joined the congressional majorities in support of a postwar world peace organization. Instead, "unilateralism" became the foreign policy of the Republican Right. It was, in Taft's words, "the policy of the free hand." Unilateralists shied away from alliances that committed the United States to any advance action. The United States must "go it alone" in its foreign dealings. Right Wing Republicans relied on air and naval power as the means to safeguard American independence. Unilateralism also meant economic self-sufficiency. "We must look out for our own economic interest," said Taft, "because no one will do so for us."[12] Such an attitude partly accounts for the orthodox Republican advocacy of protective tariffs and opposition to foreign aid.

Above all, there was the Republican Right's assumption of American omnipotence and moral superiority. Paradoxically, this fundamental belief fostered an inner struggle between strict noninterventionism and spread-eagle adventurism. For some, like Taft and Hoover, American might and an oceanic moat were sufficient to shield America's superior institutions. Meddling in the affairs of others, with expanded presidential powers and federal spending, would in the long run imperil "liberty at home." Taft himself feared a "garrison state."

Other Right Wing Republicans, however, championed the benefits of American action abroad. Senator Styles Bridges of New Hampshire had "no squeamishness about throwing our full weight at all times and everywhere on the side of freedom."[13] Nevertheless, the Republican Right urged international restraint more than adventurism in the first five years after World War II. This was a result not only of the isolationist legacy from the 1930s, but also the dominance of the Right by Taft, who lacked the "messianic impulse."[14] Yet even Taft flirted with a more militant foreign policy from time to time, thus reflecting the ambivalence of the Republican Right about foreign policy in the face of the Cold War and communist aggression in the late 1940s and 1950s.

The Roosevelt Revolution certainly brought down the whole political world of the Republican party. Republicans, first identified with the restoration of the Union and then with the post–Civil War "Full Dinner Pail" prosperity that lasted generally up to the Great Depression, had established themselves as the majority political party in the United States. Only two Democrats were elected president from 1860 to 1932, and their initial victories came when the Republican party was split. When intact, the GOP presented a formidable coalition of midwestern farmers, Negroes, urban workers, small businessmen, and corporate moguls.

But FDR and the Great Depression changed all that. Republican fortunes collapsed after 1932. Loss followed Republican loss. The Great Depression forced Herbert Hoover, the most promising of the GOP post–World War I presidents, out of the presidency in a landslide and also fixed the primary issue for the next generation: Republican culpability for the Great Depression. Franklin Roosevelt made constant capital out of it. Following 1932, Roosevelt had forged a new majority party in American politics. Consolidated by 1936, the Roosevelt coalition dominated American politics for the next generation. It had room for the Negro, who abandoned his Republican habits by 1936, and southern Bourbons, who maintained their Democratic allegiance. Roosevelt also tied the urban, ethnic machines to the Democratic party, while blue-collar labor, too, took a place under the Democratic tent. In addition, the New Deal embraced the farmer, who, although appreciative of its efforts to stabilize farm prices, was possibly the most unsure member of this coalition.

Composed of urbane intellectuals and blue-collar urbanites, hayseeds and slickers, bourbons and blacks, the Democratic party was an impossible coalition that FDR made possible. Of course, the Great Depression spurred Democratic unity, and international crises had helped hold the party together. But for many, Roosevelt *was* the Democratic party. "No other personality," admitted Westbrook Pegler (no FDR fan), "could have held together in one political household the standard, old-style Democrats of the deep South and the Communists of New York and Hollywood who constantly snarled horrendous insults, but yielded, in all showdowns to the Chief."[15]

Roosevelt was a master politician. He loved the game and played it well. FDR attended to political detail like a precinct captain, and on the hustings, in his floppy campaign hat, he was a seasoned and subtle performer. He had many moods and knew when to use them. "He's all the Barrymores rolled in one," remarked one reporter.[16] The radio airwaves supplied one of Roosevelt's most important stages; he grew up with radio and knew it required a different technique than the tub-thumper's harangue. At no time and under no circumstances could Republican opponents match his silver tone. "The Crooner," H.L. Mencken christened him. Initiated in March of 1933, FDR's fireside chats were master strokes of compassion, education, and propaganda. With his radio magic and his genius for timing and maneuver, Roosevelt bedeviled Republicans unmercifully.

Right Wing Republicans reserved a special hatred and respect for Franklin Roosevelt, who seemed to dominate American politics through the force of his personality. The depth of such sentiment manifested itself when conservatives talked of FDR as "*that* man." *Newsweek* columnist Ray Moley, who had himself broken bitterly with Roosevelt after his first term, once urged Republicans to stop spending so much time hating FDR. But GOP concentration on the Squire of Hyde Park was inevitable. A decade earlier, before the 1936 election, Roosevelt had told Moley, "There is one issue in this campaign. It's myself and people must be either for me or against me."[17] That situation never changed. As Taft grudgingly admitted in early April, "If Roosevelt lives forever, and gets re-elected, it might be hopeless. . . ."[18]

In the face of FDR's Democratic challenge, the Republican Right was determined to maintain the GOP faith. It rejected "patty-cake" politics. Republicans must oppose, not ape, the New Deal. In contrast to the liberal and moderate Republicans whose "me-too" positions blurred distinctions, the Republican Right wanted to offer fundamentally different approaches to domestic and international problems; the parties should have radical disagreements between them. Conservative Republicans correctly detected the political pitfalls of "me-too" Republicanism. Their ally in criticism of "Republican New Dealers" ironically was FDR, who constantly belittled moderate Republican claims that they could run New Deal programs better. For Republican Right Wingers, fair, efficient, and economical administration of the New Deal was intrinsically impossible. Such programs were unwise, unwanted, and unconstitutional, and politically unprofitable. As Daniel Reed, conservative Republican from upstate New York, saw it: "We cannot out-do the New Deal in a spending program of waste, extravagance and inflation."[19]

Paradoxically, the failure of GOP conservatives to nominate and the Republican party to elect a candidate after 1936 bolstered the Republican Right's political claims. Roosevelt's victories, conservatives contended, were largely personal victories, unrelated to program or philosophy. But Right Wing Republicans also held that GOP "kingmakers"—primarily from the East—had plotted over the years to persuade Republicans to name "me-too" standard-bearers who differed not at all from New Deal Democrats. This contention had real meaning for Right Wing Republicans, although it ignored the very significant non-"me-too" positions of Roosevelt's Republican presidential opponents. After unprecedented losses in the 1934 congressional elections, Republicans nominated Kansas governor Alfred Landon for president in 1936. Landon ran on a fairly liberal platform, and the voters again chose Roosevelt—overwhelmingly. Landon's failure to defend Hoover's record and his silence on constitutional issues irked the former president, who blamed these omissions for Landon's dismal showing. Landon, in turn, thought he knew what ailed the 1936 Republican campaign effort: "the appearance that the Old Guard (i.e. Hoover and his conservative backers) was still doing business at the same old stand."[20]

Despite substantial gains in the 1938 congressional elections, the Republican party was desperate by 1940 and fell prey to a savvy band of amateurs. On the sixth ballot of the 1940 GOP convention, Democratic renegade Wendell Willkie won the party's nomination before going on to lose to FDR by some five million votes. Although Willkie in 1940 ran ahead of Landon's 1936 showing, he encountered even greater hostility within the party in defeat. Willkie's lack of partisanship accounted for much of this hostility. Not only did he declare in his acceptance speech that "party lines are down," rattling Republicans who liked their politics orderly, but this former Democrat also snubbed local Republican politicos throughout the campaign. Willkie's post-convention organization was amateurish, chaotic, and ineffective—"a whore house on a Saturday night when the madam is out," claimed one Willkie aide.[21] Willkie further compounded his troubles after the election by trying to shepherd the GOP along more liberal, more internationalist lines. His *One World,* a best-seller in 1943, consolidated internal party isolationist resistance, and his inattention to political detail and local leaders reduced his weight within the party.

In 1944, Thomas E. Dewey, governor of New York since 1942, won the party's nomination but then lost to Roosevelt—the Republicans' fourth consecutive presidential defeat—as Taft and others muttered about the candidate's dawdling and about the Dewey team's predilection for "the New York viewpoint."[22] But Dewey's presidential bid impressed some. His team had begun much-needed work on the national organization. Dewey was young, and the electoral statistics had a bright side. He lost by a smaller plurality than any contender that year. Moreover, since 1924, no presidential loser had topped Dewey's 99 electoral votes. These figures, however, left one critic unmoved. "Mr. Dewey and his blueprinters had better forget about the smallest margin since 1916; it means nothing," Bernard DeVoto wrote in *Harper's* magazine. "The crucial question is whether or not the Old Guard is going to remain in power."[23]

The Republican Old Guard. The term itself had first appeared at the 1880 Republican convention when a group working for the renomination of former President U.S. Grant identified themselves by badges bearing the legend "The Old Guard." Over the years, "Old Guard" came to define regular or organization Republicans, primarily economic conservatives. The Old Guard, however much it differed from one era to the next, represented one of the critical factions in a perennial intraparty struggle.

The political and economic hard times of the 1930s obviously created many new party fissures. FDR and the challenge of the New Deal, the depleted GOP congressional ranks, and the party's repeated failures in presidential elections made united policy all the more important—and all the more difficult to achieve. Roosevelt's skilled use of divide-and-conquer tactics especially compounded GOP woes.

Indeed, so pressing was concern over GOP harmony by September, 1943, that a Republican Postwar Advisory Council met with limited success at Mackinac Island, Michigan. By the close of the Roosevelt reign, there were obviously many kinds of Republicans and many valid ways to dissect the Republican party, a condition that persisted during the years from 1945 to 1965.

The Republican party was neither as neatly nor as deeply divided as the Democratic party. The Democracy basically broke horizontally, North-South, over race and related issues like states' rights. Republican party divisions, on the other hand, were less visceral but far more complex, and any broad categories must give on specific issues. Local pressures naturally affected GOP ideological concerns, making intraparty barriers easily breached. "I doubt that any member of Congress, whatever his political philosophy in general, adheres rigidly to any mainstream of political thought," Ohio senator John Bricker once told historian Eric Goldman. Bricker also noted that his congressional colleagues would be hard pressed to describe their particular philosophy "without elaborate qualification."[24]

Yet a general kind of sorting, imprecise thought it was, was useful to Republicans themselves. Whether to designate or denigrate, terms like "Old Guard," "Conservative," "Right Wing," "Modern Republican," "Liberal Republican," "Taftite," and "Deweyite" had meaning. They helped fashion alliances and remained vital to any understanding of the battle within the Republican party between 1945 and 1965—and beyond. Generally in the 1945–1965 period, Republicans recognized themselves basically as either liberal, moderate, or conservative Republicans.

Liberal Republicans believed the party had to enter the twentieth century. Perhaps not in the same way as the Democratic party, but the GOP had to put forth programs offering the social services required by an urban, industrial people. For them, the activist state, responsible for social welfare programs, was no bogey. These progressive Republicans favored Republican legislative remedies for the ills of society. They believed that the GOP, as represented in Congress, was generally too negative. Liberal Republicans were also primarily internationalists and favored the basic approach of the Roosevelt administration in world affairs. Governors and congressmen with urban constituencies (mostly from the Northeast) filled this, the smallest of the Republican factions.

Unlike Republican liberals, the moderates wanted to check increased activity by the federal government. GOP moderates accepted, rather than approved of, New Deal innovations. They wanted no wrecking of New Deal contributions like the Tennessee Valley Authority (TVA) or Social Security; their constituents would not like that. But the moderates did favor reduced appropriations for New Deal welfare programs, coupled with lower taxes, a balanced budget, and more efficient administration. Sometimes called "garden variety" Republicans, these moderates were partisans, who, although unready to assault the New Deal structure, pounced on Democratic soft spots—communists in government, high taxes, crippling government regulations, corruption, and so on. Republican moderates readily supported internationalist foreign policy but were quicker than their liberal brethren to exploit Democratic blunders. Moderate Republicans constituted the largest and most important GOP group and held the balance of power within the party. They were also the most sensitive meters of public opinion.

The willingness of liberal and moderate Republicans to go along with New Deal-like policies made them "me-too" Republicans, according to their conservative kin. Conservative Republicans—loosely dubbed "the Republican Right"—chose few of their many other names: Rock-Ribbed Republicans, the Dinosaur wing, Mossbacks, Hardshells, Standpatters, Neanderthals, and, until the young conservative influx of the early 1960s, the famed Old Guard.

If one heeded professional political pundits, however, the Old Guard was a cold corpse indeed by 1945. During the Roosevelt era, the Old Guard had often been left for dead. The 1936 convention, wrote Irvin S. Cobb at that time, was the "quiet interment for the Old Guard." After election day, political sages could agree on one thing, as *Newsweek* noted: "the Old· Guard brand of Republicanism was dead." Republican triumphs in 1938 were judged a repudiation of the Old Guard, and the Willkie and Dewey nominations were hardly considered Old Guard victories. Still, GOP conservatism was alive in 1945—commanding the party in Congress and dominating national and state party machinery. Even the hostile remarks of Bernard DeVoto in January, 1945, attested to Old Guard durability: The Republican party "can choose the Old Guard and die or choose someone else and live, but it must choose soon. The sun is well past midafternoon and winter days are short."[25]

For the Old Guard, Congress remained the primary key to its continued survival. As Harrison Spangler wrote, "In our successful days, the policies and philosophies of the Party were evolved by and through the Republican members of Congress . . . that is the only practical way they can be worked out."[26] Policy worked out there, of course, would bear the Old Guard impress, and in 1945 Robert Taft was seeing to it that congressional Republicans set policy.

After his 1944 defeat, New York's Governor Dewey had pressed for the announcement of a specific Republican legislative program, inviting GOP congressional leaders to New York to talk about it. The Republican congressional command worried that such a program might spur Democratic unity and Republican disunity, as well. Besides, with the war in Europe winding down, the times were too unsteady to set a legislative agenda with authority, and any Republican program would also require Democratic backing—a dubious prospect. More important, a program fashioned by the defeated standard-bearer would mean the surrender of power by congressional Republican leaders—leaders who were suspicious of Dewey's liberalism anyway and proud of their own orthodoxy. In the end, they convinced the New York governor of the dangers of a specific legislative program.

By April, however, Taft was attempting to fashion some policy statement "so the country may know where we stand." Dewey would have no part in this effort. Taft's labors came to a successful end in early December, 1945, when House and Senate Republicans issued "a statement of aims and purposes." After gaining Republican National Committee (RNC) approval, this statement was intended to serve as a blueprint for the 1946 campaign.

Although the input came mainly from conservatives, the statement was no conservative manifesto. Rather, it supplied balm for all factions and banality for its readers. The statement pledged Republican support for the United Nations and other international assistance, provided American self-interest was protected. The Republicans also eschewed partisanship, "secrecy, inefficiency and drift" in American foreign policy. On the domestic front, they assailed radicalism, regimentation, bureaucracy, deficit spending, and machine politics. Equality of opportunity and economy in government got unsurprising endorsements in the Capitol Hill document. The Republicans also declared their support for collective bargaining that recognized reason, fairness, and the rights of the general public. Most significant for the upcoming campaign were the words "Wartime limitations, restrictions and controls must be removed." Hardly a war whoop, the declaration was, Taft even admitted, "satisfactory, though not inspiring."[27]

But the bland Capitol Hll document dissatisfied some hard-line Republicans from the Middle and Far West who threatened to fight for the inclusion of greater blasts against radicalism and labor. At the opening of the RNC meeting in Chicago, Illinois governor Dwight Green expressed their resentment: "Our party has failed nationally chiefly because it has not been true to the faith that is in us."[28] Nevertheless, a day later the RNC approved the congressional principles, but not without a concession to party hardliners. At the urging of Illinois committeeman Werner P. Schroeder, national Chairman Herbert Brownell created a seven-man committee to revise the statement as events dictated. The RNC then unanimously endorsed the Taft-sponsored congressional statement.

While the liberal *Nation* bewailed Old Guard dominance at Chicago, the *Chicago Tribune* thought the congressional statement "wishwashy" and advised the Republicans to unearth some "fresh platitudes."[29] Despite the *Tribune*'s displeasure, Republican solons had wisely pussyfooted on the statement of principles. The postwar scene was too unsettled, party unity too important for the victory-starved Republicans. Caution was good politics. Besides, the Old Guard still retained control in party councils and had yielded only slightly to preserve party harmony. And with the creation of the seven-man subcommittee, even more determined hard-liners were given a voice in the future statement. (Four months later, the National Committee accepted this subcommittee's update—a peppery catalogue of Democratic failings.) Moreover, noneastern influence was acknowledged not only in the conference's handiwork but outside the official proceedings, as well. Taft's and Bricker's names, for example, were on many tongues at Chicago as possible 1948 presidential candidates.

The various sectional, ideological, and personal strains within the GOP became evident again when Herbert Brownell—a Dewey campaign holdover—indicated in early 1946 that he would resign as national chairman in April in order to devote more time to his law practice and his family. With a Democrat in the White House, the party chairmanship—a control post of the national party machinery—was especially prized, and news of Brownell's departure naturally sparked talk of his successor. Tending to view the conflict in the context of 1948 presidential politics, pundits and politicos both watched developments with interest.

By mid-March, Taft was lobbying openly for Representative B. Carroll Reece of Tennessee. Reece's rival in the Dewey camp was John A. Danaher of Connecticut. Like Brown and Reece, he also had Capitol Hill ties. A former senator and now a congressional aide for the RNC, Danaher shared Reece's approach to foreign and domestic questions—an indication that at the moment differences between the Dewey and Taft camps were slight.

But, when the RNC finally met in Washington on April 1, Reece became the new national chairman on a third ballot. After his selection was made unanimous, Danaher rose and offered to help Reece—a gesture that initially underscored the amicable tone of the gathering. At this time divisions between moderates and conservatives were neither deep nor acrimonious. The two main contenders agreed on much; their differences were sectional, not political or philosophical. Besides, Reece had won with both conservative and moderate support.

In April, 1946, B. Carroll Reece was no household word. But Reece was well known in the halls of Congress and the hills of northeastern Tennessee. Lawyer, teacher, banker, and World War I hero, Reece had come to Congress at age thirty-one on the Harding coattails in 1920. And, except in 1930, Reece had won reelection ever since. In the House, he had made a staunchly conservative record in domestic affairs and a "noninterventionistic" one in the foreign field. Yet only Reece's record was staunch; a soft-spoken affability marked all his dealings in Congress.

Although news-hungry reporters naturally highlighted an exceedingly mild anti-Reece remark by unofficial presidential candidate Harold Stassen, the selection of Reece actually pleased the majority of Republicans. Dewey quickly pledged his support to Reece, and Taft immediately proclaimed the new chairman "very satisfactory." Colonel Robert R. McCormick's *Chicago Tribune* hailed the choice both as "a victory for real Republicans and a distinct setback for the Me-Too Republicans."[30] Some other papers saw in Reece's selection a win for the Old Guard, or "the champions of reaction," as the *Philadelphia Record* expressed it.[31] But Taft himself placed Reece's election in a clearer perspective: "It is really a victory for the Republicans in the House of Representatives, who felt very strongly that the campaign this fall should be conducted with a single thought to the election of a Republican House of Representatives."[32]

On April 12, 1945, the Republican Right lost a *bête noire* and gained an opportunity. In Warm Springs, Georgia, Roosevelt died, and an era closed. Vice-President Harry S. Truman became president, leaving the future of American liberalism, as historian Alonzo Hamby has written, in "a fog of uncertainty."[33] A goodwill visit by the Republican Steering Committee signaled, many believed, a new day in executive-congressional relations. "I am hopeful," Indiana's Capehart wrote Herbert Hoover, "that things may be some better under President Truman."[34]

Truman was a man of the Senate, and this encouraged hope. After the aristocratic Roosevelt, Truman's homely way appealed to the Congress and prompted early GOP goodwill. Before becoming vice-president, Truman had been a solid if inconspicuous second-term senator from Missouri. Besides conducting an unsplashy investigation of waste and corruption in the defense effort, Senator Truman had consistently voted for the New Deal. But his loyalty was to party, not ideology, and he remained friends with anti–New Deal Democrats.[35] By temperament and geographical base, the senator from Missouri was the ideal border-state Democrat, a fact that had made him Roosevelt's runningmate in 1944. A bespectacled, natty little man, Truman was popular in the Senate, but he could be intensely combative under fire. Taft admitted he was a "straightforward frank man," who had "a quality of decision which is a good thing in an executive." However, Taft also noted that Truman's decisiveness was often only "impulsiveness."[36]

Truman inherited all sorts of problems at home and abroad. In Europe, the final assault on Hitler's Germany had begun, and many new issues sprouted on the battlefield. Control of eastern Europe and growing tensions between the United States and the Soviet Union became major concerns. The San Francisco conference, which officially launched the United Nations, also became a showcase for the breakup of the wartime Grand Alliance and convinced Americans that the Soviets were to blame for most postwar difficulties.

Even as Germany was caving in and European postwar problems were emerging, Allied men and materiel were being shifted to the Pacific. Allied planners anticipated that it would take a year, perhaps longer, and a million

American casualties to crush Japan. The atomic bomb, of course, overwhelmed these plans. The blasting of Hiroshima and Nagasaki abbreviated the conflict, and by August 14, World War II was suddenly over. In the revelry that erupted, America's postwar Asian problems were temporarily obscured, especially the hope of making China a great pro-Western power. As the war ended, the Communists of Mao Tse-tung and the Nationalists of Chiang Kai-shek were preparing to resume their civil war.

But it was domestic matters that first absorbed war-weary Americans—jobs, homes, and meat on the table. The war's abrupt end added to the usual problems of demobilization. Jobs were an important matter, as the army disgorged 200,000–300,000 men a month. Yet prices not jobs, inflation not depression, proved to be the first major postwar issue. The economy quickly absorbed postwar job-seekers. Meanwhile, prices soared as the economy retooled and people began to spend their wartime savings. There were shortages and black markets. Truman's State of the Union message calling for price controls to continue for another year refueled a battle that had raged since the end of the European war in May. Business wanted to strike these wartime "shackles from American business."

Led by Taft, the Congress passed a price control bill that hobbled the Office of Price Administration (OPA) and its pricing structure. On June 25, 1946, with a blast at Congress, Truman vetoed the bill. Without any controls, prices suddenly skyrocketed. In July, 1946, the index of retail prices jumped twenty points, only ten points lower than it had risen during the entire war. In August, Congress attempted to end the frenzy with a short-term price control bill freighted with restrictions, which Truman reluctantly accepted. The index, however, climbed another twenty points by year's end.

When take-home pay failed to keep pace, trouble on the labor front inevitably ensued. Labor chieftains planned to recoup these losses as well as win raises denied during the war. The first major postwar strike occurred with the United Auto Workers struck General Motors in November, 1945. Strikes in steel, coal, and transportation followed, as 1946 became a year of labor unrest with strikes in the coal fields triggering brownouts, shortening work weeks, and causing factory closings. In the spring of 1946, stalled railroad talks so exasperated President Truman that he asked Congress for authority to draft striking railworkers. The Senate refused. When the coal miners struck, Truman seized the mines.

Although strikers often won new wage increases, the labor movement in general suffered as antilabor sentiment grew. Drastic pay demands, jurisdictional strikes, and news of communist-infiltrated unions helped shape popular beliefs on labor. United Mine Workers president John L. Lewis, pompous and arrogant, personified a labor movement that, in many eyes, had grown disdainful of the commonweal. In 1946 Congress responded through the Case bill, an attempt to remedy the imbalance in labor-capital relations by revising the National Labor Relations Act of 1935. A Truman veto killed the bill.

As the first postwar congressional elections of 1946 approached, it was clear that Truman intended to continue FDR's New Deal policies. Taft and other Republicans could only hope that Truman lacked Roosevelt's appeal.[37] At the moment, Truman and his party were scapegoats for foreign policy reverses, the high price of steak, and the misdeeds of John L. Lewis. Moreover, many issues divided the Democrats. Southerners realized shortly after Truman took over that while he downed their bourbon, his policies were pro-urban and pro-North. Liberal Democrats likewise had great doubts about Truman. He was certainly no Roosevelt. Entering the presidency, Truman had capitalized on his simplicity and his commonness. By November, 1946, however, the GOP was preparing to capitalize on the growing popular view that Harry was too simple and too common. Taft's wife, Martha, concluded, "To Err is Truman," and this pun made the political rounds. "If Truman wanted to elect a Republican Congress," Taft wrote to Dewey in the fall of 1946, "he could not be doing a better job."[38]

Arrogant labor bosses, government meddling in the economy, Democratic "cronyism," and foreign policy worries and blunders—all these were tailor-made Republican issues, particularly Right Wing Republican issues. And Democrats could no longer count on the political magic of Franklin D. Roosevelt. But the GOP was asking voters to do something they had not done for sixteen years: return a Republican majority to Congress. Writing in early 1946, Alf Landon correctly gauged the importance of the upcoming congressional election: "If the Republicans don't win the National House this year, they might as well go out of business."[39]

2

A Titanic
Ballot-Box Uprising

"What a glorious victory for the freedom loving citizens of this Republic!" crowed Daniel Reed. His fellow representative Howard Buffett of Nebraska called the returns "a titanic ballot-box uprising." *US News,* in turn, said the 1946 elections represented "a new cycle in American political history." The *Chicago Tribune* was absolutely giddy, calling the outcome "the greatest victory for the Republic since Appomattox."[1]

The Republicans had at last recaptured Congress. In the Senate, the Republicans gained twelve seats, for a 51-to-45-vote majority. In the House, they held a 242-to-188 command. The GOP carried twenty-eight of thirty-six states outside of the Solid South. Moreover, certain GOP presidential prospects won big, thus bolstering the notion that the 1946 congressional elections were only a harbinger of 1948.

The defeat of important New Dealers by conservative Republicans was added cause for revelry. In the spring of 1946, *Time* and its "political dopesters" had named the Pennsylvania Senate contest "a key race." And after election day, the Pennsylvania race did tell the story of the 1946 elections. Ardent New Dealer and state Democratic boss Joseph Guffey fell to Edward Martin. Despite a liberal record as governor of the Keystone State, Martin himself often bragged of his ties to Old Guard boss Boies Penrose and Andrew Mellon, secretary of the treasury during the 1920s; his future votes were therefore being counted on as "uncompromisingly conservative."[2]

Other avowed right-wingers came to Capitol Hill in the "Class of 1946." Delaware cashiered James M. Tunnell, a New Deal loyalist, and returned John J. Williams, a political tyro who ran against government controls. Montana sent its first Republican to the Senate in thirty-three years, electing Zales Ecton over left-wing Leif Erickson. Campaigning against New Deal bureaucracy and Pendergastism, James P. Kem crushed Frank P. Briggs, the Missouri Democrat who had filled Truman's seat since 1945. There were other winners who would later play important roles on the Republican Right. Conservative-isolationist Representative Henry C. Dworshak became Idaho's senator. In Nevada, George W. "Molly" Malone won a Senate seat by assailing the OPA. And Joseph R. McCarthy of Wisconsin hustled his way into the Senate, first edging out progressive incumbent Robert M. La Follette, Jr., in the GOP primary and then winning easily in the fall with the slogan "Congress Needs a Tail Gunner."

William Jenner of Indiana and William F. Knowland of California, both elected in 1946, also later became important figures in the Republican Right. Like others, Jenner, who had been appointed to a partial term in 1944, attacked the economics of the Roosevelt and Truman administrations. Amid shortages, jungles of bureaucracy, and high prices, Jenner had cried out on behalf of "the forgotten man." In 1945 Knowland of California had been appointed to that body by Governor Earl Warren to complete the term of the deceased Hiram Johnson. Now, Knowland walloped the popular Will Rogers, Jr., for election in his own right.

Of immediate interest, however, was the election of Ohio's Governor John W. Bricker to the Senate. Tall and handsome with premature gray hair, Bricker was an effective speaker with a melodic voice. Bricker had already served four consecutive two-year terms as Ohio governor. In 1944, with Taft's support, Bricker campaigned for the GOP presidential nomination and had to settle for the second spot on the ticket, but Bricker's claim to 60 percent of the vote in the 1946 Buckeye Senate race heightened speculation on a renewed presidential bid. Still, Bricker had his critics. Some feared his good looks and winning ways obscured an exceptionally shallow mind. William Allen White of the *Emporia Gazette* had concluded, "Bricker is an honest Harding. Thumbs down."[3] In another significant return on election day 1946, Bricker's former ticketmate, Thomas Dewey, won reelection as governor of New York by more than the half-million-vote plurality pundits had said he needed to stake a presidential claim for 1948.

Before the election, Democratic congressional boss Sam Rayburn had groaned, "This is going to be a damn beefsteak election."[4] Indeed, many Republicans of the so-called "Meatshortage Congress" ascribed their GOP victories in 1946 to resentment over the price of steak. Of course, more than meat was involved; labor problems, housing shortages, building restrictions—all the problems of reconversion—contributed to Republican victory. The candidates themselves found the major issues to be communism, the activities of labor political action committees (PACs), foreign affairs, and economy in government. "People are fed up with the bureaucratic, corrupt, conniving, Communist cabal of controls," one GOP winner flatly concluded. "The Republican ticket," he quickly added, "apparently gave assurances of trading horsemeat for horse sense."[5] A young California Republican by the name of Richard M. Nixon won a House seat in 1946 with an antilabor campaign, handing out plastic thimbles labeled "Elect Nixon and Needle the P.A.C."

"Had Enough?" the Republican slogan had asked, and apparently the voters had. But enough of what? What kind of mandate, in brief, did the GOP win? Were the voters only vexed by the headaches of postwar reconversion and the failures of Harry Truman? Or was there a more profound unhappiness with the reforms of the New Deal? Robert Taft returned to Washington convinced that beefsteak was, for the voters, only a symbol of faulty past Democratic policies. Republican winners, after months on the hustings, naturally saw in the returns an endorsement of their standard stump speeches. Among those political experts who rejected their elated musings was pollster Louis H. Bean. Warning that congressional elections seldom mandate anything, Bean found no evidence that people had voted against the social, economic, and international programs of the New Deal but instead attributed Republican victory to the rising cost of living and a small voter turnout—the upshot of apathy or discontent with Truman's reconversion policies.[6] Sharing Bean's concern that the Republicans might misread the November returns and mindful of Republican negativism during the New Deal, *Life* magazine warned, "they may be tempted to launch an orgy of mere de-controlling, repealing—a saturnalia of *sauve que peut*. If they so interpret their mandate they will regret it."[7]

But these were heady days for Republicans, and they were unfazed by such warnings. National Chairman Reece boasted that Republicans would liquidate 90 percent of the federal bureaucracy—a move that would, some scribes joked, disrupt the care and feeding of congressmen. Harold Knutsen, chairman-to-be of the House Ways and Means Committee, declared he was going to slash income taxes 20 percent for 1947. He also promised to balance the budget and trim the national debt. Ohio's Clarence Brown prophesied, "We will open with a prayer and close with a probe." Indeed, probes of almost every aspect of New Deal foreign and domestic affairs were anticipated. "Given a Republican Congress," a delighted Westbrook Pegler exclaimed, "the Pentagon Building may yet be put to good use as a prison to house the grafters and other miscreants of the long debauch. It will be a tight fit at that."[8]

On election night 1946, as Republican Joseph Martin sat in the office of his *Evening Chronicle* in North Attleboro, Massachusetts, his political career was about to take a new turn. His own reelection had been constant since he had first gone to congress in 1924, but after his 1946 victory he was slated to be Speaker of the House.

Martin had commanded House Republicans since 1938, gagging them in those early days, letting Democrats scrap among themselves, and delivering Republican votes to kill New Deal bills. A former Republican National Committee Chairman and always a possible compromise presidential candidate, Martin was so prominent that FDR had included him in his famous "Martin, Barton and Fish" litany. It was admitted that Martin would bring no flashy parliamentary skills to the Speaker's post. But he had close ties with southern Democrats and usually could count on a party discipline achieved at no cost to his casual good nature.

The post of majority leader was not so open and shut. There were several claimants. "Hell, I am the next majority leader," Charles A. Halleck had boasted in mid-November—a typical brisk and blunt Halleck remark.[9] But this fourteen-year Indiana representative had reason for confidence, since reportedly he was Martin's pick for the job. Moreover, as recent chairman of the Republican Congressional Campaign Committee, Halleck had signed campaign checks and talked to most new members.

But Halleck's election became entangled in 1948 presidential politics. Clarence Brown, Taft's floor manager in the 1940 GOP convention and Bricker's campaign manager in 1944, was also running for the majority post. Brown was popular in the House and had secured his reputation as an able strategist when he directed the RNC's election campaign. But Brown's ties to Taft and Bricker hurt him. Some House members were reluctant, given Taft's power in the Senate, to place the House also under Buckeye command. If Brown's Taft and Bricker connections put the majority leader's race in the presidential context, so did Dewey's subsequent endorsement of Halleck.

Actually, little save their backers divided Halleck and Brown; these two personal friends both opposed FDR's policies. But with Dewey behind Halleck and Taft behind Brown, the contest was naturally seen as a rehearsal for 1948. When House Republicans caucused in early January, the Taft-Brown forces, apparently realizing their weaknesses, finally let Halleck become majority leader. Yet Dewey's meddling had irked many GOP representatives. Halleck's designation was probably more of a defeat for Taft forces in the House than a clear-cut Dewey victory.

Conservative Republicans filled most of the major House chairmanships. Reforms had not yet gutted the seniority system; Republicans who had piled up seniority during the long Republican drought were usually from safe, rural districts that had consistently elected opponents of FDR's New Deal and foreign policy. Harold Knutsen, who was in line to chair the Ways and Means Committee, possessed an isolationism so deep that before Pearl Harbor he had commended Hitler's "forebearance" and had claimed that he could not see "much difference between Germany's action in Norway and the New Deal program in this country."[10] John "Meat Axe" Taber, whose thunderings against a wages and hours bill in 1940 had allegedly restored the hearing of a hitherto deaf colleague, became the self-styled "watchdog of the Treasury" as chairman of the Appropriations Committee. Jesse Wolcott, a Michigan conservative with a knack for finances and debate, took over the Banking and Currency Committee, and conservative J. Parnell Thomas of New Jersey was in charge of the House Un-American Activities Committee. The House Foreign Affairs Committee, however, was headed by Charles Eaton, a liberal internationalist. Nonetheless, Right Wing Republicans clearly controlled the House.

In the Senate the story was similar. The Old Guard dominated the high command. Taft, of course, had great power in the Senate, but he ruled through compromise and maneuver. He had his opponents—and from widely divergent elements of the party. Conservative Kenneth Wherry and liberal Wayne Morse, for example, had each said that Taft would be unacceptable as Senate majority leader, and there was talk of a "fight to the bitter end." Taft probably could have won any such skirmish, but there were good reasons to avoid it. Taft's real power in the Senate was secure anyway, and the responsibility of floor leadership would shackle him as 1948 approached. Ultimately elected as GOP Senate floor leader was Wallace H. White of Maine, an elderly New Englander who was a moderate internationalist and who planned to retire at the end of the Eightieth Congress. Since he readily deferred to Taft, the Ohioan in reality was the majority leader, and White never had any illusions about this. One wag suggested easing GOP signal-calling by placing a rearview mirror on White's desk twelve rows in front of Taft's.[11]

Taft could well afford to let White exercise nominal control, since Mr. Republican headed the important Steering or Policy Committee, where he earlier consolidated his hold on Senate Republicans, injecting them with discipline and direction. The committee met weekly and was largely composed of orthodox Republicans. Those who held other important posts added to the Right Wing tilt. Chief among them was Kenneth Wherry. In 1946 no one to Taft's right had more clout than Wherry—blunt, tough, and rambunctious. Even some of Taft's moves drew Wherry's thunder, and this sometimes posed problems for both Taft and the Republican Right. Wherry's days as progressive Senator George Norris's "errand boy" were far behind him. A staunch conservative—or, as he called it, "fundamentalist"—Republican, the former errand boy succeeded in unhorsing Norris in 1942. Wherry, an old carnival barker, was always a talker, and when he left for the Senate, his father counseled, "Ken, remember to keep your big mouth shut." Ken ignored his father's advice with such wayward intensity that over the years he peppered Senate debate with numerous "Wherryisms": verbal misfirings like "Indigo China," "the issue is clear and indistinct to me," and that Truman was "sugar-coating his red ink."[12] In spite of these malapropisms, "Lightnin' Ken" rose quickly among Senate Republicans, and the "beefsteak" election of 1946 made him majority whip.

Except for the Foreign Relations Committee, which Arthur Vandenberg of Michigan guided along internationalist paths, major Senate committee chairmanships were squarely in Old Guard hands after 1946. Styles Bridges of New Hampshire presided over the Appropriations Committee; Wayland Brooks of Illinois handled the Rules Committee; and South Dakota's Chan Gurney was at Military Affairs. By right of seniority, Taft was expected to head the Finance Committee. But Eugene Millikin of Colorado, "who looked and voted like an austere banker" and had impressed Taft, was rewarded with the Finance chairmanship. Taft, in turn, took over the Committee on Education and Labor, a hot spot, over the protests of George Aiken of Vermont, a scrappy liberal Republican who was in line for the chairmanship of Education and Labor.

Truman had said little while watching the Democrats lose Congress. But several days later, he indicated the elections had impressed him. On November 9, 1946, the president ended all wage, salary, and price controls except those on sugar, rice, and rents. Sounding like the Chamber of Commerce in citing the "market place" and the "law of supply and demand," Truman admitted price controls had lost popular favor. Then, on December 31, 1946, the president proclaimed the end of the "period of hostilities." With that, eighteen emergency powers instantly died, and thirty-three other emergency statutes would lapse in six months, among them emergency taxes and the Smith-Connally War Disputes Act. Truman's declaration also deprived Republicans of an issue in the Eightieth Congress. Republicans hailed Truman's actions but promised their own scrapping of special war powers.

There were plenty of other GOP issues. Budget and tax-cutting had a special political appeal for Republicans and allowed an indirect attack on the New Deal. During the campaign, Taber pledged to brandish a "sledgehammer" and knock $9 billion from the budget; on election night Knutsen repeated his campaign boast of lopping 20 percent off income taxes across the board. Under the new Reorganization Act of 1946, the Republican Congress did deal with the budget quickly. On January 10, 1947, Truman proposed his budget for fiscal 1948—expenditures of $37.5 billion. What Truman called "a tight budget," Republicans called "a cold shock." Although Taber was unable to remove his $9 billion, the Joint Committee on the Economy voted for a $6 billion cut over the protests of Taft and other Senate Republicans, who favored cuts of only $4.5 billion. Taft believed it a "tremendous mistake" for Republicans "to quibble" over the total reduction, the lower figure being "just as good" for political purposes.[13]

In the end Bridges and Wherry supported the Economy committee's figure, but Vandenburg, White, and Millikin backed Taft. Taft won, the Senate voting, 51 to 31, in favor of the lower Taft figure. Opposition to Taft, however, cropped up in another quarter. William F. Knowland of California wanted $3 billion earmarked for payment on the national debt. Obviously, this tactic would delay a tax cut, a Taft priority. Taft agreed to $1 billion for mandatory payment, then finally fell back to a $2 billion figure. But Knowland held firm, and Taft lost—the Senate ticketing $2.6 billion for debt payment. Ironically, after this Senate squabbling, the House ratified the joint committee's preferred figures, and when the House-Senate conference deadlocked, Congress adjourned without a legislative budget. As a result, budget reduction came through cuts in individual appropriations bills, usually with the Senate tempering the more slash-happy House.

The tax-cutting problem proved barely more solvable as Republicans again suffered from their own differences. Knutsen, chairman of the House Ways and Means committee, had already indicated on election night that he favored a 20-percent slash in taxes. Although other Republicans—Taft, for instance—agreed that total relief should be about 20 percent, they felt that such a severe horizontal cut on all taxes was too drastic. In this matter, the ardor of GOP representatives clearly outstripped that of GOP senators and, in the first month of the Eightieth Congress, an interbranch-intraparty confrontation loomed. Finally, Speaker Martin decided to intervene in this "spectacle." The Republican goal was still 20 percent, explained Martin, but GOP tax bill writers had to consider other goals like payment on the national debt and a balanced budget.

Ultimately, Knutsen's Ways and Means committee produced H.R. 1. It was not all that Knutsen had promised on election night, but it did provide for tax cuts ranging from 30 percent for the lower income brackets to 10.5 percent at the top levels. After making some revisions that gave further tax relief to lower income taxpayers, the Senate passed the House measure. The House members of the conference committee basically accepted these Senate changes on June 1, 1947. Two weeks later, calling the bill inflationary and "neither fair nor equitable," Truman vetoed it. The House failed to override. Just a month later, another Republican tax cut bill suffered a similar fate as the Senate failed by five votes to override a Truman veto.

During the second session, a tax cut was finally achieved. Presidential election-year realities prompted additional Democratic and Republican support. Furthermore, Republicans revised their tax bills in 1948, and this helped Democrats buck their president and back the proposed cuts. The new Republican bill cut tax rates to levels just below those of the 1947 proposals. It also included a number of general exemptions as well as income-splitting provisions for couples. The House approved the bill, 297 to 120. In the end, all Senate Republicans along with thirty Democrats backed the bill, which had been further revised. Truman then vetoed it, railing against its unsound economics and inequities. But this time both houses held firm and thus fulfilled a GOP campaign pledge. Still, it was a limited victory. Republicans had to pay for Democratic support by sponsoring a diluted tax bill.

Another thorny issue that appeared in the early days of the Eightieth Congress was that of atomic energy control, and it involved an old target of conservative GOP opposition to the New Deal, David E. Lilienthal. Lilienthal had been director of the Tennessee Valley Authority (TVA), the most extensive of New Deal reform efforts. Tough, able, ambitious, and articulate, he typified the New Deal bureaucrat. Now Truman was naming him to another major post as chairman of the new Atomic Energy Commission. Lilienthal was automatically sure of one Senate foe, Democrat Kenneth McKellar of Tennessee. Before the Senate wing of the Joint Committee on Atomic Energy, McKellar, a nonmember but a "guest inquisitor," badgered Lilienthal for almost three weeks, contending the former TVA administrator followed the "Communist line."

From the beginning, Lilienthal's confirmation was in trouble—and not just because of McKellar. "Mr. Lilienthal is an extreme New Dealer," Styles Bridges exclaimed in early February. In claiming this, the New Hampshire senator was indicting, not describing Lilienthal. Bridges's objections, unlike the personal ones of McKellar, were purely political. Bridges judged the last election to represent a repudiation of Lilienthal and the New Deal philosophy. The New Hampshire senator would therefore oppose the nomination of Lilienthal, who Bridges claimed could "probably spend Government money . . . faster than almost any other man in the country."[14]

There were other opponents such as Kenneth Wherry and Oklahoma Republican senator E.H. Moore. A major blow to Lilienthal's chances came on February 22, when Taft joined the opposition. The Ohio senator placed the issue squarely in the context of the previous fall's election. "Mr. Lilienthal is a typical power-hungry bureaucrat," he explained, "one of the group of men who, in recent years, dominated the thinking of perhaps half of the Government departments and bureaus in the manner seen so clearly in the administration of the OPA."[15] While Taft based his opposition on "government philosophy," Senator Bricker said the main issue was Lilienthal's administrative incompetence.

Debate on the Lilienthal nomination began on March 10, 1947. With Bricker and Taft leading the opposition, a serious Republican rift appeared in the person of Senator Vandenberg. Secretary of State George Marshall had personally sought Vandenberg's help on the Lilienthal matter. Waiting until Lilienthal's enemies had spoken, Vandenberg rebutted them. In the end, his support clinched it for Lilienthal, as seventeen other Republicans joined Vandenberg to defeat a Bricker motion to recommit the nomination. But the entire Senate GOP leadership—Bridges, Taft, Wherry, and White—opposed Lilienthal's nomination. On April 9, when the Senate voted, 50 to 31, to confirm Lilienthal, Senate Republicans were badly divided on the issue. While a conservative like Millikin voted for Lilienthal, a liberal like Flanders stuck with Taft and Bridges. Generally, however, liberal Republicans voted for Lilienthal, and Right Wing Republicans opposed the "extreme New Dealer."

Clearly, the first days of the Eightieth Congress were troubled ones for the victorious Republicans. Difficult issues, poor coordination, and rivalries within the party plagued their efforts. Republicans in Congress clashed over fundamentals and the meaning of the election. The root of GOP woes was essentially political and remained so. Writing later, liberal Senator Raymond Baldwin of Connecticut, showing his own bias, claimed, "Everyone but die-hard Republicans will admit we started off very badly."[16]

George Aiken certainly agreed. By February, Aiken was chiding party chieftains for spoiling GOP prospects in 1948 with a "narrow and reactionary" GOP program.[17] Chairman Reece, meanwhile, tried to spur Republican unity. A Reece editorial in the party's *Republican News* of March coached congressmen on team play. "A successful team . . . executes the signals called by a duly chosen quarterback," said Reece. But Reece's coaching only brought about a locker room revolt. Wayne Morse immediately called Reece the "chore boy" of the Old Guard; Reece's plea for team play was only "a brazen demand for reactionary control of the Republican Party."[18]

The Gallup poll of early March touched off more GOP wrangling—and some conservatives now joined liberal complainers. The poll indicated that 51 percent of the electorate would now vote for a Democratic president and only 49 percent would vote Republican. Truman's popularity had jumped six points since November. Conservative Harlan Bushfield, senator from South Dakota, blamed the Republicans themselves. "We have failed in everything which we promised the voters," he said. What had the Republicans done on taxes, economy in government, and revising labor laws? "Practically nothing," Bushfield thundered.[19]

At the same time, Republican rookies in the Senate griped about the seniority system as well as party policy. Sheer size made the GOP "Class of '46" unusual. The sixteen new Republicans constituted one-third of the Senate's entire GOP contingent. According to Connecticut's liberal GOP Senator Ray Baldwin, Republican freshmen were unique in their "rich background and experience." Some—Bricker, Baldwin, and Martin, for instance—had been governors, and their energies and egos chafed under Senate strictures. Since the opening of Congress, these newcomers had lunched together on Thursdays. At these luncheons, GOP rookies, liberals and conservatives alike, blamed their party's early performance—whether they deemed it too conservative or too liberal—on the leadership's failure to use their talents. The Senate Republican command treated them like "little boys," one complained. Baldwin claimed that the result of relaxed seniority rules would be more liberal policies. Conservative Republican freshmen shared Baldwin's impatience with the status quo but favored policies of the opposite kind.[20]

Such discontent finally resulted in the presentation of a round-robin letter to Millikin, the chairman of the Republican conference. One thing the "Class of '46" demanded was more conferences. Millikin indicated he would be happy to oblige. Also, the new senators were offered two nonvoting, rotating seats on the Senate Republican Policy Committee. Further, Kem and Baldwin—a conservative and a liberal—were named to the House-Senate Policy Committee.

"Not even in the latter stages of the New Deal," the *Nation* wrote in late March, "were the Democrats battling each other as Republicans are today." "Had Enough?" the *Nation* asked tauntingly. Shortly after the 1946 election, Taft had warned liberal Senator Aiken about "New Deal writers" who would undoubtedly labor to sow dissension in Republican ranks. By March, 1947, however, writers—and not just New Deal writers— needed only to report, not concoct, GOP differences. "Rumblings," "Splits that Trouble G.O.P.," and "Republican Dividing Line" were headlines that told the story. *Newsweek* wondered if restlessness might turn to revolt, and *US News* explained that no single Republican had enough power to settle the question: "How conservative shall the Republican Party be?"[21]

No single Republican did have *full* control in the Senate. Taft had enough pwoer to command attention, but not enough to rule absolutely. On domestic issues he was vulnerable at this time, both on his left and right. Republican presidential rivalries doubtless fostered GOP division in the early Eightieth Congress. Yet some of the GOP problems were beyond the party's control. As Wallace White noted, this Republican Congress was the first to grapple with the reforms of the Congressional Reorganization Act of 1946. Also, Truman had sent up many nominations in the first months, and these took up much congressional time. Considering these factors, the *Saturday Evening Post* slapped at "lame-duck columnists" who disparaged the GOP congressional effort. "Nothing is perfect," it admonished, "but . . . the Republicans don't look so bad except to those who wish they weren't Republicans at all."[22] Fortunately for the Republicans, the conservative congressional leadership's concessions to the GOP freshmen group represented a "turning point," and indeed, after the spring of 1947, such unruliness never again surfaced in the Eightieth. Differences, however, continued. The Republicans were never a whole and happy family.

No domestic issue handled by the Republicans in the Eightieth Congress proved to be more controversial or catalytic with regard to future Republican fortunes than labor relations. Yet the 1947 Taft-Hartley Act, denounced variously by its opponents as a "nightmare" and a "slave labor law," was neither in plan nor practice an Old Guard Republican triumph.

Some kind of labor legislation was inevitable in the Eightieth Congress. For a decade there had been attempts to reform the Wagner Labor Relations Act of 1935, a New Deal mainstay. Postwar labor problems and the 1946 election had moved such legislation that much closer. Even Truman asked Congress for labor law reform. On the opening day of the Eightieth, solons placed seventeen labor bills in the legislative hopper; by mid-March, that number had grown to over sixty-five.

Fred A. Hartley, Jr., was an unlikely coauthor of a major piece of labor legislation. Until 1947 few knew of him outside the New Jersey district that had reelected him since 1928. Moreover, the American Federation of Labor (AFL) had even supported his reelection in 1940. When congressional conservatives removed unfavored liberal Republican Richard Welch from the chairmanship of the Labor Committee, Hartley was next in line.

Hartley's committee obviously knew the kind of bill it wanted, for it began writing it before the close of investigative hearings. As in tax and budget cutting, early House action with regard to labor reform was more drastic than the Senate's. The House bill contained several extreme provisions that were inserted, Hartley later claimed, to draw fire and make the Senate measure appear more reasonable and thereby veto-proof.[23] In any case, the House, after brief debate, approved the Hartley bill, 308 to 107, with twenty-two Republicans opposed.

Things were different in the Senate. There, the Taft-led Education and Labor Committee was dominated by Republicans, eight to five. But the makeup of the GOP group posed problems for Taft. To his left were two unruly Republicans—Morse and Aiken—and one Dewey loyalist, Irving Ives, a liberal Republican from New York. As for potential trouble on his right, Taft also had to move warily. Joseph Ball of Minnesota favored harsher measures than Taft and had twenty to thirty likeminded senators behind him. Finally, there was for Taft not only the reality of a slender GOP majority in the Senate, but the prospect of a Truman veto in the end.

One early Taft move to preclude a successful Truman veto was to present an omnibus labor bill, and not a series of labor reform bills. The bill that emerged was Taft's handiwork; he knew when to abandon severe restrictions and when to acquiesce in milder demands. For example, Taft had supported the right of employers and employees to seek injunctions in secondary boycotts and jurisdictional strikes, but when faced with committee opposition, he did not press the issue on the floor. When Joseph Ball persisted in doing so, Taft simply abandoned him as the Senate then passed a more moderate Taft substitute. Even in defeat, Taft always worked to enhance the chances of overriding an expected presidential veto. For instance, in committee Taft offered an amendment restricting industry-wide bargaining, which Ives and Morse opposed. On the Senate floor, when Ives barely mustered votes to beat Taft on this issue, Taft accepted defeat and congratulated Ives.[24] On May 13, 1947, the Senate finally passed the total Taft package, 68 to 24. Morse and William Langer of North Dakota, two Senate mavericks, and Nevada's conservative freshman, Senator Malone, were the only Republicans opposing.

Quickly and decisively, Congress accepted a House-Senate conference report that left out certain House provisions, such as a ban on industry-wide bargaining and subjection of unions to antitrust laws, but accepted House bans on strikes by government workers and campaign contributions by unions. Then, on June 20, the last possible day for such action, Truman vetoed the resultant Taft-Hartley bill. The House, 331 to 83, overrode the president's veto that same day. Three days later, Taft-Hartley became law when the Senate voted 68 to 25 to override. Mavericks Morse and Langer continued to be foes of the measure in the Senate. George Malone also voted against Taft-Hartley simply because he opposed all federal regulation of labor. This, he claimed, was the states' domain.

The Taft-Hartley Act outlawed certain unfair labor practices like jurisdictional strikes, secondary boycotts, and the refusal to bargain in good faith, and it banned the closed shop. A union shop, in which a worker had to join a union after a certain period on the job, was provided for, but states could prohibit compulsory membership in a union. These right-to-work laws, allowed under Taft-Hartley's section 14b, quickly became identified with conservative policies, and state right-to-work movements thereafter sprouted in various areas of the country. Also, Taft-Hartley required union leaders to sign noncommunist affidavits and unions to make yearly financial reports to the Labor Department and to their members. Perhaps the most important feature of the Taft-Hartley Act allowed the president to seek a court injunction for a cooling-off period in strikes threatening a national emergency.

"You have restored representative government to mastery in its own house," former President Hoover wrote to Taft after the successful passage of the Taft-Hartley Act.[25] Following this display of Taft political skill, Republicans on Capitol Hill talked with renewed enthusiasm about a Taft presidential bid. But many conservative Republicans and businessmen quickly found fault with Taft-Hartley, claiming that Taft had coddled the unions. Such complaints belied a knowledge of the political process in general and the realities of congressional power in 1947 in particular. Taft-Hartley had successfully revised a key tenet of the New Deal labor policy. It had also taken aim at one of the sources of New Deal political power: organized labor. Certainly it was the Republicans' most specific and important assault by the Eightieth Congress on the New Deal legacy. But as illustrated by the grumblings of numerous conservatives, it was hardly the Old Guard triumph that some liberal critics claimed. On the other hand, Taft's prudence and willingness to compromise—qualities essential to putting Taft-Hartley on the statute books—may have in the long run harmed Taft's bid for the GOP presidential nomination precisely because some Old Guardsmen saw Taft's maneuvering as cowardice and backsliding, not smart politics.

Taft-Hartley was not the only instance during the Eightieth Congress when Taft confounded some Right Wing Republicans. Although a conservative himself, Taft was a "rounded" conservative. Certainly his basic principles and preferences were conservative: fiscal restraint, a balanced budget, state over federal authority, and so on. But Taft was no ideologue, and this irked the most conservative Right Wing Republicans. Part of the problem was the way Taft's mind worked. He studied each problem and valued the facts more than his preconceived notions. With these facts, Taft then fashioned solutions that he hoped would complement his political principles. In explanation, Taft once wrote, "If the free enterprise system does not do its best to prevent hardship and poverty, it will find itself superseded by a less progressive system which does." [26]

Housing was one such example. The caustic slogan "Under Truman: Two Families in Every Garage" pointed up the postwar shortage of housing for families with low and moderate incomes. After thorough study, Taft had joined Allen Ellender of Louisiana and Robert F. Wagner of New York, the Senate's "Mr. New Deal," in late 1945 to sponsor housing reform. The Taft-Ellender-Wagner bill (T-E-W) provided federal support for middle- and low-income housing, slum clearance, and urban renewal. The cost of the public housing section of the measure over the next four years was a projected $90 million. For this reason, the head of the National Association of Real Estate Boards called Taft "a fellow traveller held captive by the bureaucracy which is running this government." "We will take Taft's presidential nomination away from him on this issue," he added. [27] The Senate finally passed T-E-W by voice vote in 1948. In the House, however, Jesse Wolcott, the conservative-dominated Rules Committee, and the House leadership combined successfully to kill T-E-W. This failure to promote major housing legislation was, historian Susan Hartmann has concluded, the Eightieth Congress's "most notable failure." [28]

The House also foiled Taft's federal aid to education initiatives. In 1948 Taft reintroduced a bill providing aid to poorer states for upgrading public education. It called for an outlay of about $300 million, as well as federal aid to parochial schools where states allowed it. Despite opposition from many quarters, the Senate finally approved Taft's proposal, 58 to 22, on April 1, 1948. Twenty-seven of the forty-four voting Republicans supported Taft. Although GOP conservatives like Albert Hawkes of New Jersey and James P. Kem of Missouri opposed Taft, numerous conservatives voted for federal school aid. There were some surprising foes, too. Raymond Baldwin and Henry Cabot Lodge, Jr., though liberals, had big Catholic constituencies, and they opposed Taft's measure. Nevertheless, after favorable Senate action, Taft's bill languished in the House Labor and Education Committee, never to come to a House vote during the Eightieth Congress.

Obviously, Taft's moves in housing and education vexed those conservatives who worshipped the "let the devil take the hindmost" philosophy, as Taft put it. Perhaps, if pressed, some of these conservatives might have grudgingly conceded, as did Taft, that the federal government had to "put a floor under the essential things to give a minimum standard of living and all children an opportunity to get a start in life."[29] But no other Right Wing Republican except Taft was willing to lead the way. And, given the prospect of additional taxes and an expanded bureaucracy to achieve such goals, few followed him.

But these housing and education initiatives made good conservative sense to the Ohio senator. "I believe in the principles of insurance to everyone unless he refuses to work," Taft had explained earlier in his career, "but it must be held within a reasonable cost, without setting up a vast Federal bureaucracy, without destroying local self-government, and without removing the incentive. . . ." Taft's biographer, James Patterson, has said that Taft was "consistent and seldom uninformed" in applying this philosophy. Taft believed that even if Congress lacked specific constitutional authority to spend money for general welfare, the practice was "well established" and would be ruled constitutional. Taft admitted that there was a "theoretical argument" against federal aid in matters of health, housing, and relief. But, he wrote, "I am quite sure that any party that took that position would have only a short tenure of office and the opposition party would soon enact the legislation anyway, in a much more extreme form."[30]

Many rock-ribbed conservatives, of course, did not agree with Taft's reasoning. The real estate lobbyist's tirade quoted earlier was to be expected, rooted as it was in special interest. But the criticism of Taft by some conservatives marked highs in political stupidity. For hard-liners on the right, Taft's mild housing and education proposals were already "extreme forms." These measures had a New Deal smack. John Taber claimed Taft had no popular touch and was "seeking to establish himself with the public by rackets" like T-E-W. Bricker reportedly offered a crisper explanation: "I hear the socialists have gotten to Bob Taft." Wherry also saw a "touch of socialism" in the senior Ohio senator.[31]

On March 18, 1947, Nebraska Congressman Howard Buffett told the House: "I am not happy talking about foreign affairs. I would prefer to leave that field to others."[32] Buffett spoke for many Right Wing Republicans who had isolationist roots and believed the real battle for America should be waged primarily on American shores against New Deal blueprinting, deficit spending, and the Roosevelt coalition. The advent of the Cold War, however, forced the Republican Right to confront foreign policy questions whether it really wanted to or not.

The lines of command in the Senate with regard to foreign policy clearly reflected the Republican Right's emerging role. Senator Vandenberg dominated foreign policy in the Senate, just as Senator Taft led in domestic affairs. This arrangement—tacit and informal—was natural. Taft's paramount interest was domestic policy. He showed talent here, but on foreign policy, said William S. White, he lacked a coherent view. Furthermore, Taft thought Congress could have little impact on foreign policy.[33] Besides, there was Vandenberg. Long on seniority, political know-how, and vanity, the Michigan senator had definite ideas about foreign policy and the desire to fight for them. The former isolationist's conversion to internationalism, coming as it did in a much-ballyhooed speech at the war's end, made Vandenberg's position that much more important. The Truman State Department realized this and openly courted him. For rising above party, Vandenberg was hailed a statesman, and as his power grew so did his reputation for selfless nonpartisanship.

Vandenberg used his power to advance the hazy concept of bipartisanship. Bipartisanship stressed interparty agreement on the essentials of American foreign policy and no retreat from international commitments. Bipartisanship related primarily to European affairs, Asia and Latin America largely remaining outside of it. As Vandenberg once put it, "Partisan politics stopped at the water's edge." Differences over foreign policy should not "root themselves in partisanship."[34] But even for well-wishers, bipartisanship posed problems. Where was the line between constructive criticism and partisan harping? And would not the harshest foreign policy critic always claim that his judgments looked to the national good and not to partisan gain?

Bipartisanship had many GOP foes. These Republicans flatly rejected bipartisanship: it menaced the national and Republican interest. Herbert Hoover privately fretted over "Republican crumb-eaters of the State Department."[35] Although Wherry spearheaded open opposition to Vandenberg's leadership, only Taft had the intellectual and oratorical wherewithal to bring off such a challenge, and he had no desire to do so.

The Taft-Vandenberg dyarchy was not without its stresses. From the outset of the Eightieth Congress, there were reports of trouble in this arrangement. Taft believed the duty of the Republican opposition was to oppose—in both domestic and foreign affairs. And Taft often found fault with the direction of American foreign policy. But a Taft-Vandenberg break never actually occurred, for both men worked hard for harmony. Taft kept busy with domestic legislation and once told columnist Dorothy Thompson that he did not wish "to promote a major battle among the Republicans of the Senate over foreign policy."[36] Further, Taft leaned heavily on southern Democratic support on domestic issues, and a sally against a foreign policy that most Bourbons favored might have proved costly on the home front. Hard-line conservative Republicans deplored such caution on the part of Taft and bluntly attacked him for it. Vandenberg, wrote *Chicago Tribune* publisher Robert McCormick, had long since sold out to the internationalists and "eastern bankers," and now Taft was doing so too.[37]

In foreign affairs, postwar Republicans faced a difficult situation. Relations between the United States and the Soviet Union had deteriorated rapidly at the end of the war. Total war had not brought total peace. In early March, 1946, Winston Churchill had spoken of an "Iron Curtain" across Europe, and by mid-1947 many spoke of the "Cold War." For Americans who eyed Soviet activity in Poland, Rumania, and Germany, there was supreme disappointment, followed by rancor. As Howard Buffett said, "Even yet it is hard to believe that 400,000 American boys died for the Atlantic Charter and that instead their sacrifice was used to expand communism over two continents."[38]

To stop communist expansion would obviously require American aid. The most immediate problem was Greece. A corrupt, reactionary, and unpopular monarchy, propped up by Britain, was under fire. A guerrilla element opposed the Athens regime, and that movement was dominated by communists who, Western diplomats erroneously assumed, took their orders from the Kremlin.

On February 21, 1947, the British minister in Washington told Secretary of State George C. Marshall that the British, financially strapped at home, were pulling out of Greece in thirty days. Though hardly unexpected, the news sparked a crisis in Washington. Greece's strategic position in the Mediterranean was crucial—a communist Greece might serve as a gateway to Soviet influence in Turkey, the Middle East, and perhaps western Europe.

The upshot of this assessment came on March 12, 1947, when Truman asked the Eightieth Congress for $400 million in military and economic aid for Greece and Turkey. Forewarned by Vandenberg to "scare hell" out of the American people, Truman painted the clash between communist totalitarianism and democracy in stark colors. He proclaimed that the new global mission of the United States was that it must "support free people who are resisting attempted subjugation by armed minorities or by outside pressures." This was the Truman Doctrine, which one historian has called "a form of shock therapy."[39]

Was the voltage high enough to galvanize cost-cutting, isolationist Republicans of the Eightieth into backing this new departure? Vandenberg had already promised his support. But Right Wing Republicans were another matter. In the previous major foreign policy test on Capitol Hill, Senate Republicans had voted overwhelmingly but unsuccessfully against a loan for Britain. In the present situation, Taft realized that the Congress must back the president, but the senator fretted over the Republican majority's loss of honor if it accepted "goods as packaged at the White House." Not so concerned were other conservative Republicans like John Taber. He remained convinced that we should "first put our own house in order before we attempt anything else."[40]

Opposition to Greek-Turkish aid made for strange bedfellows. Democratic liberals like Florida's Claude Pepper and Idaho's Glen Taylor joined Right Wing Republicans generally from the Midwest. These Republicans were as anticommunist as anyone, but they worried about the aid's impact on the domestic economy. American resources were limited, they contended, and huge outlays might require the reestablishment of wartime economic controls. Further, such political and economic commitments might suck America dry, leaving it prey, said Jenner, to a "bloodless Soviet takeover."[41] The Right, with its isolationist legacy, nevertheless remained puzzled over how to fight communism yet stay free of political and economic commitments. It had been easier at the war's end, when anticommunism had merely meant yanking back lend-lease or opposing a postwar loan to the Soviets. Now anticommunism required positive action.

Strangely, some of these conservative GOP guardians of American shores suddenly spoke as defenders of the United Nations. Kem of Missouri chided Truman's "fatal mistake" of ignoring the United Nations, and Clarence Brown called the Greek-Turkish aid bill a "dagger aimed at the very heart of the United Nations."[42] In view of some of their past remarks and actions, the conservatives' concern for the United Nations was ludicrous. Still, the criticism had potential punch, and Vandenberg, seeking to block the "neoisolationist line of retreat into the United Nations," offered an amendment allowing the U.N. General Assembly or Security Council, with the United States waiving its right to veto, to end the Greek-Turkish aid program.

Because it was crisis-bred and also represented a blow against communism, the Greek-Turkish aid request ultimately overwhelmed its foes. In the end, Taft, with no desire to "discredit" the president while Truman bargained with the Soviets, indicated he would vote for Greek-Turkish aid. The Senate passed it, 67 to 23, after relatively harmonious debate. Taft joined thirty-four other Republicans in support of the president. Sixteen diehard GOP senators voted against it.

There were also problems in the House. House GOP leaders had to intervene in order to get the Greek-Turkish aid bill out of the Right Wing–dominated Rules Committee and on to the floor. There, the leadership promised, the bill would be no test of party loyalty. As a result, on May

9, the Greek-Turkish aid bill won House approval by a vote of 287 to 107, with ninety-three Republicans on the losing end. Then, when the aid request reached the House Appropriations Committee, John Taber brandished pencil and paper and did what he called some "fifth grade arithmetic." The upstate New York banker's math was severe. He and the Appropriations Committee slashed $3 million off the appropriation. Taber had made his point. At a White House powwow, Taber agreed to restore all funds only after the administration promised not to spend the $3 million, but merely announce the sum for propaganda purposes.[43] In such fashion the Eightieth Congress approved aid to Greece and Turkey.

The larger problems of war-torn Europe still remained. The ravages of two wars had left the continent financially and spiritually bankrupt. Supplies of food and raw materials were low; the capital equipment of Europe was rundown; industry was stagnant. The severe winter of 1946–1947 compounded European economic and spiritual woes. Millions were jobless, and across the continent people starved. In this setting, Communist party ranks swelled; in Italy, a quarter of the electorate was Communist, and in France, the figure was one-third. If the Communists did not initiate strikes, they at least exploited them. This was their moment; civil disturbances and parliamentary disruptions were opening gambits to governmental control.

At Harvard's June commencement in 1947, Secretary of State George Marshall presented the administration's plan for the economic rehabilitation of Europe and prevention of further Communist exploitation. Marshall called on the nations of Europe—east and west, Communist and non-Communist—to prepare a plan for the economic recovery of all Europe. Marshall pledged American aid to this collective enterprise. Three weeks later, European leaders met in Paris to discuss Marshall's idea. The Russians quickly decided to withdraw, dragging the east Europeans with them.

What ailed Europe and what could be done? Conservative Republicans had their own prescriptions. Freshman Senator George Malone of Nevada had addressed Europe's troubles even before Marshall. At Malone's first GOP caucus, he explained: "All these sons-of-bitches need is a referee in bankruptcy."[44] In that kind of gathering such a remark raised few eyebrows. With the unveiling of the Marshall Plan, Republicans of more seniority also had something to say. Herbert Hoover feared the Marshall Plan was "an invitation to gang up on the United States." "Of course, we all want to do what we can, but we do not want to exhaust this country," concluded the former president in a letter to Taft. Complaining of the administration's lack of economic analysis and its propensity to give in to the "unreasonable demands" of the Europeans, Taft muttered to Hoover, "We always seem to be begging them to let us help them as if it were to our financial or economic advantage to do so."[45]

Such comments indicated that the European Recovery Program (ERP) would be a major issue on Capitol Hill. Another indication came in late 1947 when a special session of the Eightieth Congress took up the administration's request for interim aid—$597 million in stopgap funds for France, Italy, and Austria. The request passed, despite hefty midwestern GOP opposition and conservative bids to alter and cut the aid.

Truman, meanwhile, formally proposed the European Recovery Program. He asked Congress to appropriate $17 billion for its first four years. The call for a four-year commitment drew fire immediately, as Right Wing Republican resistance to the proposal mounted rapidly. Taft, who called the plan a "global WPA," worked quietly for the formation of an Anti-Marshall Plan Committee, or a committee to lobby for reduced ERP funds. Said Taft, "The State Department is smearing us with propaganda just the way it did on the British loan."[46]

As an unannounced presidential candidate, Taft had to be wary. Polls showed growing public support for the Marshall Plan idea. Moreover, key tallies indicated congressional Republicans were badly split over the matter. Whatever the Republicans did, Taft, as a presidential candidate, desired GOP harmony as 1948 approached.[47] Such unity seemed unlikely, when news leaked that a group of twenty GOP senators was meeting secretly at a downtown Washington hotel to discuss the Marshall Plan. The bulk of them were conservatives with isolationist credentials—Bricker, Brooks, Jenner, Capehart, Kem, and others. But a few—Knowland and Ball, for instance—were internationalists who basically favored the Marshall Plan. Taft himself stayed away from all this. If the group had any objective, it was to scale down Marshall Plan funds. As a result, the Washington hotel meetings produced no band of party insurgents, and the group merely chose a committee of five to take its thoughts to Vandenberg.

Little that was new appeared in the Right Wing critique of the Marshall Plan. Again, safeguarding the American economy was mentioned as being foremost—the drain on the United States would leave American institutions vulnerable. As Taft wrote, "I have found that the Secretary of State is always more anxious to give American money away than he is to preserve the economy of this country."[48] This "globaloney" would bring high prices, high taxes, and ultimately, Senator Kem predicted, dry up the middle class as a capital source. In addition to new taxes, there would have to be new controls and regimentation—"a police state at home," warned Wat Arnold, conservative congressman from Missouri.

But more than the American economy concerned the Republican Right. The continued debasement of the European economy was feared, too. Like Taft, Jenner branded the Marshall Plan a "boondoggling PWA," which, like its domestic kin, would prove no final solution. Their remarks illustrated the link between Right Wing international and domestic outlooks. So did their emphasis on self-sufficiency and initiative—equally as important for nations as for individuals. "They [the Europeans] are not doing their part," Taber complained. "They work four days a week in France and they are on strike a lot of the time."[49] If European nations failed to balance their budgets, reduce their expenses, and stabilize their currencies, they would continue to wallow, no matter how great the infusion of Yankee cash.

The possibility of European governments' taking the kind of action that would please most members of the Old Guard was slight. Their nationalized industries placed these governments even to the left of FDR's New Deal. This fact irritated. Noting the "strange paradox" of fighting Marxist communism while subsidizing Marxist socialism, Senator Kem later tried unsuccessfully to deny aid to nations that further nationalized their basic industries. (Taft had doubts about this intrusion in the inner workings of other nations.) Homer Capehart, meanwhile, offered a complete alternative to the Marshall Plan, which he thought was "socialistic on both the procurement and distribution end," since it involved government-to-government aid. Capehart proposed instead to raise the lending power of the Reconstruction Finance Corporation and create an international division that would assess foreign industries in need of aid and would then buy preferred stock in qualified foreign corporations. The beauty of the plan, Capehart believed, was that one nation's private enterprise would help another's. However, only twenty-two senators ultimately voted for the Capehart plan.

In the fall of 1947, Vandenberg worried most about possible trouble from Taft. But the primary concern of Taft and many of the other Right Wing Republicans was the "lavish distribution of dollars" envisioned in the Marshall Plan. How much would the Congress give the European Recovery Program? Vandenberg himself soon realized the importance of this issue and responded by pruning the administration's request of $6.8 billion for fifteen months down to $5.3 billion for twelve months. The Senate Foreign Relations Committee accepted Vandenberg's figures on February 13, but Right Wing Republicans wanted still greater cuts. Finally, as Vandenberg had feared, there was trouble with Taft. The Ohio senator, although basically sympathetic to the goals of the Marshall Plan, introduced along with Wherry a measure to cut the Foreign Relations Committee's figure to $4 billion for the first year.

If the GOP trimmers ever had the votes, they were surely gone after a coup drove Czechoslovakia behind the Iron Curtain in February, 1948. Herbert Hoover, for example, in an open letter to Speaker Martin, subsequently backed the full $5.3 billion authorization. Still, GOP conservatives in the Senate showed surprising strength in the March 12 showdown on the Taft-Wherry amendment. The Senate rejected this cut, 56 to 31, Republicans accounting for 23 negative votes—the maximum Senate opposition to foreign aid in the Eightieth Congress. Then the Senate, Taft included, approved the Marshall Plan with the original authorization of $5.3 billion. Ultimately, the House, too, passed the $5.3 billion dollar allotment by an overwhelming vote.

After the Marshall Plan became law, Taber's House Appropriations Committee again posed a problem. In recommending the enabling legislation for the plan's funding—almost a year after the Harvard address—the Appropriations Committee made cuts almost equal to those rejected by the Senate in March. A new battle between isolationists and internationalists loomed. On the House floor an attempt to shorten the agreed-upon time period from fifteen to twelve months—and thereby reestablish the original appropriation—failed as the House GOP leadership, unwilling to advertise party splits on the eve of the Republican convention, backed Taber's Appropriations Committee proposal.

Over in the Senate, Vandenberg reacted quickly. Permitted by chairman Styles Bridges to speak before the economy-minded Senate Appropriations Committee, Vandenberg persuaded it to maintain all the funds originally authorized, and the full Senate then ratified this action. Only ten senators opposed Vandenberg, who even got support from Taft and Wherry. If Taber and other Marshall aid House slashers had a strategy, it was the belief that the senators would finally yield and accept the House Appropriations Committee cuts in order to depart for the Philadelphia convention. Yet Taft, an earlier advocate of cuts, now declared he would hold Congress in session until it backed the original "moral commitment." Such opposition was too much for Taber. House conferees began to buckle, and finally Taber did too. On June 20 the House followed the Senate in keeping the original funding intact.

The Republicans went off to Philadelphia in June, 1948, and the Congress went down in history as the "Do-Nothing, Good-for-Nothing Eightieth." That was unfair, but then Truman, the chief name-caller, was scrambling for the presidency and was hardly a disinterested bystander.

The Eightieth Congress, in fact, accomplished much in foreign affairs. Among its other achievements, it extended the Reciprocal Trade Act, a mainstay of New Deal foreign policy, and it generally continued to practice bipartisanship. Foes of these actions consistently included Right Wing isolationist Republicans, but they offered no real threat. European troubles demanded action, and conservative GOP opponents offered almost nothing. Furthermore, Senator Vandenberg was at the peak of his power. Indeed, the passage of the Vandenberg Resolution, which cleared the way for later American participation in NATO, capped his mastery of foreign affairs in the Eightieth Congress. The Senate passed, 64 to 4, the Vandenberg Resolution just before the Republican convention in June, 1948, with its opponents generally avoiding debate and roll calls. Such surrenders led the *Chicago Tribune* to grumble: Republicans "no less than the New Dealers, are in the control of the Wall Street crowd and all the other economic interests which seek to turn the foreign policy of the United States to private profit."[50]

But that was foreign affairs. On the domestic front Republicans had acted independently and now had to bear the consequences for such actions. Was the domestic record of the Eightieth, as historian Eric Goldman has claimed, really "an assault on the legislation and tendencies of a Half-Century of Revolution?"[51] Perhaps oratorically, but GOP action amounted to only a foray, at most. In the end, Old Guard fulminations against the New Deal gave way to practical politics, as tax laws and Taft-Hartley attested. There were some minor Old Guard triumphs. The Eightieth Congress passed, and Truman accepted, laws nullifying workers' portal-to-portal claims, laws excluding some workers from Social Security coverage, and cuts in funds for soil conservation and crop storage. Generally, however, it was in its obstructionist capacity that the Eightieth earned its "Do-Nothing" tag. Still, Truman was imprecise even here. House Republicans, in blocking action on such matters as housing and school aid, actually were repudiating the Republican Senate as much as the White House, along with the leadership of Robert Taft.

Truman's broad swipes, however, were good politics, and historians have generally agreed with his analysis. Congressional Republicans, historian Susan Hartmann has concluded, failed to express the dominant views of their own party and to recognize the appeal of "social welfare" legislation. In so doing, they appeared to oppose the reforms of the past fifteen years.[52] Conclusions like Hartmann's, of course, were made long after the 1948 presidential election. At the time, Right Wing Republicans, before and even after that surprising election, sincerely believed that voters had firmly rejected "social welfare" and New Deal programs. For them, the 1946 congressional elections had proved this beyond doubt. During the Eightieth Congress, such Right Wing Republicans were absolutely certain of their mandate, and only Washington political realities tempered their attacks on the New Deal structure. "A vast amount of New Deal rubbish will have to be removed before even the outline of our free institutions will become visible," Daniel Reed had written after the 1946 elections. "The task . . . rests with Congress, and that which cannot be accomplished now because of Executive interference will be made possible by voters in 1948."[53]

3

The Philadelphia Story

At Philadelphia in June, 1948, Dwight Green gave the Republican convention's keynote address. "We are here," the Illinois governor boomed, "to nominate the 34th President of the United States."[1] He did not have to rummage far through the attics of political bombast for that one. But Green's use of such a stock phrase was understandable. Things looked good for the GOP in 1948, and had for some time.

All Republicans had presumed that the 1946 elections heralded a GOP presidential victory in 1948. One Democrat, Senator J. William Fulbright of Arkansas, wanted a Republican in the White House even sooner, suggesting in 1946 that Truman step down and let a Republican take over. Indeed, Democratic woes accounted for the sunny Republican picture. In September, 1946, Henry A. Wallace, the former vice-president, had been forced to quit as commerce secretary after attacking the administration's "get tough" policy toward the Soviet Union. Popular among certain Democratic liberals, Wallace had launched a presidential drive at the end of 1947. Other liberal Democrats who were dissatisfied with Wallace had initiated their own "dump Truman" movement. Further, Truman could not count on the backing of Bourbon Democratic conservatives, since his civil rights proposals had upset the South.

The spectacular Republican gains of November, 1946, and spirited Democratic squabbling all added luster to the 1948 Republican presidential nomination. The race began early. The GOP had its first official candidate by December, 1946. Harold E. Stassen's announcement indicated that he was still a man in a hurry. Winning the Minnesota governor's race at the age of thirty-one, he had become the youngest man ever elected governor in the United States, and he had been reelected twice. After wartime duty as Admiral William Halsey's assistant chief of staff, Stassen had returned home to resume his political career—with a run for the Republican presidential nomination.

A quick start was what Stassen needed, and he began to campaign for progressive Republican candidates around the nation. Stassen evoked the liberal Republicanism of Wendell Willkie, and this provoked Old Guard suspicion and fear. There was cause for concern. As a Young Republican and as a gubernatorial candidate in 1938, Stassen had taken on the Old Guard and had won. Now, on December 29, 1946, when the tall, blond, and blue-eyed private citizen with the winning smile formally announced for the presidency, he pledged "to move the Republican party along the path of true liberalism." In fact, Stassen differed hardly at all from most Republicans. Theoretically, his nebulous, if not meaningless, liberalism called for the "maximum . . . freedom . . . consistent with the same degree of freedom by his or her fellow man." Practically, Stassen positions that set him apart from his GOP rivals for the nomination amounted to the few trivial caveats he had made in endorsing the Taft-Hartley Act and his belief that the Communist Party, U.S.A., should be outlawed. Writing at the time, Arthur Schlesinger properly found Stassen to be an "appropriate partner of Senator Taft." Nonetheless, Stassen's "cosmopolitan approach" to national and international problems and his aggressive pursuit of the liberal tag were enough to make him the "liberal Republican" candidate in the 1948 Republican nomination struggle.[2]

The Stassen announcement was widely regarded as the opening shot in the Republican presidential wars, and GOP eyes quickly focused on Ohio. Ohio—Mother of Republican Presidents—had two GOP hopefuls, and the Ohio Republican organization was faced with the problem of an embarrassment of riches. Would John Bricker or Robert Taft be the Buckeye presidential favorite come 1948?

By late December, 1946, some of Ohio's riches had diminished. The fortunes of freshman Senator Bricker had indeed fallen since election day. His off-the-record Gridiron Dinner speech in mid-December, according to Arthur Krock in the *New York Times,* led many listeners to question the new senator's "perception and judgment."[3] Afterward, Bricker's stock suffered in the eastern press, and this troubled even staunch midwestern Republicans. Bricker was also a victim of his own senatorial election success. He now found himself in the Senate, where Taft dwarfed him. As one Republican expressed it, the main result of Bricker's move to Washington was to "blanket Bricker."[4]

Not that there were any serious personal problems between Bricker and Taft. In fact, they got along well. Reportedly, they had had an earlier agreement regarding presidential politics. Bricker had supported Taft's 1940 bid, and Taft had "let John try it" in 1944. But 1948 was another matter, and neither was the other's uncritical admirer. Taft's sometimes "leftish" tilt distressed Bricker, and Taft doubted Bricker's political skill and sagacity. Taft had privately criticized Bricker's 1944 campaign and was not convinced that Bricker could beat Dewey or Stassen.[5]

In early 1947 Taft told one supporter that he had had no final talk with

Bricker, "although [Bricker] apparently has every intention of withdrawing and has told many people so."[6] But Bricker's delay in publicly bowing out fired speculation, and reporters began to wonder if he would ever do so. Bricker ultimately ended speculation on July 31, 1947, by pledging to support Taft. Subsequently, on October 24, Taft informed Ohio Republican officials that he wanted the backing of the Buckeye delegation at the GOP convention. He named Congressman Clarence Brown of Ohio and Katharine Kennedy Brown to represent him in the preconvention delegate drive, since Senate duties, he claimed, would keep him from campaigning for the nomination.

For many, Robert Taft with his balding dome and hornrimmed spectacles embodied the conservative statesman. Neither tub-thumper nor gladhander, Taft was shy, industrious, and, most of all, dependable. However poorly these qualities translated in presidential politics, his background had certainly prepared him for public life. Son of President William H. Taft, graduate of Yale College and Harvard law school, Taft had done his political apprenticeship in Ohio politics, serving as majority leader in the Ohio Assembly and later going on to the Ohio Senate.

Although the son of an influential father and a graduate of the finest schools, Taft lacked the stuff of Camelot legacies. Indeed, *Time* had tagged him the "Dagwood Bumstead of American Politics" after some public relations blunders in his 1940 presidential bid. Taft always appeared cold, stiff, and dogmatic. The public never saw the warm, private Taft, and he resisted efforts to "humanize me." Some of the attempts that he acquiesced in were painfully amateurish. The "selling job," one aide told Taft at the end of 1947, was "STINKO."[7]

Taft had other problems, too. His speeches, which he insisted on writing himself, were "clumsy, dry, and disputatious."[8] Yet, tucked among the arid facts, figures, and logic were ideas or ways of expressing ideas that sometimes sparked controversy. Here was irony—the colorless Taft was also highly controversial. The Nuremberg trials, Taft told a Kenyon College audience in 1946, violated American principles of law. At a beefsteak banquet, Taft addressed the problem of the rising cost of living by admonishing his listeners to "eat less." Such gaffes and Taft's lack of political glamor fortified the argument that haunted him throughout his career—"Taft can't win." His friend and advisor Ben Tate encountered this belief everywhere on a political scouting trip in late 1947. Taft obviously rejected the "Taft can't win" thesis, but he realized its impact and the difficulty of combating it in a systematic way.[9]

"Taft can't win" would also describe the nature of Taft's leadership in Congress. Taft's power was so great in the Eightieth Congress that *Time* wrote of "The Age of Taft." Even the *Nation* concluded: Taft's "willingness to assume responsibility is poles away from those former G.O.P. New Deal critics who were merely willing to attack."[10] But in winning such praise, Taft paid dearly. Moreover, certain Senate GOP colleagues resented all the attention paid to Mr. Republican.

Taft's cool, abrupt manner compounded the usual hazards of strong congressional command. But the direction of Taft's rule, as seen earlier, troubled archconservatives most. The initiatives that won acclaim from the *Nation, Time,* and others set Right Wing Republicans muttering—and Taft knew this. He once lamely tried to explain his actions to conservative Senator John J. Williams of Delaware by saying: "Probably you think I have been somewhat too liberal with government money in the positions I have taken, but I was most anxious to maintain a unified party during this period in order that we might reach the one essential goal of ousting the present gang from control."[11]

On January 16, 1948, Thomas E. Dewey announced as candidate for the Republican nomination, thereby testing Alice Roosevelt Longworth's wisecrack on Dewey: "You can't make a souffle rise twice." The New York governor cut a more dashing figure than Taft. Short, with dark good looks, Dewey had piercing brown eyes, heavy eyebrows, and a mustache. He was *almost* a matinee idol. As district attorney for New York County, Dewey had earlier won national attention by busting rackets figures such as Lucky Luciano and Dutch Schultz. But Dewey had his problems, too. Many found him stiff, conceited, and pompous. Conservative philanthropist Sterling Morton, for example, described Dewey as a self-made man who worshipped his creator.[12]

Dewey himself had wondered if a defeated presidential candidate could rise again, and he had surrendered control of the national party organization after his 1944 defeat. But Dewey's stunning 1946 reelection as governor of New York and Truman's low ratings had encouraged him to make another run for the presidency. His gubernatorial victory reportedly had even boosted his strength in the Midwest.

Most political observers agreed that the major divisions of the GOP centered on Robert Taft and Thomas Dewey. Few could pinpoint the precise reasons; no issues really separated Dewey and Taft in 1948. Taft and his followers constantly worried that Dewey might accommodate the New Deal. He might do so, said Taftites, because Dewey was inclined to pander to what was popular. The New York governor, said Herbert Hoover, lacked deep intellectual commitment. "A man couldn't wear a mustache like that without it affecting his mind," he once told an associate.[13] Taft, for his part, believed that Dewey had muffed his chance for the presidency in 1944, and now it was Taft's turn. Clearly, at this time, there was no deep-seated hostility between the Taft and Dewey wings, and estimates of voter appeal were determining GOP alliances more than were weighty questions of policy.

If his Albany post helped Dewey keep clear of any early GOP preconvention wrangling, General Douglas MacArthur's Tokyo base offered a similar advantage. But an Asian military headquarters had disadvantages, too. In the summer of 1947 the *New York Times* reported a Republican presidential boom for MacArthur, the overlord of the Allied occupation of Japan.[14] Although a professional military man, the hero of the Pacific had figured in GOP presidential politics before, finishing second in the 1944 Wisconsin GOP primary. Now, MacArthur-for-President clubs began sprouting up again in Wisconsin. In a straw poll at the Wisconsin Republican State Convention, the general amassed 157 votes—eye-catching when compared with Taft's 97.

MacArthur speculation intensified when the *Chicago Tribune*'s publisher Robert R. McCormick toured the Far East in October, 1947, and stopped in Tokyo "to look Mac over."[15] Upon returning home, however, McCormick disappointed those expecting him to bring back word of MacArthur's candidacy. He denied ever urging MacArthur to run and told reporters that only in a convention deadlock would he, McCormick, switch from Taft to MacArthur.

If McCormick and MacArthur discussed a possible MacArthur candidacy, that kind of talk was not new at Tokyo headquarters. MacArthur coveted the Republican nomination, although the general did not want it to seem that way. He followed an "ambiguous and disingenuous" strategy that allowed him to encourage backers but eschew any personal political ambition.[16] In October, 1947, citing the increasing flow of letters from nearly every section of the country, MacArthur privately asked General Robert E. Wood—former America First Committee chairman and GOP conservative—for political counsel.[17] At the same time, a highly placed member of MacArthur's staff told Hanford MacNider, an Iowa MacArthur booster, that he had talked with MacArthur about running and believed him "willing."[18]

On the home front, the MacArthur-for-president drive rapidly advanced. On November 25, 1947, MacArthur backers met at the Chicago Club with Wood, MacNider, and newspaper mogul Frank Gannett, among others. Many participants were wealthy midwestern businessmen and retired army officers with ties to conservative and old isolationist organizations. No doubt they relished the assurance of Colonel H.E. Eastwood, their Tokyo-based liaison, that MacArthur was a "dyed-in-the-wool Republican and feels everyone of consequence knows this."[19] One notable MacArthur enthusiast, however, thought otherwise. Phillip La Follette, the one-time governor of Wisconsin and a progressive who had served on MacArthur's staff during World War II, believed that the general's occupation policies in Japan revealed him to be a "liberal." La Follette and the "dyed-in-the-wool" Republicans at Chicago did have one thing in common, however—a belief that MacArthur could handle foreign policy matters.[20]

At the Chicago Club parley, the MacArthur boosters mapped a strategy built around a deadlocked GOP convention. But MacArthur had to first prove his popularity among Republicans, and almost all the Chicago strategists believed the general had to return home in the spring or his cause would founder. Yet even before the Chicago powwow MacArthur had dashed that prospect, believing that a preconvention homecoming would "crystallize bitterness in other Republican camps" and would be "indulging in the cheapest form of theatricals." A disappointed Wood could only hope that "the very fact that you [MacArthur] choose a course contrary to all accepted ideas of political strategy might be the wisest course of all."[21] MacArthur nevertheless cooperated with his backers in all else.

"The big test," MacArthur called the Wisconsin primary, where his strength was supposedly greatest. But when Phillip La Follette opened the MacArthur-for-president campaign in that state in late January, there were already problems. Two days earlier General Eisenhower had removed himself from consideration for the presidency, saying that nothing in the international or domestic scene especially qualified a military man for the presidency. A factional battle in the Wisconsin GOP further hampered MacArthur's chances. Led by boss Tom Coleman and Senator Joe McCarthy, the Wisconsin machine supported Stassen. McCarthy, with Coleman's backing, had beaten Robert La Follette, Jr., in the 1946 GOP Senate primary, and the Coleman machine deeply resented this new La Follette challenge. There were also rumors that MacArthur was only a "stalking horse" for Taft and would decline the GOP nomination in favor of the Ohio senator. In addition, questions persisted regarding MacArthur's stand on the issues. Although Tokyo provided the illusion of remoteness from political combat, it also helped keep MacArthur "the Great American Enigma," or as Lindesay Parrott of the *New York Times* concluded, "the darkest of the political dark horses."[22]

The Coleman machine—and Stassen with it—won the Wisconsin primary on April 6. Stassen captured 40 percent of the popular vote and 8 delegates. MacArthur ran second with 36 percent of the popular vote and 8 delegates. Dewey got 24 percent of the popular tallies and no delegates. Wood told MacArthur that the outcome indicated no change in the general's strategic position. A convention deadlock was still the main hope. Most analyses, however, said Wisconsin doomed MacArthur. His fame and favorite-son status had demanded an extraordinary showing, and this he did not receive.[23]

Nor did MacArthur get it elsewhere. The Nebraska preferential primary was the next test for all GOP hopefuls, since all contenders were on the ballot. The odds were with Taft. Nebraska was in the isolationist heartland, and Taft had use of Senator Hugh Butler's state organization. Senator Wherry reportedly also favored Taft but remained ostensibly neutral since he himself was running for reelection. Yet Stassen surprised everybody by amassing a winning plurality of 16,000 over Dewey and 60,000 over Taft.

Stassen's victory in isolationist country suddenly made him something more than the choice of party liberals. Taft, who had only campaigned four days in the state, was "naturally disappointed." But MacArthur was the big loser. He limped in fifth, behind Vandenberg. As a result, Wood now urged the general to return home quickly, for the GOP organizations disliked Stassen, and other candidates, hoping to block Stassen, might be willing to accept MacArthur as a "compromise candidate."[24]

Talk of compromise candidates and dark horses did indeed begin after the Nebraska voting, but MacArthur's name seldom came up. Stassen's triumph had obviously "rocked" the Old Guard. Arthur Krock reported that Taft and Dewey forces had started to discuss forming an anti-Stassen coalition. Party regulars dusted off the old saying, "Primaries indicate, conventions nominate," and Taft himself said that primaries have "no great influence in determining the result," statements that led to charges that Taft and Dewey were plotting to keep the nomination "within the GOP Old Guard."[25]

On January 26, 1948, Harold Stassen had announced that he would enter the Ohio Republican primary. Stassen wanted "a test on foreign and domestic issues" on Mr. Republican's own turf, where he could highlight his position as a GOP liberal. While warning that this Stassen gambit was "contrary to the usual practice among those interested in maintaining Republican harmony," Taft called it Stassen's "greatest mistake," for "if a primary battleground must be chosen, I am delighted he has selected Ohio where he has no chance of success."[26]

Stassen's campaign had plenty of drive coming out of Wisconsin and Nebraska, and Taft's campaign manager, Clarence Brown, returned to Ohio "petrified" by "the Stassen thing."[27] Both Taft and Stassen stumped hard throughout the state, but as James Reston pointed out, it was hardly a "test on fundamental issues." At best, the Ohio contest presented voters with a broad choice between age and youth, liberalism and conservatism. On election day, Taft got 14 and Stassen 9 of the 23 contested delegates. Both claimed victory. In fact, neither made a dramatic showing. Stassen had reduced Taft's strength in the Ohio delegation from 54 to 44 but had gained only 9 votes and much enmity from within the party for himself. Thereafter, Stassen's difficulties in securing delegates grew. Taft, in turn, had failed to carry his home state convincingly, and after the Ohio primary the Old Guard—at least those uncommitted to Taft—looked anew for a proven vote-getter.

Oregon, where Stassen and Dewey next squared off, provided Republicans—Republicans of all kinds—with a potential winner. Dewey garnered

53 percent of the vote and 12 delegates. Even though Taft was not in the Oregon race, the results there also further clouded his candidacy. Reports out of the Taft camp told of disappointment: a Stassen victory in Oregon, instead of a sweeping one for Dewey, would have allowed them at least to make a pitch for Taft on the basis of party regularity. Now even that argument was gone.

In June, 1948, the Republicans descended on Philadelphia for the GOP convention. The city was ready. Red, white, and blue lights decorated Chestnut Street. A giant rubber elephant stood atop the Bellevue Stratford's marquee, although once it collapsed and had to be reinflated. (No portents were noted.) Happily, cool temperatures spared the delegates from the sauna that summertime Philadelphia can become. Furthermore, designers, working for a cool "psychological effect," had decked out Convention Hall in "sylvan garb." There was, of course, some traditional bunting, but designs of flowers and greens mainly filled the convention site.

Columnists Stewart and Joseph Alsop wrote on convention eve: "The stage is set at Philadelphia for the final struggle between isolationists and men of the Vandenberg school, between backward looking and modernminded Republicans."[28] But instead of a titanic clash between good and evil, delegates had to settle, according to most preconvention analyses, for one merely between Taft and Dewey. Campaign managers' forecasts aside, each of these two men had between 277 and 300 votes. Stassen had about 150, and favorite sons harbored what remained of the 1,094 votes. As the convention opened, Dewey had the edge. But it was only slight, and a deadlock was a real possibility.

The likelihood of deadlock enhanced the positions of the favorite sons and dark horses. MacArthur still hoped the convention would turn to him. The conservative biweekly *Human Events* trotted out Senator Bricker as a compromise candidate.[29] California Governor Earl Warren was mentioned as a possible nominee, as was Senator Edward Martin of Pennsylvania. But most talk centered on Vandenberg and House Speaker Joseph Martin.

Vandenberg, the much-ballyhooed leader of GOP internationalists, had let others boost him for the presidency. His silence had given him leverage in the Senate and provided reporters with something to scrutinize at the convention. Many observers believed him to be the "most available" compromise choice. But Vandenberg was unpopular among Taft followers, for he had defeated Mr. Republican on the Lilienthal nomination and on various foreign policy questions. A day before the convention began, Michigan Governor Kim Sigler announced that Vandenberg was available.

Joseph Martin, on the other hand, had been available for some time. Despite his great support in the House, he had nevertheless resisted calls to take the House floor and make a speech highlighting his presidential qualifications. Martin was more acceptable to Taft enthusiasts than Vandenberg. He was, in fact, a perfect compromise candidate. But as permanent chairman of the convention, Martin's ability to drum up support for himself was limited and, to his credit, he worked scrupulously to do nothing to bring about a deadlock.

Another Martin also figured highly in the GOP presidential derby. "If I was Taft," Alf Landon had written after the 1946 elections, "I would give Martin of Pennsylvania . . . a lot of attention."[20] By the start of the Republican convention, everyone—journalists, politicians, and presidential aspirants—was closely watching Senator Edward Martin and the entire Pennsylvania delegation. At the moment, the Republican party in Pennsylvania was badly split between the Grundy and Duff forces. In the 1920s, Joseph P. "Uncle Joe" Grundy had succeeded Boies Penrose as boss of the Keystone State GOP, and he ruled it from his perch as chairman of the Pennsylvania Manufacturers Association (PMA). This devout Quaker, who wore staid dark suits and filled his talk with the traditional "thee," had founded the PMA in 1909 as a business lobby. It soon became an adjunct of the Pennsylvania GOP. It championed high tariffs and low taxes, and displayed a repugnance of all reform. In 1946, with Grundy's support, James Duff had been elected governor of Pennsylvania to replace Edward Martin, a Grundy loyalist who had lured Duff into politics and had himself just been elected to the Senate. The Grundy-Duff alliance, however, was short-lived, and at a PMA retirement banquet for Uncle Joe in 1947, Duff had hailed a new day of enlightened politics in Pennsylvania. "Cigars shifted," noted *Time,* and a bitter patronage battle ensued.[31]

There had been plans in early 1948 to unite the Pennsylvania delegation to the convention behind House Speaker Joe Martin. But these efforts had collapsed when Duff became excited by the Vandenberg-for-president talk. Although Duff had no specific candidate, he was definitely against New York Governor Dewey. Dewey's agents immediately spotted an opportunity. They approached the Grundy faction through Senator Edward Martin and National Committeeman G. Mason Owlett, plying the Grundyites with anti-Taft propaganda. The overtures succeeded. A week before the convention, Grundy reportedly branded Taft "a socialist."[32]

On Sunday—convention eve—the Pennsylvania delegation caucused and gave 72 favorite-son votes to Senator Martin and one vote to Vandenberg. Following the first three or four ballots for the presidential nomination, the delegation planned to caucus on the floor. Duff was reported to have 45 to 52 votes ready to switch to Taft at that time in order to stop Dewey. Dewey strategists, however, believed that as a result of their work the Grundy faction actually commanded a majority of the Keystone State delegates.

Tuesday afternoon, following a meeting with Dewey, Senator Edward

Martin stunned the convention by announcing his withdrawal as a favorite son and his decision to nominate the New York governor. Martin's withdrawal sparked many rumors—a Dewey-Grundy patronage deal had been sealed, Dewey had assured Grundy on future tariff policies, and the new Republican National Committee Chairman would come from Pennsylvania. (Later in the week, Dewey did choose Pennsylvania Congressman Hugh Scott as the new Republican national chairman.) "I moved," Martin said at the next day's Pennsylvania caucus, "because I did not want a debacle like we had eight years ago." (At that time, Willkie had won the GOP nomination without Pennsylvania's help.) Martin later said his fear that a convention deadlock would leave the party in shambles for the campaign had prompted his quick action. Actually, there was nothing spontaneous about his move. His admiration for Dewey was longstanding and well known. Moreover, Martin had devised his convention plans even before departing Washington for Philadelphia.[33] Whatever the explanation, the Dewey forces had snared a key conservative bloc.

Clarence Brown of Ohio, Taft's campaign manager, declared that Martin's Tuesday announcement represented "the height of the New York Governor's blitz." Actually, it only got the Dewey bandwagon rolling. Wednesday—the day of the nominating speeches—saw the full impact of Martin's move. The Pennsylvania delegation met, and after Martin silently endured the blasts of some furious delegates, it gave Dewey 41 first-ballot votes. Duff, whose endorsement of Taft was purely an anti-Dewey gambit, carried only 26 Pennsylvania delegates to Mr. Republican. Stassen and Vandenberg picked up one vote each, and three delegates expressed no preference. Grundy, Owlett, and other Pennsylvania GOP leaders stood behind Dewey, while Joseph Pew and state chairman Harvey Taylor stuck with Duff and Taft. The damage to Taft was irreparable.

This happened late Wednesday. Earlier, New Jersey's Governor Alfred E. Driscoll had announced that he would release his 35-member delegation after the first ballot and that he himself would be voting for Dewey. Governor Robert Bradford of Massachusetts stated that after his delegation's complimentary vote for Senator Leverett Saltonstall, he, too, would urge Dewey's nomination. Numerous conservatives also joined the Dewey bandwagon. James P. Kem was one. This rookie senator from Missouri was far more conservative than Taft, yet he declared for Dewey on Wednesday. Explaining his action later, Kem stated that no leading candidate entirely satisfied him, but that Dewey promised an "efficient and business like job of cleaning house" and was "a great vote-getting candidate."[34] Kem subsequently carried the bulk of the Missouri delegation to the New York governor. Also, early on Wednesday evening, amid gossip of a deal for the vice-presidential spot, Charles A. Halleck revealed that Indiana's 29-member delegation with an estimated 10 votes for Taft would vote unanimously for Dewey on the first ballot.

A quick stop-Dewey coalition was Taft's only hope. A Taft-Stassen ticket was one possibility, although Stassen's attacks on the Old Guard's "Maginot-line type of reactionary thinking," delivered at the Union League Club of Philadelphia just before the convention opened, made such a "shotgun marriage" seem unlikely. Still, Martin's blockbuster and its fallout sparked a flurry of stop-Dewey meetings. Taft, Stassen, and Governor Kim Sigler, Vandenberg's representative, met three times on Wednesday about the situation. Taft insisted that they all back him. After their Ohio combat, however, Stassen could hardly knuckle under to Taft. Stassen suggested they support Vandenberg instead, but Taft refused. In the end, the talks got nowhere. Stassen then angered Taft by telling reporters afterward that a Taft-Stassen ticket was "impossible," thus breaking their agreement to make no comments.

The weather turned hot and muggy on Thursday, and in the afternoon the balloting began. Dewey showed surprising first-ballot strength. He won 434 votes to Taft's 224, Stassen had 157, and Vandenberg totaled 62. On the next ballot, Dewey scored gains in Iowa, Kansas, Kentucky, Massachusetts, and so on into New Jersey, which gave him 33 of its 35 votes. Dewey was on the move. At the end of the balloting, Vandenberg held at 62, Stassen fell to 149, and Taft climbed to 274. But Dewey shot to 515—just 33 shy of the nomination. Despite the pleas of Connecticut's Senator Ray Baldwin to hold up the official announcement until Connecticut could caucus, Martin recognized Pennsylvania's Governor Duff, who asked for a recess until the early evening. New York delegation chairman William F. Bleakley confidently agreed over the boos of other Dewey supporters, and the Republican convention recessed.

At the Ben Franklin Hotel, Taft contacted Stassen once more and asked him for his delegates. Stassen refused but said he might reconsider after another ballot. Back in Convention Hall, as the third ballot was about to begin, the convention buzzed with word that Earl Warren was freeing his California delegates and many would vote for Dewey. Aware of this and the impending release of the Connecticut delegation, Taft decided to withdraw. Shortly after 7:30 P.M., John Bricker read Taft's statement. Senator Wiliam F. Knowland did the same for Warren, and Sigler for Vandenberg. Then, Stassen bowed out. "The unanimous nomination," exclaimed the *Chicago Tribune*, "ended one of the greatest party battles ever waged."[35]

The *Tribune*'s owner, however, had not stayed for the finish. Before the band could strike up "Hail to the Chief," McCormick had left Convention Hall, wanting neither to join nor spoil the unanimous vote, and sputtering, "Well, it might have been worse; it might have been Vandenberg."[36] Inside, Dewey addressed the by-now riotous gathering. Accepting the nomination, he pledged, "I come to you unfettered by a single obligation or promise to any living person."

Charles A. Halleck, House majority leader from Indiana, had reason to doubt this. He believed that the Dewey forces had promised him the vice-presidency. In addition to the House majority leader's other successful pro-Dewey efforts, Halleck had delivered the Indiana delegation to the New York governor. Halleck thought this was part of a deal. On Wednesday, Halleck had told his Indiana delegation that he would be the vice-presidential nominee if they followed him to Dewey. Dewey personally had not talked to Halleck, but J. Russell Sprague, his advisor, had. According to Halleck's biographer, Dewey later admitted that Sprague had told Halleck that he would urge Halleck's nomination. Yet Dewey also stated that he learned of this Sprague-Halleck conversation only on the night of his own nomination.[37]

Recently there has been much criticism of the way vice-presidential candidates are chosen. With the nomination won, the exhausted presidential nominee repairs to a hotel suite, where he and other politicos ruminate through the night and into the early morning. Then, for a variety of reasons, they pick a runningmate. Thus it happened in 1948, and it killed Halleck's chances of becoming Dewey's vice-president. Halleck's name came up for consideration at such a gathering. Dewey later recalled his own favorable response to Halleck's name, which Sprague advocated.[38] But Halleck's isolationist past made him unacceptable, and the group quickly dismissed him. Taft, who declined an invitation to this parley, had suggested Bricker or Illinois governor Dwight Green, but they were also passed over. "Tom's whole concern seemed to be about carrying the Atlantic seaboard," Taft later told Green, "and he seemed to be afraid of all midwestern candidates because they were too isolationistic!"[39] Early Friday morning, the meeting settled on Governor Earl Warren of California.

Later that day, when the convention learned of the choice, Clarence Brown leaned over to Halleck to say, "You've been doublecrossed." Halleck agreed.[40] The Indianan later dubbed it "The Philadelphia Story." For others, such action merely underscored the continuing importance of "New York kingmakers" within the GOP. The June 25 *New York Times* editorial entitled "Surely not Mr. Halleck" was later accepted as proof by Phyllis Schlafly in *A Choice Not An Echo* that "certain powers" intent on maintaining the Roosevelt foreign policy had "stepped in to scotch" a Dewey-Halleck ticket.[41]

The platform also passed with smoothness and dispatch. It triggered no Alsopian "final struggle." Instead, the platform reflected the existing duality of authority in the Senate. Its domestic section was a Taft document, and its foreign policy section was Vandenberg's. The planks on civil rights and housing were the most troublesome domestic issues. Southerners wanted to soft-pedal civil rights, and one concession to the South was the exclusion of a plank favoring a permanent Fair Employment Practices Committee. But the platform did include planks supporting an antilynch law and the abolition of the poll tax. On the housing issue, unlike in the previous Congress, Taft's position prevailed. The platform acknowledged that private enterprise was the best remedy for the housing problem but advocated federal aid for slum clearance and low-rent housing. In reference to education, however, the mention of federal aid was omitted in deference to hard-line party conservatives. While calling for a minimum of government controls, the Philadelphia platform did recognize the federal government's responsibility for a long-range farm program, public health, old-age security, and conservation.

Vandenberg worked with Henry Cabot Lodge, Jr., the Resolutions Committee chairman, to insure the GOP platform became no isolationist manifesto. He and Lodge inserted several provocative statements in the committee's working paper, including a condemnation of House Republicans for not appropriating the necessary ERP funds.[42] As expected, these provisions drew the fire of isolationists, who, led by Senator Brooks of Illinois, knocked them out of the final draft. In the end, the convention roared its approval of the final document. Taft and Dewey found it acceptable, as did Vandenberg. The GOP platform even pleased the liberal Senator Wayne Morse, who termed it "the death knell of the Old Guard."[43]

The Old Guard—Republican conservatives—had had a tough time at Philadelphia and had split badly. Among the midwestern-dominated Taft Republicans, there were many who, more conservative than Taft himself, had doomed any compromise stop-Dewey movement. James Reston of the *New York Times* had noted even before the flurry of stop-Dewey conferences on Wednesday that the idea of the Taft forces' throwing their support to Vandenberg, as Stassen had urged, was doubtful.[44] Could even Taft have promised that his delegates would follow him in such a venture? Actually, Taft's problems had appeared long before this. Directed by Clarence Brown, "a small-town operator," according to William S. White, Taft's campaign had already floundered.[45] His headquarters' order of 10,000 copies of "This Week in Philadelphia," an entertainment guide with Dewey's picture on the cover, was just one of the Taft operation's many blunders.

Dewey's nomination had really been won before the delegates met in Philadelphia. The Nebraska, Ohio, and Oregon primaries had mattered far more than any convention week mistakes or the difficulties of the stop-Dewey movement. And the evidence contained in these springtime contests had influenced the Right Wing's calculations of electability more than the mere delegate count. Taft later admitted that his own optimism had flagged after the Nebraska primary, because that outing had given "some reality" to the "Taft can't win" thesis. Although Taft did not say so, his unspectacular showing in Ohio also had bolstered this belief. Taft himself realized that the "basic reason" for his loss at Philadelphia was that Republican politicians in general lacked confidence that he could be a winner.[46]

Significantly, many of these Republicans were Old Guard conservatives who, at this particular moment, saw little difference between Dewey and Taft politically or philosophically. Their belief that Dewey was a winner, along with their own chances for political gain, eased their switch from Taft to Dewey. Such an attitude among the Old Guard naturally helped defuse the tension at the Philadelphia convention. It was not the "greatest party battle ever waged," as the *Chicago Tribune* claimed. Taft had lost the nomination, but the platform generally reflected his views, and he accepted it. He also admitted later that Dewey's political beliefs were "about the same as mine."[47]

Still, defeat stung. Taft wrote of his "resentment over the defection of the conservatives like the Pennsylvania Manufacture [*sic*] Association, the Duponts and Senator Kem."[48] And as an indication that Taft was not finished as a presidential possibility, this note, scrawled on the announcement board in Taft's Ben Franklin headquarters, greeted departing delegates: "Taft in '52."

Three weeks later in the same city of Philadelphia, Harry Truman sat in a steamy off-stage room, waiting to address the Democratic convention. His cause appeared hopeless. Southern Democrats, enraged over the passage of a strong civil rights plank, had bolted the Democratic convention and would soon launch their own Dixiecrat or States' Rights party with South Carolina's Governor J. Strom Thurmond as their standard-bearer. On Truman's left were the Progressives, who later, also in Philadelphia, would select Henry Wallace as their presidential nominee. The kind of news that Truman could consider good indicated his plight—a "dump Truman" drive at the convention had failed largely for lack of a suitable candidate.

Well past midnight, Truman stepped before this divided and downcast convention. "Senator Barkley [Alben Barkley, Truman's runningmate] and I will win this election and make those Republicans like it—don't you forget that," he declared. Suddenly the dispirited delegates perked up. Citing national needs and GOP platform promises, the president then announced that he was calling the Eightieth Congress back into session. This ploy was no simple soapbox inspiration, but the result of much White House deliberation. A special session, Truman believed, would advertise the "lacklustre" record of the Eightieth Congress and compel the GOP ticket—a non-Washington duo—to confront squarely the issue of the GOP Congress. Further, it would divide the Republicans on major issues and spotlight "the neanderthal men of the Republican party . . . who will embarrass Dewey and Warren."[49]

Truman's action was blatantly political. "It's the same old New Deal Stuff," said one Ohio Republican, "a synthetic emergency warmed over once more in a last desperate bid to spend and elect." Nevertheless, the call for a special session did pose problems for the GOP. Some, like Vandenberg, favored further major legislative action. But others resisted. Iowa's Representative Ben Jensen suggested the lawmakers assemble and immediately adjourn. Taft, affronted by Truman's "abuse" of his office, told a meeting of GOP leaders, "No, we're not giving that fellow anything." As a result, no major measures—minimum wage, aid to education, or public housing—passed the special session. As Halleck told a friend: "We do not want to open the Pandora Box of legislation."[50]

After the close of the special session in mid-August, the presidential campaign turned listless. Dewey was a sure winner, and the campaign became memorable only after the returns were in. In the area of foreign policy, the 1948 contest witnessed a "peak" of bipartisanship. Despite his early intention to make the administration's foreign policy a major campaign issue, Dewey announced on July 24 that he was committed to Vandenberg's concept of bipartisanship. In doing so, historian Robert Divine has pointed out, Dewey gave up an issue that polls showed held promise as a vote-getter for a Republican candidate. Further, Dewey's decision freed Truman to concentrate on blistering the "Do-Nothing Republican Eightieth."[51]

As a result, Truman and Dewey avoided foreign policy debate until almost the last week of the campaign. Even areas normally outside the scope of bipartisan cooperation—Latin America and the Far East—escaped partisan wrangling. The crisis in Berlin, of course, provided the backdrop of the 1948 election and put a premium on national unity. Moreover, the Republicans—all Republicans—were certain of victory. Dewey, in turn, seemed to have unilaterally initiated a bipartisan domestic policy. His speeches were high-sounding calls for national unity and "American Destiny," and they lacked punch. On the other hand, Truman's whistle-stopping blasts against the Republican Eightieth Congress provided the only real campaign fire, and to these Dewey offered no defense.

Overconfidence only partly explains Dewey's toothless 1948 campaign style. The New York governor believed that his 1944 presidential campaign had sputtered after he switched to a scrappy prosecutorial approach on the hustings. In 1948, therefore, he began by trying to avoid his earlier mistakes. Sometime in October, however, Dewey came to fear that his campaign needed a lift. But Republican leaders counseled against a change in tactics, fearing it would be seen as a sign of weakness. So Dewey continued his lofty campaign. Dewey's own criticism of congressional Republicans and his knowledge that Taft still had their basic loyalty also helps to explain the New York governor's failure to rebut Truman's "Do-Nothing" barbs.[52]

During the campaign, Dewey's style had its critics, but not many among Republicans. House Speaker Joe Martin later recalled that he had urged Dewey to defend the Eightieth Congress. In fact, as he and Dewey stumped together, Martin's own newspaper, the North Attleboro *Evening Chronicle,* ran an editorial that was critical of Dewey's campaign speeches. "A newspaper accident," Martin tried to explain at the time.[53] During all of the campaign, however, there was virtually no direct, public Republican criticism of the Dewey campaign effort, and the many manuscript collections of Right Wing Republicans reveal no private fault-finding *before* election day.

Although H.L. Mencken concluded that Dewey's recitations sounded like the "worst bombast of university professors," a majority of the nation's editors and commentators praised the Dewey unity tactics over "Give-'Em-Hell" Harry's whistle-stop performances.[54] For them, Dewey spoke like "a president." Political seers everywhere awaited his triumph. Several days before the election, the New York governor even leaked the names of his future cabinet officers to the press. Such GOP confidence extended far beyond the Dewey campaign train. Taft, for example, predicted a record vote and a Dewey victory. Long before this, the Republican Eightieth had voted the money for a gala Republican inauguration.

Ohio did it. The Mother of Republican Presidents—Taft country—vacillated all during election night, then finally fell to Truman. Dewey had lost. No election since 1916 had been closer. Truman was still president. He won 24.1 million popular votes and twenty-eight states, for 303 electoral votes. Dewey garnered 22 million popular tallies, sixteen states, and 189 electoral votes. Thurmond and Wallace each won less than 1.2 million popular votes, but the Dixiecrat gained 39 electoral votes, while Wallace got none.

GOP losses were nationwide. In the House, Democrats picked up seventy-five seats and now boasted a 262-to-172 majority. Republican losses were big in Pennsylvania and Ohio, where eight GOP solons fell. Traditionally Republican seats in farm states also went Democratic. Important House Republicans were stunned. Harold Knutsen, Ways and Means chairman and tax-cut advocate, lost. George Bender was one of the Ohio losers. Charlie Halleck's normal victory margin was cut considerably. In the Senate races, the Democrats doubled their top preelection forecasts. Gaining nine seats, they now enjoyed a 54-to-42 edge over the Republicans. Although Wherry and Bridges were reelected and Representative Karl Mundt won a Senate seat from South Dakota, Right Wing Republicans incurred heavy losses. In Minnesota, Joseph Ball, who was becoming increasingly conservative, lost his Senate seat to Hubert Humphrey, the liberal mayor of Minneapolis. Senator Brooks of Illinois lost his reelection bid, as did Governor Green. Also toppled were Edward V. Robertson of Wyoming, Chapman Revercomb of West Virginia, and Henry Dworshak of Idaho. In Tennessee, former national chairman Reece came up short in his Senate race with Democrat Estes Kefauver. Nor did Republicans fill the seats of retiring conservatives Edward Moore of Oklahoma, Albert Hawkes of New Jersey, and Harlan Bushfield of South Dakota.

The outcome at all levels was a shocking surprise. Dewey and Taft and Republicans of all stripes could at least agree on that much.

A New Set of Guts

Dewey's loss stunned the Republican party. Joe Martin returned to Washington in "deep gloom." Taft was almost "beside himself." "A national tragedy," moaned former National Committee Chairman B. Carroll Reece. Walter S. Hallanan, the temporary chairman at Philadelphia, thought the election "may be the turning point to national socialism."[1]

Hallanan accepted some of the blame for the November loss himself. He wrote to Pennsylvania's Edward Martin, whose bolt had triggered Dewey's convention bandwagon: "Our defeat . . . showed that we made a grievous blunder at Philadelphia." Though Martin acknowledged no error, other Republicans did. Senator Kem of Missouri reportedly admitted his mistake in switching to Dewey at Philadelphia, and Taft told of "quite a few recantations" by Republican politicos.[2]

There was indeed plenty of GOP interest in solving what Arthur Krock called the "political whodunit" of the century. John Sherman Cooper, GOP liberal defeated in the Kentucky Senate race, believed the defeat spotlighted the need for new leadership and an "affirmative constructive philosophy." Another liberal, Senator Henry Cabot Lodge, Jr., of Massachusetts, saw hope for a modern Republican party in the 1948 returns. Believing modern political parties resembled political "service stations," Lodge wanted to make sure the "gas, oil, and water and windshield cleaning we offer is better than the other parties."[3]

Conservative Republicans naturally rejected Lodges filling-station metaphor, as well as the liberal analyses of the Dewey defeat. Lodge's gas station smacked of the Dewey campaign's "me-too" approach, and after 1948, conservative and moderate Republicans alike joined to reject "me-tooism" and Republican "pussyfooting." For C. Budington Kelland, the conservative Republican national committeeman from Arizona, there was no mystery about the Dewey smashup. On November 5 he wrote his fellow Republicans that the 1948 campaign—"a private Albany enterprise"—was "smug, arrogant, stupid and supercilious." Kelland had wanted the Republican party to draw a "definite line of demarcation" between Republican and Democratic tenets. This Dewey had failed to do.[4] Numerous other party members seemed to agree with Kelland and demanded that the GOP stand staunchly for principles, though there was little agreement on what those principles should be.

Virtually every aspect of the Dewey campaign bothered conservative and other Republicans. Kelland groused about the Dewey unity pitch. Hallanan criticized its "milque toast character" and Dewey's "repetitious monotone." "The people," Kem concluded typically, "were not interested in his pious platitudes and his faith, hope and Dewey stuff." Taft, in turn, believed that he and even Dewey could have won the White House with any kind of fight.[5]

Most Republicans held that better "salesmanship" had been, and was now, necessary. In early 1949 Senator Homer Capehart of Indiana, who had made his fortune marketing jukeboxes, told Republicans that they were the "world's worst salesmen." The Eightieth Congress was the primary Republican product that could have been peddled as an "affirmative asset." Harry Truman had maligned Republican goods at every whistle-stop—and all without rebuttal from the GOP standard-bearer. As a result, Kelland said, Republicans allowed themselves to be attacked as the party of "special interests, entrenched wealth" and "mossbacks dominated by the mythical Old Guard."[6]

According to conservative Republicans, Dewey had not only allowed Truman to abuse the Republican Eightieth, but he had also snubbed particular GOP candidates for reelection. Wayland Brooks of Illinois, Chapman Revercomb of West Virginia, and Edward B. Robertson of Wyoming were allegedly victims of the Dewey brand of Republicanism. Further, Reece suspected that a "strange trick" by Dewey campaign manager Herbert Brownell had aided the Dewey group in Tennessee that "concertedly knifed" him in his unsuccessful Senate bid.[7]

All losing candidates for the presidency, H.L. Mencken once urged, should be quietly hanged, "lest the sight of their grief have a very evil effect upon the young." Dewey had remained generally quiet since the November disaster, but at the Lincoln's Birthday meeting on February 8, the New York governor finally broke his silence. "The Republican party is split wide open," he told Republicans gathered at Washington's Mayflower Hotel. "It has been split wide open for years, but we have tried to gloss it over. I am a living example that that doesn't work." A minority of Republicans who confused personal prejudice with party aims, Dewey continued, seemed to "make all the noise" and, if triumphant, would make the GOP "the deadest pigeon in the country."[8]

Dewey was hardly blowing the bugle for party unity, and the Lincoln's Birthday celebrants gave him "less than deafening" applause. In fact, on this unhappy Lincoln's Birthday most Republicans could hardly see what right Dewey had to read anybody out of the GOP. While most Republicans had been surprised by Dewey's recent defeat, they ultimately found little mystery in it. Krock's "political whodunit" had quickly become a "hedun-it"—Dewey.

The contrary analyses of political pundits—and later historians—had little impact on most Republicans during this period of rumination following the election. Defeat—so habitual, yet this time so surprising—had left the majority of Republicans frustrated, bitter, and desperate. Moderate Republicans generally accepted the conservative critique of the Dewey campaign, which signaled a new drift for the GOP. "These boys [Deweyites] have wrecked the party in three different elections," said one Old Guardsman. "Now it's only fair to give us a chance to wreck it our way." [9]

He was only half-kidding.

"There is no time for recrimination or alibis," said the RNC chairman in a letter of early December.

But the chairman, Hugh Scott, was already a party to the most notable squabble arising from the Dewey defeat. Actually, Scott was more a pawn than a full-fledged participant. Before becoming chairman in June, 1948, he had been an unheralded congressman from Pennsylvania. Few doubted Scott's energy and enthusiasm as national party chief, but many believed he had allowed the Dewey "clique" to disregard the national party apparatus throughout the campaign of 1948. A combination of Taft and Stassen loyalists now wanted Scott's gavel. Scott, however, believed he had a four-year contract.

Scott's lack of political identity underscored the symbolic stakes of the conflict. For the Taft wing, Scott was inextricably tied to the ill-fated Dewey campaign. For Dewey supporters, Scott's retention was naturally important. For the Pennsylvania organization, the post of national chairman was regarded as a prize for its key role at the Philadelphia convention, and in December, Pennsylvania's Senator Edward Martin assured Colonel McCormick of the *Chicago Tribune* that Scott "was at heart one of us." [10] Indeed, the suspicion that Scott, despite his ties to Dewey, was actually an emissary of Uncle Joe Grundy's "reactionary" Pennsylvania machine did confuse many party liberals. As a result, the Old Guard and liberals alike were divided among themselves on the Scott matter.

Scott had prominent enemies—among them former RNC chairman Harrison Spangler of Iowa and the recently deposed Reece, who allegedly wanted another stint as GOP boss. Joseph Martin was also anti-Scott, for the Pennsylvania upstart had "more or less" ignored the former House Speaker during the campaign. But Taft, who later called Scott "a compete screwball," initially balked at his ouster. The Stassen–Vandenberg–*New York Herald Tribune* crowd, he feared, would then install Everett Dirksen, a recently retired congressman from Illinois who was regarded as an internationalist. Taft suggested that Scott relinquish either the chairmanship or his seat in Congress, and merely allow Taftites to help in the selection of the RNC executive committee.[11] Scott, however, refused to budge or to "deal" with the Taft forces. In fact, he named his own executive committee, packing it with Dewey supporters and excluding such heavyweights—from different party factions—as Ralph Cake of Oregon, Sinclair Weeks of Massachusetts, and Clarence Brown of Ohio.

In late January, the RNC met at Omaha in, appropriately, the Black Mirror Room of the Hotel Fontenelle. There, Scott denied responsibility for the 1948 campaign and announced an end to "me-too" Republicanism, said Dewey "should not, could not and will not be a candidate in 1952," but simultaneously rebuffed party "cliffhangers" who would take the GOP back to Garfield, not forward to victory.

Scott, who offered to negotiate everything except his own resignation, was sure his foes lacked the votes to sack him, divided as they were over a replacement candidate. Furthermore, it soon became known at Omaha that Scott had taped his fall conversations with GOP politicians who had approved of the Dewey campaign. Anonymous messages that such tapes existed mysteriously found their way under the delegates' hotel doors. Clarence Brown immediately yelled "Blackmail." Scott, in turn, denied any intention to use these tapes to stay in power and denounced the "high school" tactics of the opposition. But he did confess that he had brought transcripts of the tapes to Omaha—"to keep the record straight." Thus began, some may claim, a Republican preoccupation with transcripts and tapes. In the end, anti-Scott forces, led by Clarence Brown, failed to unseat Scott, although they did force him to agree to unstack the executive committee.

But the Scott story was not over. C. Budington Kelland of Arizona was one conservative who saw to that. Actually, Kelland had left Omaha "pretty well content," pleased by the new executive committee and the powwow's anti-Dewey tone. Still, Scott had to go. "I think we have abolished Albany," Kelland wrote, "but we really won't get moving until Hugh Scott surrenders the citadel." Shortly after the Omaha meeting, therefore, the Arizona committeeman initiated a drive to make Guy Gabrielson, a New Jersey committeeman whose "thinking is a hundred percent right," the next Republican national chairman.[12]

In mid-July, Kelland and Gabrielson surfaced in Pittsburgh. They were among the twenty-five national committeemen—strange bedfellows that included Taft and Stassen supporters—who met at the Duquesne Club to plot Scott's ouster. The Duquesne group, convinced that it now had the votes to dump Scott, gave him three days to resign. In the face of such pressures, Scott finally bowed to what many believed was inevitable, and quit. Remarked one GOP veteran, "Hugh Scott promised to make us Republicans a fighting party, and he sure has succeeded."[13]

It was hoped that Scott's departure would bring peace to the troubled GOP. Dewey and Taft were reportedly conferring to avoid further party discord. Taft hoped that Gabrielson's New York connections would help him unite all wings of the party, and there were reports that Gabrielson was talking to the Dewey people. But two weeks of maneuver brought party harmony no closer. Gabrielson became an active candidate with only the Taft wing behind him. The former Scott backers—Dewey lieutenant Russell Sprague and G. Mason Owlett, national committeemen from Pennsylvania—working to find a candidate, forged ties with RNC members from the West and came up with Axel J. Beck of Elk Point, South Dakota. A Swedish immigrant, farmer-lawyer Beck was an American success story. But Beck's thick accent proved a liability in his bid to become GOP national spokesman, and Gabrielson ultimately won by a narrow 57-to-47 margin.

The new chairman had come far from his Iowa beginnings. Heavy set, with hornrimmed glasses, Gabrielson was a polished Wall Street lawyer with corporate ties. His selection was hailed by the political pundits as a Taft victory—but not by Taft. Certainly Mr. Republican respected Gabrielson— "although he comes from the East"—and believed the new chairman would join the battle against Truman. But the real issue, Taft maintained, had always been Dewey's continued control of the National Committee.[14] Gabrielson's election was mainly an anti-Dewey move. Still, after the November smashup, that was enough.

The shocks of election day 1948 also reverberated on Capitol Hill during the first days of the Eighty-first Congress. Joe Martin's minority leadership in the House went unchallenged, but Republican rumblings began shortly after election day over in the Senate. Party liberals wanted to sack Taft as GOP Senate boss. Led by New York's Irving Ives, who believed the party under Taft had remained "in a state of suspended animation," a group of so-called Young Turks wanted the GOP to offer constructive, intelligent remedies for national and international problems. Henry Cabot Lodge was their choice to replace Taft as Policy Committee chairman. California's William F. Knowland would take over for Wherry as floor leader, and Leverett Saltonstall of Massachusetts was the Young Turks' pick for party whip. But these "liberals" had little chance of winning. Actually, according to Arthur Krock of the *New York Times,* they were only after favorable press notices, which they hoped would result in giving them greater weight in party councils.[15]

They got little of either. At a caucus on January 3, 1949, Senate Republicans again made Taft the chairman of the Policy Committee. He received 28 votes to Lodge's 14. In his bid to become floor leader, Young Turk

Knowland lost to Wherry by the same margin. Then, Taft supporter Hugh Butler of Nebraska nominated Saltonstall for party whip, and he won by acclamation. GOP leaders also voted to enlarge the Policy Committee, and Ives and Saltonstall filled these two spots. "Not much of a gesture," said one of the leaders of the revolt, but it was enough to keep the Young Turks off balance.[16]

Compounding Young Turk woes was the bad publicity generated by the revolt. Their concern with style over substance quickly became apparent. When Taft appeared before reporters with the voting chart of the liberal *New Republic,* the point was firmly made—Taft was generally as liberal as his Young Turk foes. Taft himself believed the Young Turk move had advanced his cause. The Ohio senator's only trouble, noted writer John Chamberlain, was that he could never be cast as a "streamlined" Republican.[17]

Postelection tremors also shook party doctrine. After all that "Dewey stuff," many Right Wing Republicans yearned for a clear statement of party principle. Said the busy Kelland, "The Republican Party must go to the operating room and get a new set of guts."[18] But congressional GOP conservatives resisted. Clarence Brown maintained that Republican policy would be found in congressional tallies—and nowhere else. Still, pressures mounted for a new, conservative GOP manifesto, and in July, 1949, the National Republican Round-up formed to promote unabashed orthodox Republicanism. Also, there were reports that some GOP conservatives were withholding contributions until the party shaped up. One example was Sterling Morton, who told Alf Landon, "The National Committee will get no contributions from me until I find some signs . . . the Republican Party is to present an alert and active opposition, and not to constitute themselves into a board of ratification of the actions of Truman and his associates."[19] The party's half-million dollar deficit for 1949 suggested similar tightfistedness on the party of other wealthy GOP conservatives.

The trend within the GOP soon became more obvious when the RNC strategy committee met in Chicago in December, 1949. The committee chairman, Arthur Summerfield of Michigan, a Vandenberg supporter in 1948, now called for an end to "me-tooism." The strategy for the 1950 campaign would be uncompromising opposition to Democratic programs and proposals, and the committee appointed a group to flesh out this position by the RNC's February meeting. Reminded that Taft supported some administration proposals, one strategist snapped, "Well, that will be just too damned bad for Taft."[20]

This December development demonstrated that the movement for a statement of Republican principles had overtaken Taft and other congressmen. In early February, House and Senate GOP representatives met, however reluctantly, with the emissaries of the drafting committee to hammer out a policy declaration.

On February 7, 1950, Republicans gathered at the Uline Arena in Washington to celebrate another Lincoln's Birthday. The 11,000 Republicans got a "poor man's" box supper of fried chicken, followed by the unveiling of the "Statement of Republican Principles and Objectives." The paramount issue, proclaimed the new document, was "Liberty against Socialism." It rejected Fair Deal features like "socialized medicine," deficit spending, and the administration's proposed farm program, the Brannan Plan. The GOP statement advocated a balanced budget, further rural electrification, expanded Social Security, federal aid for "subsistence, shelter, and medical care," and freer world trade, provided industry and farmers were protected from the products of "underpaid foreign labor." The GOP also endorsed a tightening of the Truman administration's loyalty program. Bipartisan foreign policy should continue, said the document, but the administration must supply necessary information, and secret diplomacy must end.

This 1950 "Statement of Republican Principles and Objectives" only updated the declaration of 1945. Although the 1950 model was longer and more specific, the tone was identical. In fact, the 1950 authors ransacked whole phrases from the earlier version. Both statements were conservative but contained room for government action on certain social problems.

Even before its official unveiling, the policy declaration had sparked GOP dissension. Illinois committeemen Werner Schroeder had tried unsuccessfully to include an official repudiation of continued bipartisan foreign policy. The *Chicago Tribune* had labeled the declaration "dismal, weak and inadequate." "The best that can be said of this statement of lack of principles," it continued, "is that it will soon be forgotten."[21] Even party liberals shared the *Tribune*'s judgment that "The Republicans Lay an Egg" and offered their own substitute declarations.[22]

That the statement did not bring unity became clear only two days after Uline. Dewey, while delivering lectures on "The American Political System" at Princeton University, chided those who attacked party candidates with the epithet "me-too." These "croaking voices," charged Dewey, were conservative, isolationist, or both.[23] Thus, on two successive Lincoln's Birthdays, Dewey had seized the occasion to focus on the growing gap between himself and conservatives. In doing so—and he certainly had some cause to be defensive—he helped to widen that gap, intensifying and personalizing the continuing hostility within the GOP.

The Ohio Women's Republican Club would unveil no official statement of principle at its Lincoln's Birthday observation in 1950. Instead, an inconspicuous first-term senator from Wisconsin—identified with no particular issue—had been invited to address the ladies.

What Joseph R. McCarthy came to Wheeling, West Virginia, to talk about was Communists in the U.S. government. Exactly what he said was debatable. According to one report, McCarthy stated: "I have here in my hand a list of 205 that were known to the Secretary of State as being members of the Communist Party and who nevertheless are still working and shaping the policy of the State Department."[24] There was, however, no debating the impact of whatever McCarthy said. He had unveiled a Republican manifesto of another kind. Within weeks, RNC Chairman Gabrielson was declaring the uncovering of Communists was the GOP's major new business. McCarthy and this issue would rock American politics—and the Republican party—for the next five years.

The "Commie issue" was far from new in American politics. Most recently, amid the investigative craze of the Eightieth Congress, the House Un-American Activities Committee (HUAC, originally created in 1938) had won notoriety for its probe of subversion in the motion picture industry and the indictment of the Hollywood Ten. HUAC had then capped its work in the Eightieth Congress with some splashy revelations. Whittaker Chambers, a former Communist and currently a *Time* editor, charged that Alger Hiss, the current president of the Carnegie Endowment for International Peace, had been a Communist during the 1930s. Conservative columnists such as Fulton Lewis and Westbrook Pegler had long charged that New Deal officialdom was honeycombed with Communists, and Hiss, as a high-level State Department official, had been an FDR advisor at Yalta and an organizer of the San Francisco Conference on the United Nations. With the subsequent unearthing of the famous Pumpkin Papers—microfilmed copies of State Department reports that Chambers claimed Hiss had passed to him—the charge against Hiss escalated to Communist espionage. Coming as the Cold War continued to rage, and given the anticommunist tone of Truman's foreign policy, the Hiss charges naturally gave rise to suspicions that Communist foul play in Washington had undercut American foreign policy from Europe to China. Mao's Communists had just run Chiang's Nationalists off mainland China. The nation learned in September, 1949, that the Soviets now had the atom bomb. A month after a jury convicted Alger Hiss of perjury in January, 1950—the statute of limitations having expired for espionage—Canadian authorities arrested Klaus Fuchs, a German-born physicist accused of being a spy. FBI agents followed months later with the cracking of the atomic spy ring that included Julius and Ethel Rosenberg. The stage was well set for McCarthy.

Legend has it that Senator Joe McCarthy, hungry for an issue to shore up a deteriorating Wisconsin political base that would be tested in two years, discovered the communist issue over a strategy dinner at Washington's Colony Restaurant in December, 1950. But the careful researches of historian Michael O'Brien make plain that McCarthy had begun exploiting the communist issue a full three months before, when he attacked a Wisconsin newspaper and its city editor on this basis. This strike generated a good deal of favorable McCarthy publicity and led to similar incidents before McCarthy's "discovery" of anticommunism. Although he entered the Senate in 1947 labeled a liberal Republican and backed the liberal Stassen for the Republican presidential nomination in 1948, McCarthy's early voting record frustrated attempts at categorization. He had voted with Vandenberg on foreign policy matters and Taft on most domestic issues. In December, 1949, *Chicago Tribune* correspondent Walter Trohan had written of McCarthy as a "me-too" member of the "Eastern Seaboard internationalists," but "Tailgunner Joe" was mainly a Senate Republican backbencher with a doubtful Senate future. McCarthy's Wheeling remarks changed all that. Prior to Wheeling, the Wisconsin senator had been a largely indistinguishable garden variety Republican. Within months, McCarthy's name became synonymous with the anticommunist crusade. He offered what earlier anticommunists lacked—flamboyance, tenacity, and a knack for self-promotion. Moreover, the gentlemanly rules of the Senate just could not contain McCarthy.[25]

The Hiss conviction, the spy revelations, and other accompanying events made McCarthy's charges seem plausible. Post-1948 GOP desperation made them seem politically profitable. What McCarthy required most of the Republican command was tolerance. This he received, along with varying amounts of encouragement. Returning to Washington after his Lincoln's Birthday junket to West Virginia (along the way he changed the number of Communists in the State Department to 57), McCarthy spoke to the Senate on February 20 about the State Department's Communist problem. Two days later, the Senate unanimously voted to investigate McCarthy's charges. The resultant committee, headed by Millard Tydings, a conservative Democrat from Maryland, began its probe in March.

Anticommunist Right Wing Republican senators found McCarthy's crusade at once attractive and repellent. Taft initially described one McCarthy performance as "perfectly reckless, and unfounded charges could prove embarrassing to the GOP." Wherry reportedly confided to one State Department officer, "Oh Mac has got out on a limb and kind of made a fool of himself and we have to back him up now." Wherry later denied saying this, but according to his biographer, he hated demagogues like McCarthy, who "would not put his cards on the table."[26]

Nevertheless, the Wisconsin senator's stature in the GOP grew during the first half of 1950. GOP fortunes were low with Dewey's loss. Right Wing Republicans had fretted for years over the "socialist-tainted" New Deal bureaucracy. And anticommunism was now a hot issue. Moreover, foreign policy setbacks encouraged the search for culprits—and scapegoats. Republicans who were worried about Asian affairs naturally applauded when McCarthy set about investigating America's China policy. Taft, for his part, allegedly told the Wisconsin senator to move quickly to another cause if one did not work out. He also passed along possible subjects for McCarthy to investigate. McCarthy often went too far, but the partisan Mr. Republican found McCarthyism hard to resist. Perhaps Bricker best expressed the Right Wing attitude when telling McCarthy: "Joe, you're a dirty son of a bitch, but there are times when you've got to have a son of a bitch around, and this is one of them."[27]

A knot of GOP senators agreed heartily that McCarthy was a "dirty son of a bitch" and could find no excuses for his unconscionable buccaneering. On June 1, 1950, Margaret Chase Smith and six other moderate GOP senators issued a "Declaration of Conscience" that scolded nameless Republicans who exploited "fear, bigotry, ignorance, and intolerance" for political gain. Robert E. Wood angrily informed Smith that the "Declaration" "pretty well illustrates the deep gulf between . . . Eastern Republicans and the Midwestern Republicans."[28]

The Tydings committee report, issued in July, 1950, momentarily prevented additional wrangling among Republicans over McCarthy's activities. Even before the report's official appearance, Republicans as a whole were calling the Tydings hearings "Whitewash Incorporated." Actually, the report made McCarthy, not his original charges, the major issue. It accused the Wisconsin senator of perpetrating a "fraud and a hoax"—rough language to use against a Senate colleague. The report closed Republican ranks and made for an ugly partisan mood in the Senate, even triggering a brief shoving match between Senator Wherry and Edward P. Morgan, the Tydings committee counsel and the report's author. In the end, the Senate endorsed the Tydings committee's findings, but along straight party lines. Lodge, a committee member, filed his own "Individual Views." Even some of the most liberal signers of Smith's "Declaration of Conscience" expressed their dissatisfaction with the Tydings report and their support for McCarthy's ends—but not his means.[29] "McCarthyism" was now clearly a political issue, and the Tydings report made sure that it stayed that way.

A "conservative revival" is sweeping the nation, declared *Life* magazine in the spring of 1950. The "conservative revival" cut across party lines, but as *Life* advised, "The obvious opportunity of the Republicans is to develop a small-c conservatism which can be explained to the country as something different and more constructive than the old special interest standpattism."[30]

Right Wing Republicans may have suspected that *Life*'s "enlightened conservatism" was not really their brand of conservatism. In some important GOP primaries in 1950, Right Wing hopefuls had failed to unhorse liberal or moderate opponents. Party renegade Wayne Morse of Oregon overwhelmed primary challenger David I. Hoover, a professed ultra-conservative who had tried to link Morse and communism. In New Hampshire, Wesley Powell, the thirty-five-year-old former aide to Styles Bridges and the beneficiary of his organization, challenged incumbent Charles Tobey. "I'm proud to be a conservative," declared Powell, who branded the liberal Tobey a "Truman Republican." But Tobey squeaked by. Only in South Dakota did a truly Right Wing Republican, Francis Case, topple a less staunch incumbent. Case had campaigned against bipartisan foreign policy and his rival's spending record. Still, even the springtime successes of Earl Warren in California prompted *Life*'s somewhat confusing conclusion that "enlightened conservatism" was "causing a ruckus" in the GOP.[31]

The national gaze focused particularly on the ruckus in Pennsylvania in 1950, where observers looked for clues to the national GOP drift. The "Battle of Pennsylvania" pitted Governor James Duff against the Old Guard Republican machine of Joseph Grundy, now headed by G. Mason Owlett. Duff wanted the Republican Senate nomination. Duff was heavily favored against the Grundy outfit's selection, Representative John C. Kunkel. Realizing this, the Grundyites therefore decided to concentrate on the nomination for governor. Their candidate was the former GOP chairman of Philadelphia, Jay Cooke. Duff backed Judge John S. Fine of Luzerne County. Knowing that a victory for himself would mean little if the Grundy-Owlett faction controlled patronage in Harrisburg, Duff declared he would not run if Cooke were his fall ticketmate. Actually, Cooke was no cog in Grundy's Old Guard, but Grundy's backing nevertheless made Cooke the candidate of the Grundy Old Guard machine. Indeed, many other contrary considerations complicated "The Battle of Pennsylvania." Taft, for example, privately preferred Duff and Fine, partly out of gratitude for Duff's convention aid in 1948.[32]

Political observers and stump speakers generally disregarded these fine points. "The Battle of Pennsylvania" pitted Duff's "liberalism" (*Life*'s "enlightened conservatism") against GOP Old Guard "standpattisms." Born of bitterness, this power struggle degenerated into a meaningless volley of denunciation, charge, and countercharge. The issue, said Duff, was "Grundyism"—government by the few, for the few, and at the expense of the many. He lambasted the "high-button shoes" Old Guard reactionaries—"old fogies and sourpuss fakers." The Grundy forces, in turn, said that Duff was "power mad" and "a would-be Caesar" whose politics were New Dealish, not Republican. They charged that Duff used the state police for political bullying, and that Fine had winked at gambling and vice and made an alliance with a "whisky ring" when he was county political boss.

Duff's two-to-one victory margin over the Keystone State Old Guard, wrote Frederick Nelson in the *Saturday Evening Post*, "started a wave of speculation all over the country." Duff emerged as one of *Life*'s "conservative revivalists." *US News and World Report* discerned a swing to the political middle. But given the complexities of the Pennsylvania GOP infighting and the confusions of political labeling, there was relatively little the 1950 GOP primary season could presage. If anything, the GOP was settling for a position between "hell, no" and "me-too," a position eschewing Dewey's meek partisanship and embracing McCarthy's anticommunist charges, if not his methods. [33]

That exact position became clearer during the fall congressional campaign. The GOP slogan for 1950—"Liberty against Socialism"—was pure conservative Republicanism. Despite hopes in some quarters for an enlightened conservatism, this was the spirit that had governed the GOP in the aftermath of the Dewey defeat. In ascribing Dewey's setback to insufficient partisanship—"me-tooism"—Right Wing Republicans insured that the 1950 canvass would be spirited indeed. Actually, it turned into a political brawl, with McCarthyism and foreign policy questions highlighted by the Korean war, which made the combat all the more intense.

Out of all this came Republican victory—"indisputably Republican," judged the *New York Times*. [34] Republicans gained twenty-eight seats in the House, leaving the Democrats with a 234-to-199 command. Republicans won eighteen of thirty-six senatorial contests, for a total of five new seats. Senate Democrats maintained only a 49-to-47 edge. A southern Democrat–Republican alliance was expected to block all future Fair Deal reform on Capitol Hill. Moreover, Republicans had toppled two key Fair Dealers, majority leader Scott Lucas of Illinois and majority whip Francis Myers of Pennsylvania. GOP conservatives had promised big gains with a partisan campaign, and they delighted in them. The *Chicago Tribune* boasted, "The national election showed that our kind of middlewestern Republicanism is the winning kind." [35]

Such Republicanism certainly won in Illinois, where national GOP trends were clearly apparent. Ambitious and voluble Everett Dirksen had been a highly regarded representative with international tendencies before eye problems had forced him to retire from Congress in 1948. His medical troubles over, Dirksen in 1950 sought the GOP Senate nomination. He then displayed his well-known political flexibility. By concentrating on Democratic threats to individual freedom and even repudiating his prior vote for the Marshall Plan, which he now tagged "Operation Rathole," Dirksen finally won both the backing of the *Chicago Tribune*'s Robert R. McCormick and the GOP nomination.

Dirksen was now a certified Right Wing Republican. In the general election he blasted Democratic foreign policy bungling, had McCarthy campaign for him, and walloped majority leader Scott Lucas. In explaining Dirksen's victory, Old Guard Republicans chose to overlook Lucas's considerable campaign difficulties and instead credited Dirksen's new-found rightish ways.

Conservative Republicans were also successful elsewhere in the Midwest and Far West. Homer Capehart was reelected in Indiana, as were Bourke Hickenlooper of Iowa and Alexander Wiley in Wisconsin. Idaho replaced Glen H. Taylor, Wallace's 1948 runningmate who had lost in the primaries, with Herman Welker, a McCarthy admirer. In South Dakota, conservative Representative Francis P. Case won promotion to the Senate. Wallace Bennett, the former president of the National Association of Manufacturers, knocked off Elbert Thomas, a Fair Deal senator from Utah. In Colorado, Eugene Millikin held off a stiff challenge from Fair Deal Democrat John Carroll. Another classic liberal-conservative battle resulted in California's Congressman Richard Nixon's advancement to the upper chamber. Nixon, who had won notoriety for his pursuit of Alger Hiss while a member of HUAC, had successfully made an issue of the Truman administration's Asian policy and his opponent Helen Gahagan Douglas's liberal record.

There were some disappointments. Missouri's conservative Forrest Donnell failed in his reelection bid. And despite the much-noted victory of John Marshall Butler over McCarthy foe Millard Tydings in the Maryland senate race, the GOP trend throughout the East was largely liberal. Duff, slayer of the Pennsylvania Old Guard, defeated majority whip Francis Myers in a rugged battle. In New England, Senators Aiken and Tobey held their own. John Lodge, the Massachusetts senator's brother, was elected governor of Connecticut, and New York Governor Dewey again won reelection. The "only problem" for the Republican future, Wood wrote in his postelection roundup to MacArthur, was the continuing "gulf" between midwestern Republicans and these eastern ones: "The Eastern Republicans are almost as much New Deal and Fair Deal as the Democrats themselves."[36]

A giddy Taft was making no such distinctions after election day 1950. "All the eight new senators look to me like stalwarts," he wrote to Styles Bridges. Taft did not know how the Senate picture could be better for the GOP.[37] Mr. Republican had even greater reason to cheer. His own reelection bid against the fired-up opposition of organized labor had turned out well. Labor had had a ready war chest and had fielded zealous political workers against him in Ohio. Taft faced a popular opponent in state auditor Joseph T. Ferguson. Although Ferguson's reputation as a lightweight caused pundits to treat his candidacy as a joke and encouraged speculation that the Truman White House, wanting Taft as the GOP standard-bearer in 1952, had connived in "Jumping Joe's" selection, Taft had awaited nobody's help— shoring up his Ohio organization, working to win over the press, and grudgingly surrendering to public relations advice. He also labored hard on the hustings, taking his "Liberty against Socialism" pitch to hospitable and to hostile crowds, alike.

On election day, Taft beat Ferguson by almost 550,000 votes, scoring one of the great triumphs of Ohio's senatorial history. Robert McCormick and the *Chicago Tribune* spoke for many in proclaiming Taft to be "the logical" Republican presidential candidate. "People who are lukewarm towards you said you would have to have a smashing victory to be nominated," McCormick wrote to Taft. "Well, you have had it." Had this victory really finished the "Taft can't win" bogey? Taft himself put off all presidential talk but exultantly concluded that Republicans could recapture the White House in 1952 by employing the 1950 general strategy.[38]

Clearly, the Republican Right as a whole was encouraged. Sizing up the 1950 congressional races, Senator James Kem of Missouri, who would be up for reelection in two years, concluded that "clear and outspoken," "no-holds-barred" criticism of certain Truman administration policies had assured GOP victories.[39] The extreme expression of this administration opposition was anticommunism, and GOP winners believed that its impact was indeed powerful. James Reston's campaign sampling led him to see the importance of McCarthyism. Even Republicans like Duff had echoed McCarthy's charges during the campaign—and some Democrats had also joined in. In the end, the electoral defeat of Maryland senator Millard Tydings, whom McCarthy had personally campaigned against, gave the Wisconsin senator an undeserved reputation as a national political power. McCarthy himself was one of many Republicans who saw visions of 1952 in the 1950 congressional returns. Wrote McCarthy, "I sincerely hope we can continue on now, and elect a real *American* president in 1952."[40]

No issue mattered more to Americans in the 1950 elections than foreign policy, especially American foreign policy in the Orient. Republicans as a party had a longtime traditional interest—emotional and political—in the Far East. American triumphs there—the acquisition of the Philippines, the Open Door notes, and the Treaty of Portsmouth—had come with Republicans in the White House. Far Eastern trade had boomed during GOP times, and American missionaries in the Orient largely had been recruited from and reported back to the Republican Midwest.

Although the GOP was no Asian party, as some suggested, it did include a cluster of "Asia Firsters." Republicans like Wherry, Bridges, Jenner, Judd, and Knowland often charged that the Truman administration's European-oriented foreign policy slighted the Orient. While Knowland and Bridges said they only wanted greater balance in American foreign policy, some prewar isolationists like Taft and Wherry consistently displayed far greater interest in Asia than Europe. These men were frequently so much less interventionistic about the Far East than about Europe that some of them embraced, in the words of William S. White, an "Asian Cult."[41]

With the passage of the Marshall Plan, Republicans—initially Right Wing Republicans—quickly turned to the Far East. Since American foreign policy in that area lay outside the limits of bipartisan cooperation, here was partisan pickings aplenty. Beset by revolution, China had been the major Far Eastern concern since V-J Day. By the fall of 1949, Mao's Communists had pushed Chiang's Nationalists off the mainland and established the People's Republic of China. Moreover, Mao himself had aligned China with the Soviet Union in the Cold War.

The State Department's White Paper on China, issued in August, 1949, blamed Chiang's downfall on the internal failures of the Nationalist movement, not the inadequacy of American economic and military aid. Senators Bridges, Wherry, Knowland, and Democrat Pat McCarran of Nevada immediately branded the White Paper "a 1054-page whitewash of wishful do-nothing policy." The Nationalists had had no guns to fight with, and Democratic administrations were responsible for that failure, they said. Late in 1949, when the *New York Times* reported the administration's decision to stop American military aid to Chiang's Nationalists on Formosa, GOP conservatives exploded. "Cowardly bungling and groveling," declared Bridges; the policy of a "small group of willful men in the State Department," charged Taft and Knowland.[42]

"Who Lost China?" Right Wing Republicans had found their answer well before the fall of 1949, and other Republicans were in varying degrees of agreement. "The New Deal coddled communism in China from the start," explained Daniel Reed.[43] Conservative Republicans gave their unstinting support to the Nationalist Chinese. They blistered the Roosevelt and Truman administrations for compromising Chinese sovereignty at Yalta, for pressuring Chiang to form a coalition with the Communists, and for limiting military and economic aid to the Nationalist Chinese. America might have been able to keep China from the Reds, their argument continued, but "willful men" in the State Department—the "China Hands"—had subverted American might. This "conspiracy theory" had, of course, gained currency beginning in June, 1945, when an FBI raid on the New York office of the leftish Asian affairs journal *Amerasia* led to the arrest of, among others, China Hand John Service (who was later exonerated of these particular espionage charges). Senator McCarthy, although never before linked with the Republican Right, gave this conspiracy theory its fullest and timeliest expression in Wheeling in February, 1950.

·Korea was another Far Eastern concern that soon dominated newspaper headlines, as the North Korean army invaded South Korea on June 25, 1950. Although Secretary of State Dean Acheson had failed to include South Korea within the American defense perimeter in January, 1950, the United States attempted quickly but unsuccessfully to stem the North Korean advance with air and sea forces. With the Soviet Union boycotting its meetings, the U.N. Security Council voted to repel the North Korean advance by force.

GOP conservatives, Asia Firsters, and prewar isolationists—all generally applauded President Truman's quick deployment of American troops to Korea and of the U.S. Seventh Fleet to patrol the waters between Red China and Formosa—all done without the authorization of the Congress or the United Nations. It was high time for such action. Still, there was no cease-fire in the Old Guard's condemnation of administration foreign policy. Democratic presidents were still disregarding established constitutional channels. Moreover, the rough early going of U.N. forces under General Douglas MacArthur also prompted GOP muttering over the administration's lack of preparedness and aggressiveness. Along with increased grumbling about the containment policy came Republican calls for the reunification of Korea. And frustration on the Korean battlefield bred further ideas of conspiracy at home. Senator George Malone of Nevada, for instance, saw a deliberate pattern of "losing strategic means throughout the world."[44]

MacArthur's stunning amphibious assault at Inchon on September 5 and the subsequent rout of the North Korean army broke this pattern. After Inchon, the Truman administration made a reunited Korea under a freely chosen government its own goal. For the GOP, the Inchon landing created, according to historian Robert Caridi, "rather spectacular visions" of the potential of more aggressive policies.[45] By mid-October, U.N. forces seized the North Korean capital, Pyongyang. As the congressional elections approached, these gains helped focus Republican criticism on the administration's general bipartisan foreign policy, and for the most part away from its Korean War effort.

After election day, however, the character of the conflict quickly changed. In late November the Chinese entered the war and ultimately overwhelmed the U.N. forces, driving them deep into South Korea. Chinese intervention forced the administration once again to limit its war aims only to a free South Korea. But Right Wing Republicans now saw the Korean conflict as a full-fledged Sino-American war, and they rejected the concept of limitation. Either declare war on China or bring American boys home, and Right Wing Republicans advocated both policies simultaneously. The root of this seeming inconsistency was their belief that Truman, as Jenner put it, "blundered, tricked and betrayed us into a war." Truman's half-hearted prosecution of the war made withdrawal that much more attractive.[46]

MacArthur also rejected the concept of limited war and pressed the administration to expand the conflict by blockading the Chinese coast, bombing Chinese targets, and using Chinese Nationalist troops. Rebuffed, the general complained of administration restrictions in a letter to Joseph Martin. When the House Republican leader made the general's letter public on April 5, 1951, the president was forced to meet this constitutional challenge. Truman stripped MacArthur of his command.

MacArthur's stature in the GOP and the belief that "there is no substitute for victory" prompted the Republican Right to take up MacArthur's cause immediately—although it continued to talk of withdrawal. Jenner saw the MacArthur sack as the work of a secret inner coterie directed by the Soviet Union, while the Right's new ally, Joe McCarthy, cited another reason for the sack of MacArthur: Truman—"the sonofabitch"—had acted after a night "of bourbon and benedictine."[47] With news of MacArthur's dismissal, Republican Capitol Hill leaders huddled in Joe Martin's office. Afterward, Martin announced that the GOP conference had resolved to investigate American foreign policy and to ask MacArthur to address Congress. Martin told reporters that possible impeachments had also been discussed. Americans, as frustrated as the general with containment and limited war, welcomed him home as a messiah. MacArthur, in turn, did not disappoint his Capitol Hill hosts. His "Old Soldiers Never Die" speech brought some solons to tears. One Right Wing Republican was absolutely spellbound. "We heard God speak here today," claimed Representative Dewey Short, "God in the flesh, the voice of God."[48]

But this was MacArthur's high point. After the long congressional investigation, the conclusion grew that MacArthur wanted, in the words of General Omar Bradley, "the wrong war, at the wrong place, at the wrong time and with the wrong enemy." In the end the Republican Right only challenged the wisdom, not the right, of Truman's move. They supported MacArthur's bid to widen the war, but, failing that, they wanted American withdrawal. Either get on with the fighting or get out, alternatives represented in the two unsuccessful resolutions of Washington's Senator Harry P. Cain.

The MacArthur-Truman clash, with all its complications for American policy in the Far East, was only part of the larger debate over bipartisan foreign policy. Dewey's extension of bipartisanship into new foreign policy areas during the 1948 campaign left the concept extremely vulnerable upon his loss. Bipartisanship, said its critics, was nothing more than "me-too" foreign policy. Even Vandenberg, the chief architect of bipartisan foreign policy, puzzled over its political impact. "How is it possible to have a dynamic party system when paramount questions are to be exempted from politics?" he wondered.[49]

Although the 1948 electoral debacle amply answered such questions for Republicans of many different persuasions, more than GOP political needs helped to undermine bipartisanship. The Truman administration had become increasingly independent, consulting with Republicans only when absolutely necessary and, complained Republicans, withholding necessary foreign policy information. For example, the designation of Dean Acheson as secretary of state was sprung on the Republicans without prior consultation. Worse, post-1948 foreign policy setbacks and alleged Democratic blunders—China, for instance—jeopardized a policy that had been built on earlier international triumphs such as the Marshall Plan. Finally, bipartisanship depended on delicate personal bonds, and Vandenberg, now dying of cancer, was often absent from the Senate.

By mid-1950, even before the Korean War, the Republican assault on bipartisanship was already mounting. Senator Bridges said that it was high time for a "showdown" on bipartisan foreign policy. In May, 1950, Senator Jenner charged that bipartisan foreign policy had resulted in "a disgraceful abandonment of our vital interests, a vicious undermining of our economic and financial solvency, and the flagrant neglect of even the minimum requirement for an impregnable national defense."[50] A "chorus of disapproval" of Truman foreign policy came in late August when four GOP members of the Senate Foreign Relations Committee issued a manifesto excoriating Democratic failings—the past "blunders" of Yalta and Potsdam, as well as present American military weakness. Among the fault-finders were H. Alexander Smith of New Jersey and Lodge, both of the "Vandenberg school." From a hospital bed in Michigan, Vandenberg himself indicated his "general agreement" with this manifesto.[51]

The fall campaign of 1950 merely hastened the neo-isolationist drift. "On the political stump [the Republicans] sound angry enough to make Joe McCarthy Secretary of State," reported James Reston.[52] Republicans did hit the administration's foreign policy all along the line. Only in its exultant tone was the *Chicago Tribune* different from other quarters of opinion in predicting a "wholesale revision of our foreign policy." At the very least, the 1950 congressional returns signaled the emergence of foreign policy hardliners as the "major political force" in the GOP—a power shift symbolized by the departure of internationalists such as Vandenberg, Ives, and Margaret Chase Smith from the Senate GOP Policy Committee.[53]

By December, 1950, a "Great Debate" had begun. In that month, the administration made public its decision to send American troops to Europe as part of its NATO commitment and to appoint General Dwight D. Eisenhower as the head of NATO forces. Conservative Republicans were outraged. Why beef up Europe when American boys were on the run in Korea? they asked. Far Eastern events had only served to heighten their latent hostility toward Europe. Britain, for example, had recognized Red China, and the failure of the allies to support United States policy in Korea was taken as proof of European unfaithfulness. "The old 'empire' has doublecrossed us at every turn," Representative Daniel Reed wrote, "and the tragedy . . . is that we are paying for it with the lives of our boys. . . ."[54]

On December 20, 1950, Herbert Hoover made a nationwide address that expressed the foreign policy beliefs of many Right Wing Republicans. Korea was obviously a defeat for the United Nations, said the former president. In fact, the United Nations had become "a forum of continuous smear on our honor, our ideals and our purposes." Great Britain was "flirting with the appeasement of the Communist bloc," and Europe had failed to develop "unity of purpose." The United States must realize the futility of throwing ground troops into war against the Communist land mass. The defense of continental Europe was a European matter, Hoover believed. America could neither create nor buy with money the spiritual force that Europe needed. The United States must arm "to the teeth" air and naval forces in order to control the Atlantic and Pacific and to guard against a possible Communist invasion of the Western Hemisphere. Hoover noted that this hemispheric approach would ultimately reduce costs, allow for a balanced budget, and free the United States from "inflation and economic degeneration." In short, Hoover would make the Western Hemisphere the "Gibraltar of Western Civilization."[55]

On Capitol Hill, the central issue of this Great Debate became clear when Taft took the Senate floor on January 5, 1951: Did the legislative or executive branch control the commitment of American troops abroad? Well into his full-fledged attack on bipartisan foreign policy, which he claimed had ended with the 1948 election, Taft turned to the content of American foreign policy. Despite some private doubts about Hoover's hemispheric approach, Taft defended the former president's general stand. Moreover, while dissenting from those who would abandon the rest of the world and rely solely on continental defense, Taft reiterated his strong belief in a strong sea and air defense. The United States should not try to be a controlling power on the European land mass. Hence, Taft opposed the stationing of American troops in Europe at this time. But whatever was to be the policy, concluded Taft, Congress must have an equal role in determining it. Foreign policy was not, as Truman maintained, the absolute right of the president.[56]

Among Republicans, eastern internationalists such as Lodge, Saltonstall, Dulles, and Duff immediately criticized Taft's address. They tended to support the essentials of the administration's diplomatic moves and to grant the executive, not the legislative branch, the right to control the stationing of American troops. Dewey judged the latter to be "a job for experts, not politicians." Right Wing Republicans, on the other hand, lauded Taft and stood against the president's claim to an absolute right to station troops, as well as to determine the foreign policy that required such action. Conservative hopes along this line ultimately rested on the Wherry Resolution. Introduced on January 8, this resolution prohibited the sending of American troops to Europe until the formulation of a *congressional* policy. According to Wherry and other Right Wing Republicans, "Congress must recapture its own responsibilities, which New Deal Presidents usurped."[57]

But Right Wing Republicans also took this opportunity to flog Truman's basic foreign policy, especially with regard to our allies. Reflecting the current American experience in Korea, Senator Kem declared, "We need friends with cool hands, not cold feet." The longstanding Right Wing concern about overcommitted American resources also persisted. The Truman-Acheson containment policy, exclaimed Bricker, "would bleed us white both physically and financially."[58]

The most forceful presentation of the administration position came on February 1, 1951, when General Dwight D. Eisenhower spoke before a joint session of Congress. Eisenhower, who was highly esteemed in both parties, urged that the Congress place no limits on the number of troops that could be sent to Europe. Eisenhower further recommended that the United States arm Europe on a scale comparable to that of lend-lease days. While most Republicans remained deferential to Ike during investigative hearings, Taft stood out in his vigorous questioning of the general.

Actually, the Ohio senator was showing considerable flexibility on the troops-to-Europe issue, finally agreeing to accept more than three divisions "to show Europe we will participate." But the constitutional issue still remained. On the troop question, at least, Taft proved to be a stand-in for Vandenberg among Republicans.[59]

When Democratic leaders in the Senate also proved willing to compromise over troops for Europe and the legality of it, the Great Debate sputtered to a close in early April. The Senate passed, 49 to 43, the McClellan amendment, which stated that it was the sense of the Senate that no troops in addition to four earmarked divisions could be sent to Europe without specific Senate approval. Only eight Republicans, all from the East, opposed the McClellan Resolution—a clear sign that the "neo-isolationist" assumptions of Hoover, Taft, Wherry, and other conservatives had a strong grip on the GOP by 1950. Later, Taft joined the majority in voting, 69 to 21, to table the Wherry Resolution, which would have prohibited *any* troops from being sent until Congress set a policy.

Taft was quite happy with the result; the McClellan amendment was no law, but he believed that it represented a "clear statement" of the Senate's right to pass on the sending of troops to Europe to implement NATO. The Truman administration, having opposed the proviso for further congressional approval, rejected Taft's interpretation. Acheson called the McClellan Resolution "a present for everybody," without legal force.[60] The Great Debate thus left the constitutional question unsettled—and the McClellan Resolution would never be tested.

However valid, the McClellan Resolution represented an important concession to Taft and the Republican Right on the issue of executive-legislative prerogatives. Democrats—at least those on Capitol Hill—realized that if bipartisan foreign policy was to be continued, the legitimate concerns of its foes would have to be addressed. Although Taft and other Right Wing Republicans had recognized the need for American troops in Europe, the Europe-first, internationalist, bipartisan policy had lost considerable ground since 1948. The defeat of Dewey and the effective departure of Vandenberg hampered a policy that was already hurt by mounting foreign policy reverses and the Truman administration's deteriorating political position. Most significant, events in the Far East shifted the focus of national attention after the 1948 election, and this clearly redounded to the benefit of the Republicans, particularly Right Wing Republicans. Still, there was no certainty that the Old Guard's foreign policy—inconsistent, confused, narrow, and negative as it sometimes was—offered an appealing alternative for the American people.

The story was similar on domestic policy in the four years after the 1948 election. By early 1951, according to historian Alonzo Hamby, President Truman's Fair Deal represented "more of an inspirational banner than a real political program."[61] It was getting nowhere on Capitol Hill. Symbolically, there was no repeal of the Taft-Hartley Act, the main achievement of the Republican Eightieth Congress. A combination of GOP gains in the 1950 congressional elections and China's entry into the Korean conflict had merely secured the anti-Fair Deal work of a coalition of southern Democrats and Republicans.

But GOP conservatives offered no real program of their own to replace the Fair Deal. As far as they were concerned, the 1950 election returns proved that crying "socialism" about the Truman program was enough. Subsequently, tales of influence peddling, petty corruption, and political cronyism in the Truman administration made an aggressive, negative approach all the more inviting—and the Republican Right responded with gusto. After 1948, even Taft, who had always distinguished himself by his broad, reform-minded conservatism and his political integrity, entered what his biographer, William S. White, called his "sad, worst, period"—a time of negativism and even political cynicism.[62] This kind of disposition, along with a sincere belief in anticommunism, ultimately led the Republican Old Guard to support McCarthy and McCarthyism, despite the realization by some Right Wing Republicans such as Taft that the Wisconsin senator's political swashbuckling posed definite hazards.

Right Wing Republican assumptions clearly held sway in the GOP in the years following the Dewey debacle. Nowhere was this more obvious than in the Great Debate. But if the Great Debate clearly demonstrated that the Republican Right had gained commanding power in the GOP, it also spotlighted the nature and severity of the ideological and sectional cleavage in the party. Along this line, GOP presidential politics complicated matters, especially when Taft and Eisenhower differed so markedly over the troops issue. Both had been mentioned as possible GOP standard-bearers in 1952, and their clash fueled political gossip. James Reston thought this "one of the most interesting aspects" of the Great Debate.[63]

If the Elephant Remembers

Sometime during the Great Debate of early 1951, Senator Robert A. Taft had an appointment at the Pentagon. Upon arriving at a secondary entrance, Taft was met by two Pentagon officials who whisked the senator to the office of General Dwight D. Eisenhower. Eisenhower had initiated this secret meeting and Taft had quickly accepted, even offering to come to the Pentagon. As Eisenhower later recalled, he had hoped that their meeting would produce assurances from Taft that collective security would remain a "definite feature" of future American foreign policy.

Their talk was long and friendly, although Eisenhower noted that Taft seemed a bit suspicious. During the discussion, Taft kept returning to the central question of the Great Debate—the specific number of American troops to be sent to Europe. Taft would give no direct pledge on the future of collective security, and this increased Eisenhower's fears about the strength of isolationism in Congress and the Republican party. The general's fears were in turn damaging to the presidential hopes of Robert Taft. Assurances from Taft on the future of collective security might have allayed Eisenhower's fears and encouraged him to drop any political ambitions for himself. Eisenhower intimated as much and had already prepared a statement that he believed would squash all speculation regarding any Eisenhower presidential candidacy. But because Taft had made no explicit promise, Eisenhower finally decided to destroy this statement after their meeting.[1]

At the conclusion of the Great Debate in the spring of 1951, Eisenhower departed for Europe to set up the NATO command. Senator Taft remained on Capitol Hill to chart another bid for the GOP presidential nomination. Speculation continued, however, regarding a possible Taft-Eisenhower contest for that prize.

On October 16, 1951, Senator Robert A. Taft officially became a candidate for the Republican presidential nomination. He promised a "vigorous presentation" of such principles as "liberty of the individual," state and local control, and economic freedom. As he again reached for the GOP presidential nomination, Taft displayed "a kind of quiet confidence."[2] He had reason for such confidence. This was his third bid; the signs were favorable. Dewey's 1948 setback had left the party more open than ever to a conservative takeover. Conservatives claimed that Taft could do no worse than the four prior GOP "me-too" standard-bearers. Taft's 1950 landslide victory in Ohio, many believed, had buried the "Taft can't win" argument. Indeed, this win helped Taft to strengthen his hold on organization Republicans around the country as well as the GOP congressional delegation. There was talk of a "New Taft"—one radiating confidence and personal warmth.

Also fueling the bandwagon was the Taft organization, seasoned and determined not to repeat earlier blunders. This organization boasted some GOP bigwigs. Former national chairman B. Carroll Reece joined the Taft camp, as did John D.M. Hamilton, GOP chairman from 1936 to 1940. A big catch for the Taft side was Tom Coleman, Wisconsin GOP boss and engineer of Stassen's primary triumph there in 1948. What the Taft organization had in experience, however, it lacked in breadth. There had been no effort to bring in political professionals from the East. As a result, Taft was surrounded mainly by midwestern right-wing advisors. The Taft team remained confident. And, although opponents doubted the validity of this optimism and refused to believe Taft's claims that as of February, 1952, he had 635 delegates, there was still much concern in liberal quarters about the boom for Mr. Republican.

Not even all conservatives had confidence in either Taft's electoral prospects or his policies. The Ohio senator's independence, of course, had troubled some conservatives for many years. Senator George "Molly" Malone of Nevada was one GOP hard-liner who was especially rattled by Taft's irregular ways. Malone constantly favored a return to high protective tariffs, and he often urged Taft to take a similar stand. "Bob badly needs some positive program," Malone told a Taft aide in early 1951. Later that year, one scout reported that "Molly is still carrying a peeve" because Taft had once voted for reciprocal trade extension.[3]

Outside of Washington, Taft's waywardness also disturbed conservatives. George Creel, who had been a Wilson administration official and was now a dissident California Democrat, was interested in South Dakota Senator Karl Mundt's scheme to join together southern conservative Democrats and Republicans. Taft was one possible candidate for such a union, and Taft supporters hoped for Creel's help. But the Ohio senator's "adventures in me-tooism" distressed Creel. When Mundt tried to ease Creel's worries by explaining some of Taft's legislative stands, even he had to admit that Taft was "a little on the socialistic side" on the public housing issue.[4]

Creel also complained that Taft lacked the "evangelical fervor that wins enthusiasm." Indeed, many conservative Republicans who supported Taft's public policies had doubts about his chances for electoral success, especially in the new television age. Conservative newspaper mogul Frank Gannett thought that television would merely advertise Taft's lack of "political sex appeal." Even Taft supporters often winced at what television brought into their living rooms. One expressed shock upon watching the Ohioan thoughtlessly push aside a little girl on his way to a New Hampshire campaign appearance. Taft well-wishers recommended that the senator see a public relations specialist.[5]

In the meantime, two personalities with plenty of political sex appeal were presenting Taft and the conservative cause with problems. Wisconsin's Senator Joseph McCarthy had expressed no presidential ambitions, and there had been no serious talk of a McCarthy run. But McCarthy would certainly figure in the GOP presidential equation. Exactly how became a critical question in late 1951, when reports circulated that Republican leaders were attempting to drop the McCarthy issue. Taft himself indicated as much by a speech in Des Moines, Iowa, criticizing McCarthy's attack on General George Marshall. Taft claimed that the Wisconsin senator had gone too far in this instance, and he expressed doubt that communism would be an issue in 1952.

Ambivalence had always marked Taft's attitude toward McCarthy, and publicly Taft had basically kept quiet. Now was certainly no time for a clash with the Wisconsin senator. Although McCarthy's general popular appeal had never been tested, he did have a loyal and vocal following. Many conservatives, even critics of McCarthy's slam-bang approach, believed that any attack on his methods would seriously undermine anticommunism. George Creel, for example, complained of the constant "note of deprecation" in Taft's references to McCarthy.[6] Moreover, McCarthy had considerable clout in Wisconsin, an important GOP primary state.

Robert Taft feared any potential McCarthy trouble and asked Tom Coleman for help. As Wisconsin GOP boss, Coleman knew that conditions had changed since he had engineered McCarthy's Senate victory in 1946. By late 1951, McCarthy had developed a "Christ-like complex," Coleman reported. McCarthy told Coleman that Taft would have to support him totally before he would endorse Taft. Taft nevertheless informed Hoover that Coleman still believed that he could bring McCarthy around.[7] It was Taft, though, who seemed to make "amends with McCarthy." Taft gave McCarthy a strong plug in early 1952. McCarthy, for his part, remained silent, and there were even reports he favored General Douglas MacArthur as the next GOP presidential candidate. In the end, however, the Wisconsin GOP backed Taft in the primary.

It was inevitable that General Douglas MacArthur would also figure in the 1952 nomination battle. He simply would not fade away. A war hero and a great orator, MacArthur was a demigod to those who seethed at the stalemate and indecision in Korea. Paradoxically, he had become a favorite of both isolationists and internationalists. Since his homecoming, he had also trumpeted the conservative virtues of individualism and self-reliance. And despite his public repudiation of political aspirations, political speculation concerning the general persisted. Gannett maintained that television would be crucial in the upcoming presidential campaign, and unlike Taft, MacArthur was superb on television.[8] South Dakota's Senator Karl Mundt, in turn, believed that a MacArthur-Taft ticket would be a "wonderful tonic for America."[9]

Although MacArthur insisted throughout that Taft should be the Republican choice, his public statements often proved vague and inconclusive. Some MacArthur moves appeared to be either politically self-serving or just plain foolish. In September, 1951, he spoke in Cleveland of Ohio's historic role in national leadership—a role, MacArthur added, that may increase "in the not too distant future." Political observers and some Taft partisans saw MacArthur's words as a definite endorsement for Taft.[10] But Taft campaign operative John Hamilton was not satisfied and took up the matter with MacArthur. The general maintained that the speech had been a Taft endorsement. Perhaps it was, wrote Hamilton, but it seemed that way only to some. "A substantial group must have their answers spelled out for them and cannot rely on their powers of deduction." Hamilton wanted a bolder declaration. Several days later, the *Milwaukee Journal* reported that MacArthur had urged Wisconsin backers to get behind Taft in the spring primaries. Two weeks later came the news that MacArthur's aide, Major General Courtney Whitney, had informed one MacArthur enthusiast that the general would enter no presidential primaries.[11]

Still, this was hardly the kind of support Taft's managers had in mind. MacArthur's ambiguity vexed Taft supporters, as did the activities of newly hatched MacArthur-for-President clubs in the key primary states of Wisconsin and Minnesota. In December, 1951, Hamilton met with MacArthur to discuss these matters. The result of their meeting, Hamilton reported, "could not have been more disheartening." The general believed that to squelch these pro-MacArthur movements would be "a most harmful influence," since they were along "conservative lines." He also claimed an inability to keep people from organizing MacArthur clubs if they wanted to. These movements, which had already put up primary delegate slates in Minnesota, would not divide the conservative vote, MacArthur claimed; rather, they would split up those voters who wanted a general for president, thus cutting into Eisenhower's support. "Unbelievable," wrote Hamilton.[12]

The MacArthur-Hamilton conference obviously settled nothing. Either MacArthur was being coy or had left his knack for strategy on the battlefield.

Just what was MacArthur up to? Conservative columnist George Sokolsky, believing that all the mail he had received on the subject gave him a right to know, went to MacArthur's Waldorf Astoria suite to find out for himself in December, 1951. The general assured Sokolsky that he was *absolutely* for Taft—an assurance Sokolsky quickly relayed to the Taft camp. [13] In the end, Taft and Herbert Hoover got MacArthur to ask all Minnesota delegates favorable to him to withdraw. Even so, there was no outright MacArthur endorsement of Taft. MacArthur remained, wrote Arthur Krock, the "political x of 1952." [14]

A far more definite political factor by early 1952 was General Dwight D. Eisenhower. MacArthur's former underling was on the minds of most Republicans, since this military hero was a political natural. With an easy way and an infectious grin, Eisenhower had the common touch and, unlike MacArthur, never aroused the public's fears about a military man in the White House. If Eisenhower was a natural politician, he also seemed apolitical. Unlike MacArthur, he carried no political battle scars. Indeed, the question was constantly asked: Was Ike a Democrat or Republican? In 1948 some members in both parties had wanted Ike to top their ticket, but he stayed out of politics for that season. Presidential talk nevertheless persisted, becoming louder and more Republican as time went on. A year later, *Kansas City Star* president Roy Roberts gave assurances that Ike, who had grown up in Abilene, Kansas, was "a good Kansas Republican." Not only that, said Roberts, but Eisenhower would accept a draft and might be persuaded to run.

Subsequently, at a crowded news conference on January 5, 1952, Henry Cabot Lodge, Jr., of Massachusetts announced that Eisenhower's name would be entered in the New Hampshire primary. Next day came word out of NATO headquarters in France: The general would indeed accept the Republican nomination, but he would neither seek the nomination nor join in any preconvention political activities. The *New York Times* and the *Chicago Sun Times* quickly joined *Life* and other publications in support of Ike. Taft, for his part, interpreted Eisenhower's statement to mean he would not be an active candidate, although he would accept a draft. MacArthur, in turn, viewed the Eisenhower candidacy within the framework of his own unsuccessful presidential bid in 1948. "Eisenhower's absence will be a telling factor against him," wrote MacArthur. [15]

The battle lines for 1952 were finally shaping up. There were, of course, other aspirants. California's Governor Earl Warren was an active candidate, as was Harold E. Stassen (although Taft managers felt sure that the latter was only a "hatchet man" for Eisenhower). But the main contenders were Taft and Eisenhower, and shortly after the Lodge announcement, the Taft camp joined the battle. "Hero worship is no substitute for faith based on known performance. Neither is glamour, or sex appeal," Taft aide David Ingalls told the RNC in early January, 1952.[16] Ingalls's remarks presaged the rough political combat ahead.

Hero worship, glamor, sex appeal—were these all that separated Taft and Eisenhower? Not entirely. There were differences of political style and strategy. Where Eisenhower's Republicanism had to be vouched for, Taft's was unassailable. While Taft relished political battle, Ike shunned it. After 1948, Right Wing Republicans—especially those who had supported Dewey at the 1948 convention—were certain that the GOP needed a fighting standard-bearer. Ike would blur party lines in the Willkie tradition, while Taft would sharpen them. General Albert C. Wedemeyer reported that, although a "capable army officer" and "lovable character," Eisenhower was "an appeaser, an individual either incapable or unwilling to meet issues head on."[17]

Yet it was precisely this ability to dull political differences that Ike's boosters claimed the GOP needed, since, as a minority party, the GOP had to lure independents and disaffected Democratic voters into its ranks—voters who would be put off by the Old Guard's negativism and partisanship. Conservatives naturally rejected this notion, mainly because they disputed the premise that independent votes were automatically liberal votes. Right Wing Republicans like Taft believed that the independent voter was only waiting for the Republicans to offer a real choice—that is, a conservative choice. Finally, the makeup of Eisenhower's support annoyed Right Wing Republicans. Scott, Duff, Lodge, and Dewey—this was an Old Guard enemies list. Wrote John Taber, "Eisenhower has the support of the crowd, who, three times before, have been back of a 'me-too' campaign."[18]

Taft's suspicions that an Eisenhower presidency would result in a Republican New Deal administration with as much spending and socialism as under Truman stemmed only from his appraisal of Ike's character and backers, since there were few other clues to the general's attitudes. Naturally, Taft people hoped Ike would lose support as he took specific policy stands. Eisenhower's early primary wins made this haziness all the more tormenting for the Taft camp. One Taft aid suggested revising the popular phrase "I Like Ike" into "But What Does Ike Like?"[19]

When Ike finally returned home and began discussing domestic policy, it proved a mixed blessing for Taft. Eisenhower told a news conference in early June, 1952, that the 1950 GOP statement of principles was "the best statement" of his own political beliefs. Taft, of course, had been largely responsible for that document, as the Ohioan quickly pointed out. But in the end, domestic policy questions never really became important in their preconvention clash. Any distinction ultimately rested not on specific policy proposals, but on tone or emphasis and on the makeup of each candidate's supporters. Taft had battled Democratic presidents and programs since his arrival on Capitol Hill. Yet Taft, himself, was not ready to dismantle the New Deal structure. In some cases, he had even advanced proposals of a liberal character. Still, Taft continued to rail against Democratic New and Fair Dealings. This fact, along with his conservative following, helped maintain Taft's conservative image. On domestic matters, Eisenhower conveyed and retained the more progressive or liberal reputation.

On foreign policy matters, however, there was much less mystery about the differences between them. And these were basic to the nomination struggle. Taft and Eisenhower had clashed before over the basics of American foreign policy, and supporters of each predicted dire results for American foreign policy should the other win the nomination. While both agreed that the nation's NATO obligation must be met and that the United States must aid in the rearmament of Europe, Taft-Eisenhower differences over this specific American role in Europe were especially wide. Further, Eisenhower championed the infantry's role in military policy; Taft stressed air and sea power. Eisenhower still had faith in the United Nations; Taft thought it a failure. Overall, Taft shared the Republican Right's preoccupation with the Far East; Eisenhower did not. Ike stressed the advantages of collective action; Taft, who had gone along with most of these efforts, focused on the disadvantages.

Political wisdom nevertheless suggested that Taft soft-pedal foreign policy disagreements with Eisenhower in the preconvention period. As the convention neared, Taft even claimed that there was little distance between him and Eisenhower on foreign policy. Privately, Eisenhower forces shared this assessment, but they felt that the differences were wide enough to be worth exploiting during the battle for the GOP nomination. Eisenhower, whose style was usually not to underscore differences in public, told reporters that Taft was an "isolationist."

The Taft-Eisenhower battle actually began in New Hampshire. Initially there was to be no test in the Granite State. Polls showed that Taft had no chance to win there, and he planned to stay out. But after canvassing the local situation, Hamilton talked Taft into entering the New Hampshire primary on the last possible day. The Taft camp had some reasons for hope, but even these had a dark side. The editor of the Manchester *Union Leader,* William Loeb, who was on his way to becoming a conservative fixture, had come to support Taft after failing to interest MacArthur in the fray. For its part, the Taft team was wary of Loeb. Fearful of his "bad personal reputation" and his paper's "vitriolic personal attacks," the Taft group wanted his goodwill, but they did not want him to lead any Taft drive.[20] Nonetheless, the *Union Leader* became the trumpet of the Taft candidacy in New Hampshire.

Since the polls forecast a victory for Ike, who also boasted a star-studded delegate slate, Taft and his handlers downplayed their chances for success. Even so, Eisenhower's election victory was impressive. He amassed 46,661 votes to Taft's 35,838 to win full control of the fourteen-member Granite State delegation. Some Taft supporters were dismayed, believing Taft had made a grave mistake in challenging Eisenhower in New Hampshire. Clarence Brown, for example, had urged Taft to stay out of this race and now complained, "The whole situation is a story of too many cooks spoiling the broth—and that nobody can actually manage the candidate."[21]

The next blow to Taft came in Minnesota. Stassen won control of the delegation, but Ike won the headlines by garnering 108,000 write-in votes to the 24,000 of Mr. Republican. The results prompted Eisenhower to "re-examine" his political position, and two weeks later Eisenhower asked to be relieved of his NATO command. Adding to Taft's woes at this time was the action of Governor Alfred Driscoll of New Jersey. On the eve of the Minnesota vote, Driscoll had announced his support for Eisenhower. Senator Taft seethed over this bad news from the East, for he believed that Driscoll had pretended to be neutral only until Taft could no longer legally withdraw from the New Jersey primary. Knowing it would be senseless to battle the Garden State Republican organization, Taft tried to withdraw anyway, but a court ruled his name had to remain on the New Jersey ballot. "The eastern seaboard," Brown wrote, "is enemy territory."[22]

After New Hampshire and Minnesota, even Taft's managers conceded that a loss in Wisconsin would virtually knock their candidate out of the race. On April 2, however, Taft won over Stassen in Wisconsin and over Eisenhower in Nebraska. Suddenly Taft saw the makings of a midwestern groundswell. This dual win did buck up the Taft campaign and helped set a pattern for the drawnout springtime struggle for the GOP nomination. Taft went on to score primary victories in Ohio and Illinois, and he also triumphed in the state conventions in West Virginia, North Dakota, Wyoming, and Indiana. But Eisenhower piled up wins in New Jersey, Pennsylvania, Massachusetts, and Missouri, as well as in Oregon, Rhode Island, and Vermont. The last Taft-Eisenhower primary contest came in South Dakota. Taft won South Dakota's 14 delegates, nosing out Ike in the winner-take-all primary. This contest also brought another important advantage to the Taft drive. General Douglas MacArthur had personally written to former South Dakota governor Leslie Jensen, asking him to help Taft.

By this time, events in Texas attracted national attention and eventually proved to be the single most important factor in the preconvention struggle. Small and designed to stay that way, the Republican party in Texas was fairly typical of GOP outposts in Dixie, organizations that were basically "personal preserves" of the national committeeman—patronage dealerships when a Republican sat in the White House. But small as it was, the Texas GOP was split. Longtime Texas GOP boss Colonel R.B. Creager had died in 1950, and now Henry Zweifel—a Taft man—and J.H. (Jack) Porter—an

Eisenhower man—were battling for control. Early on, Taft campaign strategists expected problems in Texas, and the precinct and county caucuses in early May, 1952, confirmed their worst fears.[23] At both stages, the Porter faction swamped the Zweifel-led Taft forces by using Texas Democrats favorable to Ike. Zweifel tried to block this approach by requiring delegates to sign a loyalty pledge to the GOP, but Porter countered by instructing his forces to sign the pledges—they were unconstitutional anyway, he claimed. In response to this "near revolutionary movement" of Porter's "One Day Republicans," the Zweifel-Taft forces held rump precinct and county caucus sessions.

Henry Zweifel was one Republican who admitted openly that he would rather lose with Taft than win with Eisenhower. He now decided to play rough so that he would have to do neither. When the state convention met in late May at Mineral Wells, the mood was bitter and ugly. Zweifel was even charging that Eisenhower had the backing of the communist *Daily Worker*. The Texas state executive committee stood by Zweifel in rejecting the Porter delegates' claims of GOP loyalty. At the convention, the Zweifel forces then put together a 38-member national convention delegation that, while technically uninstructed, included 30 to 34 Taft supporters. The Porter faction, in turn, held its own gathering in Mineral Wells and formed a national convention delegation that favored Eisenhower, 33 to 5.

The Eisenhower forces immediately branded the Mineral Wells episode the "Texas Steal." Phrases like "Rob with Bob" and "Graft with Taft" peppered reports out of Mineral Wells. Eisenhower himself claimed that "Rustlers stole the Texas birthright instead of Texas steers." Although Zweifel followers believed that the Taft-dominated National Committee would "barrel-house 'em through," Taft, whose aides B. Carroll Reece and David Ingalls bore some responsibility for events in Texas, was not yet ready to go this far.[24] Compromise over the contested delegates was still possible, Taft remarked at the Indiana state Republican convention in early June.

Taft and his team remained confident despite the Texas difficulties. Taft's offer to compromise on the contested Texas delegates was, after all, nothing more than his first step in uniting the party for the fall canvass. Upon returning to the states in June, Eisenhower eased any Right Wing worries with the general's first nationwide address from his hometown of Abilene, Kansas. A general ramble of platitudes, the speech was seen as a dud. Snorted B. Carroll Reece, "It looks like he's pretty much for home, mother and heaven."[25]

But Taft's campaign tactics, not Ike's hazy policy stands, became the main issue in the month before the July convention. The Eisenhower camp kept the image of a Taft "steamroller" alive. Initially, Eisenhower had welcomed Taft's compromise offer on the Texas situation. But Lodge, the mastermind of the Eisenhower campaign, spotted a hot issue. He therefore framed the Texas problem in moral terms and undercut all hope for a negotiated settlement. "It's never right to compromise with dishonesty," he said.[26]

The announcement of the convention agenda prompted further charges of a Taft steamroller. The Taft-dominated RNC had packed the convention agenda with pro-Taft speakers. MacArthur was slated to give the keynote address. The next evening, former President Hoover was scheduled to speak. There were also to be talks by Bridges, Kem, and McCarthy—a Right Wing spectacular. Only two of the twenty-five GOP governors were placed on the list of speakers. Moreover, the convention officials—permanent chairman Joseph Martin and temporary chairman Walter S. Hallanan—were known Taft supporters. Charges of strongarm tactics grew even louder when the RNC, against Taft's wishes, barred television cameras—but not reporters or other media representatives—from its hearings on contested delegates. On the steamroller matter, Taft stood firm, branding such charges "a fake issue."

Taft was already complaining about the opposition of GOP governors when the National Governors Conference assembled in Houston practically on convention eve. The GOP governors were a stronghold of Eisenhower support, and some of them wanted to do something at Houston to further the general's cause. But three of the GOP governors at Houston were strong Taft backers, and without unanimity, any such move would have been seen for what it was: a pro-Ike gambit. But the pro-Ike governors were undaunted. Led by Colorado's Dan Thornton, they fashioned a manifesto calling on the GOP convention to prohibit contested delegates from voting on the seating of other delegates. When an utterly bamboozled Taft supporter, Governor H. Bracken Lee of Utah, signed this manifesto, the other Taft governors—Len Jordon of Idaho and Norman Brunsdale of North Dakota—followed suit. So unwitting was Lee that he even read the manifesto's first page—a harmless call for honor, fairness, and integrity at the GOP convention—at a joint news conference with Thornton. After Lee then rushed off to catch a plane out of Houston, Thornton continued the press conference, delivering the bombshell on page two—the GOP governors' proposal for a change in party rules. In Chicago, Chairman Gabrielson immediately rejected the governors' move as "contrary to all customs and former rulings." But the issue was far from dead.

Despite the Houston handiwork and the current Gallup poll that showed Taft, unlike Eisenhower, running behind possible Democratic candidates, Mr. Republican beamed confidently as he arrived in Chicago. He claimed 537 delegates; the Associated Press gave him 534 delegates to the 425 of Eisenhower and the 131 of other hopefuls. The magic number for the nomination was 604.

Chicago. There would be no GOP jubilee. The carnival aspect of American political conventions was largely absent. Convention sidelights inevitably returned to a central theme—bitter and intense intraparty warfare. Reminding delegates of Texas shenanigans, one sound truck blared, "Thou shalt not steal." Another ricocheted its bitter message off Windy City buildings: "Two-time loser Dewey wants to be president by proxy. Phooey on Dewey." Taft enthusiasts brandished buttons with the Republican Right's credo since 1948: "No me-too in 1952." Intoned the *Chicago Tribune,* "If the elephant remembers, he should be all thru with 'me too.'"[27]

Even before the opening gavel of the convention, chairman Guy Gabrielson had to arbitrate what was called the "battle of the banners"—a surprisingly grim fracas over poster space at the Conrad Hilton hotel, site of the Taft and Eisenhower headquarters. There was one report that Eisenhower workers, unappreciative of some serenading by young Taftites, booted them down a stairwell of the Conrad Hilton. Other testimony only confirmed what occasional delegate fisticuffs demonstrated—the preconvention struggle had left Republicans unnerved, and this promised to be a mean convention indeed.

The gathering itself was to be held in the International Amphitheatre. The arena had been built for livestock shows and rodeos, where, unlike political parleys, the bull generally threw the men around. In fact, before the newly installed air conditioner went on, the hall "smelled like the old bull ring at Juarez," according to writer Gene Fowler.[28] At the west end of the hall, a blowup of Lincoln's sober gaze reminded the *Chicago Tribune* that Lincoln was a rail- not a party-splitter.[29] Chicago seemed ready for battle. "There is more than a personal battle that is going on here," Reston observed; "the conservative wing of the party is fighting for its life."[30]

On Monday the delegates waited an hour for the proceedings to begin. Five minutes before the convention was scheduled to start, Lodge unveiled a "Fair Play" amendment in the chairman's office behind the stage. This amendment was an offshoot of the Houston manifesto and provided that no temporary, disputed, or alternate delegate be allowed to vote until the convention had decided on that delegate's legitimacy. Unlike the Houston manifesto, however, it exempted delegates previously certified by over two-thirds of the RNC. The Taft camp wanted to avoid a floor fight, and they offered a compromise: the exemption of seven Louisiana delegates from Fair Play provisions. Louisiana was a truly special case, since the state's GOP committee had legally approved these delegates. But the Eisenhower strategy depended on a floor fight, and Lodge, afraid the Taft forces might accept the Fair Play resolution, rejected any compromise.

The Fair Play resolution caught the Taft managers off guard, and poor communication on the convention floor made matters worse. As soon as the convention opened, Gabrielson promptly recognized Senator John Bricker, who moved that the 1948 convention rules be in effect. It was obviously a mistake for the Taft camp to make this first move; Bricker had even declined Gabrielson' earlier backstage request to do so.[31] But once at the podium, the chairman called on Bricker anyway, and the startled senator complied. Immediately, Governor Arthur B. Langlie of Washington introduced the Fair Play amendment.

This led to uproar. Clarence Brown, one of the Taft strategists, edged his way to the podium. The jammed aisles hampered communications between Brown and Coleman, the Taft floor manager. The Taft team had left the chairman's office believing that Gabrielson would rule favorably on their point of order to exempt the Louisiana delegation from Fair Play provisions. Once on stage, Gabrielson apparently told Brown that he had changed his mind. Brown broached the point of order, but amid the boos of the Ike supporters, he offered instead an amendment excluding the Louisiana delegates from the Langlie provisions. Taft, watching on television, exploded in anger and frustration: the proposed Brown amendment would require a convention vote and would thus provide an early test of strength between Eisenhower and Taft forces.

A furious two-hour debate ensued. Bricker offered to swap acceptance of the Langlie resolution for the Brown amendment. The Eisenhower camp would not budge on what New Hampshire governor Sherman Adams said was a "moral issue." Finally the convention spiked the Brown amendment, 658 to 548, and then passed Langlie's Fair play resolution by acclamation. The vote had exposed latent Eisenhower strength: California and Minnesota gave all their votes to Ike; Pennsylvania—again a key delegation—voted 57 to 13 against the Brown amendment; Michigan voted 45 to 1 against. Although Taft managers nevertheless smiled to the end, one Taft worker recalled that the "psychological defeat" was "overpowering."[32]

Taft followers suffered other disappointments on convention Monday. During the Brown amendment debate, Bricker had urged a quick solution in order for the convention to hear from "that most gallant American in history except George Washington," General Douglas MacArthur. The keynoter was known to be friendly to Taft, and Taft supporters hoped for an emotional plea for Mr. Republican. Appearing out of uniform in a dark blue suit and tie, the general flayed the Democrats but blew no bugle for Taft. It was one of MacArthur's worst speeches. "One could feel the electricity gradually running out of the room," wrote C.L. Sulzberger of the *New York Times*. "I think he cooked his own goose and didn't do much for Taft."[33] On opening day, about all Taft won was the applause sweepstakes, a sign that Taft owned the hearts if not the minds of Republicans at Chicago.

By Wednesday the convention was hopelessly behind schedule. Despite the appeal of Styles Bridges for an end to the fighting and bitterness, it was still too early for that. Properly accredited delegates were still the main issue.

The Saturday before the convention, the RNC had ruled on the disputed delegates. Its most important decision came when it accepted the Taft compromise formula and split the Texas delegation, 22 to 16 in favor of Taft. The second level of appeal was the Credentials Committee, which met the following Tuesday and ratified most of the RNC's Saturday rulings. Here, in a goodwill gesture, the Taft forces abandoned their Louisiana delegation in favor of Ike's contingent.

But Lodge and the Eisenhower forces still would not deal. On Wednesday evening—originally slated for nominations—the Credentials Committee reports on disputed delegates went to the convention floor. Here, Lodge continued the fight over the Georgia and Texas delegations. Georgia came first. Again, Taft followers believed that the pro-Taft delegation had legitimate claims, claims legally recognized by the Georgia secretary of state and the Georgia Superior Court. But whatever they thought, the Georgia issue quickly became another test of strength between the Taft and Eisenhower forces.

The debate instantly became sharp, with Senator Everett Dirksen's action capping it. In upholding the claims of the Georgia pro-Taft delegation, he pointed a finger toward Dewey in the New York delegation's section and said, "My friends on the eastern seaboard, re-examine your hearts on this issue because we followed you before and you took us down the path to defeat." The convention went wild. Convention eyes turned to the stone-faced Dewey. Some delegates booed Dirksen, but they were drowned out by the shrieks and bellows of the Taft partisans. Suddenly, there was a commotion in the Michigan delegation, and the police had to rush in to restore order. Astonished by his own handiwork, Dirksen then scolded Republicans for booing other Republicans. By now the GOP Chicago convention had become a true political slugfest, the inevitable product of emotions that had simmered for almost four years.

After this Old Guard catharsis, the convention voted just before midnight. By a margin of 607 to 531, the convention voted to seat the pro-Eisenhower delegation from Georgia. "Some of the Taft delegates," Taft explained later, "couldn't or wouldn't recognize that Georgia was the first vote for the nomination."[34] Afterward, not wanting to further advertise their delegate strength, the Taft forces accepted the Credentials Committee's minority report calling for the seating of the pro-Ike Porter delegation from Texas.

Unfortunately, there was still more bad news for Taft in a strategic spot. For days there had been convention rumors that Pennsylvania governor John Fine was leaning toward Ike. In fact, Fine and Michigan GOP boss Arthur Summerfield had agreed early to stand together for Eisenhower but to withhold news of their pact. Fine, who had come to Chicago determined "not to miss the boat," declared for Eisenhower immediately after the Georgia tally.

The Pennsylvania delegation then caucused before television cameras and gave Eisenhower 51 votes, with 16 going to Taft and 3 to MacArthur. Following this Keystone State action, the Associated Press estimated that Eisenhower commanded 501 delegates and Taft only 485. The other candidates split up 111 votes, and 109 delegates were still undecided.

Thursday—the day of the nominating speeches—brought conservative desperation and more intraparty acrimony. The day began with fresh rumors that MacArthur had returned to Chicago from New York. Previously, most MacArthur talk had centered on the vice-presidential post. Even Taft had hinted publicly that MacArthur would be his pick for the second spot and privately told Bricker that he planned to choose the general.[35] Some Right Wing Republicans, though, preferred MacArthur at the top of the ticket and hoped a deadlocked convention would ultimately turn to him. By Thursday, a MacArthur-for-President boom appeared to some to be the only hope of the Old Guard. South Dakota's Senator Francis Case was openly urging the general's nomination. Taft, of course, was the key, since MacArthur insisted he would never "stab Taft in the back."[36]

Faced with this dilemma, a group of GOP conservatives met in Herbert Hoover's suite at the Conrad Hilton on Thursday morning. Conservative columnist George Sokolsky and Albert C. Wedemeyer were among the participants. Taft could not now win the GOP presidential nomination, and he must therefore throw his support to MacArthur, Hoover told them. The group decided to dispatch Wedemeyer to talk with Taft.

Later that afternoon, Taft received Wedemeyer's suggestion "in good faith" but replied that he would not switch to MacArthur on the first ballot. No first-ballot victory was possible for anyone, Taft believed. Besides, he wrote later, such a move would have been a surrender of principle and "a betrayal of thousands of workers and millions of voters." Taft did say that he might reconsider on later ballots. Then, according to Wedemeyer, Taft had him call MacArthur in New York with three questions. Would MacArthur announce his all-out support for Taft? No, said the general; this might be seen as an act of weakness and desperation. Would MacArthur accept the vice-presidential spot on the ticket? Certainly, replied the general. Then, Taft had Wedemeyer ask MacArthur if he would accept the presidential nomination if Taft switched to him. "Al," answered MacArthur, "Bob Taft is our captain and we must do whatever he wants us to do."[37]

Convention tensions flared again on Thursday. Taft's campaign manager David Ingalls penned a vitriolic handout urging delegates to "SINK DEWEY." The sheet branded Dewey "THE MOST COLD-BLOODED, RUTHLESS, SELF-SEEKING BOSS IN THE UNITED STATES TODAY." That evening when Dirksen stepped to the rostrum to nominate Taft, Dewey walked out of the hall.

Prior to the first ballot on Friday morning, many rumors ran through the International Amphitheatre. There was talk of a stop-Ike movement. Had not Taft called California's Governor Earl Warren and Harold Stassen? Speculation about MacArthur persisted. Reports that the Ohioan would switch to Warren marked the silliest prevote babble. Actually, the only real hope for conservatives rested upon stopping Ike on the first ballot and then acting on a tentative agreement with Warren and Stassen to recess the convention after that.

As the balloting was about to begin, Taft made a last-ditch effort to contact California senator Knowland on the convention floor in order to work something out at the end of the first ballot. But the Californian informed his Senate boss that there would be only one ballot. Knowland called it. The Eisenhower forces shot ahead quickly. With 604 votes needed to nominate, Ike rolled up 595 first-ballot votes to Taft's 500—before switches. Minnesota quickly provided Ike with 19 new tallies, and he was over at 614. The bandwagon rolled on, with pro-Taft votes beginning to change in Pennsylvania. "These bandwagon people," snarled one Taft delegate as he headed for the exits, would find they were boarding a hearse.[38] When Joseph Martin finally announced the first-ballot totals, Eisenhower had 845 votes to the 280 remaining Taft stalwarts. Warren held on to 77 delegates and MacArthur 4. Then, for the third time in twelve years, Bricker conceded for Taft and moved that Eisenhower's nomination be made unanimous. Bricker also announced that Taft and Eisenhower had already met, and that Mr. Republican had pledged to support the general.

With victory assured, Eisenhower had indeed immediately called on Mr. Republican at his Blackstone Hotel suite. Enduring the boos and catcalls of overwrought Taft workers as he arrived, the general conferred with Taft and secured his support. By the time the two men emerged for pictures, a Taft worker had successfully pleaded with his fellows to supplant their jeers with cheers.

But one thing neither Eisenhower nor his managers did to mend the party breach was to offer Taft a spot on the ticket. In their various discussions, Taft had been mentioned as a vice-presidential possibility but the suggestion had gone nowhere. Taft, in turn, was known to favor Dirksen, but this possibility was regarded as ludicrous. Ultimately, the Eisenhower camp's vice-presidential choice was the young first-term senator from California, Richard M. Nixon. Although Right Wing Republicans appreciated Nixon's anticommunist credentials, his selection was hardly a concession to them. While committed to Warren in the nomination battle, Nixon had worked quietly for Eisenhower. Yet Nixon did see himself as a party healer and therefore asked Bricker to second his nomination. The Ohio senator declined, however, because of "what they [the Eisenhower faction] have said and done to Bob Taft."[39] Nixon nonetheless praised Taft in his own acceptance speech.

"The Old Guard never surrenders," Bernard DeVoto wrote shortly after the Chicago convention, "but that does not matter for it has lost the climactic battle." Then DeVoto, whose smugness exceeded his political sense, added that the men who have restored the party's "sense of reality" would certainly "bar and triple lock the door" against the Taft wing's "rural barbershop mind of 1880."[40]

There was indeed much talk of a new GOP day, revolutions and party "rebirth," and the "New Guard" Republicans, who were liberal, young, many of them governors, and likely to be closer to Ike than the existing congressional command. Many New Guard cheerleaders were giddy from the events of Chicago, but it was really too early for such rejoicing. After all, similar talk of revolution had accompanied the earlier GOP convention triumphs of Willkie and Dewey. As in the past, a November loss would dash all hopes of revolutionary change. And the vanquishment of the Old Guard or Republican Right remained highly doubtful. A new face at the top of the party was one thing. Instilling the party with a new philosophy and overhauling the party machinery—at all levels—was another.

Besides, just what had the New Guard won at Chicago? It had snared the nomination, but little else. "It was clear from the time the first throng began to gather in the lobby of the Hilton," Richard Rovere reported, "that a lot of [Republicans], including a large number who wore 'I Like Ike' buttons the size of saucers, really didn't like him at all and were supporting him only because they had been sold on the Taft can't win theory."[41] Natural impulse would have normally led them to Taft. Fine, Summerfield, and other such GOP politicos had done their electoral figuring. Cold logic alone led them to Ike.

Chicago hearts were still chiefly Right Wing hearts. The loudest convention cheers had gone to MacArthur and Hoover. Further, the platform, passed without protest, was no revolutionary manifesto. Indeed, Wayne Morse claimed that it was written under "reactionary domination."[42] The foreign policy section, over which a fight was expected, satisfied both Eisenhower and Taft. Its calls for the liberation of enslaved peoples rested on "neo-isolationist assumptions." And even on domestic policy, questions about where Ike stood persisted. Clearly, the platform was a product of compromise, and it remained Eisenhower's to interpret.

Eisenhower's Chicago victory prompted a reassessment by Right Wing Republicans on their role in the GOP. They remained convinced that their kind of Republicanism had the support of most Republicans and most Americans. The Eisenhower forces had simply shanghaied the Chicago parley. Analyzing the Chicago convention, Taft brushed aside his team's tactical errors and identified three major forces that defeated him. First was "the power of the New York financial interests and large number of businessmen subject to New York influence." Second were the influential newspapers, four-fifths of which, Taft contended, became virtual "propaganda sheets" for Eisenhower. Finally, there were the governors, who had greater sway with the delegates than Washington lawmakers, most of whom were friendly to Taft.[43]

Some Right Wing Republicans went even further. Where Taft talked generally of the "power of the New York financial interests," others claimed that Wall Street and eastern media "kingmakers," had torpedoed Taft, swapping vice-presidential and Supreme Court posts for California votes in key Chicago delegate contests. The alleged wrongs of the Eisenhower forces at Chicago quickly became another chapter in the Republican Right's continuing saga of convention frustrations and, in the end, helped undermine the New Guard's claim on the Republican party. Ike had won the Republican nomination. Now he would have to win the Republican party.

In the meantime, what was the Old Guard up to after Chicago? It continued, of course, to seethe over "the methods of the Dewey-Lodge crowd." The Republican Right was also waiting and making itself scarce. Taft, for instance, immediately left for a vacation in Canada. Herbert Hoover went fishing. "I fear we are on uncharted waters," he told many, referring to the GOP, not his fishing trip. Hoover advised General Wedemeyer to "remain quiescent."[44] Disaffection rapidly spread through Right Wing Republican ranks. Tom Coleman reportedly declined an offer to manage the Eisenhower campaign. In Massachusetts, a group of Taft supporters went to work for John F. Kennedy, the Democratic rival of Lodge, and there were widespread reports that Taft followers were shunning campaign duty even at the local level. Party contributors had tight fists. Yet despite Colonel McCormick's talk of forming a new Right Wing "American Party," *US News and World Report* correctly noted early in August that there was more sitting on hands than open rebellion in the GOP.[45]

Meanwhile, the Republican Right waited for clues as to the men and message behind Eisenhower's fall campaign. Conservative Republicans, certain that Ike was only a reflection of his advisors, grew edgy over the possible campaign roles of Dewey, Hoffman, the Lodge brothers, and Duff. Hallanan, in turn, noted the absence of Taft men among Eisenhower campaign braintrusters. "If they think they can win this election by having the Eisenhower pre-convention crowd run the show alone," he wrote, "they will be rudely awakened in November."[46]

Eisenhower, in fact, was acting swiftly to mend party rifts. A week after the convention, he told Paul Hoffman, the former Marshall Plan administrator who had big ideas about Ike as a party remodeler, to stop "pouring salt in the wounds of the defeated."[47] Eisenhower also kept Dewey and Herbert Brownell in the background of the campaign effort. In Illinois, Ike told former Taft supporters to cherish their old loyalties and pledged that "every section of the party would receive his support." This pledge was actually part of a deal with the new national chairman, Arthur Summerfield, who made it a condition for his accepting the post.[48] Summerfield was one of the many wise selections for national campaign positions. Capitol Hill GOP conservatives Charles Halleck and Karl Mundt were named to head the Speakers Bureau. Also, Dirksen, the old Chicago firebrand, was asked out to Denver to meet Ike and quickly accepted a spot on the top campaign strategy committee.

Despite these peace offerings, the Eisenhower campaign was dragging by late August. Ike was pussyfooting on the major issues, grumbled numerous Right Wing Republicans. A Scripps-Howard editorial said it best: "Ike is running like a dry creek."[49]

Nebraska senator Hugh Butler's remedy for GOP campaign woes was a meeting between Eisenhower and Taft. The Eisenhower handlers had wanted such a meeting for some time. Taft's positive aid remained crucial, if only as a signal to many conservative Republicans, especially campaign workers. "Until Bob Taft blows the bugle," explained Cale J. Holder, the Indiana state chairman, "a lot of us aren't going to fight in the army."[50]

Their leader, however, was in Canada. It was there that he wrote his postconvention analysis of his Chicago loss. His ruminations were sometimes bitter; one *Chicago Daily News* scribe reported after a visit to Taft's northern retreat that Ike's chances of enlisting the senator were "about zero."[51] Brooding over Chicago and complaining about the makeup of the Eisenhower campaign team, Mr. Republican planned to hold off cooperating until early September. "By that time I think the Eisenhower people might be fairly scared as to the result," he wrote, "and there may be a more bonafide effort to make real concessions on the running of the campaign and the setting up of the new Administration."[52]

Taft made it clear that his role in the fall canvass would ultimately be determined by Eisenhower's response to specific Taft demands regarding future administration policy and personnel. He wanted no appearance of a sell-out of his own principles or "my friends to the purge that so many Eisenhower supporters seem to plan for them." Without such assurances, Taft would stump only for certain senatorial candidates, and his speeches would "not be too enthusiastic for the national ticket."[53] Furthermore, without assurances, there would be no Taft-Eisenhower meeting.

Taft sent a list of these desired guarantees to Dirksen, who was to "sound out" the Eisenhower camp. Some of the demands, wrote Taft, might be made public, others not. Among the demands, Taft wanted an Eisenhower commitment to cut the budget to $60 billion for 1955 so there could be a tax cut by the spring of 1954. He desired Eisenhower's promise to support the Republican platform's Taft-Hartley section and to oppose flat 90 percent farm price supports and the Brannan plan (the Truman Administration's plan to guarantee fixed minimum incomes to farmers raising per-

ishable crops), which Congress had rejected. Further, the Ohio senator required equal representation for Taft supporters in the Eisenhower cabinet.
More specifically, he wanted neither Dewey nor "a spender" like Paul Hoffman as secretary of state.[54]

After some haggling and delay, Eisenhower and Taft did finally meet in
New York at the general's Morningside Heights residence on September 12.
During their breakfast conference, Eisenhower examined a statement that
Taft had prepared for later distribution to the press. After making some
minor suggestions, Eisenhower approved the document, and the photogra-
phers were called in. Their meeting ended when, standing on the steps of
Ike's headquarters, both were asked if they saw eye-to-eye on McCarthy. Ignoring this question, they shook hands and parted. Eisenhower went back
inside, and Taft walked to the King's Crown Hotel for a press conference.

There, Taft read his statement urging full support for Eisenhower. Taft
called their foreign policy differences only "differences of degree." On the
homefront, both Eisenhower and Taft agreed that the major domestic issue
was "liberty against the creeping socialization of every domestic field." The
statement committed Eisenhower on budget and tax matters, as well as Taft-
Hartley. Missing, however, were Taft's strictures on the cabinet.

Taft had blown the bugle. "I could see no choice except to support
him," Taft wrote afterward. "It seems to me my job is to keep him as far on
the conservative side as possible." Yet Taft men such as Tom Coleman and
Ben Tate believed that Taft had knuckled under to Eisenhower. Ike, too,
was promptly criticized for his harmony bid. Moderate Republicans dubbed
the affair the "Surrender of Morningside Heights."[55] Ike's "great crusade,"
said his Democratic rival, Illinois governor Adlai Stevenson, had become a
"great surrender."

After the Morningside Heights conference, Congressman Howard Buffett was one "deeply disappointed" conservative who sought aid and comfort from General Douglas MacArthur.[56] But in doing so, Buffett was seeking support from a soldier who had at last decided to fade away. Despite his
entreaty, the Nebraska congressman got no reponse from the general.
MacArthur retreated politically to his Waldorf-Astoria redoubt. With the
August announcement of the general's appointment as chairman of the
board of the Remington-Rand Corporation, came word that MacArthur
would play no role at all in the fall political canvass.

Some MacArthur role, however, was unavoidable. Right-Wing splinter
parties such as the Christian Nationalist and Constitution parties had put
MacArthur's name on the ballot in a number of states. Political observers
believed that MacArthur's unauthorized candidacy might hurt Eisenhower
in both Texas and Washington. Taft, Hoover, Wedemeyer, and others
urged the general to disavow these movements and plump for Ike. But
MacArthur baffled old friends and supporters by remaining silent. One

MacArthur intimate privately explained that one reason for the general's noninvolvement was his lack of confidence in Ike's "training, experience and natural abilities."[57] In any case, for the public and many friends, MacArthur still remained what he had always been on the postwar political scene: "The Great American Enigma."

Even without MacArthur's aid, Dwight Eisenhower's crusade at last began to move ahead. The Middle West—stronghold of the Republican Right—had posed serious problems for Ike and his advisors. Controversial senators Joseph McCarthy and William Jenner were only the two most publicized Right Wing candidates causing unease for the Eisenhower campaign.

Attempting to "harmonize" these matters as much as possible at Indianapolis, Eisenhower declared that Republicans were not "servile puppets" to any party line and, without naming Jenner, endorsed the entire GOP ticket for Indiana. Senator Jenner, who was aware that he could not be elected independently of the national ticket, was instantly up on his feet, embracing the general. This camera-conscious clutch galled Ike, and his managers found it "most embarrassing." As for McCarthy, he was clearly on the minds of the Eisenhower entourage as its campaign train rolled into Wisconsin. Eisenhower had found McCarthy's earlier attacks on General George Marshall outrageous. But Ike, again aware of the need for party unity, called for McCarthy's reelection, saying that he and McCarthy differed only over the method of their anticommunism. Not only that, but it was reported that Ike had scratched a defense of Marshall from his Milwaukee speech—at McCarthy's urging. Ike's advisors at first denied these reports, but Eisenhower admitted subsequently that he had bowdlerized his Milwaukee remarks—but only at the insistence of Wisconsin governor Walter Kohler, not McCarthy. In fact, McCarthy himself had little to do with these editorial changes. Kohler, along with Eisenhower aides Sherman Adams and Jerry Parsons, had persuaded Ike to delete his Marshall remarks for fear of upsetting Tom Coleman and other Taft Republicans in such a politically important and unpredictable state as Wisconsin.[58]

Other Right Wing Republicans, some of them archfoes of collective security, also gained Eisenhower's stamp of approval in 1952. For example, the general backed the senatorial reelection bid of James P. Kem of Missouri, and also of Chapman Revercomb in West Virginia, whose candidacy Dewey had refused to endorse in 1948.

The Eisenhower crusade sounded increasingly right-wingish as it came out of the Midwest. The formula, K_1C_2—Korea, Communism, and Corruption—represented the main campaign themes; it was the brainchild of Senator Karl Mundt, a preconvention Taft backer. By early November, Taft could say that Eisenhower was championing policies "I've been preaching for 14 years." Taft claimed that his own failed bid for the 1952 GOP nomination had succeeded in shaping the issues of the fall campaign. Crowed Indiana's Senator Homer Capehart in October: "In another two weeks, General Eisenhower will be thinking and talking just like Senator Taft."[59]

The Republican Right noted some problems in Eisenhower's newfound conservatism. The *Chicago Tribune* grumbled about the general's tendency "to trim and waver."[60] For Albert Wedemeyer, Ike's new ways merely confirmed old Wedemeyer impressions—Ike had "no strong convictions in the national and international fields because he has not read, discussed, or thought through . . . present policies."[61] Such concerns lingered, but ultimately even one ultra-conservative chronicler of GOP history was forced to admit that the 1952 canvass did offer the voter "a choice not an echo."[62]

In the end, the Republican Right finally fell in behind Eisenhower. In mid-October former President Hoover spoke out for the national ticket, and others followed. Howard Buffett and Wedemeyer both enlisted in the Eisenhower crusade. McCormick's *Chicago Tribune* came around, too. Reluctantly, and aware of Eisenhower's debt to the "undesirable element in his party," the *Tribune* advised readers to vote for Ike—if only to bolster the "anti-Socialist" Republican vote in Congress. The Republican Right's backing for Ike never revealed real fire.[63] In Right Wing Republican eyes, Ike was clearly superior to the Democratic Stevenson. Moreover, conservative Republicans were certain that they would control the GOP in Congress. In short, Right Wing support for Eisenhower largely amounted to pure political accommodation. In any case, on election day the GOP was, if not entirely happy, at least temporarily united.

And finally victorious. Eisenhower—the Republican standard-bearer—won the White House and helped Republicans gain control of Capitol Hill. Moreover, the GOP claimed thirty governorships after election day, for a net gain of five. Eisenhower won in a landslide, capturing 55.4 percent of the popular vote to Stevenson's 44.4 percent. He piled up 442 electoral tallies; Stevenson gained only 89. The cracking of the Solid South made Ike's electoral figures even more impressive. Florida, Virginia, Tennessee, and Texas, where old-line Democrats dug in, all fell to the general. He topped Hoover's 1928 popular vote in the South. William S. White proclaimed "the beginnings at least of a two-party system below the Potomac."[64]

Taft, for his part, believed that the public had voted primarily to end the New Deal and its "tax-spend" philosophy, and he maintained that he could have amassed "substantially the same" majority as Eisenhower. Later analysts disagreed. Samuel Lubell, for example, concluded that Taft—or any Republican—could have won, but not by the Eisenhower margin. Ike had run well among normally Republican groups, but he also managed to corral large numbers of white-collar voters, who would have been scared off by the isolationist tone of Taft. The Chicago battle, in highlighting the differences between Ike and Taft, had proved a boon to the general, and Ike's campaign effort to bind the party together may have been a mistake, costing him heavily among the young and other groups.[65]

The congressional results underscored Ike's personal triumph. He ran about 5 million votes, or 16 percent, ahead of Republican congressional candidates, contributing heavily to GOP majorities on Capitol Hill. Republicans gained twenty-one seats to win control of the House, 221 to 211. In the Senate, the party won twenty-three of twenty-five races, leaving Republicans with a 48-to-47 edge. "The election represents," wrote a delighted Herbert Hoover, "a turning away from bad taste, corruption, Communism, and to some extent from socialism."[66]

Despite the elation of Hoover and other GOP conservatives, the Old Guard, itself, suffered on election day. Taft, for one, held Eisenhower responsible for simply giving Republican conservatives "a formal pat on the back." They were then "pretty well left out on the limb," where they were targets of a "general smearing from General Eisenhower's eastern friends."[67] One can perhaps understand Taft's conclusion, since Right Wing Republicans sorely needed a scapegoat. James Kem of Missouri, Harry Cain of Washington, Zales Ecton of Wyoming, and Patrick Hurley of New Mexico— all Right Wing Republicans—lost their Senate races.

Later analysis would reveal that twelve of thirteen Old Guard senatorial candidates ran behind Eisenhower. Most liberal Republican candidates for the Senate, on the other hand, ran ahead of the general. The average vote of Old Guard candidates for the Senate was only 51.6 percent, while moderates and liberals claimed 54.3 percent.[68] Right Wing winners such as Edward Martin in Pennsylvania and George Malone in Nevada were clearly beholden to Ike's popularity. In "one of the most startling upsets," Barry Goldwater knocked off Senate majority leader Earnest McFarland of Arizona—a result Goldwater attributed to Eisenhower's coattails. In two closely watched races, Jenner and McCarthy both won, but ran far behind the national ticket, and there were doubts they could have won without Ike's support. Jenner, for instance, ran 150,000 votes behind Eisenhower's Indiana plurality of 300,000.

Whatever later evaluations and analyses might reveal, Eisenhower had run and won as a Republican. And the GOP, along with the Old Guard, had won along with him. Election day 1952 was therefore no time for nitpicking or sober self-scrutiny. It was a time for universal Republican revelry—and it had been a long time coming.

6

Mr. Republican

It was also time for the Republicans to brawl. So went the political wisdom of Will Rogers, who had once observed that Democrats battled each other before elections, and Republicans afterward. There was reason enough to expect a postelection GOP breakup. Eisenhower and Taft, McCarthy, Jenner, and others had soft-pedaled their differences during the fall campaign. Now the demands of agenda setting, the prerogatives of the executive versus the legislative branch, and the dictates of personality, all menaced future Republican harmony. No sooner was the election finished than many pundits were prepared to declare that the GOP honeymoon was over.

Eisenhower and his advisors, however, labored to keep the party together. Shortly after the election, one of their first moves was to invite Colorado's Senator Eugene Millikin to visit Eisenhower in Augusta, Georgia. This preconvention Taft supporter, who was slated to be the chairman of the Finance Committee in the new Congress, was Ike's first official visitor. His Augusta pilgrimage underscored the importance of fiscal matters and also Ike's intention to live up to agreements made with Taft at Morningside Heights. In another goodwill gesture, the Eisenhower command asked for Taft's suggestions on executive appointments and established a committee through which he could channel recommendations. Still, as the *New York Times* said, the dominant question remained just what program Eisenhower would lay down and whether it would bring a collision with Taft.[1]

For Right Wing Republicans, in particular, the link between policy and personnel was tremendously important. They feared, as they had during the campaign, that the politically innocent Ike would become "captive" to his advisors. Eisenhower might hold basically conservative views on certain issues, Taft conceded, "but he does not seem to understand . . . that New Deal policies always dress themselves up in conservative argument." As a result, the character of Eisenhower's advisors and cabinet officers was viewed as crucial. If placed in key spots, worried Right Wing Republicans, the likes of Henry Cabot Lodge, Earl Warren, Paul Hoffman, and Thomas Dewey might ply the new president with too much "me-too" advice.[2]

Given these Right Wing fears and the makeup of Eisenhower's preelection team, some public squabbles within the party were inevitable. Eisenhower's selection of new secretary of labor, Martin Durkin, prompted one of them. Durkin, who was head of the AFL's plumbers union and a Democrat, had once advocated the repeal of the Taft-Hartley Act. Worse, he had supported Adlai Stevenson in the recent election. Taft called his appointment "incredible." He believed that this "terrible" choice would "make any job regarding Taft-Hartley infinitely more difficult."[3] The wisdom of the appointment was questionable enough, but Eisenhower aides had even failed to inform Taft or Everett Dirksen—Durkin's senator—of the selection beforehand. Taft hoped that his blast would "check the tendency toward a New Deal Administration with a Republican label."[4] Journalists, in turn, used their flashiest headlines on the Durkin controversy. "The honeymoon is over," *US News and World Report* proclaimed, "and the battle lines are being drawn."[5]

Although political seers read too much into Taft's criticism of Durkin's appointment, other Eisenhower cabinet selections were little more comforting to Taft. The choice of Arthur Summerfield as postmaster general and Ezra Taft Benson (a distant Taft relative) as secretary of agriculture appealed to him, but Taft was known to be hostile to the new secretary of commerce, Sinclair Weeks—a traitor to the Taft cause before the Chicago convention— and to the new attorney general, Herbert Brownell—political guru of the Dewey wing. For Taft, the considerable ties between General Motors and the government made the appointment of Charles Wilson as secretary of defense a mistake. In fact, Taft privately complained about "so many businessmen in the Cabinet."[6]

The treasury portfolio especially concerned Taft. The new secretary of the treasury, George H. Humphrey, should have pleased the senator. Humphrey was a former Taft enthusiast and, in his own words, "a hard shell, non-progressive." He had been president of the Mark Hanna Company and a leading GOP fundraiser in Cleveland. But the Humphrey appointment disappointed Taft. First, the Eisenhower people had failed to consult with Taft on it. More important, Taft had his own candidate for the treasury post—Senator Harry Byrd of Virginia. Byrd, of course, was a Democrat, but he was a southern Democrat and a diehard fiscal conservative. Taft wanted, among other things, to consolidate the recent GOP gains in Dixie, and Byrd's appointment was part of his own southern strategy. Eisenhower, however, had explained earlier that he could not appoint a Democrat, an excuse that "looked foolish" to Taft after the Durkin selection. Taft explained to one southern backer, "For some reason the Dewey [–Eisenhower] group . . . never had any interest in the South because it interferes with their idea that we should appease the minorities of the North."[7]

It soon became apparent that Taft's advice mattered only when it jibed with the Eisenhower camp's goals. Taft rapidly came to regard the appointments committee as a farce. Although Taft conceded that the Eisenhower cabinet was basically conservative, he doubted that it would oppose "any truly liberal proposals."[8] Other Old Guard Republicans also detected the "machinations" of Tom Dewey within the administration. For example, Senator Henry Dworshak of Idaho noted that such "pets of F.D.R." as Nelson Rockefeller and Arthur S. Flemming were taking places in the new Republican administration.[9]

Obviously, the same problem remained that had existed from the beginning of the 1952 nomination battle—who actually had Ike's ear? This question was especially critical, said Taft, because Ike never read anything. Mr. Republican continued to hope that it would prove impossible for the Dewey people to keep the president "shut off" from noneastern influence once Eisenhower got to Washington.[10] That failing, there was still the Republican Right's strength on Capitol Hill. Eisenhower's appointment of FDR pets convinced Senator Dworshak by early December that steps must be taken to insure against the domination of Senate Republicans by the Dewey wing. Clearly, as Republicans prepared for their first administration in twenty years, a few party members anticipated fighting against, not for, other Republicans.

Taft was not among them. Although the Durkin appointment had alarmed him, and he worried that Ike might become a prisoner of poor counsel, Taft wanted to make the new Republican administration a success. Taft believed he could help by becoming Senate majority leader. Taft had spearheaded Senate Republicans for years anyway. Now, after the election, he let it be known that he wanted the title. The Ohioan believed that his selection afforded the "only chance for developing a harmonious program." He could present "both viewpoints" to Eisenhower, and arguments could be settled before they became public.

The Eisenhower camp, in turn, reportedly wanted William F. Knowland to lead Senate Republicans, and Taft to remain as head of the GOP Policy Committee. Taft realized, however, that the White House and not the Policy Committee would henceforth set Republican policy. He therefore offered Knowland, who was low in seniority, the Republican Policy Committee chairmanship, and the California senator quickly accepted. Taft's next obstacle was Senator Styles Bridges. Since the Durkin conflict, pressure had mounted on the conservative internationalist from New Hampshire to become majority leader. Dewey forces were said to favor him, and, for a time, political observers billed the leadership contest as one between Taft and Bridges.[11]

But no clash of GOP Senate giants resulted. Bridges wanted to be president pro tempore of the Senate—a position he had the seniority to fill.

Moreover, the New Hampshire senator did not want to give up the important Appropriations Committee chairmanship in order to gain the floor leadership. Bridges would also be up for reelection in two years and feared a possible challenge from Sherman Adams, the state's governor, who was resigning to become Eisenhower's White House chief of staff. Ultimately, Taft and Bridges agreed that the post as president pro tempore would free Bridges to shore up his New Hampshire base. Taft promised his help and quickly asked publisher William Loeb of the Manchester *Union Leader* to give Bridges "all the favorable publicity you can." [12]

On December 16, standing in front of Ike's New York headquarters at the Commodore Hotel, senators Frank Carlson and H. Alexander Smith told reporters that they were backing Taft as majority leader. Smith and Carlson were close to Eisenhower, and the site of their announcement suggested that Ike approved of Taft's designs. Indeed, days later, Arthur Krock of the *New York Times* reported that Ike had authorized the Smith-Carlson endorsement. [13]

Three days after the Smith-Carlson plug, Taft publicly announced his candidacy for the majority leader's post. His legislative knowhow was well known, as were his ties to southern Democrats. More important, there was his standing as Mr. Republican. Making him a team player on Capitol Hill was only slightly less important now than it had been before Morningside Heights. Taft's cooperation would help Ike on Capitol Hill and across the country. The Ohioan, in turn, had assured Carlson of his desire for understanding within party ranks and his absolute loyalty to President Eisenhower. Paradoxically, his outburst over Durkin, which had initially hampered his bid for the Senate post, ultimately helped him. Ike's continuing failure to consult with other senators on appointments irked Taft's colleagues, and many came to back Taft as a champion of senatorial prerogatives. And hence, when Senate Republicans caucused, Taft won unanimous approval.

Under Taft's direction, Right Wing Republicans dominated the congressional chairmanships in the Eighty-third Congress. In the Senate, the GOP Policy Committee was loaded with Taft followers. Everett Dirksen ran the Republican Campaign Committee. Styles Bridges, of course, was Appropriations Committee head. Joseph McCarthy chaired the Government Operations Committee; and William Jenner, the Administration and Rules Committee. While Wisconsin's Alexander Wiley—a domestic conservative but a convert to internationalism—took charge of the Foreign Relations Committee, Taft gave up a seat on the Finance Committee for one on Foreign Relations, in order to watch over Wiley. Finally, Millikin headed the Finance Committee. The Colorado senator was one of the most powerful GOP conservatives in the Senate but, like Taft, was ready to get along with the new administration. As Millikin wrote to Senator Frank Carlson, "I do not see any insuperable reasons against effective cooperation between the Congress and President Eisenhower."[10]

In the House the situation was similar. The GOP leadership wanted the new administration to succeed, and again the committee heads were mainly older conservatives. As in the Eightieth Congress, Joseph Martin would be Speaker of the House. He clearly saw himself as a soldier in Eisenhower's crusade—whatever that entailed. Martin liked to tell House colleagues what Senator Richard Russell had told him at a Washington cocktail party: "Joe, we've got to make the Eisenhower Administration a success. We've all got to cooperate to this end, because if it fails, the next administration will be a radical one."[15]

Martin was not the only House Republican ruler with leadership experience gained during the turbulent Eightieth Congress. Charles Halleck would again utilize his considerable legislative skills as GOP majority leader. Crusty, economy-minded John Taber of New York was back as chairman of the House Appropriations committee, as was Jesse Wolcott at Banking and Currency, and Leo Allen at Rules. Hard-line conservative Clare Hoffman now headed the Government Operations Committee, and Daniel Reed took command of Ways and Means. Finally, Robert Chiperfield, a conservative and an Old Marshall Plan foe, pounded the gavel in the House Foreign Affairs Committee. Ironically, like Chiperfield, most of these GOP committee heads had for years stood against what would shortly become the Eisenhower policies. For them, this would pose a personal political dilemma that would have ramifications for the Republican party as it entered a new era.

Nothing could spoil the first Republican inauguration in twenty years. Held under sunny skies and mild temperatures, it was an excellent day for new beginnings.

But Eisenhower proclaimed no new day. In a comparatively short inaugural address, the thirty-fourth president basically called for greater international cooperation and more world trade. This was certainly not the kind of crusade many Republicans thought Ike had promised on the hustings, and the *Chicago Tribune* said so. "So far as the intellectual content of the address is concerned, it might have been written at Mr. Truman's orders," grumbled the *Tribune*.[16] Yet few newspapers echoed these complaints. Nor did Ike's internationalist message prompt much Capitol Hill grousing. Indeed, Right Wing Republicans fairly bubbled over Ike's new start.

Shortly thereafter, Eisenhower's State of the Union message provided additional cause for Old Guard applause. The president's program for "progress toward free enterprise" and "natural economic law" included an end to Korean War wage and price controls and steps toward a balanced budget. Further, the administration promised to achieve maximum national security at a minimum cost. The foreign policy section of Eisenhower's State of the Union address was especially pleasing to the Republican Old Guard. Eisenhower outlined the beginnings of a "new positive foreign policy." The American Seventh Fleet, Eisenhower stated, would no longer "shield" Red China from Chiang Kai-shek's Nationalist forces on Formosa, thereby "unleashing" Chiang. Also, Ike called on Congress to repudiate any secret concessions made to the Russians at World War II conferences. This "sure and substantial start" for his administration, as Ike called it, won a rousing GOP reception on Capitol Hill. House Speaker Joe Martin called the address "an outstanding exposition of clear thinking and sane policies," and Taft hailed it as a "great speech." [17] Given the right-wing tone of Eisenhower's message, it was only fitting that Ike left the chamber arm-in-arm with Taft.

The State of the Union address did have some bad news in it for conservatives of a tax-slashing bent. All tax reduction, the president stated, could come only after the achievement of a balanced budget at a later date. The *Chicago Tribune* complained only of this section, and Eisenhower's Capitol Hill hosts met his tax-cut strictures with little applause. The news especially disappointed one GOP House member. Without consulting the White House, Ways and Means chairman Daniel Reed had already introduced H.R. 1—a proposal for personal income tax cuts. The administration, in turn, had miffed Reed by failing to confer with him before the State of the Union message, as it had with Senate Finance Committee chairman Eugene Millikin. [18]

Opposing presidents was nothing new for Dan Reed, who had come to Congress in 1919 after coaching football at Cornell University. Now Reed was ready to hold the line against a Republican president in behalf of traditional GOP economic doctrine that stated that tax reduction would stimulate the economy, thus raising revenues and ultimately bringing a balanced budget. Reed and other tax-cut proponents feared that with the Korean War winding down and the attendant decline in military spending, a recession was imminent. Conversely, the Eisenhower administration saw inflation as its major economic concern.

On February 16, Reed's Ways and Means committee approved his H.R. 1, 21 to 4. All Republicans supported the committee report, which declared that "tax relief must be the first order of business for this Congress." Eisenhower had already taken his stand against tax relief and now maneuvered against Reed. As a result, House Speaker Joseph Martin directed the Rules Committee to pigeonhole Reed's tax-cut proposal.

Reed retaliated by next turning his attention to the abolition of the excess profits tax on business. The president, for his part, wanted to keep revenues high from both income *and* excess profits levies. Moreover, Eisenhower recognized the potential political damage to the Republican party—commonly regarded as the party of big business—if corporations gained tax relief before individuals. Reed, too, acknowledged that this would be "disastrous politically," but this realization only made him more determined to gain *both* personal tax relief and the end of the excess profits tax, which was scheduled by law to lapse on June 30, 1953.[19] Reed therefore announced that his Ways and Means Committee would sit on the White House's request for the extension of excess profits legislation as long as H.R. 1 remained bottled up in the Rules Committee. For a time, Reed, who had failed to get enough signatures on a discharge petition for H.R. 1, blocked excess profits consideration by refusing even to convene his Ways and Means Committee. As Reed once said upon leaving the White House, "When I fight, I fight."[20]

As this conflict dragged on, news broke of additional GOP dissension over tax and budget matters. Senator Robert Taft was at the center of this struggle. Unlike many Republicans, Taft remembered the promises made at Morningside Heights. He counted on a balanced budget for fiscal 1954, followed by a budget reduced to $60 billion accompanied by a considerable tax cut for fiscal 1955, but had little faith that the new administration would actually do so. Ultimately, Congress would probably have to lead the way. Taft gave the White House until May to "make recommendations for substantial reductions."[21]

Time ran out at the end of April when Eisenhower informed congressional leaders that he would be unable to balance his first budget. The administration could prune only $4.4 billion from the $9.9 billion deficit estimated in Truman's 1954 budget, mainly because of military considerations. During Ike's briefing, Taft sat in "grim silence." Then he exploded. "With a program like this, we'll never elect a Republican Congress in 1954," he thundered, pounding his fist on the cabinet table. "You're taking us down the same road Truman traveled. It's a repudiation of everything we promised in the campaign." Military men had hoodwinked the president, Taft charged.[22] Eisenhower, flushed and furious, sat silently—astonished by what he later deemed the "demagogic nature of [Taft's] tirade." After Taft's flare-up, a thick silence filled the room. It was only the small talk of Treasury Secretary George Humphrey and others that allowed the president to cool down. Then, Eisenhower calmly reviewed rising military costs and dissented from Taft's dire political predictions.[23]

Taft's brief but bitter words were astonishing largely because up to that point he had been a prime exponent of GOP teamwork. Obviously, the demands of cooperation and certain prior disappointments still weighed heavily on Mr. Republican. Despite Eisenhower's belief that this tirade "undercut Taft's leadership position," the Ohioan was merely voicing the concern of many Old Guardsmen under the new party command. Still, Taft's budget blowup heralded no open break with the Eisenhower White House.

Meanwhile, Daniel Reed remained dug in on Capitol Hill. Some of his trenchmates, however, were deserting him. For instance, budget-minded Congressman John Taber complained to Reed that his mulish obstruction was "designed practically deliberately" to elect a Democratic Congress in 1954. Reed disagreed. He told Taber that they were both fighting the same battle for a balanced budget and tax relief. But, said Reed, the stakes were even greater than that. Claimed the former football coach, "I am fighting on a matter of principle to preserve the integrity of each chairman, the prestige of the committee and the dignity of this House."[24]

Reed's words had the ring of a good pep talk, but he was competing against heavy odds. The administration finally resorted to the Rules Committee in order to force excess profits legislation to the House floor. This power play unsettled other committee heads, but there was still a premium on party cooperation in these early days, and the Ways and Means Committee ultimately reported out the excess profits tax bill over the opposition of its chairman. In the end, Congress approved it, and the president signed the bill for excess profits continuation on July 16, 1953.

For Eisenhower's budget, the victory was of little importance, since the total revenue gained from the excess profits levies was slight. Nor were the president's political gains that clear-cut. Initially, Arthur Krock had reported that White House "muscle-flexing" had made an impression on Eisenhower's GOP opponents, especially those with reelection campaigns in 1954. But Ike's subsequent actions raised doubts. Hoping to alter the GOP through conciliation, Eisenhower had basically winked at Reed's half-year rebellion. In early August Ike purposely downplayed the administration's difficulties with Reed, even calling him an administration "wheelhorse" on most other Capitol Hill issues.[25]

Perhaps Ike was wise to soothe the Ways and Means chairman, but such leniency also characterized his dealings with other more recalcitrant lawmakers. Word naturally circulated on Capitol Hill that GOP solons could buck the White House and go unpunished.

For Republicans, foreign policy was still the most explosive issue. The 1950 and 1952 campaigns had shown that a surface unity could be achieved, but differences remained deep and volatile. With American boys still fighting in Korea and the Cold War dragging on, Eisenhower's State of the Union message on foreign policy was not enough to change that.

Skirmishing within Republican ranks began as soon as Ike took office. Indeed, Eisenhower's foreign policy appointments became the first targets of Right Wing Republicans. With the Democrats ousted, GOP conservatives wanted no more of "Acheson's Architects of Disaster." As a result, the confirmations of General Walter Bedell Smith as undersecretary of state and James B. Conant as high commissioner to Germany encountered great difficulty. These two appointments finally got through the Senate. On the other hand, Paul Nitze's appointment as undersecretary of defense never made it.

But the major GOP foreign policy scuffle came in the first months of the Eisenhower administration over Charles P. Bohlen. "Chip" Bohlen had been a career officer in the State Department and had served as Franklin Roosevelt's translator at the Yalta conference. Now Eisenhower had chosen Bohlen as the new ambassador to the Soviet Union. Bohlen's continued endorsement of the Yalta accords made him something more than just a State Department Russian-language specialist. Bohlen maintained that the violation, not the construction of the Yalta accords, was the basic problem— precisely the position of past Democratic administrations.

Bohlen thus personified past Democratic foreign policy failures in the eyes of many Republicans. His appointment drew heavy fire. Right Wing Republicans were horrified. "When Bohlen, the exponent of appeasement and containment is elevated to the vital role of Ambassador to Moscow," Senator Styles Bridges remarked, "the cause of freedom suffers the world over."[26] Taft believed that opposition to Bohlen was "perfectly reasonable," and, had Bohlen's prospective post been more important, Taft would have joined the opposition himself.[27] But Taft, still laboring for party harmony, voted with all the other Senate Foreign Relations committeemen to approve Bohlen. The conflict then mushroomed outside of the committee room. Secretary of State John Foster Dulles allegedly had earlier tried to appease McCarthy by making Scott McLeod, a fierce anticommunist and former aide to Senator Bridges, the State Department's new security officer. McCarthy and other Senate opponents shortly thereafter contended that Bohlen had flunked McLeod's security investigation.

The Bohlen issue now became a classic confrontation between the Congress and the executive, especially after McCarthy and other Right Wing Republican senators demanded to see Bohlen's FBI security files. In response to their demands, majority leader Taft agreed to go to the White House with Mississippi's Senator John Sparkman, a Democrat, and check Bohlen's file. Two days later, Taft reported back to the Senate that Bohlen's file was clean. Despite Taft's report and support, eleven Republicans continued unsuccessfully to oppose Bohlen's confirmation when the Senate voted on March 27. Bridges, Bricker, McCarthy, Dirksen, Goldwater, and others rejected the Bohlen selection without apology. Conservative columnist David Lawrence spoke for many disgruntled Right Wing Republicans when he called the Senate's confirmation of Bohlen "a tragic chapter in American history."

Even Taft reportedly told the White House, "No more Bohlens." The administration subsequently did make more careful diplomatic appointments.[28]

Although Taft won praise in some quarters for his display of loyalty to the administration during the Bohlen controversy, his position among GOP conservatives suffered considerably. The mood of the Senate lobbies among the Old Guard was "gloomy." "Taft—you can have him," exclaimed one senator, a former Taft backer.[29]

Bohlen's designation as American ambassador to Russia was only part of the GOP's problems flowing from Yalta. The 1952 Republican platform had pledged to "repudiate" all secret agreements made at World War II conferences and had specifically mentioned Yalta. President Eisenhower had asked for the same in his State of the Union message. The conservative position on this matter was clear. Although to repudiate Yalta by joint action of the president and Congress would not undo the evil that was wrought there, it would mark a real break with the Democratic past. To this end, five resolutions disavowing Yalta were offered in Congress by the end of January.

The Eisenhower administration offered its own Yalta antidote, known as the Enslaved Peoples Resolution, on February 20, 1953. The administration's proposal rejected any interpretation or execution of secret agreements that had been "perverted to bring about the subjugation of free people." However, there was no challenge to the fundamental validity of these prior pacts. Nor was there any mention of Franklin D. Roosevelt or the wartime conferences themselves. The administration appeared to be condemning only the Soviet Union's violation of the wartime accords. This fit precisely with Democratic views and, consequently, the Senate Democratic Policy Committee rapidly approved the Eisenhower proposal. Actually, the Eisenhower administration had designed this vague and toothless resolution to secure just this support. Eisenhower deeply desired the continuation of bipartisan foreign policy and knew the Democrats would abide no stronger language regarding Yalta, other wartime conferences, and past Democratic foreign policy. Moreover, the administration feared that an explicit denial of specific wartime accords might jeopardize certain favorable Western rights granted in those accords—for example, access to West Berlin.

GOP congressional leaders gave the Enslaved Peoples Resolution a frosty reception. But the general tone and temper of Republican foreign policy was obviously beginning to change. Between 1949 and 1952, conservative neo-isolationist opinions had held sway in the GOP. During that period bipartisan foreign policy had come under fierce attack from Republicans of all kinds. The Republican platform of 1952, which had denounced the Truman administration's containment policy as "negative, futile and immoral" and had called for the liberation of captive peoples, was a showcase of this neo-isolationist sentiment. But now that the party had won the White House and had the primary responsibility for the nation's destiny, party moderates began to move away from the harsh foreign policy stands associated with GOP hard-liners. This shift to a more moderate position first became apparent on the Enslaved Peoples (Yalta) issue. Moderate Republicans overwhelmingly backed the president, while Right Wing Republicans staunchly opposed the White House move.

This time, Taft stood by GOP conservatives. Not long after Eisenhower's Enslaved Peoples Resolution went to Capitol Hill, Taft told the president that GOP support for it would be limited without certain revisions. Taft and Republican senator Bourke Hickenlooper of Iowa later offered one such change. Their amendment stated that the Enslaved Peoples Resolution should not be construed as a congressional determination of the validity of the secret wartime agreements. The Senate Foreign Relations Committee accepted this Taft-Hickenlooper reservation, but Senate Democrats quickly made known their opposition. Stalemate ensued.

By March 9 no solution was in sight, and congressional leaders counseled the president to put off action on the administration's proposal. As a result, the Enslaved Peoples Resolution was sent back to the Senate Foreign Relations Committee. The death of Soviet ruler Joseph Stalin provided a good excuse for such a move. Despite William S. White's claim of a "subtle and negative little victory" for Taft, Eisenhower had actually won by keeping Democrats friendly, precipitating no war in the GOP, and edging the party away from the issues of the past.[30]

Eisenhower had kept one foreign policy campaign promise even before inauguration day. His October pledge to go to Korea won him headlines and ultimately votes, holding out hope for an end to the Korean impasse. Still, neither Eisenhower's November trip to the Asian front nor his December meeting with General MacArthur brought any real change in the American position in Korea. Peace came, but it was indistinguishable from what the Truman administration could probably have achieved—except that it was achieved without the accompanying howls of the GOP. The armistice agreement, signed on July 27, 1953, left North Korea in essentially the same position as before the war. Even under a Republican administration, total military victory in Korea never became the American goal. The Eisenhower administration said that it would fight for the unification of Korea only at a political conference following the armistice. There would be no liberation of North Korea.

Disgruntled by the Korean settlement, Right Wing Republicans mainly turned to blaming our selfish and irresolute European allies. Foremost among the critics was Robert Taft. In late May, 1953, he caused a stir by voicing dissatisfaction with both the impending Korean settlement and with the European allies. Taft was ill and had to have his son read his speech before the National Conference of Christians and Jews, but the Cincinnati message lost nothing in the transmission. Taft traced the unfavorable Korean truce to the need to appease the United Nations. He concluded, "I believe we might as well abandon any idea of working with the United Nations in the East and reserve for ourselves a completely free hand." Was an Eisenhower-Taft face-off at last in the making? At the news conference following Taft's speech, Eisenhower admitted Taft's right to his own opinion and even admitted his own irritations and frustrations in foreign policy matters. But the president stopped there. Those who wanted to "go it alone" in one place, he explained, had to "go it alone" everywhere.[31] Occurring simultaneously with congressional moves to withhold funds from the United Nations if Red China were to enter, the Taft speech caused a considerable flap. *US News and World Report* wrote, "In Congress, the lines are drawing tighter." This marked the "deepest rift yet" in GOP ranks.[32]

Mr. Republican was largely unprepared for the speculation that followed his Cincinnati address. He subsequently rejected Eisenhower's reading of his remarks. The Cincinnati speech had said nothing about going it alone, Taft told Herbert Hoover. All he wanted was a "freer hand." Taft insisted that he favored alliance building, particularly with Great Britain. "But," said he, "I don't think it is wrong to point out the difficulties of holding together such an alliance of nations whose heart is not in the job."[33]

As seen previously, Eisenhower's early foreign policy moves had cheered Taft. By early July his frustration had grown to the point where he could write, "I don't suppose we could be in a bigger mess in foreign affairs than we are."[34] Nevertheless, he kept his displeasure largely to himself after the Cincinnati address, unobtrusively joining a handful of old isolationists in Congress who were growing increasingly sour but were remaining basically quiet.

On foreign and domestic matters both, Senator Taft was primarily responsible for the lack of conservative GOP carping about Eisenhower. His December pledge to cooperate with the incoming administration had proved sincere. Paradoxically, his sustained team play accounted for the headlines that followed his infrequent public criticisms.

The attitude of the Eisenhower White House clearly helped Taft ease into this new role. Eisenhower had instructed subordinates to treat Taft with presidential deference. For Taft, White House doors were always open. Ike even chided the formal senator for making appointments. Moreover, both men grew more comfortable with one another as the months passed, learning where they agreed and disagreed. On international matters, Eisenhower discovered that he and Taft never disagreed when discussing "theoretical or academic" foreign policy essentials. Their clashes came only over specifics. Concerning domestic policy, Eisenhower liked to tell of Taft's reply to his remark that the Ohioan was "twice as liberal as I." "Oh, you know how that is," said the senator, "a label like that gets applied to you and afterwards you just have to live with it."[35] By the beginning of April, 1953, Ike could write in his diary, "I think it is scarcely too much to say that Taft and I are becoming right good friends."[36]

Taft, for his part, early came to appreciate the respectful treatment he received at the White House. Eisenhower still failed to understand what issues deeply divided politicians, Taft thought. But Taft believed that he had at least saved Ike from the counsel of the party's Dewey wing. Late in June, 1953, Taft wrote, "I am quite convinced that Eisenhower is essentially conservative and if we keep working with him and pushing him in the right direction, we will make real progress."[37]

Major political observers, meanwhile, began to comment on Taft's new clout and statesmanship. William S. White watched Taft's growing influence in the White House and concluded, "This is an era that has raised possibly the longest bridge in the shortest time in American politics. . . ."[38] That bridge between the Republicans on Capitol Hill and the White House was Robert Taft.

Comments like these prompted the conservative *Human Events* to remark, "The scribes and Pharisees . . . are apparently seeking to create a Taft myth—a myth of an amiable, but shortsighted fellow who had been rather sporting about his nomination and rather obliging towards Ike since January."[39] However valid this comment, Eisenhower did come to value Taft. "His loss would be a little short of calamitous," he wrote in early June, 1953.[40]

Ironically, just two months earlier on April 19, 1953, Taft had conferred with Eisenhower in Augusta, Georgia. Golf being part of the presidential routine during the Eisenhower years, and with their legislative business out of the way, Eisenhower and Taft took to the links. It was a mark of their growing friendship, as well as their mutual enthusiasm for the game. On that day, however, Taft had complained of pains in his hip. Several weeks later, Taft learned that he had cancer. Keeping his exact medical problems private, he turned over his leadership duties to William F. Knowland of California for the remainder of the congressional session. By a tragic turn of fate, just as his effectiveness was increasing, Mr. Republican was on his way out—a situation that, according to the *Washington Post,* was a real "blow" for the administration.[41]

Taft had long since secured his place as Mr. Republican. The "Taft Myth" of the committed helpmeet of President Eisenhower, on the other hand, was new. Like any myth, this one was based on some truth. The Ohioan had worked to quash antiadministration sentiment among Right Wing Republicans, and by mid-1953, no major break had occurred in Republican ranks. Taft's partisanship and political realism helped to explain his cooperation with the new administration. Eisenhower was, after all, a Republican president, and Taft wanted him to succeed. Furthermore, during the early days of the administration, not only did Taft become more aware of Eisenhower's essential conservatism, but he also learned of the perils and restraints of governance from the vantage point of a Republican White House—an education few Republicans had had.

By helping and defending the Eisenhower administration, though, Taft had suffered in certain right-wing quarters. Ironically, the same tart GOP partisanship that had led Taft to flay Democratic presidents and proposals to the delight of the Republican Old Guard now led him to defend a Republican president whose policies were at best suspect from an orthodox GOP standpoint. Taft's latest activity was, to some GOP conservatives, positively "unRepublican." In short, Mr. Republican's sense of political reality and partisanship had won out over strict adherence to right-wing party doctrine of the New and Fair Deal days. This sense of reality had rankled some GOP diehards even in earlier times. Taft's legislative responses to critical postwar problems had already been variously denounced as socialistic and "adventures in me-tooism" by his more conservative brethren.

But Taft insisted that conservatism did not mean constant opposition to change or a failure to respond to problems that people were asking the federal government to address. Taft recognized, too, that far less conservative elements would quickly fill any political void left by "do-nothing" Republicans. The Republican Right's failure to match the wisdom of Taft was its greatest mistake in the 1945–1953 period, a result of its constant rigidity.

Still, to the end, not much separated Taft and the Republican Old Guard. Indeed, for over two decades Taft was not only Mr. Republican, but Mr. Republican Right in the popular mind. And during the early postwar years, nobody to Taft's right—not Kenneth Wherry on Capitol Hill or Douglas MacArthur across the nation—had Taft's political expertise or significance. Furthermore, Taft generally supported the Republican Right in its opposition to Democratic policies and "me-too" Republicanism. Despite Taft's liberal legislative efforts in housing, education, and medical care, the popular picture of Taft remained that of a stalwart foe of Democratic domestic and foreign policies. Unfairly, but understandably, Taft had often been portrayed as a cranky antagonist of *all* reform—cold and callous to the troubles of the less fortunate. This was due in part to Taft's harsh and overblown partisan rhetoric, as well as his dreadful public relations. *This* Taft was something of a myth, too—but one that the general public embraced. Unfortunately, Taft's efforts to advance federal housing and education were often forgotten, but his inflation-fighting advice to "eat less," easily remembered.

This conservative Taft, of course, fit neatly into the Republican Right image. The Republican Right generally failed to identify with the aspirations of a considerable segment of the American public. Although Old Guard Republicans often belabored the political machinations of Wall Street, the Republican party itself was commonly regarded as the party of big business. When conservative Republican fears about government controls, high taxes, and the excesses of organized labor did coincide with those of the public, voters had responded favorably to them, as in 1946. But generally, in the postwar period, the Republican Right had offered no sustained, integrated program. It proved most successful in its obstructionist role. From 1945 through 1952, the Right had consistently combined with southern Democrats to block Harry Truman's Fair Deal and other similar reform proposals. Taft had, at times, been both a benefactor and a victim of this success.

In foreign affairs, the Republican Right (Taft included) was also similarly negative. Faced with the realities of the Cold War, the Republican Right seemed content to declare its anticommunism, call for strengthened air and sea defenses, and wait for the Democrats to leave office. With few exceptions, theirs was a policy of remedyless carping. Although the Republican Right's warnings about the limits of American power might by themselves seem prophetic in post-Vietnam America, they were hardly in keeping with the relative world position of the United States after World War II. In that period, the Right's fears about American overextension were unsubstantiated or simply a smokescreen for a parochial isolationism. And, many Old Guard predictions never came true. For example, the Marshall Plan, far from sapping the American economy, as GOP conservatives had fretted, gave it a boost. Moreover, in view of their stand on international cooperation, the Right's concern over its potential harm to the United Nations in such ventures as the Greek-Turkish aid program was hardly credible—and even ludicrous.

The Republican Right's Asian policy also suffered from confusion. Its preoccupation with communism in the Far East came late, leaving it open to charges of political opportunism. The Old Guard's China stand failed to acknowledge present or past power realities with respect to Mao's Communists or Chiang's Nationalists. Regarding Korea, conservative Republicans had been partly responsible for cuts in aid to South Korea before the outbreak of hostilities. During the conflict itself, the Republican Right's simultaneous calls for all-out war and withdrawal, while expressing general public frustration with the new concept of limited war, illuminated the Right's failure to set realistic and steady goals for the Korean involvement. With some justification, critics could charge that the Republican Right's vacillation was at once irresponsible and hypocritical.

By 1952 the Republican Right had proved unable to turn the public's obvious frustration and disappointment with American foreign policy to its lasting advantage. It simply offered no coherent and balanced foreign policy alternative. Significantly, the Eisenhower wing, which offered no radical break with Democratic foreign policy, was able to capitalize on this right-wing, neo-isolationist sentiment.

Politically, the Republican Right failed in the 1945–1952 period to nominate, much less elect, one of its own for president. Robert Taft had been the only real Right Wing hope, yet, ironically, Old Guard Republicans themselves were partly responsible for his persistent failure. In 1948 Taft's liberal legislative moves had angered some Right Wing Republicans sufficiently that they switched to Dewey. Even in 1952, when most GOP conservatives clearly wanted no repeat of Dewey's "me-too" disaster of 1948, their fears regarding the "Taft can't win" thesis led many of them to support Eisenhower.

Still, Taft's losses in 1948 and 1952 were widely, and correctly, regarded as defeats for the Old Guard. A majority of Right Wing Republicans had never brought the "Taft can't win" theory and had stuck with Taft to the end. They believed that if Republicans would only eschew "me-too," hordes of conservatives—who were normally electoral no-shows—would reward the party for offering " a choice not an echo." Although Right Wing opponents claimed that stay-at-home voters were more likely to favor Democratic candidates and that Taft had far greater strength in the Republican party conventions than in the nation at large, real flesh-and-blood voters in a general election for president were never given the chance to prove the "Taft can't win" thesis or disprove the Republican Right's political speculation. Therefore, Right Wing Republicans continued to talk of the latent power of conservative "stay-at-homes." As Richard Rovere observed in the *New Yorker* shortly after the 1952 Chicago Republican convention, "The selection of Taft would at least have got him off the Republican conscience, where he is to remain whether or not Ike loses."[42]

That Taft never got a chance to present a "clear alternative" was solely the fault of the eastern Republicans, claimed Right Wing Republicans. Political buccaneering on the part of the Dewey faction had denied the GOP nomination to Senator Taft and the Republican Right. The Republican Old Guard had ample reason to think unfair some convention moves of its adversaries, especially in 1952, but the Republican Right's broad charges that Wall Street and Madison Avenue forces had bought, bartered, and bally-hooed the nominations of Dewey and Eisenhower remain unsubstantiated. Certainly, the methods used by Eisenhower backers at Chicago galled the Republican Right and were remembered for a long time.

Taft's continual losing battle for the GOP nomination and the presidency also confirmed numerous Right Wing Republican fears about presidential politics. Taft had been a victim of image politics, which had rewarded FDR, Dewey, and Eisenhower. Taft simply lacked the stuff of *mass* appeal. Even one diehard Taft enthusiast later recalled that one had to know Taft well to understand him.[43] Such a personality was at a tremendous disadvantage in democratic politics. GOP conservatives believed that Taft's lack of the popular touch, as well as his unrelenting truth-telling, doomed his presidential hopes. He was simply no match for the reigning hucksterism of the East. Yet to many in the Old Guard, Taft had failed to gain the White House for all the right reasons and had made the proper enemies in doing so.

With the departure of Taft from the Senate in June, 1953, William S. White wrote, midwestern conservative Republicans "stand at a twilight turning."[44] Clearly, these were dark days for the Republican Right. Old Guard ranks on Capitol Hill had dwindled with the last election. In the Senate the GOP leadership had been a bastion of conservative Republicanism for years. Taft had been much responsible for this, putting down periodic revolts by "liberal" GOP elements. Now, with one of these former insurgents, William F. Knowland, at the head of the Senate GOP and Eisenhower in the White House, Old Guard domination was in peril. Worse, the RNC, another traditional Right Wing stronghold, was coming increasingly under the sway of the White House. Moreover, as Taft himself realized, the national media was predominantly hostile to conservative Republicanism, and right-wing commentators like Westbrook Pegler and George Sokolsky possessed only narrow followings. Finally, the Old Guard had even less of a claim on the intellectual "egghead" vote than Eisenhower.

Taft's departure further complicated matters for the Republican Right. While he had stifled dissent among Republican hard-liners, Taft had also carried the orthodox position to the White House. He had also been the most skillful legislator of the Republican Right and had shouldered much of the parliamentary burden for his Senate colleagues. His ties to southern Democrats in the Senate had been very close, and Taft's absence made the ongoing relationship between Republicans and southern Bourbons questionable.

Thus, Taft's exit was a blow for the Republican Right, as well as for the Eisenhower administration. Although the relationship between Taft and the Republican Right had often been anomalous, Taft had always regarded himself as a GOP conservative. And the Republican Right, in turn, could never ignore him. As William S. White wrote in his prize-winning biography of Taft, [conservative Republicans] "wanted him whether they understood him always or not, sometimes they even wanted him when they did not at all approve of him."[45]

On the afternoon of July 31, 1953, John Bricker, who had conceded for Taft at three GOP conventions, rose on the Senate floor. Shaken, his voice barely audible, Bricker informed his colleagues that Robert A. Taft had just died in New York City. At the White House, Eisenhower mourned his "wise counselor and valued friend." The flag on Capitol Hill was lowered to half-staff, and the House rose in silent tribute. The Senate quickly adjourned out of respect for Mr. Republican.

Stick with Ike

Republican instability was inevitable after the death of Robert Taft. Ironically, Mr. Republican had won a greater voice for the Republican Right Wing in the GOP administration by keeping it muzzled. Now, the fragile peace that had existed between the Eisenhower and Old Guard Republicans since the 1952 Chicago convention was in jeopardy. Were the Republicans on the verge of committing hara-kiri?

After Taft's death, maneuvering began immediately over William F. Knowland's ongoing leadership of Senate Republicans. GOP-watchers could recall that Knowland had joined with anti-Taft rebels in 1949 and had been mentioned as "Ike's candidate" for majority leader in late 1952. Observers also variously described Knowland's record as "middle of the road" or a "little to the left of the Republican Party." But despite Capitol Hill "corridor rumors" of a possible Right Wing challenge, the Senate Republicans (with seven absent) unanimously chose William Knowland as their new majority leader on August 4, 1953.

The *New York Times* regarded this selection as a "significant victory for Eisenhower," and Knowland himself bolstered this view by publicly rejecting the Right-Wing contention that the Eisenhower administration was proving too hospitable to past Democratic foreign policy. Knowland won, however, without active White House support, since Eisenhower had instructed administration officials to keep out of this Senate Republican business. What really clinched it for Knowland was that Taft had picked him as majority leader in one of his last Capitol Hill acts. This undoubtedly helped the Senate GOP to avoid civil war at this time.

If Knowland's moderate reputation put off some GOP conservatives, his own Republican credentials were reassuring. Twelve-year-old Billy had made speeches for GOP presidential candidate Warren Harding. He subsequently became the RNC's youngest member by age twenty-six. As a California state lawmaker, Knowland had maintained close ties with liberal GOP governor Earl Warren, who appointed him to fill the Senate term of the deceased Hiram Johnson in 1945. Although initially seen as a liberal

Young Turk, the California senator was difficult to categorize—especially after 1949, when he became convinced that American foreign policy was slighting the Far East in relation to Europe. In fact, Knowland subsequently made the case of the so-called Asia-Firsters with such fire that critics soon dubbed him the "Senator from Formosa"—a nickname he deeply resented because he had consistently backed European aid measures.

Knowland unquestionably had the respect of his Senate colleagues on both sides of the aisle. Nobody doubted his integrity. But Knowland was stiff, humorless, and ill at ease in the Senate cloakroom, where he was known as a "young fogey." He had yet to learn the value of a well-stocked liquor cabinet in doing Capitol Hill business. In fact, he rarely talked with fellow senators. Like Taft, Knowland had a precise, logical mind, and little political pizzazz. Unlike Taft, he lacked parliamentary know-how or prudence.

Knowland's helmsmanship and influence with the Old Guard received its first important test in connection with the so-called Bricker Amendment in 1953–1954. Ohio Senator John Bricker had already proposed a constitutional amendment during the Truman years that would have reasserted Congress's primacy over treaties and executive agreements, and thus forestall a repetition of Yalta-like diplomacy. The 1952 Republican platform had touched on this issue, promising that no treaty or executive agreement would "deprive our citizens the rights guaranteed them by the federal constitution." Therefore, when Bricker reintroduced his amendment in the Eighty-third Congress, forty-five of the forty-eight Republicans were among its sixty-three cosponsors. Such groups as the American Medical Association and the American Bar Association supported the Ohio senator's constitutional proposal.

One particularly controversial feature of the Bricker Amendment was the "which clause." It stated that a treaty would become effective only by legislation "which" would be needed in the absence of a treaty. This highly ambiguous phrase raised vital questions about the role of the states in the treaty-making process. This clause, which Eisenhower believed to have been introduced "insidiously," prompted the administration to oppose the Bricker Amendment. Ultimately, the administration saw Bricker's proposal as a symbol of the conservative Republicans' disinclination to have America assume its global responsibilities. Given the administration's stand, many moderate Republicans, who had supported the Bricker Amendment when it was first introduced during the Truman years, began to cool in their desire to shackle the president's treaty-making powers. Bricker, in turn, blamed administration hostility to his amendment on "certain forces" in New York.[1]

Despite administration efforts to achieve some compromise with Bricker, the first session of the Eighty-third ended in stalemate over the

Bricker Amendment. Eisenhower had come to believe that the constitutional proposal merely represented the senator's "one hope of achieving at least
a faint immortality in American history."[2] When the Congress reconvened
in January, 1954, Eisenhower informed Knowland of his continued opposition.

The Bricker Amendment thus remained a major point of GOP contention, and never more so than after the sudden firing of Clarence Manion.
The president had earlier selected the pro-Taft former dean of Notre Dame
law school to head the President's Commission on Inter-Governmental Relations. But as the Senate debated the Bricker Amendment in mid-February,
1954, news came of the forced resignation of Manion from the commission.
Manion and the Right Wing charged that this action pointed up the White
House's "fatal disposition to ride the saddle of faction" against anti–New
Deal Republicans. The White House countered that it had known of Manion's "orthodox" beliefs before his appointment, and that he was asked to
leave simply because of his failure to devote the necessary time to the commission. But Robert Donovan's inside account of the administration later
made clear that Manion's "extreme right wing views" were largely to blame
for his departure.[3]

By the close of Senate debate on the constitutional issue, Bricker agreed
to the Senate GOP command's request to knock out the "which clause"
from his amendment. The Senate, in the end, turned to a substitute known
as the George Substitute. Named after the Democratic senator from Georgia, this proposal was so similar to the Ohioan's original amendment that
Bricker gave it his approval. Predictably, the Eisenhower administration opposed the George Substitute. But the proposal did enlist one surprising supporter—William Knowland, who temporarily left his seat as majority leader
to speak for it during the debate. Despite what Ike later called Knowland's
"ridiculous spectacle," the Senate killed the George Substitute—but only
by one vote less than the required two-thirds needed to propose a constitutional amendment. There were thirty-two Republicans among the George
Resolution's supporters. For the *Chicago Tribune*, the administration's resistance showed that New Dealers had hijacked the GOP and that conservative Republicans needed to find a new party.[4]

During the 1952 presidential campaign, commentators had written that
the election of a Republican president would serve to check Senator Joe
McCarthy and McCarthyism. With Eisenhower in the White House and Taft
riding herd in the Senate, the prospects did indeed seem bright. The Senate
Republican leadership quickly decided that Indiana senator William Jenner's Internal Security Committee would have sole responsibility on the Red
issue; McCarthy, in turn, was left to assume the chairmanship of the relatively minor Committee on Government Operations and was expected to

use its Permanent Subcommittee on Investigations to probe government corruption. Said Taft, "We've got McCarthy where he can't do any harm."[5]

But there soon was trouble. Not only did Jenner allow the Wisconsin senator's committee to encroach consistently on his turf, but the Bohlen controversy, mentioned earlier, quickly showed that McCarthy's anti-Red crusade was nonpartisan and not necessarily confined to the committee room. McCarthy simply could not be muzzled—even by Republicans. That he would continue to grab headlines became obvious only a few days after Bohlen's controversial confirmation. Standing before television cameras, McCarthy baldly announced that he had just "negotiated" a pact with Greek shipowners that got them to halt trade with Communist China and North Korea.

Although the administration's foreign operations director, Harold Stassen, initially asserted that McCarthy "undermined" administration efforts by such negotiating activities, Secretary of State Dulles shortly thereafter claimed that McCarthy's exploits were actually in the national interest and that Stassen had really meant to say "infringed," and not "undermined." At this moment, administration flexibility seemed worthwhile in order to establish goodwill with McCarthy and Capitol Hill Republicans, who were themselves disgusted with the allied trade with the Communist enemy. Taft, for example, believed that McCarthy was at most guilty of a little grandstanding.[6]

Eisenhower, on the other hand, could bring himself to take public exception to McCarthy committee aide J.B. Matthews, who identified the clergy as "the single largest group supporting the Communist apparatus in the United States today." Indeed, throughout his first year in office, the president vacillated between opposing and appeasing McCarthy. What some regarded as a pitiful lack of leadership on Ike's part, others saw as a cagey program designed to give the Wisconsin senator "enough rope" to hang himself. In public, Eisenhower insisted that he would not discuss personalities whenever McCarthy's name came up. "I will not get down in the gutter with that guy," the president once told his staff.[7] Such a stricture obviously made White House leadership extremely difficult on an issue that was one chiefly of personality.

From time to time, the administration actually tried to outgun McCarthy on his own turf. The administration issued periodic reports on its security risk dismissals, and in November, 1953, Attorney General Herbert Brownell charged that in 1945 President Truman had named Harry Dexter White as head of the International Monetary Fund while knowing that FBI reports indicated that White was involved in espionage activities. But this approach contained certain dangers. When Truman responded that the Eisenhower administration had stooped to McCarthyism, the Wisconsin senator quickly demanded equal time and attacked the present as well as the past White House occupant. He charged that the Eisenhower administration had failed to fire enough security risks and chided it for allowing the "blood trade" between Red China and the allies to continue.

While one Eisenhower aide termed this McCarthy speech "a declaration of war against the President," at least one Right Wing Republican urged the White House to heed McCarthy. McCarthy was "gaining rapidly," South Dakota's Senator Karl Mundt wrote to Republican national chairman Len Hall in late November, 1953. "We MUST keep the [Democrats] on the defensive on Communism . . . afterall, what other issue have we." Later, in December, Mundt observed that it was a "shame Ike cooled off" on Brownell's Harry Dexter White speech. "Check for yourself," he added, "the McCarthy viewpoints are popular and Dulles and Ike should have a talk with Joe. Work out an armistice and working arrangement and *stop* supporting the unpopular side of issues."[8]

But the Wisconsin senator was a creature of controversy, a public figure who fed on headlines, and by February, 1954, the Eisenhower administration and McCarthy were locked in their greatest confrontation. At the root of the trouble was an army dentist, Irving Peress, a member of the left-wing American Labor party. Hauled before McCarthy's committee, Peress refused to answer questions regarding his political views. When the army later gave Peress an honorable discharge, McCarthy demanded an explanation. Brigadier General Ralph Zwicker, however, refused to divulge the names of officials involved in the Peress matter, and the Wisconsin senator publicly berated Zwicker as "not fit to wear that uniform." Even the *Chicago Tribune* thought the senator had gone too far.[9]

Although Secretary of the Army Robert Stevens immediately refused to allow Zwicker to appear again before McCarthy's committee, the administration still hoped to mend the breach between the army and McCarthy. As a result, Secretary Stevens and senators Dirksen, Mundt, and McCarthy met for the famous "Chicken Luncheon" of February 24, 1954, regarding a compromise. When Karl Mundt announced the luncheon's "memo of understanding," it appeared that Stevens had eaten crow, not chicken, since he gave in to McCarthy's demands and gained none of the safeguards he had wanted. McCarthy exacerbated matters by telling one reporter that Stevens could not have surrendered "more abjectly if he had got down on his knees."[10]

McCarthy's triumph proved short-lived. On March 11, the army released information detailing attempts by McCarthy and his aide Roy Cohn to gain preferential treatment for army private G. David Schine, another McCarthy assistant. Although these charges had first appeared in the press in mid-December, 1952, McCarthy now claimed the army was trying to "blackmail" him. There was also a mounting political challenge to McCarthy from within the GOP. On March 9, Vermont Republican senator Ralph

Flanders attacked McCarthy, characterizing him as a "one man party" who was doing his best to shatter the GOP. Even more significant, President Eisenhower now appeared ready to talk "personalities." At a news conference, Ike praised Flanders's "service" and pointedly warned of the "great danger" to the Republican party from "individuals seeking after personal aggrandizement."

Clearly, McCarthy's support was falling off. Conservative John Taber was beginning to find McCarthy's statements to be "ridiculous." "I do believe," Taber continued, "that the country would be better off everywhere if all of us, including Joe, would devote our attention to rooting [Communists] out rather than talking quite so much about sidelines."[11] Finally, Vice-President Nixon publicly chided McCarthy for "reckless talk" that hampered the anticommunist cause.

Angst-ridden Republicans had to watch in the spring of 1954 as the Senate investigated the army's charges against Senator McCarthy. The Democrats had insisted on public, even televised hearings, and, as a result, the army-McCarthy hearings became a national spectacle, as an estimated 80 million Americans tuned in. The confrontation was indeed dramatic but generally inconclusive as far as the specific charges were concerned. McCarthy did, however, manage to alienate most of his moderate backers, and he began to tumble badly in the public opinion polls.

Even before the close of the army-McCarthy hearings in June, Senator Ralph Flanders of Vermont, a liberal Republican, introduced a resolution in the Senate that proposed to punish McCarthy for various transgressions by stripping him of his committee chairmanships. Making it impossible for Republicans to duck the McCarthy issue any longer, the Flanders resolution posed great dangers for the GOP, and majority leader Knowland publicly labeled it a "mistake"—unjustifiable and an obstacle to the administration's legislative program. By mid-July, however, seeing that Flanders had won increased support by altering his original resolution to call only for McCarthy's censure, not the removal of his committee chairmanships, Knowland was forced to offer his own compromise resolution to create a special bipartisan committee to examine McCarthy's activities. Although Flanders opposed this move, the Knowland measure passed, 75 to 12. Specific charges were added to the resolution, as well as a key amendment by New York Republican Irving Ives that required the special committee to report back before the end of the Eighty-third Congress—a provision Knowland approved only grudgingly.[12]

Named after chairman Arthur V. Watkins, a conservative Utah Republican, the resultant special committee included two other Republicans and three Democrats. All six were fairly conservative and known as "Senate types." The McCarthy matter was locked behind closed doors—for the time being.

The McCarthy matter was, of course, only one of the problems plaguing the GOP in 1953–1954. Republicans had not ruled the White House in twenty years, and political savants often pointed out that only fourteen GOP House members remained from Herbert Hoover's day and not one senator. The Republican party was basically an opposition party that was no longer in opposition. Worse, the new president, however much a natural politician, was a military man and unfamiliar with the intricacies of civilian politics in Washington. In this environment, congressional–White House misunderstandings were bound to occur, and as Ike complained of being "kicked in the shins" by Capitol Hill Republicans, they groused about "Just A Republican New Deal."[13]

The GOP's Lincoln Birthday bash of 1954 in Washington signaled a marked intensification of party troubles. There were many empty seats and "mountains" of unclaimed box suppers. Ike's remarks to the gathering were met with "less than deafening" applause. At about this same time in the *American Magazine*, C. Budington Kelland of Arizona held forth on administration shortcomings. The crusty national committeeman from Arizona claimed that the Taft wing of the GOP had been restless since the senator's death, and the administration—especially the White House chief of staff Sherman Adams—was not helping to allay Old Guard fears.[14]

Old Guard criticism of the administration mounted throughout 1954. Bricker and McCarthy continued to cause problems for Ike. North Dakota senator Milton Young groused publicly about the White House, or the "Palace," where "you feel like an outcast."[15] Right Wing Republicans grumbled that the Eisenhower administration was calling on Congress to extend, not repeal, the old "Truman-Roosevelt" program. The concern that most Right Wing Republicans felt was revealed in Hoffman's letter to RNC boss Hall: "Some of us here want to help Ike and go along on every possible occasion, but will not do a right-about-face on policies we have taken for 25–40 years."[16]

Conservative opinion makers gave Eisenhower—"a Fifth-Column Democrat"—an even rougher going-over. "He's a picnic pitcher in the world series," wrote Westbrook Pegler. Justifying the battering Ike was regularly receiving in his *Chicago Tribune,* Colonel McCormick said, "We treat Eisenhower as he deserves, and right now he doesn't deserve much."[17]

There was nothing surprising about this GOP wrangling. The fundamental problem in the party was still a basic lack of agreement on what the GOP's 1952 victory meant. When the Eisenhower administration brought no rollback of New Deal structures or scrapping of Democratic foreign policy, the howls and shrieks of conservative hard-liners naturally ensued. Eisenhower himself was partly to blame. His vague and honeyed words during the 1952 canvass had allowed GOP conservative imaginations to run wild. For the moment, Republicans of all types came to believe their own campaign rhetoric about a united party. Many Right Wing Republicans temporarily forgot why they had opposed Ike before the Chicago GOP convention in 1952—a result, perhaps, of their belief that all the general needed was the proper advisors, which he would get in Washington.

Also bothering Old Guard Republicans was the nonpartisan tone and style of the Eisenhower administration. The administration was just not battling Democrats, which they had been doing for the last twenty years. Of course, the administration felt that the slimness of GOP majorities on Capitol Hill militated against "indiscriminant attacks on Democrats as a group." Such an approach rankled orthodox Republicans who, finding little positive to say about the Eisenhower administration, had to resort to maligning Democrats.

Old Guardsmen, like Kelland and Mundt, also correctly griped that administration patronage was not going to old-line, "regular" Republicans, but to political "late comers" instead. Patronage was badly handled in the first years of the administration, with many available jobs going to men of questionable Republicanism, and this galled old-time party wheelhorses. On the other hand, Eisenhower seldom used political patronage to punish Republican opponents. His light touch with the political lash stemmed from his belief that a conciliatory approach to party problems would help isolate and "reduce to impotence" the GOP extremists of the "McCarthy-Malone" axis. A related Eisenhower shortcoming by 1954 concerned his role in the upcoming elections. Under pressure from GOP leaders, Eisenhower maintained that he would set forth the Republican record and that there would be a pat on the back and a picture with the president for all GOP House and Senate candidates. Political pundits quickly observed that Eisenhower had surrendered a great deal of political leverage by giving such a blanket endorsement. After a while, one top administration official realized that the White House needed a "ruthless s.o.b. to run its politics."[18]

Although journalists highlighted GOP differences, in reality the Republican party at the time was not all claws and fangs. In fact, during the Eighty-third Congress, the administration enjoyed its share of good news. Not all Old Guard Republicans were at war with the Republican White House. In the House, Eisenhower could count on the team play of Joseph Martin and Charles Halleck. Surprisingly, Senator Homer Capehart and representatives Leo Allen and John Taber were GOP hard-liners who generally cooperated with the White House. There was also Dan Reed. After his initial tax rebellion, Reed proved extremely helpful on certain tax bills and successfully shepherded Social Security extension through the House, despite the fact he had opposed the latter program since its inception in 1935. "I am part of the Administration," he now boasted.[19]

While the approaching 1954 congressional election prompted increased support for President Eisenhower—both in the Congress and on the hustings—intraparty wrangling remained. A case in point was Chicago businessman Joseph Meek, a GOP hard-liner running for the Senate in Illinois against Democratic incumbent Paul Douglas. In order to gain Ike's campaign support, Meek agreed to endorse the whole Eisenhower program and not invite McCarthy into the state. This latter prohibition especially irritated Meek, who complained further of the administration's continued coolness toward him. In the end, Meek believed his concessions to Eisenhower made him a "Johnny-Come-Lately" to "Eisenhower people" and "suspicious" to "Taft people" in Illinois. Internal splits also continued to rack the Republican party across the nation. For example, a bitter New Jersey GOP primary left progressive Clifford Case the party's senatorial candidate and caused a great deal of apathy on the part of New Jersey's Right Wing Republicans in the fall campaign.[20]

A big Republican win would be Eisenhower's "greatest weapon" in future combat within the party, while a loss would bring intensified Right Wing criticism and perhaps all-out intraparty war. There was, however, no real political jackpot for any GOP faction on election day 1954. Only one thing was certain in its aftermath—the Republicans had lost control of Congress. The Democrats took a 49-to-47 edge in the Senate, and they also won control of the House by a 232-to-203 majority.

What did these tallies mean for the GOP? Right Wing Republicans, pointing to the reelection victories of Bridges in New Hampshire, Mundt in South Dakota, and the defeats of such liberal incumbents as John Sherman Cooper in Kentucky and Michigan's backsliding Old Guardsman Homer Ferguson, concluded that future GOP unity had to be based on "conservative terms." Party liberals, however, saw the victory of GOP progressive Clifford Case in New Jersey and the defeat of hardshell Joe Meek in Illinois as proof that the Republicans could no longer run on the record of William McKinley.

Senator Joe McCarthy had lost most of his party support even before candidates mounted the stump in 1954. A cluster of party bosses in the Midwest—supposedly the McCarthy heartland—requested that McCarthy stay off their turf. Although anti-McCarthy sentiment was far from total and the party's hard core deeply resented the administration's handling of the McCarthy issue, the general consensus was that McCarthy and his crusade had won nothing on election day.

Nevertheless, William S. White of the *New York Times* reported shortly after election day that McCarthy was the catalyst for "the largest emergence and coming together of right-wing groups since the United States entered World War II."[21] The belief was common that the Republican Right was backing the Wisconsin senator only in hopes of recapturing the Republican party. Eisenhower, for his part, realized that McCarthy's voting record did indeed separate him from the GOP's "revolutionary fringe." "However," Ike added, "the members of that [Old Guard] gang are so anxious to seize on every possible embarrassment for the Administration that they support him."[22]

Whatever the fall's election returns indicated, confronting the McCarthy issue at last became unavoidable. The Watkins committee bipartisan review had proceeded deliberately during the summer of 1954. Unlike the army-McCarthy hearings, its closed hearings were relentlessly undramatic— and also conclusive. On September 27, 1954, the Select Committee recommended that the Senate censure Senator Joseph McCarthy on two counts— contempt of the Senate for his failure to appear before the Subcommittee on Privileges and Election and his "reprehensible" abuse of General Zwicker. Knowland, of course, had gladly yielded to Republican pressure to delay full Senate consideration of the charges until after the congressional elections.

When the debate finally began on November 10, 1954, the McCarthy censure question was in reality a test of what faction would control the future "tone and spirit" of the Republican party. South Dakota conservative senator Francis Case offered the first compromise proposal—a call for a simple McCarthy apology. Case's and other such subsequent conservative compromise solutions highlighted the Old Guard belief that the McCarthy controversy was just a problem of personality. Bricker, who had urged McCarthy "not to swing his shalaghley so wildly," believed that McCarthy's indiscretions toward his fellow senators were primarily responsible for the censure movement. During the censure debate, Jenner told McCarthy that he had to restrain himself, and McCarthy agreed. But it was not long before he was on his feet challenging Watkins and the Select Committee. McCarthy's outbursts proved costly. After he branded the Watkins committee as the "unwitting handmaiden" of the Communists, Senator Wallace Bennett of Utah, GOP conservative and former head of the National Manufacturers Association, tacked on an amendment condemning McCarthy for contempt of the entire Senate.[23]

As the censure debate continued, Right Wing supporters ultimately came to equate McCarthy's cause with the Congress's investigative authority—a traditional Old Guard principle. Of course, Right Wing Republicans also believed that McCarthy and an anticommunist stance were inseparable. As Barry Goldwater of Arizona said, "a field day against Senator McCarthy in the Senate may well turn out to be a field day against America's global anti-Communist policy."[24] According to his backers, McCarthy was a marked Red hunter, for he had relentlessly attacked the "sacred cows of American politics." Bricker maintained, "The pack which hunts the hunters of Communists has caught the smell of blood."[25]

Blood was also on Senator Goldwater's mind, but it was the blood of the GOP. "We have the spectacle of cannibalism holding forth," the

Arizona senator declared. "We find the Republican Party . . . busily chewing on itself." Out of this spectacle, said Goldwater, only the Democrats could emerge winners. Old Guard Republicans tried to use this theme as a means to find some way out of the McCarthy dilemma. Their hope was to construct some solution that could win moderate Republican support. If the McCarthy matter could become a partisan issue only, the Senate might have to drop it.[26]

A potential break for pro-McCarthy forces came in early December as the harsh and vindictive debate reached a close. After a night of "prayerful consideration," majority leader William Knowland, who had differed with McCarthy in the past, announced his opposition to McCarthy's censure. McCarthy's major offenses had occurred during an earlier Congress, and his reelection had wiped the slate clean, explained Knowland. Knowland's support, however, brought compromise no closer, and on the night of December 2, after a day of parliamentary maneuver, the Senate at last voted to censure Senator McCarthy. The vote was 67 for and 22 against. All Democrats and independent Wayne Morse voted to ground "Tailgunner Joe." Senate Republicans, on the other hand, split right down the middle. The list of censure opponents—Bridges, Bricker, Dirksen, Jenner, Welker, Goldwater, Malone, and so on—read like a roster of the Republican Right. Indeed, all Senate Republican leaders, except Leverett Saltonstall, voted for McCarthy. Following the vote, Right Wing Republican senators, in a mocking and derisive way, haggled over the resolution's exact meaning. This seamy ending to the whole Senate affair did not fool McCarthy, who later told reporters, "Well, it wasn't exactly a vote of confidence."[27] The Republican party's McCarthy drama ended two days later at the White House. There, Eisenhower, who had stayed clear of the Senate battle, congratulated Select Committee chairman A.V. Watkins on a "very splendid job."

The McCarthy affair left Right Wing Republicans and conservatives in despair. Hearst columnist George Rothwell Brown predicted that the hunt for Red hunters would go on, with Indiana senator Jenner being the next victim. As for Jenner himself, the McCarthy affair demonstrated the "high political mortality of anti-Communists in Congress." Former President Hoover also feared for the future of anticommunism since any such movement would be henceforth tarred as McCarthyism.[28]

On November 15, 1954, Senate majority leader William Knowland interrupted the McCarthy censure debate to speak urgently about recent events at home and abroad.

Prior to this, Eisenhower administration moves in the national security area had prompted few complaints by Right Wing Republicans. Indeed, the major policies and pronouncements of Secretary of State John Foster Dulles genuinely appealed to the nationalistic wing of the GOP. For example,

Dulles announced in December, 1953 that there would be an "agonizing reappraisal" of the United States European commitments if the European alliance failed to bring in West Germany. A month later, Dulles declared that the United States would meet any new aggression with "massive retaliatory power." This policy combined with a "New Look" defense strategy of enhanced air and sea power and reduced levels of ground troops to yield, in the phrase of the day, "more bang for the buck." Further, Eisenhower's appointment of Admiral Arthur Radford as chairman of the Joint Chiefs assured that a Taft favorite would oversee the new military stance. But was the stillness of the Right Wing on foreign and defense matters about to be shattered as Knowland—the Republican Old Guard's new ally in the McCarthy censure battle—took the Senate floor?

Knowland expressed grave fears that the administration was about to be duped by the "Trojan Horse of co-existence" being advanced by the Soviet Union. Then he called upon the Congress to investigate current American foreign and defense policy. Days later, after Communist China announced its imprisonment of thirteen Americans captured during the Korean War and fired on the Nationalist-held island of Wuchiu, Knowland urged an immediate blockade of Red China. When Knowland subsequently sided with Senator McCarthy, pundits believed that he had gone over to the Republican Right, severing all connections with the Eisenhower administration.[29]

Actually, relations between Eisenhower and Knowland had been strained for some time. The majority leader, choosing to believe Ike's platitudes on the integrity of the coordinate branches of government, acted more like the Senate's representative to the White House than vice versa. The Senate's GOP leadership, Knowland said in late November, 1954, should not be "gagged and silent." For his part, Eisenhower spent much time brooding over Knowland's shortcomings as a party leader, especially after the majority leader's defection on the Bricker Amendment in February, 1954. By the middle of the year, Eisenhower concluded that Knowland was the "biggest disappointment of his political life."[30]

Knowland's various proclamations on foreign policy had also rankled the administration. Although he suggested that the administration break diplomatic ties with the Soviet Union, Knowland's Asian policy drew most attention. As one of the leaders of the Asia Firsters, Knowland took the Senate floor in July, 1954, to declare that if Red China were admitted to the United Nations—seen by many as the first step toward United States recognition of the Peking regime—he would quit as majority leader and work full time to sever all United States ties with the United Nations. It was a grand gesture, and Knowland repeated it periodically. "Knowland has no foreign policy except to develop high blood pressure whenever he mentions the words 'Red China,'" wrote Eisenhower.[31]

The administration rejected Knowland's demand for a China blockade, and Eisenhower stated that he had no interest in leading the GOP "off in extremes." Both Eisenhower and Knowland stressed that their disagreement was mainly over methods, and not principle, but most observers remained unconvinced. Adlai Stevenson impishly suggested that Ike sign "a nonaggression pact" with Knowland and find some way of "peaceful coexistence with a large segment" of the GOP.[32]

More trouble for the administration along this line seemed to appear on December 16, 1954, when McCarthy lashed out at Eisenhower's Asian policy. Like the Wisconsin Tailgunner's previous sallies and unlike Knowland's criticism of the administration, McCarthy's blast was bitter and personal. He accused Eisenhower of a "tolerance of Chinese Communism" and a "shrinking show of weakness toward Red China." But McCarthy went too far by publicly apologizing to the American people for supporting Ike in 1952. RNC chairman Hall said that "even greater" GOP unity would follow McCarthy's salvo, and even pro-McCarthy senators of days before rushed to disassociate themselves from the Wisconsin renegade. Ironically, McCarthy's actions temporarily served to bring the party back together—and make any Knowland-McCarthy axis impossible.

If McCarthy continued to lose support for himself, Knowland marshaled none with his antiadministration foreign policy statements. Big Bill nevertheless remained the GOP Senate chief. The administration lacked enough influence among Senate Republicans to make a sure move against Knowland, and an unsuccessful one would leave anti-Ike forces in an even stronger position. For both Knowland and the administration, there was no alternative to an uneasy truce. *Time* correctly stated that Knowland "will simply continue as the Republican non-leader in the Senate."[33]

Against this backdrop, GOP conservatives assembled in Chicago in mid-February, 1955, when the Abraham Lincoln National Eisenhower Club sponsored meetings to address the question: "What Must the Republican Party do to preserve the Republic and itself?" Over 1,700 participants from twenty-six states awaited answers from speakers such as senators George Malone, Everett Dirksen, and Joe McCarthy, as well as Governor J. Bracken Lee of Utah.

Chicago conservatives roared as Joe McCarthy assailed the Eisenhower administration's foreign policy of coexistence and Everett Dirksen vowed to fight the president on the Bricker Amendment. Luncheon speaker Governor Bracken Lee of Utah boldly charged that the Eisenhower administration had taken the nation further to the left in two years than it had ever moved in its history. Claiming that "the leadership in Washington hasn't been loyal to the Republican Party," Lee then declared that real Republicans and Democrats might have to "sit down together and put somebody on a ticket who is going to run on the kind of platform we like."[34]

A few days after this Chicago gathering, the Abraham Lincoln Club launched a national campaign to recapture the GOP from the "Eisenhower New Deal Wing." Yet Dirksen quickly came out against any third-party drive, and even McCarthy said that he hoped the administration would "co-exist" with him for a while. For Right Wing Republicans, the Eisenhower administration's betrayal—both real and perceived—was great. But the Chicago meeting and its aftermath also illustrated that Right Wing fortunes were, as the administration's Henry Cabot Lodge judged, "at the bottom of the barrel."[35]

Just how low these fortunes were became apparent on the issue of Eisenhower's role at the Big Four conference at Geneva in the summer of 1955. Geneva became a primary challenge to the Republican Right's neo-isolationism. The fundamental issue was the desirability or possibility of "peaceful coexistence" with the Soviet Union—a policy that was in theoretical conflict with the administration's own policy of "liberation" of people living under communism.

By early spring, 1955, McCarthy's own hoped-for coexistence with the Eisenhower administration was proving impossible, and he now took up the cause of the liberation of eastern Europe by offering a resolution to prohibit the president from discussing any other subject at Geneva until the Soviet Union resolved the "satellite question." This measure would, according to Senate Democratic majority leader Lyndon Johnson, "straightjacket" the president and torpedo the Geneva summit. Despite Knowland's opposition, Democrats on the Senate Foreign Relations committee shrewdly forced McCarthy's resolution to the floor.

There, after McCarthy attacked the administration and fought with Knowland over his anticommunist credentials, the Senate finally voted to spike the McCarthy resolutions, 4 to 77. Democratic support for the president forced a high degree of GOP opposition to the McCarthy resolution, as only Republicans Jenner, Malone, and North Dakota maverick William Langer stood with McCarthy to the end.

By the close of the first session of the Eighty-fourth Congress, Right Wingers were in retreat and disarray. Ike himself now believed that on Capitol Hill there was "more cohesion on principle and greater dedication to our cause" than ever before.[36] In the Senate, where Right Wing Republicans had been so unruly, the GOP now became relatively peaceful. The Geneva question had shattered any possible entente between Knowland and McCarthy, and by midsummer, 1955, McCarthy was almost alone in rebellion against the administration. His crusade had become a caper. Knowland, for his part, remained the GOP Senate leader, but in name only. Despite his help on the Geneva matter, the administration generally sought the aid of other senators who had some connections with the Republican Right.

Ironically, the demise of Knowland and McCarthy—whose ties to the

Republican Right were actually new and tenuous—helped to undermine the Old Guard. Indeed, the power of the Republican Right had reached its lowest point since 1952.

When the lights went on in the guestroom of Mrs. John Doud in Denver in the early morning hours of September 24, 1955, the Republican party suddenly faced a political crisis. Mrs. Doud's visitor was her son-in-law, President Dwight D. Eisenhower, and he had just suffered a moderate coronary thrombosis. Thereafter, Ike would remain at Fitzsimmons Army Hospital near Denver until November 11, 1955, while an anxious nation awaited his return to Washington.

Political prospects immediately changed for Right Wing Republicans. L. Brent Bozell, columnist in the lively new conservative journal *National Review,* believed that Eisenhower's illness gave the Republican Right Wing a "new lease" after being finished as an important political factor just the preceding summer. Still, there was no quick grab for power, only a quiet stirring, causing Bozell to lament that the Right was experiencing "trepidation and misguided notions about good taste," instead of properly exploiting the situation.[37]

Eisenhower's heart attack was not, however, the first event to raise questions about a possible Republican presidential contender for 1956. In fact, only weeks earlier in the same city of Denver, Ike had reminded the RNC that "you never pin your flag so tightly on one mast that if a ship sinks you cannot rip it off and nail up another." Such talk had made even hard-boiled party professionals jumpy. Most Republican politicos—liberals, moderates, and conservatives alike—had already pinned their hopes for a 1956 GOP victory on Eisenhower in the belief that the Republican party was not strong enough to win without Ike. When asked about the possibility of an Eisenhower-less ticket in 1956, chairman Hall replied, "When I get to that bridge, I'll jump off."[38]

William F. Knowland was a notable exception to these gloomy Republicans. He rejected the "doctrine of the indispensable man" and did not believe that the party needed a reluctant candidate. Indeed, Capitol Hill colleagues and pundits had long regarded Knowland as the Republican Right's possible candidate for 1956, and conservative journals were touting him for the top spot. Political gossip therefore spread on November 1, 1955, when Knowland urged the president to announce his intentions concerning reelection by early winter at the latest.

Knowland's possible candidacy was really never a challenge to the convalescent president. It grew instead from widespread Old Guard fears of a possible "squeeze play." Allegedly, some Dewey-Eisenhower men wanted Eisenhower to delay any decision until perhaps mid-March so that they could round up an alternative "Dewey-Eisenhower wing" candidate in case Ike chose not to run for reelection. Some senators fretted as GOP presidential talk focused on the president's brother, Milton, the head of the Pennsylvania State University. There were also disconcerting sightings of Milton Eisenhower campaign buttons.

Against this background, Knowland confirmed in mid-January that he would run for the Republican nomination if the president did not announce his political plans by February 15. Later in January, the Californian indicated that he would not discourage a pro-Knowland slate of delegates from running in the New Hampshire primary. Eisenhower, for his part, remained silent about his intentions and ignored Knowland's deadline. Any Eisenhower decision, of course could come only after the doctor's go-ahead, which he got on February 15. But the medical report settled nothing. The president immediately flew to the Georgia plantation of Secretary of the Treasury George Humphrey for some dove hunting, golf, and political reflection.

So the wait continued. Knowland reportedly believed there was only a 50–50 chance that the president would run and was therefore gearing up his own campaign. Yet Knowland's mid-January announcement triggered no popular groundswell and no influx of campaign contributions. In fact, Right Wing circles remained cautious and tightlipped about the Knowland candidacy. Big Bill Knowland nevertheless was prepared to press on.

On February 29, Eisenhower ended all speculation by announcing for reelection. Instantly ending his unofficial campaign and predicting an Eisenhower reelection victory, Knowland publicly warned Ike how important it was "to consolidate" the Republican party. Many in the "Taft Wing," said Knowland, "feel they have not been made so much a part of the team as their long service in the party warrants." Knowland urged the RNC to use these Republicans more fully and even suggested that Ike name a Taft Republican as a vice-presidential runningmate instead of Nixon.[39]

Representation and voice—these were Knowland's goals from the beginning. Right Wing Republicans realized that there could be no fight with Ike in 1956. Yet take Eisenhower away—certainly a gloomy prospect for the party in 1956—and it was back to the trenches. Knowland's potential challenge was actually the first volley of the post-Eisenhower era of the Republican party. It demonstrated that the Right Wing was not dead, and that the GOP was far from Eisenhowerized.

The GOP political drama next centered on the vice-presidential nomination. Eisenhower's health naturally made the office the object of renewed attention and political yearnings. Knowland heightened the drama by suggesting the possibility of a Taftian stand-in for Nixon, but Eisenhower himself sparked political speculation by maintaining that he could not properly endorse any runningmate until after his own nomination was secured. "Dump Nixon" talk began almost immediately. A week later, Eisenhower told reporters that he had directed Nixon to "chart his own course"—Nixon could remain as vice-president or take some cabinet post in order to gain more experience and exposure.

Nixon and Eisenhower had indeed discussed this possibility before, and the vice-president told RNC chairman Leonard Hall he believed that this was Ike's way of dumping him. True enough for any seasoned politico, said Hall, but Ike was hardly that. Perhaps Hall really wanted Nixon to remain on the ticket. Or perhaps Hall lacked the political sophistication to ease Nixon off the ticket. Earlier, Eisenhower and Hall had discussed the possibility of a major realignment of American political parties—a "turning point in history," Hall had called it. The plan was to name a conservative Democrat for the GOP second spot, and Ike and Hall considered a number of possibilities. But the question remained: What about Nixon? Hall said it would be best to get Nixon off the ticket "willingly," making him a "hero" in the process. Eisenhower agreed. "Talk to him, but be very gentle," Ike told Hall.[40] Was Ike really serious in this discussion with Hall? Eisenhower's well-known directions to Nixon and his silence in naming a runningmate made such an apparent "dump Nixon" desire highly plausible. If Eisenhower was truly serious, at the critical moment, Hall was either too gentle with the vice-president or acted as a political double agent.

One contemporary observer judged that Eisenhower was only keeping the vice-presidential nomination open until Nixon's standing in the party could be tested. Nixon's exact place in the GOP had puzzled observers for some time and would continue to do so. One thing was certain by early 1956—he was hardly "the darling of the Old Guard" that some writers claimed. In fact, his embrace of the Eisenhower program, which made for the first "New Nixon," rattled Right Wing Republicans and undercut his conservative support. When Eisenhower's own candidacy was in doubt, an ensuing Nixon "boom" began not among Old Guard Republicans, but Dewey forces. Indeed, Nixon-watch journalists—conservative and otherwise—had come to appreciate Nixon's pragmatic approach to GOP politics.

Given Hall's failure or disinclination to ease Nixon off the ticket, the mid-March New Hampshire primary, where the vice-president amassed a surprising 22,000 write-in votes, provided ample evidence of Nixon's standing with the party electorate. Eisenhower now modified his earlier strictures regarding any early endorsement, saying that he would be happy to run with Nixon. When, on April 26, Nixon announced that he would accept the vice-presidential nomination, Eisenhower said he was "delighted."

Everyone assumed the vice-presidential problem was settled—until a month before the GOP convention. Then, on July 22, administration disarmament advisor Harold Stassen suddenly launched his own "dump Nixon" movement. He favored Massachusetts governor Christian Herter as Ike's next vice-president. Not only did the allies have more confidence in Herter, but, said Stassen, independent voters did, too. He brought forward a poll showing that an Eisenhower-Herter ticket was about six percentage points stronger than the present GOP combination—an important difference for GOP House and Senate candidates. Although Stassen stated that he was not speaking for the president, he did indicate that he had talked to Eisenhower, who said he would be glad to run with Herter.

There was no doubt about the Republican Right's position on this second "dump Nixon" move. Conservative support for the vice-president was solid. "Republicans will resent the unwarranted arrogance of Harold Stassen's attempting to suggest a Vice Presidential candidate," said Senator William Jenner. Further, Styles Bridges countered with his own poll showing Nixon's strength. Nixon had certainly done no political somersaults since the earlier period of Right Wing coolness. But now he had the right enemies. Stassen was an Old Guard adversary, and his anti-Nixon announcement was seen as another GOP liberal gambit to revamp the party.

Yet Stassen's campaign was in trouble from the beginning. A day after the Stassen declaration, Christian Herter himself stated that he would not campaign against Nixon but would in fact nominate him at the GOP convention. This latter arrangement was the master stroke of chairman Hall. Then, when Stassen got lost on the way to the opening session of the GOP convention in San Francisco and had to be escorted to the Cow Palace by a taxicab full of reporters, it only dramatized how comic his "dump Nixon" bid had finally become. After finally arriving, he was confronted by Nixon's solid delegate count and Dewey's firm support for Nixon—reportedly part of a deal that required the vice-president to tone down his speeches in the fall. Stassen got nowhere, and after three convention days he surrendered. His seconding speech for Nixon—a price Stassen paid for a meeting with Ike—was a tribute to the Eisenhower-Nixon party balance and the disarmament advisor's folly in trying to wreck it. Eisenhower remained above the GOP factional battle, while Nixon was caught in the middle. The Republican Right Wing, riled by the pretensions of Stassen and his liberal cohorts, had aligned itself firmly with the vice-president.

In his welcoming address to the Republican National Convention, California's GOP governor Goodwin Knight declared that the Republicans would leave San Franciso "marching arm in arm." They would indeed. Stassen's activities served only to unite the GOP. The Eisenhower grin by now seemed to have infected the entire party. "Not since the Democratic convention of 1936," wrote James Reston, "has a President dominated a political rally the way the President is dominating this one."[41] Senator Knowland praised the president's "constructive record of accomplishment" and called upon "the spirit of Bob Taft" to guide all Republicans in the campaign ahead. Unlike the 1952 slugfest in Chicago, the Republican gathering in San Francisco turned out to be a political lovefeast, with Taft's ghost being used as a unifying element in the "long tribute" to Ike.

Although the San Francisco convention witnessed the formal unveiling of the "New Republican Party," observers were noting well before the gathering that GOP state chairmen in forty-one states had been replaced with Ike men, and two-thirds of the RNC was new since 1952. Taft wing warhorses such as C. Budington Kelland, Werner W. Schroeder, Harrison Spangler, and Guy Gabrielson had faded from the GOP organizational scene. After four years, Ike's magic was even working on Capitol Hill, where, according to one Eisenhower braintruster, "conservative" congressional leaders like Knowland and Martin were at last "coming around." Those failing to do so, the *National Review* remarked, were being "consigned to outer darkness." "With such skill have [Ike] and his associates conducted the movement," the *National Review* continued, "that it has become quite clear what the Republican Party is not: it is not the Party of Senator Taft."[42]

A change in national party leadership, however, was only one component of the new Eisenhower GOP. By the time of the San Francisco convention, a new party credo was ready, too. The basics of this philosophy were set forth in Arthur Larson's *A Republican Looks at His Party,* published in July, 1956. Former dean of the University of Pittsburgh Law School and now an assistant secretary of labor, Larson had taken it upon himself to delineate the ideas animating the Eisenhower administration. His book quickly gained Ike's approval.

Although *A Republican Looks at his Party* had the whiff of campaign propaganda, it represented a serious attempt to define the Eisenhower program. The "New Republicanism," according to Larson, represented the "Authentic American Center" in politics. Under the New Republicanism, the central government would undertake those tasks that the states or citizens could not do for themselves—a paraphrase of a Lincoln quotation that Eisenhower often repeated. Arrayed against the New Republicanism were the opposition forces of 1896 and 1936. The opposition of 1896, with its stress on states' rights and laissez faire economics, represented "bad conservatism." Unlike the good conservatism of the Eisenhower administration, it worshipped only the "shell of the past."[43]

Larson's New Republicanism, however, was extremely general and inclusive. It lacked real meaning. Stewart Alsop pointed out that Franklin Roosevelt had often quoted the same Lincoln words favored by Ike. Conservative comment further attested to the looseness of Larson's thesis. In the *National Review,* Willmoor Kendall noted that no conservative could object to New Republican principles.[44]

Eisenhower's San Francisco acceptance speech was pure New Republican language. In tackling the problems of today, declared Ike, Republicans still believed in long-range principle over political expediency, and though their concern for the citizen was warm, it was not paternalistic. Eisenhower's San Francisco address and Larson's book accomplished the same result by separating Ike from the Republican party. One reviewer of *A Republican Looks at His Party* suggested that a more accurate title might be "A Republican Looks at His President," and Eisenhower's San Francisco performance elicited similar comments.[45]

Still, there was hardly a mumble at San Francisco. Instead of a floor fight over the New Republicanism, the Republicans honeyed over their differences. Believing "old scars healed" and past issues obsolete, *Life* hailed "The New Republican Harmony."[46] Actually, there was no New Republican party. Such talk was little more than campaign oratory that some Republicans came to believe. In San Francisco, the GOP appeared too peaceful, too united, and too quiet for a party undergoing such transformation. Where was the old Right Wing fire?

At the time, of course, any Right Wing attack on Eisenhower would have been pointless, unless Republicans desired political suicide. Ike was the *one* Republican hope in November, and political wisdom demanded a united front. Besides, Larson's and Eisenhower's words meant nothing as far as Right Wing Republicans were concerned. It was true that Eisenhower had temporarily recast the GOP's public image and had broken the power of the Taft wing nationally. But Eisenhower had hardly routed the Republican Right within the party. Even if the Old Guard was not in command, it was still secure on Capitol Hill. Far more important, Right Wing Republicans still held power in numerous state GOP organizations across the country and represented a sizable minority in others. Indeed, in some state contests during 1956, Right Wing factions had clobbered Ike supporters who were hurt by the president's unwillingness to meddle in these contests.

Clearly, the Right's hopes for the Republican future—a future of "unhyphenated" Republicanism—had not waned. As one convention-watcher wrote, "The stillness at San Francisco was less that of an enemy vanquished or even cowed than of one patiently biding its time."[47]

It was a chilly fall for the Republican Right. In the public mind, the GOP was Eisenhower's. The *National Review* had written shortly after Eisenhower's reelection announcement, "The decisions that must be made before November are dreadful ones." Perhaps this was so for conservative intellectuals, who debated through the autumn whether to support Eisenhower, but the decision for most GOP politicians was not so agonizing. They would, as the new Republican slogan went, "Stick with Ike," as they quickly boarded the "Coattail Express."

One conservative rider was Senator George Bender, who was up for reelection in Ohio. This old Taft bugle-blower rapidly converted to Eisenhower Republicanism, a philosophy he now claimed to have espoused "before I knew there was such an individual."[48] Another "Coattail" passenger was Everett Dirksen of Illinois, who again proved a good gauge of GOP political trends. Dirksen, of course, had been the major pro-Taft firebrand at the 1952 Chicago convention. Subsequently, the Eisenhower administration, noting Dirksen's basically friendly attitude in contrast to Knowland's, had worked hard to make Dirksen a Taft stand-in among GOP senators. By the summer of 1956, the Illinois senator was spearheading the administration's Senate forces on the issue of aid to Yugoslavia. With a reelection campaign coming up in 1956, Dirksen's shift was politically smart and in keeping with the actions of many other GOP conservatives who decided to stick with the Republican party, where a "healthy tendency" toward conservatism still existed.

Such knuckling under to Ike by GOP candidates irked the *National Review,* which had begun to worry about the tendency to "Caesarize" Ike, characterizing Republicans who subordinated themselves to Eisenhower as "self-immolators." The *National Review* remarked, "We hope that enough of the self-immolators will be defeated to remind the balance of the basic character of our political system."[49]

Despite the "stick with Ike" sentiment, all was not harmony for the Republican party during the 1956 campaign. When Leonard Hall announced the new RNC executive committee appointments in the fall of 1956, for example, Old Guard anger erupted. Excluded from this new group, former national chairman B. Carroll Reece sent a bitter letter to Hall, as did Ohio national committeewoman Katharine Kennedy Brown, an old Taft ally. Brown noted the injustices being visited upon the friends of Taft and told Hall, "You thus make yourself a spokesman for the cult who seek to purge all conservatives who carried the torch for the Republican Party during the lean years."[50] Her letter eventually appeared in Drew Pearson's newspaper column.

At another point during the campaign, the Old Guard became enraged over what the president's friend and political advisor Paul Hoffman wrote in October's *Collier's* magazine. In "How Eisenhower Saved the Republican Party," Hoffman stated that Ike had succeeded in transforming the GOP in spite of a number of Republican troublemakers, whom Hoffman divided into two groups—the "Faint Hopes" and the "Unappeasables." Hoffman quoted Ike as saying, "There are some people you cannot afford to have as friends," and he even revealed that Ike had sometimes considered breaking away from the GOP and running as an independent.[51]

The controversy aroused by the Hoffman article naturally raised concern in an election year. Knowland and Bricker both lamented the potential political damage that it offered. "Faint Hope" Barry Goldwater demanded a fast explanation from the administration.[52] The "Unappeasables," mean-while, reacted typically to what Welker, who had a tough battle for reelection in Idaho, called Hoffman's "hatchet job." Malone immediately branded Hoffman "an international socialist." McCarthy began a probe of a former Hoffman aide and eventually had Hoffman appear before his committee "so that the American people could better understand your hatred for those you feel in your arrogance you can read out of the Republican Party."[53]

Eisenhower, when asked about Hoffman's *Collier's* article at his next news conference, finessed that American political parties were state organizations. They, and not the president, decided who is or is not a Republican. But Ike hinted that Hoffman was not far off the mark by conceding that there were certain party members he had learned not to depend on. Later, discussing the matter with Senator Malone, the president upheld Hoffman's right to express his own opinion, adding that he (Ike) had not even read the article. This was a smart political parry, but hardly true. Hoffman had asked Ike to read his piece and make suggestions and comments. The president had done so, pointing out only a few minor factual errors, since he had no desire to gag Hoffman in any way.[54] Never at issue, however, was Hoffman's right of political expression. Ike had not been reluctant in the past to tell Hoffman to tone down his divisive political pronouncements, and Ike would never have allowed such an article to threaten the Republican campaign effort in 1952.

That Hoffman's article gained White House clearance in 1956 illustrates the change in Eisenhower's relationship to the GOP after four years. The 1956 Eisenhower canvass *was* different than the one four years before. Ironically, the intervening years had widened, and not narrowed, the gap between the president and his party. Eisenhower's campaign managers made their pitch for Eisenhower, not Eisenhower *and* the Republican party. There was, for example, only one reference to the GOP in the final election eve campaign appeal—and Nixon made that. This caused Richard Rovere to observe that in a sense Eisenhower's handlers were "reading him out" of the Republican party.[55]

Still, Eisenhower did not attempt to eliminate Old Guardsmen from the Republican party, as a strong party leader might have been tempted to do. Even the most obstreperous Right Wing Republican could obtain Eisenhower campaign support. Welker discovered this when he asked Ike for help in countering the effects of Hoffman's article.

Thus, GOP conservatives backed the president in 1956 and banked on his great popularity. Eisenhower still carried the Republican label, and next to the horrors of the Democratic program, the Eisenhower "middle way" looked safe. Further, Democratic candidate Adlai Stevenson made Eisenhower appear and sound conservative by comparison. Finally, it was not that difficult or dangerous to tack and trim with Eisenhower in the White House. "Much that sails under the banner of Republicanism today is certainly not Republicanism as we know it in Ohio," John Bricker had written earlier. "However, if we keep our places in the crew, we can probably have some influence in determining the final post reached by our good Ship of State."[56]

On election day 1956, Eisenhower won big, amassing 35.5 million popular votes to Stevenson's 26 million. The president won forty-one states for 457 electoral tallies, while Stevenson carried seven states for 73 electoral votes. The win was nationwide, as Eisenhower extended his 1952 inroads into Dixie. Still, Eisenhower could not haul the Republican party along with him. The Democrats held on to a 49-to-47 edge in the Senate and beefed up their House majority by thirty-three seats to make it 232 to 199. Eisenhower told election night GOP revelers, "Modern Republicanism has now proved itself. And America has approved Modern Republicanism."[57]

"Modern Republicanism"—the phrase caught on quickly. The electoral returns, however, belied Ike's claims, and even he later admitted that voters were still uncertain that Modern Republicanism was the new beacon of the entire GOP. Although George Aiken in Vermont and John Sherman Cooper in Kentucky were victorious, other Ike-minded Republicans lost. An original Eisenhower booster, Pennsylvania senator James Duff, failed in his reelection bid, as did the most notable convert to Eisenhower Republicanism, Ohio senator George Bender. Douglas McKay in Oregon, Dan Thornton in Colorado, and Arthur Langlie in Washington were all Modern Republicans whom Eisenhower had encouraged to run for the Senate, and they all lost.

Right Wing Republicans could hardly send up cheers either. Political flexibility clearly paid off for conservative incumbents like Dirksen, Capehart, Butler, and Francis Case. But Colorado voters replaced retiring GOP conservative senator Eugene Millikin with John Carroll, a Fair Deal Democrat. In Idaho, Democrat Frank Church knocked off GOP diehard Herman Welker. Welker blamed the New York "kingmakers" for his defeat, claiming, "The boys from New York put me out of politics and work."[58] Conservative Utah governor J. Bracken Lee, one of Eisenhower's harshest critics, also failed to win reelection. Commented William S. White after the election, the Taft wing "lies in ruins."[59]

The nation still liked Ike, but the entire Republican party, including the Republican Right, was in bad shape.

8

Go Down Grinning
with Ike

"I won't give a damn about Ike the day after the election," an old Taft partisan said earlier in the summer of 1956. "He's our meal ticket now. Once we're in, the hell with him."[1]

Such sentiment led many GOP watchers to expect trouble on the right for the Eisenhower administration during the second term. Not only have presidents had more success in passing their programs during their first terms, but Eisenhower was the first president to be affected by the Twenty-second Amendment, which prohibited a president from serving more than two terms. This was expected to weaken his power. Moreover, Eisenhower's failure to carry along the Republican party in the 1956 elections wounded him as a party leader. As for Ike's prospects for further reforming the GOP, one observer concluded, "Fat Chance."[2]

Eisenhower's 1957 State of the Union message presaged trouble. Gone were the conservative clichés of Ike's first State of the Union message. Now, Eisenhower's new requests for public health and welfare programs, as well as increased school construction, seemed to reaffirm Modern Republicanism. Days later, in presenting the administration's budget, Eisenhower called for a new budget that was $2 billion higher than the previous one, bringing the total request to $71.8 billion—a record for peacetime. These figures raised concern even within the administration. Treasury secretary George Humphrey warned publicly that future budgets of this magnitude could bring "a depression that will curl your hair."

The Eisenhower budget instantly became a political "battle flag" for GOP conservatives. Ranking Republicans in budget-related committees on Capitol Hill all promised some pruning, and minority leader Knowland publicly tossed around billion-dollar figures that might be cut from the proposed budget. GOP rebel Joe McCarthy said that the administration's budget "far out does" former President Truman in "his wildest spending spree."[3] The conservative outcry was even louder beyond Capitol Hill. William Loeb's Manchester *Union Leader* initiated a vicious personal attack on President Eisenhower, calling him a "stinking hypocrite." Major business organizations such as the National Association of Manufacturers and the Chamber of Commerce joined with the *Wall Street Journal* in protest.[4]

Conservative House Republicans, however, led the charge, which rapidly expanded to include an assault on Modern Republicanism in general. In mid-January, 1957, Richard Simpson, chairman of the Republican Congressional Campaign Committee, said that the GOP itself was wasting away under the "warm glow" and "great name" of Eisenhower. His House colleague, Clare Hoffman of Michigan, stated that Republicans had gone "dizzy" under Ike and warned that the president's "left-wing, free-spending, international one world advisors proposed to disinfect, fumigate, purify, renovate, unify and remake the Republican Party."[5]

This conservative House revolt was only beginning when the RNC met in January, 1957, to select a successor to the retiring Leonard Hall, chief GOP face-lifter under Ike. Administration forces were able to torpedo Old Guard hopes of electing an old-line chairman and to get unanimous RNC agreement on H. Meade Alcorn, Connecticut national committeeman, who was the president's choice and an enthusiastic Modern Republican. Nevertheless, this RNC meeting, which took place on the day of Ike's second inauguration, had its share of Right Wing bellyaching. For example, after Maryland governor Theodore H. McKeldrin exhorted Republicans to follow the Eisenhower path, Oregon committeeman Robert Mautz was instantly on his feet. He ticked off a series of 1956 Eisenhower Republican losers and said that unless the party got some "old-fashioned Republicanism," it would find itself "dead as a dodobird." "He's talking Ohio's language," old Taftite Clarence Brown said of Mautz. Such fierce expressions obviously indicated that times had changed since the campaign, and when the newly elected chairman Meade Alcorn pledged to fight for Modern Republicanism, GOP observers forecast an inevitable clash between him and the Old Guard.[6]

Indeed, the issue of "Real Republicanism versus Modern Republicanism" preoccupied the whole GOP throughout much of 1957. The Republican Right dominated the debate on "Just What is a Modern Republican?" Its definitions were not intended to please the Eisenhower administration. If Modern Republicanism were not a "form of bribery," it was simply a mere campaign "catch phrase" that had served its purpose. Even liberal Republican George Aiken of Vermont urged the party to drop the term, because it was "misleading, badly misused and subject to misinterpretation."[7]

In the midst of this development, a strong new voice of antiadministration sentiment came forward in early April, 1957. In the past, Arizona senator Barry Goldwater had only quietly differed with the Eisenhower administration, and in 1956 he had even urged the president to run for a second term. Goldwater was certainly not a member of what Richard Rovere termed the GOP's "zany faction" that included Jenner and Welker. This gave Goldwater's April 8 pronouncement added weight. On that day, he stood in the near-empty Senate chamber and publicly broke with the Eisenhower administration. It was, Goldwater later recalled, "the hardest thing I ever did."[8]

Goldwater began his Senate speech by applauding the administration's first term. Then he came to the point. Goldwater charged that the Eisenhower White House was suddenly lured by "the siren of socialism." "Foreign giveaways" and "slavish economic indigence" at home were part of the new order as the administration "aped New Deal antics." The Arizona senator rebuked Eisenhower for failing to keep his 1952 pledges and for the 1956 budget—a budget that "subverts the American economy." Goldwater then added, "The citizens of this country are tired of the New Deal now more than in 1952, when they made the first attempt to throw it over."[9] Goldwater grabbed headlines. *Time* immediately called him conservatism's "most articulate spokesman" and added that "the Republican Old Guard is back on its feet."[10]

The Republican Right at this moment actually had more active vocal chords than political muscle, and even the *National Review*'s Bozell concluded in late May that talk of a right-wing revival was just "nonsense."[11] Still, the Republican party remained clearly split. One indication of this was the party's suffering coffers. From the League of Republican Women came reports that Old Guard and Modern factions were "close to hairpulling." Further, Young Republicans were adopting some antiadministration resolutions. When addressing GOP leaders in June, 1957, Ike learned about the GOP divisions firsthand. These Republicans still liked Ike, but only when he talked generally or lambasted Democrats. His bid to drum up support for specific legislative proposals prompted few cheers.

The United States Information Agency (USIA) thus became a natural target for antispending GOP conservatives. Eisenhower had rewarded Arthur Larson for his 1956 political labors on the administration's behalf by making him director of the USIA. Not only did Larson's ties to Modern Republicanism make USIA funding an obvious Old Guard target on Capitol Hill, but some extremely partisan Larson remarks had also angered Democrats, especially majority leader Lyndon Johnson. Despite these obstacles, administration supporter Jacob Javits planned to force a roll-call vote on the USIA appropriations request. But Bridges persuaded Javits that he did not have the votes, and the New Yorker dropped his plan. Hearing of these GOP maneuvers and wanting to embarrass the Republicans, Johnson himself brought the USIA funding question to the Senate floor. There, the Senate voted, 61 to 15, to cut USIA funding from $144 million to $90.2 million. In the end, only fourteen Republicans stuck by the president.

The USIA cuts became, however, the "highwater marks" of congressional independence in the budget-making process in 1957. The president's position generally triumphed on Capitol Hill. The big issue proved to be foreign aid, with Right Wing Republicans continuing to rail against what they saw as the futile attempt to buy global friendship. But even the more independent Senate, after a thirteen-hour session, defeated all bids to alter or slash foreign aid funds and gave the president his full request of $3.6 billion. The vote was 57 to 25 in favor, with thirty-one Republicans backing Eisenhower. The eight Republican foes included Bricker, Jenner, and Dworshak. Writing at the close of the "Battle of the Budget," the *National Review* concluded that conservative budget-slashers lacked "relevant leadership."[12]

The Old Guard could lose the "Battle of the Budget" without surrendering in the "Battle of the GOP." For the Old Guard, the "Battle of the Budget" was just a battle, while the struggle for the GOP was the war. The Republican Right had used the Eisenhower budget to sound off against Eisenhower's Modern Republicanism; actual budget cuts seemed only secondary. This was basically a political battle, with the structure and control of the post-Eisenhower GOP being the primary issues.

Whether the Republican Right's new crusade would be acceptable to the voters remained to be seen, and political pundits and Right Wing Republicans looked to developments in Wisconsin in 1957 to offer an electoral clue. In a special August election to fill the Senate seat of Joseph McCarthy, who had died in early May, Democrat William Proxmire trounced Republican governor Walter Kohler by 122,000 votes, taking 56.7 percent of the vote. The upset left Democrats with a 50-to-46 Senate margin and dealt a much-publicized blow to Modern Republicanism. The Wisconsin governor had advertised himself as an Eisenhower Republican, and the president dispatched Interior secretary Fred Seaton to Wisconsin to stump for Kohler. Kohler's unpopularity with the Wisconsin Old Guard became obvious as soon as the returns were in. An estimated two-thirds of the Republicans who had voted in 1956 stayed home in this 1957 election.

Eisenhower deemed the Kohler result "a bad licking" and explained that Wisconsin voters had "allowed themselves to be misled by a lot of slogans and catch words that really have no validity in our politics." In private, Eisenhower faulted Old Guard Republicans who indulged "their personal animosities" against Kohler. Right Wing Republicans, in turn, blamed Modern Republicanism for Kohler's loss. Former president Hoover wrote that party conservatives were "putting on sitdown strikes" against this newfangled Republicanism, and Barry Goldwater proclaimed that Proxmire's victory threw "the last clod of dirt on the coffin of Modern Republicanism."[13]

Proxmire's upset of Modern Republican Kohler symbolized Right Wing resurgence in 1957. The Wisconsin loss and Eisenhower's Capitol Hill difficulties prompted *Business Week* to conclude: "New Republicanism at New Low." Even the *National Review*'s usually cautious L. Brent Bozell wrote in November, 1957, "The prospects of conservatives capturing power are brighter today than at any time since 1952."[14]

During this Old Guard renaissance, the Republican Right was again beginning to nurse some presidential hopes. Senator William Knowland of California was the chief prospect. In early 1957 he had announced that he would not seek reelection to the Senate at the close of his term in 1958. Despite the senator's claims that personal reasons lay behind his decision, "political cynics" expected Knowland to run for governor of California in 1958 and use that post as a springboard to the 1960 GOP presidential nomination. "Knowland, Nixon: Race for Ike's Job is On," ran the *US News and World Report* of January, 1957. In fact, by August, Knowland was telling Capitol Hill colleagues from California that he intended to run for governor. According to John Bricker, Knowland's move away from the Senate upset some conservative senators, who believed the minority leader was "making a good record" right there.[15] Knowland, however, remained typically tight-lipped about his long-range political moves.

Knowland needed some kind of quick boost to realize his ambitions. Eisenhower preferred Nixon to Knowland as the future GOP standard-bearer—and Knowland knew this. The president, according to administration insider Emmett Hughes, promised to support Knowland for governor, "but not a damn thing higher than that."[16] Further, Nixon showed higher support and recognition than Knowland in public opinion polls. A successful governor's race might help Knowland remedy this problem and also give him considerable influence as head of the California delegation at the 1960 GOP convention.

As Senate leader, Knowland had also recently worked to win new friends and improve relations with the Eisenhower administration. Much to the *National Review*'s dismay, Knowland had remained relatively quiet during the "Battle of the Budget," and he even opposed anti-Eisenhower foreign aid foes in one Senate shoot-out. Moreover, his rabid foreign policy pronouncements tapered off. Knowland also inched away from a traditional conservative position in another area when shepherding the 1957 Civil Rights Act through the Senate—some said because California had a considerable black population. Knowland, whom the *National Review* called "the nation's ranking political conservative," was definitely displaying considerable flexibility as 1957 closed.[17]

But winning popular support posed real problems for Big Bill. Hard-driving and meticulous in his Senate leadership, Knowland lacked political spark. Only lately had Knowland tried to cultivate his California constituency, and when Big Bill appeared at a picnic in an unbuttoned sport shirt, some party-goers were surprised and shocked. The *National Review* held that a California gubernatorial win in 1958 would put Knowland in the 1960 GOP presidential race right to the finish. Still, doubts remained about any ultimate Knowland presidential triumph.

Knowland had some immediate problems in the California GOP, which was beset by deep ideological differences and powerful personal allegiances. Knowland and Nixon were familiar enough California figures, with the senator generally seen as being to the right of the vice-president. But there was also the current Republican governor of California, Goodwin J. Knight, a liberal. As Knowland began laying his plans for the California gubernatorial race, "Goodie" Knight was promising to "fight to the finish." Meanwhile, the state's Democratic party had done some rebuilding and had a popular candidate in attorney General Pat Brown. As a result, political soothsayers did not think much of Knight's gubernatorial reelection prospects.

In November, 1957, Governor Knight traveled to Washington to arrange a "political truce." After a White House meeting, the California governor announced that "for the good of the Republican Party," he would run for the U.S. Senate. Although this obviously left the GOP gubernatorial spot open for Knowland, Knowland insisted that Knight's withdrawal completely surprised him. In fact, Knowland and most other observers believed that Nixon and *Los Angeles Times* publisher Norman Chandler had pressured Knight to bow out. The *National Review*'s Bozell maintained that Nixon did so in order to "whittle down" the impact of a future Knowland victory.[18] Ironically, Knight's withdrawal hurt Knowland rather than helped him. Had Knowland won after a lively contest for the GOP governor's nomination, he would have gained considerable stature with the California electorate. Moreover, Knight's "retirement" announcement was not enough to end the GOP feuding, and there were reports that both the Knowland and Knight camps were drumming up votes for the other's Democratic rival.

The biggest source of California GOP wrangling involved the right-to-work issue. Under the Taft-Hartley Act of 1947, states could determine for themselves whether to allow the so-called union shop or outlaw it. California voters had defeated an antiunion right-to-work proposition in 1944, but conservative business groups were ready to try again in 1958. Knowland backed such legislation in his 1958 campaign, and his position terrified less extreme Republicans. Knight claimed that Knowland's endorsement of this "non-Republican" issue freed him from supporting Knowland. The California governor even hinted that many Republicans might want to consider voting Democratic. Some obviously did in the spring GOP California primary, since both Knight and Knowland ran far behind their Democratic counterparts in the open primary. Brown, for example, amassed 662,000 votes more than Knowland.

Nonetheless, Knowland identified himself even more strongly with the issue after the spring primary by getting California Republicans to scrap their earlier anti–right-to-work plank of 1956. Right-to-work was, of course, a traditional right-wing issue, and Knowland's steadfastness thrilled conservatives. In *Newsweek,* for example, Ray Moley lauded Big Bill for "speaking to the minds and not the prejudices and emotions of the voters." [19] For pundits and old-line politicos alike, Knowland's crusade recalled Taft's 1950 reelection campaign in Ohio. Conservative GOP congressman B. Carroll Reece looked to that earlier race as a guide for both the California and conservative future. Voters still wanted a real choice, explained Reece, and in Knowland's position they could find it. [20]

As the 1958 elections approached, the Republican party as a whole was in trouble over right-to-work and other issues. California was not unique. Ohio was another state where right-to-work movements complicated the GOP outlook. There, John Bricker, who faced reelection, and Ray Bliss, the state GOP boss, at first pleaded with right-to-work forces—normally conservative business allies—not to press the issue. That failing, Bricker then tried to minimize the issue's potential damage to his campaign by refusing to appear with the Republican gubernatorial candidate, William O'Neil, a champion of right-to-work legislation.

Bricker and O'Neil's problems in Ohio were mild by comparison with other GOP factional battles between the Old Guard and Modern Republicans throughout the nation. In Utah, personal and political differences led former Governor H. Bracken Lee to mount a third-party challenge to incumbent conservative Republican A.V. Watkins. Out of New Jersey came reports that disgruntled party hard-liners were withholding contributions from the Republican candidate and sending them instead to Knowland in California. Back in Washington, Republican Capitol Hill campaign committee bosses were publicly advising GOP congressional hopefuls that running on the Eisenhower record was not necessarily politically wise. Many Republicans not only doubted Eisenhower's political coattails in 1958, but offered serious complaints about Ike as a party leader. "I guess we'll go down grinning with Ike," lamented Congressman Richard Simpson. [21]

In the summer of 1958 the inner agonies of the GOP came to focus on one man—Sherman Adams. Adams was Ike's White House chief of staff and his most trusted aide. He had an abrupt, if not arrogant, manner, and Right Wing Republicans had long grumbled about the "palace guard" and what they saw as Adams's favoritism in wielding patronage to advance the cause of Modern Republicanism. In any case, a House investigative committee learned in June, 1958, that Adams had interceded with a federal regulatory committee for Bernard Goldfine, a New England textile manufacturer. Goldfine, in turn, had given Adams certain gifts, including oriental rugs and a vicuña coat.

Ike's own continuing popularity kept hostile Republicans from directly attacking him, but the Goldfine revelations quickly made Adams a convenient target for conservative Republicans who had chafed under six years of his Modern Republicanism. "L'Affaire Adams," B. Carroll Reece wrote in late June, resulted from the chief of staff's being "the symbol of piety" in the administration.[22] Chicago Republican Robert E. Wood demanded Adams's ouster. National Committee members overwhelmingly wanted him out. With Knowland and Goldwater publicly urging Adams to resign, the outcry for Adams's resignation mounted.

The president soon decided that Adams had to go, and on September 22 he sadly accepted his chief of staff's resignation. The Republican Old Guard immediately took credit for the sack of Sherman Adams. Within the administration, there was considerable bitterness toward "the vultures of the Grand Old Party"—the Republican Right Wing. At this particular moment, the "vulture" symbol was apt, for pundits and party workers were beginning to leave the Republican party for dead. Another metaphor was equally applicable after "L'Affaire Adams." "It's a little bit late to make all Republicans love one another or even appear to do so the way the Democrats do," the *Saturday Evening Post* admonished. "But the party leadership ought to try because people don't take passage on a ship when the officers can be seen clobbering one another up on the bridge."[23]

Republican losses in the elections of 1958 were massive. Democrats racked up their biggest gains in congressional elections since the Roosevelt landslide of 1936. The Democratic majorities were 64 to 34 in the Senate and 282 to 154 in the House. There was no break for Republicans in gubernatorial contests, as the Democrats won twenty-six such races; only fourteen GOP governors remained in office after election day.

The Republican Right suffered along with the entire party. Barry Goldwater, however, won big in Arizona, the result being largely attributed to Goldwater's attractive personality rather than his right-wing ideology. In any case, Goldwater now became the acknowledged leader of conservative Republicans, for Pat Brown badly whipped Knowland—the Republican Right's long-shot presidential hope for 1960—in the California governor's race. Running for the Senate in that state, Republican Goodwin Knight also lost to Democrat Clare Engle.

Republican losses in the Midwest underscored the party's difficulties. In this former GOP heartland, Republicans gave up eight seats in the House, two in the Senate, and also relinquished two state houses. In Indiana, high taxes, high unemployment, and his own endorsement of right-to-work legislation hurt Governor Harold Handley in his unsuccessful attempt to fill Jenner's Senate seat. Democrat R. Vance Hartke, the mayor of Evansville, was the easy winner. Next door in Ohio, Senate right-wing powerhouse John Bricker lost his reelection bid along with the Buckeye GOP candidate for governor, William O'Neil. Elsewhere, the story for the Old Guard was the same. In Nevada, Democrat Howard J. Cannon won a stunning upset over Right Wing Republican Senator George "Molly" Malone. Senate GOP die-hard Chapman Revercomb of West Virginia lost his Senate seat to Robert Byrd, a conservative Democrat whose "country corn" and fiddle playing provided the campaign difference. Utah witnessed a blood feud that left Republican conservatism the loser as H. Bracken Lee's third-party assault undid A.V. Watkins in his contest against Democratic winner Frank Moss.

Conservative Republican candidates were not the only GOP losers. Nevertheless, those few Republicans who did win had mainly a liberal tilt—new senators like J. Glenn Beall of Maryland and Kenneth Keating of New York. In Pennsylvania, the pro-Ike Hugh Scott won the Senate seat vacated by Edward Martin, a GOP hard-liner. Finally, the GOP bright spot of 1958 was liberal Republican Nelson Rockefeller, who won a 557,000-vote majority victory over incumbent New York Governor Averell Harriman, although Rocky's victory, like Goldwater's in Arizona, turned more on personality than ideology.

Economic slump across the nation, the unpopularity of Secretary of Agriculture Benson in the farm states, and "L'Affaire Adams" were frequently mentioned by political pundits as probable causes for the Republican political bust. But most observers agreed on two main factors—the GOP identification with the right-to-work movement and Eisenhower's pitiful party leadership. In Ohio, John Bricker believed that right-to-work legislation had goaded labor unions "to get out one who had never knuckled down to their demands."[24] He and Ohio state GOP chairman Ray Bliss estimated that the issue brought out a half-million new voters to the polls. Indeed, later analysis revealed that in six states with right-to-work issues on the ballot, a million and a half more Democratic voters came to the polls than in the 1954 congressional elections. Thereafter, GOP sentiment favored a move away from this political loser, as only Kansas passed a right-to-work referendum.[25]

Eisenhower, meanwhile, blamed the Republican party's electoral washout on the American people, who failed to understand the "great danger of reckless federal spending." Political observers, in turn, held Eisenhower largely responsible for the Republican defeat. Even party liberals grumbled about Eisenhower's lack of political leadership.

In the aftermath of defeat the grumbling and name-calling continued, as conservative Republicans lamented the current political situation. Congressman Clarence Brown of Ohio maintained that the voters actually favored Republicans who stood for economy and efficiency in government, and he went on to advise that conservative Republicans be given "a voice and a place in our national affairs." Brown and other Right Wing Republicans believed that the "stay-at-home" voter wanted to see a real difference between Democrats and Republicans, a difference that Modern Republicanism just did not provide. The *Wall Street Journal* indicted Modern Republicanism's "fuzzy imitation of the New Deal image" for failing to give independent voters a reason to switch from voting Democratic.[26] The *Chicago Tribune* summed it up best: "Having done its best to alienate its only possible supporters, the Republican party ought not to have been surprised when it found itself without friends."[27]

"It seems that the things I have believed in and stood for are losing pretty rapidly," wrote a downcast John Bricker after the 1958 elections.[28] Indeed, whatever the factors behind the GOP disaster, few now denied that once again the Old Guard was dead, and the term itself was seldom used after 1958. Bricker, Knowland, Malone, Jenner, Martin, McCarthy, and Welker—a roster of the conservative "Class of 1946"—had all retired or unwillingly departed by 1958 from the U.S. Senate, the Old Guard stronghold in the Capitol. Elected in the conservative swing of 1946 and reelected in the Eisenhower sweep of 1952, these "meatshortage" Republicans were gone by the end of the 1958 congressional elections. In the interim, automatic postage machines, fluorescent lights, and ghostwriters had come to the Senate, along with a gradual dulling of ideological distinctions. According to Russell Baker of the *New York Times,* the Senate had "gone gray flannel."[29]

"The day of the conservative Republican is over. The hard-shelled Republican is a social misfit," said Mayor John T. Capenhaver of Charleston, West Virgina.[30] The mood among conservatives was overwhelmingly grim after the 1958 congressional elections. "Let us conservatives not look for the silver lining," advised Brent Bozell of the *National Review.* "There is none."[31]

Senator George Aiken of Vermont was no stranger to intraparty intrigue in the wake of GOP electoral collapse. A decade earlier, after the Dewey defeat, the flinty Republican liberal had spearheaded a group of Young Turks against the Senate command of Robert Taft. Now, Aiken was at it again as the head of the self-proclaimed "Eisenhower Republicans" who met in Aiken's Senate office shortly after the 1958 elections to talk GOP politics. They traced the party's recent electoral failure to the GOP's "extreme right wing fanatical fringe." But Aiken and his visitors also pointed to *Senate* GOP problems that were clearly related to the November drubbing. Not only had there been obvious discrimination against Eisenhower Republicans in the distribution of committee assignments, but GOP liberals had less voice in Senate GOP policymaking under Knowland and Bridges than under Aiken's former enemies, Kenneth Wherry and Robert Taft. Consequently, Eisenhower heard only from the conservative-dominated Senate GOP leadership at the weekly White House legislative conferences. These Republican leaders might support the administration generally, explained Aiken and his cohorts, but party rulers often deserted Ike on the major legislative issues. In those instances, GOP liberals had to "pull Administration chest-nuts out of the fire." Aiken and his Eisenhower Republicans wanted in-creased representation in GOP Senate counsels and were ready to revolt to get it. The vacancy in the floor leader's post left by Knowland's departure offered an immediate opportunity for them.

The conservative Senate GOP command shared the belief of the Eisen-hower Republicans that the party leadership needed broadening. Compro-mise was possible. Senator Styles Bridges of New Hampshire—whom the *New Republic* now termed "the real boss of conservatives"—offered to let the insurgents control the party whip position, but the floor leader's post was out of the question. Bridges already had a candidate for Knowland's old spot. In fact, he had prepared for this eventuality two years earlier. At that time, suspecting that Knowland might be moving on, Bridges had quietly gotten the unwitting Leverett Saltonstall, a GOP liberal, to head the impor-tant Senate Republican Conference Committee and give up his job as party whip to Everett Dirksen. The party whip was the logical successor to the floor leader, and Dirksen therefore automatically became a candidate for Know-land's vacated post in early 1959.[32] It was a typical Bridges performance—accomplished without causing a stir.

Aiken immediately branded Dirksen as the Old Guard choice. Indeed he was, but the Illinois senator was no longer an Old Guardsman himself. His aid to the administration in the 1957 "Battle of the Budget" proved that Eisenhower had judged wisely in wooing the senator away from the Republi-can Right. In fact, when the Eisenhower Republicans finally settled on Ken-tucky's John Sherman Cooper as their selection for minority leader, it was discovered that Dirksen had supported the president more than this "lib-eral" candidate.

Obviously, the self-anointed Eisenhower Republicans were counting on the president's support in rounding up the half-dozen or more GOP sen-ators they needed to prevail against Dirksen and Bridges on the leadership issue. But Eisenhower quickly dashed that prospect. The president, said Bridges, intended to stay out of the leadership struggle. In reality, Eisen-hower sided with the conservatives. Not only that, but White House aides were reportedly "furious" that Aiken's group had even called themselves Eisenhower Republicans.

The combination of Ike's neutrality and Bridges's backroom dealings proved too much for the Aiken insurgents. Although they had no hope for victory, Aiken's forces still refused Bridges's compromise offer of the party whip post. So certain of victory was Bridges that he correctly predicted Dirk-sen's final victory margin of 20 to 14 in the Senate GOP caucus in early Jan-uary, 1959.

With Dirksen's floor leadership secured, Bridges still had problems, but now they were with his fellow conservatives. Angered that the rebels had continued to wage their public battle for the minority leader position knowing that their cause was futile and that compromise was possible, certain rock-ribbed Republican senators put up Karl Mundt to oppose California's Thomas Kuchel, the insurgent hope for party whip. But Bridges's earlier offer of the party whip post to a liberal represented more than a timely bargaining chip. He and Dirksen sincerely wanted to broaden the GOP leadership. As a result, after Bridges had circled the conference room and talked to certain colleagues, Senate Republicans once again voted, 20 to 14, for the rebel Kuchel.

After the January caucus, having won assurances of increased consultation, the Eisenhower Republicans pledged to cooperate with the Senate Republican leadership. For his part, Dirksen hoped to lead *all* Senate Republicans, not a single faction, and quickly began to rearrange committee assignments in a more equitable way.

It was rare for leadership fights to break out in both houses of Congress simultaneously, but this is what happened in 1959. After the ill-fated 1948 election, Republican House boss Joseph Martin had faced no challenge to his rule, and he expected none after the 1958 debacle. But, shortly after election day, about thirty-five GOP solons met at the Congress Hotel in Washington to ponder the November returns. Led by California representative Robert C. Wilson, the congressional group came to blame House GOP chief Martin for the party's electoral difficulties. They contended that Martin had lost control of the Republican House membership and no longer kept abreast of legislative business. Martin, in turn, admitted that he had lost support, but for two contradictory reasons. Fighting for the president's program left him vulnerable among anti-Eisenhower GOP lawmakers, and White House aides wanted a submissive House leader.[33]

That the Congress Hotel Group's complaints about Martin presaged no clear-cut ideological shoot-out became clear with word that Charles Halleck was the mutineers' candidate to replace Martin. Like Martin, the Indiana representative was basically conservative but had proved flexible in fighting for Eisenhower legislation. Unlike Martin, Halleck had spunk and political savvy. The Martin-Halleck clash was an Old Guard–Modern Republican face-off only in the geriatric sense.

It was a bitter battle. Halleck had been bucking for Martin's job for some time and believed that Martin had promised earlier to step down as GOP boss if the Republicans lost the House. Halleck had been ready to take over for Martin after both the 1954 and 1956 GOP congressional defeats, but Eisenhower had counseled restraint in the interest of party unity.[34] In 1959, however, Halleck had secured an implicit presidential go-ahead.

Martin finally offered to step down as head of the Policy Committee, but that was all. The longtime House leader was, in fact, generally confident, if not cocky, about the outcome of this leadership struggle. On the way to the House Republican caucus, he told reporters, "I'm going to an execution"—meaning, of course, Halleck's.[35] But on a secret, second ballot, Martin was the victim and not the executioner, as Halleck unseated him as House Republican minority leader.

Martin wept openly at the result and soon began to cry publicly about White House meddling in Capitol Hill affairs. He named administration aides who had plotted his removal and specifically blamed Vice-President Richard Nixon. Martin publicly characterized himself as the "fall guy" for the 1958 GOP election defeat. Privately, Martin grumbled that "the same forces that knocked Taft out" had done him in, too. The dump-Martin movement, he wrote, had all the "earmarks of another Dewey–Madison Avenue blitz."[36]

None of the confusions and complexities of GOP scrapping on Capitol Hill followed Republicans to Des Moines, Iowa, where the RNC met in mid-January, 1959. There, the GOP splits were clear-cut. Right Wing Republicans squarely confronted Eisenhower and his Modern Republicanism, and they vented their frustration over the direction of the Republican party under Ike. Eisenhower's pep-talk to the National Committee only touched off the controversy. Ike told the RNC that GOP political activity had to be year-round. The Republican party, said the president, was generally regarded as a "hibernating elephant" between elections. Ike urged Republicans to make an "unremitting effort" before the 1960 election. To wake up the elephant, chief Republican mahout Meade Alcorn then unveiled yet another new plan to overhaul the party.

It was mainly the congressional Republicans who took on the administration in Des Moines. Representative Richard Simpson, the House Campaign Committee chairman, challenged the president to make an "unremitting effort" himself. Simpson's Senate counterpart, Barry Goldwater, continued the challenge via a telegram from Chicago, where he was snowbound. The Alcorn plan was technically "OK," the senator noted, but party principles remained crucial to GOP electoral success. Goldwater held that the Republican elephant did indeed have to come out of hibernation, but it would first have to learn which way to point its trunk. For Goldwater, that way was to the right. Unlike Ike's remarks, the words of Simpson and Goldwater won lusty applause. Clearly the Des Moines meeting of the RNC "seethed with discontent," and the Eisenhower administration was on the defensive.[37]

Eisenhower's big budget, his lack of partisanship, his failure to dish out patronage wisely, and the Republican party's tumbling political fortunes at the polls had clearly embittered the Des Moines participants. As had not been the case in the past, Eisenhower himself came in for direct criticism. Katharine Kennedy Brown of Ohio, an old Taft supporter, jabbed at Ike and harkened back to the 1952 convention, when "those committed to a 'super facelifting' of the GOP, with their despicable untruths cut at the very heart of the Republican Party and appliqued its face with a great war hero."[38]

Some GOP well-wishers hoped that the "refreshing candor" at Des Moines would have some "salutary effects" on the Republican party. Certainly the new administration commitment to overhaul the party through the Alcorn plan held some promise. But Right Wing Republicans were correct in pointing out that ultimately this was only part of any cure. After six years under Eisenhower, the Republican party stood for almost nothing, and that had to change or the party would remain dispirited and divided. As Congressman Daniel Reed wrote in early 1959, "Our party at the moment is one of frustration and is like the General that jumped on his horse and rode off in all directions."[39]

Despite these Right Wing–Modern Republican skirmishes, as the 1960 presidential election approached, the Republican party enjoyed a brief period of greater unity than at any time since Ike took office. Eisenhower grew more political, taking a greater interest in Capitol Hill matters, as he worked closely with the new GOP congressional leaders, Charles Halleck and Everett Dirksen. The result was some Capitol Hill success for Eisenhower. The president, however, was now basically fighting conservative battles. If the president's outlook had not changed since the first term, the issues had. Liberal advisors sensed the new mood.[40] Primarily, it was the spending issue that brought "The Big Change at the White House." In 1959, for example, Republicans blocked Democratic efforts to increase funds for depressed-area legislation, housing and airport construction programs, and to expand the Eisenhower budget. President Eisenhower, himself, was now wielding the budget ax.

Politically, the status of the term "Modern Republican" reflected this change. By mid-January, Eisenhower himself asserted that he saw no real difference between Modern Republicanism and just Republicanism. Two months later, a Republican study group under Meade Alcorn recommended that "hyphenated" descriptors like "Modern" and "Conservative" be dropped. Alcorn offered quick assurance that this was no slap at Eisenhower. Actually, Modern Republicanism had died shortly after the 1956 election, and this was merely its long-overdue last rites. Another indication of the new temporary GOP harmony came in April, 1959, when Meade Alcorn resigned as national chairman for personal reasons. With little prevote dissent, Senator Thruston Morton of Kentucky, Ike's candidate, became the new Republican national chairman by acclamation.

Nor was there any real battle for the Republican presidential nomination of 1960. Vice-President Richard Nixon had a virtual lock on that. By campaigning for Republican hopefuls nationwide and riding the celebrated "rubber chicken and peas" circuit, he secured solid GOP organizational support. Moreover, the vice-president won added exposure by escaping hostile anti-American mobs in Venezuela and engaging Soviet leader Khrushchev in the Moscow "kitchen debates." Liberal Republican Nelson Rockefeller's victory as governor of New York in 1958 had made him the only obvious challenger to Nixon for the GOP presidential nomination. But a year later, Rockefeller had announced his "definite and final" decision to stay out of any presidential contest, since, said Rockefeller, "those who control the Republican nomination stand against any contest for the nomination."[41]

There was, however, a vigorous contest for Nixon's political soul. Despite some contrary assessments, the vice-president was no Right Wing Republican. Some pundits were, in fact, placing Nixon closer to the liberal Republicans. There were rumors that he had favored increased spending for social programs, against the opposition of Treasury secretary George Humphrey. Conservative sources also linked Nixon to Aiken's recent insurgent revolt in the Senate. Bozell of the *National Review* believed that the vice-president was "essentially a trimmer."[42] Nixon was certainly no ideologue. His position was hard to fix, and he reminded many observers of Robert Taft. William S. White considered the vice-president the "perfect model of the political leader who finds his inspiration and ultimate mode from the public."[43] It was therefore useless to speculate on Nixon's conservatism or liberalism. Nor did Nixon go in for intraparty labels; he had resented Eisenhower's impolitic use of the term "Modern Republicanism."

If Nixon was not the darling of the Republican Right Wing in 1960, GOP conservatives at least preferred him to Nelson Rockefeller. The Republican Right also realized that Nixon would respond to conservative pressures. The Republican Right Wing therefore sought to push him in their direction. Senator Barry Goldwater, for instance, met with Nixon to tell him of the general disappointment in the party over his failure to take firm conservative stands. Nixon, in turn, assured Goldwater of his fundamental conservatism but explained that he could not appear to be taking stands at odds with Eisenhower's. This and subsequent Nixon assurances that he would make no concessions to party liberals satisfied Goldwater.[44]

Despite Gallup poll evidence and warnings by Goldwater and national chairman Thruston Morton that he was slipping because of his failure to rouse party conservatives, Nixon waited for the mid-April, 1960, Republican primary in New Jersey to provide a clear signal of GOP trends. Liberal Republican incumbent Senator Clifford Case faced a strong challenge from conservative hard-liner Robert Morris, who had served as counsel for William Jenner's Senate Internal Security Subcommittee. The primary campaign was especially bitter, with Case labeling Morris an "irreconcilable McKinleyite" and Morris attacking Case's "unRepublican" spending record.

A Morris victory, Right Wing Republicans believed, would convince Nixon to steer a conservative course in the campaign ahead.

When Case took 63.7 percent of the GOP vote, it was a dreadful blow for GOP conservatives. "The defeat of Robert Morris in New Jersey," the *National Review* lamented, "is explainable in terms which are not pleasing to hear: a principled conservatism is not what the majority of the American people, or even, apparently, the majority of voting Republicans wants."[45] That was all Nixon needed to know.

For Nixon, counterconservative pressures continued to mount. A month after Case's victory for GOP liberalism, Governor Rockefeller, contrary to his earlier claim, said he would be available for a Republican draft. Rockefeller's self-styled "inactive candidacy" continued as he expressed his "deep" concern about the Republican platform committee's proposed planks on certain issues, such as civil rights. Hoping to avoid a floor fight that might trigger a Rockefeller presidential boom, Nixon traveled to New York on the Friday before the opening of the GOP convention in Chicago. At Rockefeller's Manhattan apartment on Fifth Avenue, the two Republicans had dinner and talked into the early hours of the next morning. Nixon offered Rockefeller the second spot on the ticket, but despite Nixon's promises to reinvigorate the office, Rockefeller declined. Their discussion, however, mainly concerned national issues. When it finally ended, they had hammered out a compromise document, which they telephoned to the Chicago convention.

The Nixon-Rockefeller pact called for "aggressive action" to abolish racial discrimination in all areas of national life and explicitly endorsed the Negro sit-in demonstrations then spreading across the South. It advocated government efforts to stimulate the economy through the free enterprise system, as well as a program of medical care for the aged. In foreign policy, Rockefeller and Nixon both supported a beefing up of American defense programs. Although the Rockefeller-Nixon agreement generally reflected Nixon's view, it became known as "The Surrender of Fifth Avenue"—Vice-President Nixon's surrender—for a number of reasons. First, the pressure that drove Nixon to Fifth Avenue had come from Rockefeller. Moreover, the language of the pact was Rockefeller's, and he made the statement public. Finally, while Nixon insisted that the statement defined their areas of mutual agreement, the New York governor treated it as a personal triumph. "If you don't think that represents my views you're crazy," he said, arriving in Chicago with the statement in his hand.[46]

The Rockefeller-Nixon pact rocked the Chicago convention. Right Wing Republicans immediately concluded that Nixon had come out of New York the loser. "Grant Surrenders to Lee," intoned the *Chicago Tribune*. The head of the Texas GOP delegation branded the Nixon-Rockefeller pact "a damned sellout." Nixon, GOP conservatives believed, had bowed to the

New York "kingmakers." The "ultra-liberal" civil rights section in particular outraged conservatives, especially the southerners, and they threatened a floor fight over it. The *National Review*'s L. Brent Bozell wrote that Nixon's Fifth Avenue retreat now made the nickname "Tricky Dick" real to Republicans.[47]

Among the angriest of the Right Wing Republicans was Arizona Senator Barry Goldwater. Believing that Nixon had double-crossed him, Goldwater exploded. He dubbed the Nixon-Rockefeller agreement "the Munich of the Republican Party" and talked about spearheading a counteroffensive on the convention floor. While Goldwater maintained that he still supported the vice-president for the nomination, Nixon's Fifth Avenue moves did alter Goldwater's convention activities. Previously, South Carolina Republicans had, without any Goldwater prodding, voted to send a pro-Goldwater delegation to the Chicago convention. Goldwater, however, had come to Chicago ready to bow out early and endorse Nixon. The news out of New York changed that. The Arizonan now directed his aide to sit on his prepared withdrawal statement.[48]

Goldwater's South Carolina backing indicated that his following had ballooned since his initial blast against Eisenhower in 1957. The first signs of a GOP conservative revival appeared in the "Americans for Goldwater," "Goldwater for President," and "Youth for Goldwater" groups that descended on Chicago. Indeed, Goldwater arrived at the GOP convention with much support as a vice-presidential candidate—an opportunity Goldwater said he would have to have "marijuana in my veins" to pass up.

Goldwater quickly became the spearhead of conservative resentment against the "Munich of the Republican Party." Certain "eager beavers" wanted him to make a move for the presidential nomination immediately, if only to advertise conservative strength in the GOP. After the "damned sellout," Texas released its delegation from its commitment to Nixon, and pro-Goldwater backers promised the senator about 287 delegate votes. Nixon strategist Leonard Hall judged potential Goldwater strength at about 300 votes.

Resurgent conservative sentiment at Chicago surprised even Goldwater. Although he knew that he had no chance of defeating Nixon, the Arizonan briefly considered remaining a candidate in order to test conservative sentiment. But, fearing that commentators might unfairly judge conservative strength by his vote total, Goldwater eventually decided to withdraw. Still, diehard conservatives in the South Carolina delegation would not give up their Goldwater votes. Goldwater therefore arranged to have someone from Arizona nominate him; he would then appear on the platform and withdraw.

As agreed, on Wednesday evening Arizona governor Paul Fannin nominated a "non-me-too" Republican—Barry Goldwater. After a spontaneous floor demonstration (Goldwater later claimed that a planned one had been squelched), Goldwater came to the podium to withdraw. He chided party conservatives for nursing grudges in the past and refusing to vote for less-than-stalwart GOP candidates. This only elected Democrats, he said. The Republican party platform was not perfect, but it certainly beat the Democrats' "blueprint for socialism." After Goldater urged the Republican Right to "grow up" and work for Nixon, he also held out some hope for the future of GOP conservatism. Declared Goldwater, "Let's get to work if we want to take this party back—and I think we can."[49] Loud cheers went up from the floor. It was the high spot of the Chicago convention.

After Goldwater's withdrawal, the convention gave Nixon 1,321 first-round votes. Louisiana voted for Goldwater on the first ballot in protest but quickly switched to make Nixon's nomination unanimous. Nixon's control of the Chicago convention was almost absolute. He had remained cool, although the "cannibalistic urge" of Republican diehards angered him.[50] His own Fifth Avenue gambit had paid off, as Rockefeller quickly announced that he would not permit his name to be put before the convention. Moreover, the platform according to Nixon and Rockefeller was accepted without debate, and Nixon selected Henry Cabot Lodge—a high priest of Modern Republicanism and an archenemy of the Republican Right—as his runningmate.

Goldwater, for his part, showed that he had a grip on Republican hearts in Chicago. But Right Wing Republican observer L. Brent Bozell found fault with the Arizonan's convention leadership. Goldwater had failed to sustain his challenge to Nixon by threatening conservative defection. Rockefeller's public challenge had swayed Nixon far more than Goldwater's private persuasion.[51] As a result Right Wing Republicans had lost the battle for Nixon's political soul—in 1960 at least.

In the end, after all the campaigning and television debates, only 112,881 votes separated the Democratic and Republican standard-bearers on election day in November, 1960. Switches amounting to 32,500 votes in Texas and Illinois would have altered the result. But after election day, John F. Kennedy was the new Democratic president of the United States, and Republican Richard Nixon, the former vice-president, was the loser.

The congressional returns also reflected the keen party competition, as well as the relative health of the Republican party. The GOP gained twenty seats in the House, but this still left the Democrats with a 259-to-178 majority. In the Senate, the Democratic majority was now 64 to 36, the Republicans having won a total of two seats. GOP conservatives had managed to hold their own in Senate races. Bridges was reelected to a fifth term, and Dworshak of Idaho, Schoeppel of Kansas, and Mundt of South Dakota were also among Right Wing GOP reelection winners. That midwestern Republicans (unlike GOP liberals such as Case and Saltonstall from the East) ran behind the national ticket could be explained by the Catholic issue, which gave Nixon an advantage in the protestant Midwest. The election of Ohio's young John Ashbrook, the former chairman of the Young Republican National Federation, highlighted only the most prominent of a new crop of young conservative House Republicans. Indeed, considering the electoral trends of the late 1950s, the election outcome had a sunny side for Republicans. GOP deterioration on Capitol Hill had been arrested, and a Republican had almost won control of the White House without the heroic Ike.

Right Wing Republicans, however, were sore losers. They blamed the GOP presidential defeat on Nixon's "pulling his punches." They had long eyed Nixon warily and were ready to fault him in spite of his near miss. Barry Goldwater, who had worked hard to drum up conservative (especially southern) support for Nixon, raised the loudest cry. Given his well-known ideas on the future of the Republican party, Goldwater's comments on the election hardly came as a surprise, although his harshness did. Goldwater blamed the Republican party's defeat on its "me-too" candidate. Nixon was just a new Dewey—another Republican loser who had eschewed conservative stands.

Goldwater simultaneously proved his point and fired the first shot of the 1964 Republican presidential wars by pointing out that Arizona had gone for Nixon while liberal Nelson Rockefeller's New York went Democratic. Goldwater clearly indicated even at this early date that he wanted to figure in the 1964 presidential picture, although not necessarily as a candidate. "But I don't want Rockefeller in that spot," he declared. "The next election," Goldwater went on, "should be contested by conservatives—not by people who ape the New Deal."[52] Bozell, however, doubted that Nixon's "liberalism" had lost the election. Bozell held that the returns exploded the Republican Right's traditional notion that electoral "stay-at-homes" were conservatives. In fact, new voters overwhelmingly tended to vote for liberal candidates—a fact that past and future surveys upheld. Considering "the country's present level of political consciousness," Bozell concluded that Goldwater's "principled offerings" would have scared away a lot of anti-Kennedy votes that went to Nixon. The conservative consciousness of the United States, according to Bozell, still needed raising.[53]

"Some years back," Leonard Hall wrote to President Eisenhower shortly after the 1960 election, "I remember that you discussed with me the possibility of doing something about the realignment of our two political parties. Perhaps this is the time?"[54] But this was hardly the time for any such venture, and this suggestion by Hall, an able political professional, remains perplexing. Eisenhower had long before stopped talking about any realigning of the American party system or even "remaking" the Republican party. In fact, his efforts to "revitalize" the GOP had left him increasingly disappointed as the end of his second term neared.[55]

Not that Eisenhower failed completely as a Republican party leader. Historian Gary Reichard has pointed out in his study of Eisenhower and the Eighty-third Congress that Ike worked GOP wonders on Capitol Hill. Not only did his domestic legislation enjoy wide support among congressional Republicans, but Eisenhower generally convinced GOP lawmakers of the wisdom of his "internationalist" foreign policy stands—a considerable political feat. Nonetheless, on dometic issues at least, Eisenhower was "reaffirming" rather than "reshaping" traditional Republicanism. Therefore, according to Reichard, Eisenhower Republicanism proved "a subtle modifier indeed."[56]

Reichard, political scientist Fred Greenstein, and others have also pointed out, accurately, that the traditional portrait of Eisenhower as the hands-off, nonpolitical president is in error. The question then becomes: What kind of political president was Eisenhower? Reichard has provided an answer as far as Ike's Capitol Hill role is concerned. But what did the Eisenhower years mean to the future of the party itself? Specifically, how successful was Ike in the major task he took upon himself—reshaping the image and texture of the Republican party?

Although Eisenhower was not the nonpolitical president that legend has it, he was also not the aggressive and sophisticated political master that Franklin Roosevelt was. In fact, Ike's political interest was never sustained. Clearly, the golf course had greater allure for the general over the long haul than politics. This was certainly not what was required of a party leader committed to recasting the GOP. Revamping a party is an arduous task. Franklin Roosevelt, who brought much more energy, skill, and commitment to the venture than Ike, discovered this and ultimately failed to fashion a "pure" New Deal party. Related to Eisenhower's lack of sustained political commitment were his refusal to meddle in GOP affairs at the state level, his reluctance to use the political patronage and punishments, his virtual slavery to the concept of established chains of command on Capitol Hill, and his overconfidence in his own ideas and powers of conciliation. Eisenhower could claim some political successes: he had maneuvered successfully against McCarthy; he had gained concessions from a hard-line Senate aspirant in Illinois; and Dirksen, Bridges, and Halleck were conservative GOP leaders who proved responsive to Ike's attentions. But these were offset by both large and small failures.

Finally, there was Eisenhower's grandest flop—Modern Republicanism. Proclaimed in the ecstacy of his 1956 victory, Modern Republicanism was a blunder for a number of reasons. It was first of all a hazy concept that left Republicans and pundits alike arguing about its true meaning. Modern Republicanism amounted to little more than a smorgasbord of liberal and conservative offerings. It lacked philosophical backbone. Nor did Ike make any real effort to build up Modern Republicanism or attend to state and local political affairs in order to bring about such a change in his political party. About the only thing that Modern Republicanism did achieve was a good deal of internal GOP ill-will. It implied that old-fashioned, regular, unhyphenated Republicanism was not good enough, and it made the Republican party an object of abuse by its own leader. Conservative Republicans, especially, resented this.

Nor had the Republican party prospered politically under Eisenhower and his Modern Republicanism. While Republicans controlled the White House, the GOP lost about 24 percent of the total offices it had held before 1953. In 1951, there were 47 GOP senators, in 1959, there were only 34; during that same period, the number of House Republicans dropped from 199 to 153, and Republican gubernatorial strength went from 25 to 14. The story was the same at the local and state levels. Naturally, conservative Republicans constantly brandished these depressing figures in making their assaults on Modern Republicanism.

In short, voters liked Ike—but not the GOP. As for the GOP, when Eisenhower left the White House, the Republican party found itself with the same configuration of internal factions as when he had arrived. Eisenhower's presence had merely postponed a decision on the Republican party's future. Actually, his reluctance to wage intraparty war for his kind of Republicanism made things much easier for conservative Republicans. Eisenhower had none of the commitment, the savvy, or the savagery that a Dewey would have brought to the task of remodeling the Republican party along more liberal lines.

As for Right Wing Republicans, they had not fared well during the Eisenhower period either. But Eisenhower was hardly to blame for this. Old Guard ranks had been decimated during the 1950s, as retirement, poor politicking, right-to-work movements, and other factors accounted for its electoral decline. Further, during this time, conservative Republicans had become the party outcasts. Most dramatically, Joseph McCarthy was both a cause and a consequence of this. Also, while conservative forces were still alive in the Republican party, they had lost what had been theirs eight years earlier—command of the GOP structure. On the other hand, the pre-Eisenhower election assumptions of the Old Guard remained intact. Conservative Republicans explained away Ike's 1952 and 1956 victories by citing his great personal popularity born of his wartime experiences. Conservatives still firmly believed that a forthright, conservative alternative to Democratic programs would insure national and presidential political success after Eisenhower.

9

A Choice Not an Echo

The Republican Right had finally found a pin-up boy—Senator Barry M. Goldwater of Arizona. Goldwater presidential talk for 1964 had begun even before election day 1960. Indeed, the senator himself took time off from stumping for the Nixon-Lodge ticket to say that he might run in 1964 should Nixon fall short in 1960. After Nixon's electoral defeat, Goldwater emerged as *the* spokesman of GOP conservatism, promising "to spend the next four years discovering why the conservative majority of this country has no effective voice against the radical minority—and doing something about it."[1]

Goldwater did that and more in the next few years. On television talk shows and the lecture circuit, in magazine feature stories and his own writings, Goldwater set forth the conservative Republican credo. The GOP had no more popular after-dinner speaker. Goldwater's newspaper column "How Do You Stand, Sir," started in 1960 in the *Los Angeles Times,* was carried by 162 other newspapers by 1962. His books quickly became bestsellers. The Republican Right—so long without an attractive advocate—now boasted Barry Goldwater, the self-styled "salesman" of the conservative view.

This being politics, the salesman quickly became synonymous with the product. Goldwater-for-President buttons began to appear everywhere. By mid-1961, a poll of 1960 GOP convention delegates and alternates showed Goldwater to be their overwhelming favorite; 49.3 percent wanted Goldwater to top the Republican ticket in 1964, while only a combined 44.4 percent favored either Nixon or Rockefeller instead. *Time* called the Arizona senator "the hottest political figure this side of Jack Kennedy."[2]

Indeed, in an age of image and charisma, Senator Goldwater stood as the perfect GOP match against President John F. Kennedy. Goldwater had "it." Tall and tan with a handsome, ruggedly sculptured face, dark horn-rimmed glasses, and wavy gray-white hair, Goldwater looked like a president. The Arizonan was so handsome, Senator Hubert Humphrey once spoofed, that he had landed a Hollywood movie contract—with *18th* Century-Fox. Even more than his good looks, Goldwater had both tremendous charm and energy or, as it was then called, "vigor." He not only flew jet planes, but, like Kennedy, he also wrote books. If Goldwater was not JFK's oratorical equal, he was at least an effective speaker in informal settings—his easy, colloquial manner ably communicating his quiet sincerity.

Comparisons between this new darling of the Republican Right and Robert Taft were also inevitable. Goldwater was the first *real* leader of the Republican Right since Taft. Through the difficult 1950s, Right Wing Republicans had remained "Taft Republicans"—a reflection on the state of the Republican Right and William F. Knowland's spiritless leadership. By 1960, however, GOP candidates were beginning to bill themselves as "Goldwater Republicans."

But Goldwater and Taft each dominated the Republican Right in different ways. If Goldwater was the salesman of conservative Republicanism, Robert Taft had been its legislator. Unlike Taft, Goldwater had no major piece of legislation bearing his name. Taft had had his greatest influence in the Senate, where Goldwater, though a member of the Senate "club," was hardly a *ruling* member. Goldwater Republicanism was, in fact, strongest in the House of Representatives.

Taft's and Goldwater's personalities mirrored their respective Capitol Hill power bases. Like the Senate, Taft had been more deliberate. While his pronouncements were often as sharp and indiscreet as Goldwater's, they nevertheless seemed to be the culmination of his thought process. Goldwater's statements, on the other hand, constantly prompted charges that he was "shooting from the hip." Goldwater, however, was a far more stalwart conservative than Taft. The Arizona senator's political canon, unlike Taft's, had little room for federal action on pressing social problems.

Ultimately, Goldwater's pure and simple message made him the Right Wing Republican best suited to the realities of presidential politics in postwar America. Taft had never been the Right Wing publicist that Goldwater was to become. Goldwater stepped forward as a kind of political celebrity, a role Taft could never have assumed. Wrote commentator Ralph DeToledano, "Where Taft was the rock, Goldwater is the flint and steel which can strike fire in the electorate."[3]

With a directness that characterized the man himself, Barry Goldwater's past helped to explain his new role on the American political scene. The senator's grandfather, Mike Goldwasser, a Polish émigré, had arrived in the New World in 1852 via England, where he had taken an Anglican bride and name. After selling hard goods and whiskey from a wagon to the miners of Sonora, California, "Big Mike" Goldwater packed off to Arizona to cash in on new gold strikes. There, in 1870, he founded the store he subsequently left to his three sons. His son Baron (Barry's father) also inherited Big Mike's business sense and built up the Goldwater enterprise. When Baron died,

Barry left the University of Arizona, where he burned more gas in his convertible than midnight oil, and returned home to run the family business. He proved a far better businessman than student, further developing the Goldwater department stores and displaying a talent for merchandizing. His design of red ants on men's undershorts—"antsy pants"—sparked a national fad.

Politics in the Goldwater tribe had been the special domain of Barry's Uncle Morris, who helped establish Arizona's Democratic party and instill Barry with his own unreconstructed Jeffersonian Democratic philosophy. In 1949 Barry Goldwater had won a seat on the Phoenix City Council on an independent ticket. A year later, Goldwater managed the successful gubernatorial campaign of radio announcer Howard Pyle, a Republican in one-party Democratic Arizona. Goldwater, however, won more notoriety than his gubernatorial candidate. As a result, Goldwater himself ran for the U.S. Senate in 1952. He upset the Senate Democratic majority leader Ernest McFarland, largely by hanging on to Eisenhower's coattails, a fact which Goldwater readily admitted.

But that was about all Goldwater depended on Ike for. He certainly took few political cues from the Republican president, moving further away from Ike during the 1950s. Goldwater fit easily in the Senate Republican club and secured an important position as chairman of the Republican Senate Campaign Committee, where he utilized his marketing skills. One fact soon became clear. Whether battling the Eisenhower administration's "me-too" trends, labor racketeers, or the Democrats, Goldwater had a knack for grabbing press space. By the end of the 1950s, politics and publicity had come together profitably for Barry Goldwater. *Time* was calling him "the salesmanager for the Republican Old Guard with a New Look."[4]

Clarence Manion, an Old Guard martyr to Eisenhower Republicanism, early recognized Goldwater's potential importance to the conservative cause and urged the senator to write down his conservative philosophy in bold and simple terms. The *National Review*'s L. Brent Bozell was recruited as a ghostwriter. Neither Manion nor Goldwater expected big sales from this undertaking, and Manion contracted with the Victor Publishing Company of Shepherdsville, Kentucky, for an initial printing of only 10,000, with the publisher to retain subsequent printing rights. Unbelievably, Goldwater's *Conscience of a Conservative* took off. Published in 1960 with little critical notice, the book had sold 700,000 copies and gone into a paperback edition by mid-1961. Sales continued to mount during the early 1960s.

Although the political Goldwater was sometimes forced to modify certain positions of the literary Goldwater, the *Conscience of a Conservative* and other early Goldwater writings expressed Right Wing Republicanism in its fullest form ever. Goldwater not only rejected the Democratic New and Fair Deals, he also attacked the "me-too Republicanism" of Eisenhower's

"Dime-Store New Deal." The senator's political beliefs remained un-abashedly pre-New Deal; he held that he could happily run for president on Franklin Roosevelt's 1932 platform with its calls for sound currency, a re-duced and balanced budget, and a slashed federal payroll.

Goldwater insisted on a strict construction of the Constitution. Since the New Deal, he claimed, the federal government had usurped the legit-imate powers of the states. The Arizonan wanted the federal government to get out of the areas of business, agriculture, and education. But Goldwater believed he offered more than the cranky Old Guard's opposition to govern-ment programs. "The weakness of conservatives is that they have been just plain 'aginners,'" he explained. "I try to be for something. I don't just say I'm against Federal aid—period. I say let the federal government reduce its costs and its burdens, and allow state and local governments to assume more responsibility."[5]

Despite this "positive" approach, Goldwater's domestic policy hardly deviated from standard Old Guard conservatism. Few basic changes could be expected, considering Goldwater's words in the *Conscience of a Conser-vative*: "The laws of God and of nature have no dateline."[6] What Goldwater *did* was to express the conservative position with clarity and consistency and without regard to practical political considerations. Goldwater ruled out any more federal welfare programs. On the contrary, he advocated a staged with-drawal—perhaps 10 percent per year—from all existing domestic programs outside of what he deemed the federal government's constitutional man-date. Social Security, Goldwater also wrote, should be made "flexible and voluntary." The Tennessee Valley Authority should be sold to private indus-try.[7] This was stern stuff that not even the most diehard Right Wing Repub-lican with political ambitions had gone so far as to advocate.

But there was more. Goldwater wanted to end all federal farm programs and return the farmer to the free market. On labor matters, Goldwater not only favored a ban on union political activities and industry-wide bargain-ing, but he supported a national right-to-work law. Goldwater even came out against the graduated income tax as "repugnant to my notions of jus-tice" and an artificial decree for "enforcing equality among unequal men."[8] Finally, Goldwater rejected federal action on two major issues of the early 1960s—civil rights and aid to education—because of his respect for states' rights and his fear of federal control of American life.

In his *Conscience of a Conservative,* Goldwater was equally direct on foreign policy questions. The Russian Communists, said Goldwater, had stated their goal of overrunning the world and imposing "slavery"—and they meant it. He insisted therefore that American foreign policymakers re-member always that the Soviet Union and the United States were at war—a cold war certainly but nevertheless a war. The United States, said Gold-water, had to proclaim immediately that its purpose remained "complete victory over the forces of international Communism." That the United States had so far failed to do so was "incredible."[9]

While the senator's foreign policy objectives never included military "victory" over Russia, Goldwater insisted on continued military superiority over the Soviet Union and held that a great power could never make the avoidance of war its chief objective. The United States had to convince the enemy, Goldwater wrote in his characteristically colorful way, "that we would rather follow the world to kingdom come than consign it to hell under Communism."[10] Such blustery Goldwater declarations actually offered little that was concrete regarding essential American foreign policy interests, but they did leave the impression of a rather "trigger-happy" anticommunist.

Along with his "Better Dead than Red" proclamations, Goldwater maintained that the United States must never surrender "another single inch" to the Communists. In fact, Goldwater wanted to help "freedom fighters" in Communist-dominated lands to retake their homelands and even suggested that the United States might initiate military opposition against vulnerable Communist regimes.

Goldwater also claimed that withdrawing recognition from "Mr. Khrushchev's murderous claque" would quickly improve the international scene. Furthermore, the United States should quit favoring the Communists with trade or technology and stop negotiating with the Soviets. As a result of such beliefs, Goldwater voted against the 1963 Limited Nuclear Test Ban Treaty, in which the United States, Great Britain, and the Soviet Union pledged to conduct nuclear weapons testing only underground.

If Goldwater was far more inclined to interfere in spots around the globe than Taft, Wherry, and earlier Old Guard Republicans with isolationist pasts, he did share their frustration with our allies and betrayed an inclination to "go it alone" in foreign affairs. Our allies, Goldwater believed, remained too fearful and cautious in this holy war with communism. He argued that the United States could not continue to conduct its foreign policy in paralytic deference to the United Nations and had to stop "humoring" neutral countries.

Goldwater also voiced traditional Right Wing criticisms of foreign aid. Along with waste and extravagance, these "giveaways," said Goldwater, fostered anti-Americanism among its proud recipients and socialism in its government-to-government mechanisms. He would give military and technical assistance only to our true friends—those countries that demonstrated the will to resist communism.

Republicans returned to Capitol Hill after the 1960 elections in a feisty mood. Political observers expected Goldwater and other Capitol Hill Republicans to battle Kennedy and the Democrats with zeal. GOP conservatives would no longer be shackled by the moderate Eisenhower administration. Moreover, Goldwater talked early in the new Congress of submitting specific legislative proposals dealing with critical national problems to show that viable conservative policy alternatives existed.

Right Wing prospects seemed especially bright in the House, where a band of young hard-liners from small towns and rural areas won seats in the early 1960s. In the Ninety-fourth Congress, for instance, forty of the fifty-eight House newcomers were Republican, most of them proud and uncompromising conservatives. These "Young Fogies," as their colleagues dubbed them, hoped to reinvigorate the free enterprise system. One of them, Donald Bruce of Indiana, hailed the "beginning of a philosophical revolution based on devotion to principle." In the late summer of 1961, Bruce and other GOP rookies launched "Operation Survival," a series of speeches that outlined their conservative views on such subjects as the growth of the federal government.

Despite the gung-ho talk of these Young Fogies, Goldwater, and other Republicans, it soon became apparent that the Republicans—especially Right Wing Republicans—were going to have difficulties on Capitol Hill. President Kennedy was hardly the "wild-eyed" Democratic blueprinter of GOP propaganda, and his moderation tempered GOP opposition. Moreover, Bourbon Democratic members of the conservative alliance were generally proving unreliable, much to the disappointment of the coalition's chief GOP drumbeater, South Dakota senator Karl Mundt. In the House, especially, Republicans had to share the blame for the failure of Capitol Hill conservatives to meet initial expectations. Early in the session, renegade liberal Republicans helped Kennedy have his way in fights over the Rules Committee, the minimum wage and depressed areas legislation, and the extension of unemployment compensation.

Inevitably, the GOP's Capitol Hill leadership came under fire. In the House, the Young Fogies faulted Charles Halleck's less-than-staunch conservatism and joined moderate GOP solons in complaining about Halleck's more general legislative shortcomings. Senate GOP minority leader Everett Dirksen also came in for some sharp criticism. The *National Review* accused him of "fawning over" Kennedy's appointments and gagging his more conservative GOP brethren. Furthermore, conservatives charged, Dirksen failed repeatedly to blast the Kennedy administration for foreign policy fiascos like the Bay of Pigs. Goldwater, for his part, criticized both Halleck and Dirksen for merely reacting to Democratic initiatives and not setting forth Republican alternatives.

Conservatives already distrusted Halleck and Dirksen for having prostituted themselves during the Eisenhower years in the "fleshpots" of Modern Republicanism. The two GOP leaders, however, soon became "the joke of the Capitol" for other reasons that upset Republicans of all persuasions.

Hoping to cut into Kennedy's monopoly of the television airwaves, Dirksen and Halleck inaugurated their own television show to rebut the president and present the GOP point of view. What became known as the "Ev and Charlie" show proved a total disaster. Mixing Republican apologetics with vapid comedy, the gruesome twosome of the GOP was no match for the attractive and witty president and the rest of the cast that would later be called Camelot. Goldwater and the young hard-liners in the House regarded themselves as attractive, dynamic advocates of new-look conservatism. "Ev and Charlie," on the other hand, presented a different image. *Commonweal* called them "wheezy and old-fashioned," a "turn of the century vaudeville act." Conservative Republicans resented both the image and the reality of Ev and Charlie's leadership.[11]

For one day in July, 1962, GOP-watchers shifted their gaze from the developing Goldwater boom and this "Ev and Charlie" show to a green and white striped tent in Gettysburg, Pennsylvania. There, former President Dwight Eisenhower played host to a GOP unity rally at his farm. The Gettysburg gathering had all the earmarks of earlier party conclaves during the Eisenhower administration. In apparent harmony and good cheer, about one hundred Republicans listened to Eisenhower pronouncements on GOP politics. Ike told them that he "hated and despised" the "shopworn and meaningless" terms "liberal" and "conservative" and recommended that these divisive labels be junked. The Republican party would move ahead, he concluded, if it "quit magnifying" its differences and stood for "progress."[12] These were the perfect words to gloss over GOP party splits, but Eisenhower's harmonics bore little relevance to the deep rifts that still threatened to tear the Republican party apart.

Far more meaningful—and divisive—were the actions taken under the Gettysburg bigtop. Plans were unveiled to establish an All-Republican Conference, a consultative body of about one hundred leading Republicans who would meet periodically to help shape party policy and do political research. While initially suspicious of any encroachment on their policymaking powers, congressional Republican leaders finally acquiesced in the establishment of the conference.

Also at the Gettysburg meeting it was decided to create a National Republican Citizen's Committee. This voluntary organization would fund the All-Republican Conference and include nonorganization Republicans, independents, and even some Democrats. For GOP hard-liners, the word "citizens" was a "dirty word" that recalled the independent groups behind Eisenhower's two presidential campaigns. They naturally feared that this "forum of meddlesome liberals" was merely the first move by "me-too" Republicans to control the 1964 Republican nomination.

Although Goldwater did not attend the Gettysburg affair, he had plenty to say about what went on there. He minced no words in speaking out against the National Republican Citizen's Committee. The forces behind this plan were the same ones "who caused our present problems," said Goldwater; "they should not be given another opportunity to lead us down the path to political destruction."[13] Goldwater and other Right Wing Republicans charged that the Citizen's Committee would ultimately siphon off funds from the Republican party itself.

In the end, the July Gettysburg rally brought little harmony to Republican ranks. The All-Republican Conference floundered from the start and eventually achieved almost nothing. Continued party splits prevented any united GOP action. If Eisenhower believed the terms "conservative" and "liberal" to be irrelevant, other Republicans had to wrestle with the reality that these labels really did mean something in GOP politics.

The Republican unity problem persisted after the 1962 congressional elections. While all Republican factions—liberal, moderate, and conservative—could claim some victories, the big electoral winners were the Democrats, who retained a 259-to-176 House majority and built up a 68-to-32 margin in the Senate.

The most noteworthy and portentous election news turned out to be the defeat of former Vice-President Richard M. Nixon in the race for governor of California. A key national Republican figure and a fairly popular bridge between the GOP's left and right wings, Nixon had returned home to California to build up the political base that most observers believed he needed. But he entered the fall campaign against the popular Democratic incumbent Pat Brown hampered by a bitterly divided California GOP and dogged by the popular belief that he was only running for governor as a way station to the presidency in 1964. Despite his disclaimers, Nixon furthered this notion by blundering late in the campaign, "When I take over as President—I mean Governor of the United States—California." After his decisive loss, Nixon went out in a blaze of invective against the press, which, he said, "wouldn't have Nixon to kick around anymore."[14]

The GOP did, however, boast gubernatorial winners in several industrial states. Former American Motors president George Romney ended fourteen years of Democratic rule in Michigan with his triumphant race for governor. One-term congressman William Scranton defeated Philadelphia mayor Richardson Dilworth to become chief executive of Pennsylvania, and in neighboring Ohio, James Rhodes ousted Michael DiSalle. Along with Nelson Rockefeller's reelection win in New York, these state house victories thrilled GOP liberals and moved New Jersey senator Clifford Case to propose an alliance between liberals on Capitol Hill and Republican governors. This progressive axis, Case believed, could develop new policies and work to influence the Republican presidential choice in 1964. But there was another view. The failure of Nixon in California and the fact that Rockefeller in winning New York ran behind his 1958 victory margin convinced conservative political strategists like the *National Review*'s William Rusher that the GOP could not defeat Kennedy in the major industrial states in 1964.[15]

There were indeed various—and sometimes contradictory—lessons in the 1962 GOP electoral returns. Americans for Conservative Action (ACA) chairman Ben Moreel, noting that 74 percent of the ACA-assisted Republican and Democratic conservatives had won their elections, hailed the "rising tide of constitutional conservatism." He and other conservative well-wishers found promise in the election of conservative Peter Dominick over incumbent Colorado senator and New Frontiersman John Carroll, and of conservative Millward Simpson over J.J. Hickey in Wyoming. Conservative hard-liners also tended to blame the defeat of Indiana senator Homer Capehart by Birch Bayh on Capehart's earlier dalliance with Eisenhower's Modern Republicanism. With GOP stalwarts such as John Ashbrook of Ohio, Donald Bruce of Indiana, and Robert Dole of Kansas also claiming or retaining seats in the House, the *National Review* suggested, "If you're going to get re-elected, it doesn't hurt to show a good conservative record to your constituents."[16]

Conservative cheerleaders could offer no more positive pronouncements on the future of American political conservatism. There was, after all, little reason for revelry. The 1962 elections were generally regarded as a defeat for the Republican Right. The newly hatched Conservative party of New York received enough votes to secure a permanent spot on the Empire State ballot but fell short of its anticipated totals. No Right Wing Republican had a greater stake in the 1962 elections than Barry Goldwater, and he found little to cheer about in the showing of conservative Republicans nationwide. Before election day, he had targeted liberal Democratic senators Joseph Clark of Pennsylvania, Wayne Morse of Oregon, and John Carroll of Colorado for defeat. Only Carroll lost. Neither Goldwater's name nor campaign aid seemed to help Republicans around the country. Sighed a disappointed Goldwater after the elections, "I can't figure it out."[17]

In the wake of the 1962 elections, all Republicans could agree on one thing: the current image of the party had to change. Also, the belief spread that the "Ev and Charlie" show had to go. One immediate result of this GOP image-changing was the replacement of Charles B. Hoevan of New Jersey as House GOP conference chairman with Gerald Ford, a handsome, young former University of Michigan football player. While some observers construed the Ford-Hoeven contest as a liberal-conservative clash, the switch amounted to little more than a party primping.

Another party preoccupation in the wake of the 1962 election returns was the GOP future in the South. Republicans posted big gains there in 1962. Most notably, five new Republican congressmen would come from below the Mason-Dixon line, and Alabama Republican James Martin almost upset veteran U.S. Senator Lister Hill. Elsewhere in the South, Republicans forced Democratic senators such as Arkansas's J. William Fulbright and South Carolina's Olin Johnston into some uncharacteristic fall campaigning. Republicans in three North Carolina counties swept all state and county offices and defeated the Democratic Speaker of the North Carolina House of Representatives. In North Carolina and Georgia, Republicans elected their first state senators since Reconstruction. "The tide is coming in now in the South," said I. Lee Potter, head of Operation Dixie, the GOP program started in the 1950s to capitalize on Eisenhower's largely personal southern gains in his two presidential campaigns.[18]

Republican inroads in the South provided the only true bright spot for Right Wing Republicans as they pondered the 1962 election outcome. These returns confirmed Barry Goldwater's belief in the coming new Republican age in Dixie. The Arizonan had heavily barnstormed the South for Richard Nixon in 1960 and later bemoaned Nixon's failure to make his political stand there. Nixon, for his part, had vacillated between appealing to the South or the northern urban-industrial areas.

The South versus the City—this Republican tug-of-war—had continued after the 1960 election, with urban advocates initially holding sway. The Republican party, they argued, had lost by narrow margins in states like Pennsylvania and Illinois because the Democrats had piled up huge majorities in the big cities where Republican organizations had all but disappeared. The first proposals of urban-oriented Republicans to close the "big-city gap" were ludicrous. Reacting to charges of political foul play in the Chicago vote in 1960, some GOP leaders discussed hiring college football players in the future to guard city polling places. More serious plans followed, however, as the Republicans prepared to follow the lead of Ray Bliss, the Ohio state chairman whose revitalized urban organizations had helped hold Ohio for Nixon in 1960.

Dixie, however, continued to have its Republican drumbeaters. They contended that the GOP must win over the 85 electoral votes of the South through a conservative appeal. Including the 70 electoral votes of the border states, GOP victory in 1964 could then come, argued GOP southern strategists, with the addition of the Midwest and the mountain states—a union, said one writer, of "the cornbelt and cornpone."[19] This southern strategy had received a big lift with the May, 1961, election of Republican John G. Tower to fill the Senate seat vacated by Vice-President Lyndon Johnson. A "conservative of conviction, not convenience" and a self-proclaimed Goldwater Republican, Tower had even declined Richard Nixon's offer of campaign help in becoming the first Republican senator from Texas since Reconstruction.

Goldwater, meanwhile, had kept up his calls for continued GOP exertions below the Mason-Dixon line. At a GOP conference on the two-party system in the South in November, 1961, Goldwater advocated watering down the civil rights section of the 1960 Republican platform. Afterward, Goldwater had to answer charges that he was "writing off" the Negro vote and the industrial urban areas. The Republicans would "write off" no group or area, said Goldwater, but it was prudent to do "our strong hunting where the ducks are flying." For him, that was clearly not among black voters since, as he had explained earlier, "We [Republicans] have literally bent over backwards to attract the Negro vote, but they don't vote for us." [20]

By early 1962, the southern strategists appeared to be gaining within the GOP. On Capitol Hill, for example, GOP opposition to the proposed Department of Urban Affairs led some observers to conclude that the Republican party had indeed settled on a southern strategy. Naturally, the 1962 electoral tallies, which showed a 244 percent rise in Republican southern strength as compared with the Democrats' 41 percent, made that decision all the easier. Kennedy appeared vulnerable in the South, which James J. Kilpatrick called "Goldwater Country," and RNC chairman William Miller promised "a major penetration" of the South in 1964.

There were several reasons for recent Republican gains in the South. The GOP was contesting more southern elections and fielding more able candidates than the post-office Republicans of an earlier era. The influx of northerners into Texas, Florida, and Virginia also helped alter southern politics. The advancing modernization and industralization of the South had attracted these Yankees, who appreciated GOP opposition to high taxes, federal spending, and government centralization. Goldwater and others contended that it was the "economic issue" that drove southerners into the Republican ranks.

Still, the specter of racism hung over the Republican Right's southern strategy. Would the new Republican party in Dixie be built on the backs of the Negro? Meade Alcorn, for one, felt that southern racists were subverting Operation Dixie, which he had launched as RNC chairman. Eastern opinion makers and liberal Republicans publicly argued that the GOP would inevitably turn "lily white" racist in "immorally" turning South. The GOP's Dixie jackpot in the 1962 elections only fueled this debate. [21]

The Republican Right fought back against these charges. Contending that "the greatest GOP gains in the past 15 years have been in the South," Goldwater characterized the charges of racism and segregation as "absurd." Actually, the progressive urban elements of the South, not the country crackers, were backing Republican candidates, countered Goldwater; Republican inroads had come in direct proportion to southern moderation on the race issue. The *National Review* pointed to critics' inconsistency in damning the Republican party as racists while saying nothing about the Democratic party with its Bourbon contingent. [22]

These conservative replies notwithstanding, the racist bogey would not go away. And it never could as long as Goldwater and conservative Republicans persisted in championing states' rights under the circumstances. However broadminded Goldwater and other states' rights Republican champions were, their doctrine meant the unrelieved suppression of the Negro. Moreover, Goldwater's talk of new southern moderation seemed strange in the face of increased Ku Klux Klan activity, gunpoint integration battles, and Bull Connor's brutalities against Negro demonstrators in Birmingham, Alabama, in 1963. Indeed, racial politics seems at least partly responsible for Republican gains in the South during this period, especially following reports of veiled segregationist appeals by some southern GOP candidates. Unlike these, the Democratic party's Bourbon contingent was a product of history, and not cynical wooing by national leaders who had advertised their willingness to appease the South on the race issue.

"On and on the Great Debate of the '60's rages: Liberal! Conservative!" proclaimed author M. Stanton Evans in 1961. "Such venerable conversation standbys as sex, religion and baseball are left trailing in its wake."[23] Although a question might be raised about how typical Evans's conversational set was, the early 1960s did witness a "conservative resurgence."

This right-wing revival had been a long time coming. The demise of the 1930s Liberty League, with its blind rage against "that man," FDR, had left American conservatism without organization and drive—an ideological shill for selfish economic "interests." By the mid-1950s, however, there was talk of "creeping conservatism," and not "creeping socialism." Ironically, Eisenhower, the right's chief Republican adversary, had contributed to the growth of the conservative sentiment; his administration had given new "currency" to the language of conservatism.[24] Mid-1958 witnessed the founding of the Americans for Constitutional Action, a lobby to "aid in the promotion and preservation of the American system of constitutional government, free enterprise and private property." The Americans for Constitutional Action rated the relative conservatism of Washington lawmakers and supplied conservative candidates with speechwriters, fundraisers, and political fieldmen. If the Americans for Constitutional Action was the conservative answer to the Americans for Democratic Action (ADA) of the liberals, so too was the newly hatched Conservative party in New York a response to the Empire State's Liberal party.

A conservative intellectual movement was well in the making by the early 1960s, its roots deeply embedded in the recent past. In 1944 Austrian Frederick A. Hayek's *The Road to Serfdom,* a bold call for individualism and limited government—classical liberalism—had quickly become an American best-seller. Subsequently, two American writers—Peter Viereck in *Conservatism Revisited* (1949) and Russell Kirk in *The Conservative Mind*

(1953)—stepped forward as proponents of the "new conservatism," with its distress over modern society's erosion of traditional religious and cultural values. Already by the mid-1950s, the American intellectual right, no longer unsure of its own existence, had entered a period of self-definition.[25]

Yet conservative intellectuals of all types wanted more than ivory-tower debate. They wanted to affect public policy, to rout American political liberalism. Only topnotch conservative weekly journals could accomplish this, John Chamberlain had written in the early 1950s. Such periodicals would prepare the public for conservative initiatives, as the *Nation* and *New Republic* had once done for American liberalism. Robert Taft, who had often griped about the media's New Deal bias, believed that conservatives had to "build up" their own "word-slingers" in order to attract articulate intellectuals.[26]

Although journals like *The Freeman* and *Human Events* existed in the decade after World War II, the concerns of Taft, Chamberlain, and others were answered with the founding of the *National Review* in 1955. This jewel of American conservative periodicals was the brainchild of William F. Buckley, a bright, young right-wing intellectual who had first gained national attention in 1951 with the publication of *God and Man at Yale,* an attack on the liberal tilt of his *alma mater.* Buckley was a brilliant, uncompromising conservative, with a literary style that effectively mixed wit and scorn. Not only did his *National Review* provide the magazine that Taft and Chamberlain had longed for, but, in Buckley, the conservative intellectual force boasted its own national celebrity—a right-wing television talk show personality.

The *National Review,* combining the various strains of conservatism—classical liberalism, "new conservative" traditionalism, and hard-line anticommunism—soon became the "cohesive intellectual force" of the postwar conservative movement.[27] A sounding board for conservative politicians and a newsletter on the politics of the Republican Right, the *National Review* also served as a springboard for such conservative newspaper columnists as James J. Kilpatrick and, later, George Will.

Despite his desire for rightish intellectuals and "word-slingers," Taft had generally remained aloof from this budding conservative intellectual movement—Taft once remarking, "I'm a politician, not a philosopher."[28] Indeed, there was only minimal contact between politicians in general and this group during the 1950s. But the gap between conservative literati and politicians closed considerably by the early 1960s. *Human Events,* for example, held a two-day conference in early 1962 on how to elect conservative candidates in the upcoming congressional elections. Ultimately, Goldwater himself became the major link between the political and intellectual worlds of the conservative movement. L. Brent Bozell, *National Review* writer and brother-in-law of William F. Buckley, helped Goldwater write his own *Con-*

science of a Conservative. Russell Kirk occasionally pitched in on Goldwater speeches. Conservative economists like Milton Friedman of the University of Chicago, Gottfried Haberler of Harvard, and Warren Nutter of the University of Virginia offered economic advice, and Professor Gerhardt Neimeyer of Notre Dame schooled the senator on foreign policy matters. Unlike FDR and JFK with their liberal advisors, however, Goldwater used these intellectuals for periodic brainstorming rather than any permanent brain trust.

Like Taft, Goldwater realized that the worlds of the philosopher and the politician differed considerably, and the down-with-the-ship attitude of some conservative intellectuals could exasperate him. Still, this new relationship between conservative politicians and intellectuals did serve to enrich the politics of the Republican Right. There was some irony in this, considering the Eisenhower administration's earlier efforts to interest "eggheads" in Modern Republicanism.

One conservative intellectual, in particular, had been working since 1953 to make one of his ideas a practical reality. Frank Chodorov had long noted the "radical movement's" emphasis on enlisting the sympathies of the young. As a conservative counterbalance, Chodorov established the Intercollegiate Society of Individualists, which distributed conservative literature to college students. Whatever the direct impact of the society's literature, conservatism among the young did spread rapidly in the 1950s. The Young Republicans, for instance, moved steadily to the right during the Eisenhower years, expressing a growing dissatisfaction with the administration's moderate policies. Given Eisenhower's oft-expressed concern for "the youngsters," this too was ironic. The extent of that irony became apparent when young college conservatives descended on the 1960 GOP convention infatuated with the Republican Right's foremost critic of the Eisenhower administration, Barry Goldwater. "Today's youngsters," remarked former Indiana senator William Jenner at the Chicago GOP convention, have "a damn sight more sense than their mommies and daddies."[29]

In thanking one of these pro-Goldwater youth groups at the close of the Chicago convention, Goldwater suggested they form a national youth organization for conservatives. That September, about one hundred young conservatives met at William F. Buckley's estate in Sharon, Connecticut. There, the Young Americans for Freedom (YAF) was launched, as participants pledged themselves to the "eternal truths" of limited government and the market economy and "victory" over international communism. This was the so-called Sharon Statement. In less than six months, the YAF claimed about 27,000 members with chapters on one hundred college campuses.

The movement grew. In March, 1961, about 6,000 young conservatives jammed the Manhattan Center in New York City to hoot at "soft-headed" liberals, President Kennedy, and even former President Eisenhower, and to howl for Herbert Hoover and Barry Goldwater. A year later, not even Madison Square Garden could hold all the young conservatives who wanted to attend a YAF rally; thousands were turned away at the door. Inside, amid the red-white-and-blue bunting, speakers like John G. Tower and L. Brent Bozell regaled the youthful right-wing hordes. The main attraction, however, was Senator Barry Goldwater, who received a five-minute ovation and acclamation as the obvious Republican presidential candidate for 1964.

This Madison Square Garden rouser highlighted the new conservative craze on American campuses. Goldwater's *Conscience of a Conservative* was enjoying brisk sales at student book stores. Goldwater badges and Goldwater clubs were making the college scene. Harvard's Student Council president was reportedly a "stern conservative." The right-wing columnist for the University of Wisconsin's student newspaper observed that the word "conservative" was no longer a "nasty word" on campus. Indeed, he added, a student now had to be an "ultra-conservative" to be truly respectable. The election of arch-Goldwater conservative Donald E. Lukens as the Young Republicans' chairman in March, 1964, only bolstered M. Stanton Evans's contention that preppy conservatism had finally emerged "full-blooded and purposeful."[30]

What had gotten into these young hard-liners? All observers, citing the age-old rebellion of the young against the old, saw student conservatives reacting against the liberal conformity of their parents and college professors. Another student hard-liner offered a fairly unconservative explanation for his own politics. "You walk around with your Goldwater button," he remarked, "and you feel that thrill of treason."[31] Of course, adult conservatives preferred to view this movement as more solidly based. M. Stanton Evans attributed campus conservatism to an "apprehension about the way things have worked out under Liberal stewardship."[32] Ascribing such good sense to the college crowd would subsequently pose problems for conservatives when the late 1960s ushered in a new fashion in campus politics—the New Left. But whatever its staying power, the preppy conservatism of the early 1960s temporarily cheered the Republican Right, so long identified as the sole, stuffy purveyor of conservatism.

An ominous aspect of the conservative scene came to light in March, 1961, when an organized letter campaign got underway demanding the impeachment of Supreme Court Chief Justice Earl Warren. By the end of the year, a new reality in American politics had emerged—the "Radical Right." Far-out right-wing groups had, of course, always existed on the fringe of American politics. But the 1960s' Radical Right was different. No longer were the fabled "little old ladies in tennis shoes" the sole members of these groups. Ultra-conservative activity, financed by the newly rich, quickly spread through the middle- and lower-middle class suburbs of the South and West. Week-long seminars on communist subversion, right-wing reading lists, and patriotic rallies were some of the signs of this Radical Right boom. In Dallas, for example, there were one hundred anticommunist study groups meeting at one time in 1961. In southern California, ultra-conservatives took their politics into the streets on automobile bumperstickers: "AMERICANISM—THE ONLY ISM FOR ME," "NO ON RED CHINA," and "SOCIALISM IS COMMUNISM."

The main message of these ultra-conservative organizations was unqualified anticommunism. All current problems were blamed on a communist plot. America's enemies were not overseas; they were at large in the United States, boring from within. The Radical Right saw the federal income tax, the proposed registration of firearms, and even attempts to flouridate community drinking water as major communist threats.

The media quickly discovered the Radical Right and, along with certain overwrought politicians, gave the phenomenon an importance out of all proportion to its numbers. Soon, the American public became familiar with the inner workings of various Radical Right organizations. There was, for example, the Minutemen, a group of some 2,400 patrioteers. Divided into about twenty-three guerrilla bands, the Minutemen intended to rely only on their firearms in the final battle against communism. In the meantime, they held "guerrilla warfare" seminars and often ran afoul of local firearm statutes. Another approach included the National Indignation Convention and Dr. Fred Schwarz's Christian Anti-Communist Crusade. Schwarz's widely televised anticommunist revivals pulled in up to 15,000 people, who came to see such stars as John Wayne and James Stewart and hear Schwarz's pronouncements on Americanism delivered in the twangy tones of his native Australia.

What became the most widely known element in the Radical Right movement began indirectly in a car traveling toward New York City in December, 1954. One of the passengers was Robert Welch, a candy manufacturer from Cambridge, Massachusetts, with a keen interest in Republican politics. On this rainy night in 1954, Welch, an unreconstructed Taft supporter, was telling his fellow travelers that Taft's 1952 conqueror, Eisenhower, had double-crossed conservative GOP candidates for the House and Senate in the recent congressional campaign. One rider asked Welch for a written account of these incredible views. Welch responded, and then later elaborated this written reply into a book entitled *The Politician*. Privately printed, the book's conclusion was that Dwight Eisenhower was "a dedicated conscious agent of the Communist conspiracy."

To combat further the grand machinations of the "Commies," Welch founded the John Birch Society in December, 1959. Welch's society took its name from a soldier from Macon, Georgia, who had been killed on patrol by the Chinese Communists—ten days after V-J Day—to become "the first casualty of World War III," a present reality for Welch and his Birchers. In this struggle against the Communists, the John Birch Society enlisted the services of a number of political notables, such as former State Department official Spruille Braden, T. Coleman Andrews, one-time Internal Revenue Service director and 1956 presidential candidate of the right-wing Constitution party, not to mention Clarence Manion, right-wing activist since being fired from the Eisenhower administration for his "orthodox" views.

The Birch Society's political first step came in early 1961, when it mounted a letter-writing campaign to demand Earl Warren's impeachment. Shortly thereafter, a John Birch Society beachhead on Capitol Hill was discovered as two California Republicans in the House—John Rousselot and Edgar Hiestand—confirmed they were Birchers. By the spring of 1962, the society had become a definite political factor in California, backing Assemblyman Joseph Shell in his GOP gubernatorial primary race against Richard Nixon, who had repudiated the organization. Despite Nixon's springtime victory over Shell and numerous other Birch Society casualties in the 1962 elections (Hiestand and Rousselot lost reelection bids), the society's membership rolls continued to swell on into 1964.

The widespread attention given to ultra-conservatism and to the John Birch Society in particular posed special problems for the Republican Right and other less fanatical conservatives. Although not directly related to resurgent conservatism among intellectuals and the young, these ultras shared major conservative fears regarding communism and big government. Hence, they had to be handled delicately. Robert Taft had always remained wary of the "nuts" on the fringe of the American Right, and now the danger seemed even greater, since the Republican Right of the early 1960s had so much to lose by a close identification with right-wing crazies. "This crowd can blow the whole bundle if we're not careful," admitted one Washington State GOP leader. But he went on to say: "If we can keep a balance, the party will come out stronger."[33]

Efforts to maintain some kind of balance came first at a political action conference by *Human Events* in February, 1962. Although the presence of chairman William Miller and House GOP campaign chief Robert Wilson pointed up the Republican attempt to capitalize on the new right-wing boom, the main theme of the meeting was that conservatives had to set realistic goals and pursue them in a reasonable manner. Texas senator John G. Tower declared that conservatives would never gain power by branding every adversary a "communist." Right-wing columnist Fulton Lewis warned right-wing extremists, "You're not going to get anymore to the right than Barry Goldwater."[34]

At the same time, John Birch Society founder Robert Welch came in for some sharp criticism. In February, 1962, the *National Review* stated that Welch was actually harming the anticommunist cause. Barry Goldwater specifically rebuked Welch in an unsolicited advertisement in the *National Review* suggesting that either Welch retire as society chairman or the Birchers regroup without their founder.

Ultimately, the major issue for conservative Republicans like Goldwater became not merely Robert Welch, but the entire John Birch Society and the Radical Right. Goldwater persistently maintained that the Birch Society was acting within its constitutional bounds and that he knew many Birchers who were fine American citizens. Still, with ultra-right leaders promoting Goldwater for president and an Old Guard warrior like Joseph Martin publicly branding the Arizonan an "extremist," the Radical Right problem would remain one that Barry Goldwater could never solve.[35]

One Republican who worked hard to keep this Radical Right issue alive was Governor Nelson Rockefeller of New York. Rockefeller had emerged an even more forceful spokesman for Eastern Republicanism than his predecessor, Thomas Dewey. According to Rockefeller, the nation's future political battles would be fought in the great urban areas, and the GOP had to appeal to city voters by offering expanded programs in housing, education, and welfare, as he had done in New York. Rockefeller Republicanism also embraced aggressive federal action in behalf of Negro civil rights—Rockefeller himself deriding the Kennedy administration's weak leadership in this area.

Many Right Wing Republicans saw "Rocky's" approach as typical "metoo Republicanism." Of course, conservative hostility toward Rockefeller was hardly new. Even before his 1958 election as governor of New York, Rockefeller's service under the Democrats had made him an "FDR pet" in the eyes of party hardliners.[36] Few GOP conservatives could forgive Rockefeller for his role in the Nixon-Rockefeller platform pact on the eve of the 1960 Republican national convention. Still more galling for Right Wing Republicans, Rockefeller, unlike Dewey, had genuine popular appeal. Rocky could rival John F. Kennedy as a political celebrity with a famous name, an engaging smile, plenty of cash for any presidential campaign, and an exciting campaign style. Soon after Nixon's presidential defeat in 1960, GOP officials around the country came to regard Rockefeller as the only Republican capable of beating JFK in 1964. There were periodic reports that Rocky's nomination drive was "unstoppable."

Goldwater, Rockefeller, and their advisors met regularly during the early Kennedy years to discuss major national issues and prevent any intraparty dogfights. Goldwater, Rocky's chief GOP rival, seemed to share the belief that Rockefeller was unstoppable and thought their talks were extremely valuable.[37] The meetings, in fact, had some effect on both Goldwater and Rockefeller as 1962 became 1963. When Goldwater remarked that Rockefeller was not "as liberal as people think," observers detected a possible mellowing on Goldwater's part. Reportedly, the Arizonan paved the way among conservative GOP professionals when Rocky toured the country in early 1963. Rockefeller, in turn began to sound increasingly conservative. In one Midwest swing, Rocky blistered the Kennedy administration and emphasized the importance of private property, individual initiative, and fiscal integrity in his own political creed. Echoing Eisenhower, the master of GOP homogenization, Rockefeller described the terms liberal and conservative as "meaningless and shopworn." He also publicly called Goldwater a "great" Republican.

Although Rockefeller's adjustment to conservative sensitivities did not diminish his high ratings in national opinion polls, there was, hanging over all of this, the public matter of the New York governor's private life. In November, 1961, Rockefeller had announced his separation and probable divorce from Mary Rockefeller, his wife of thirty years and the mother of his five children. GOP leaders expected this personal tragedy to have considerable impact on the governor's political future, divorce then being very rare among prospective presidential candidates. This situation was compounded when in May, 1963, shortly after his divorce was final, Rockefeller married Mrs. Margaretta "Happy" Murphy, an attractive young mother of four children who was herself a divorcee of only one month. Many GOP conservatives, who were already hostile to Rockefeller, now used this domestic situation as one more reason to oppose the New Yorker. Rockefeller, however, became so agitated by this new Right Wing obsession with his family life that, according to Goldwater, Rocky personally asked him to intervene with Right Wing Republicans on this matter.[38]

The unofficial Rockefeller campaign for the Republican nomination came to a standstill after the May 4 wedding ceremony. Rockefeller plunged drastically in several popular opinion surveys. Suddenly, Pennsylvania governor William Scranton and Michigan's George Romney were being mentioned as alternative GOP presidential possibilities. Against this backdrop, Rockefeller left on vacation in mid-July, 1963. Before departing, however, the governor reportedly told his aides that he was "off the unity kick" and would now run for the GOP presidential nomination as Rockefeller, and not a Goldwater clone.[39] He also left behind a 2,000-word statement for release on July 14—Bastille Day.

In this pronouncement, Rockefeller laid seige to the "Radical Right lunatic fringe," naming the John Birch Society and implicating Goldwater and the Republican Right. The Republican party, he warned, was in danger of subversion by a "radical well-financed, highly disciplined minority" that utterly rejected the heritage of Abraham Lincoln, Theodore Roosevelt, and Robert Taft. Rockefeller accused these "purveyors of hate and distrust" of having already used "ruthless, roughshod tactics of totalitarianism" to wrest control of the Young Republican convention weeks before in San Francisco.

The New York governor also found the GOP southern strategists talk of "writing off" the nation's industrial areas and minorities, specifically the Negro, to be "completely incredible." States' rights was just a "pretext" for Republican southern strategists. The "time for temporizing is over," Rockefeller declared.[40]

Rocky had clearly declared war on Goldwater. Although he never mentioned Goldwater's name in his Bastille Day remarks, the implications were obvious enough, and several days later Rockefeller said Goldwater was in danger of capture by these radical elements unless he quickly disavowed them. Goldwater, for his part, initially shrugged off Rocky's Bastille Day statement as the formal declaration of the governor's presidential candidacy. Still, Rockefeller's "double-cross" stung Goldwater, and he replied to Rocky's charges in subsequent weeks. Rockefeller, said Goldwater, was employing the old Democratic tactic of guilt by association—a statement that must have puzzled old McCarthy adversaries. The Arizonan repeated that right-wing groups like the John Birch Society were acting well within their constitutional rights and he would not disavow them. The "radical left" inside the government was a far greater menace than the "radical right" outside the government, Goldwater contended.

Goldwater's comments were mild compared with other Right Wing Republican responses to Rockefeller. Texas senator John G. Tower charged that Rockefeller had been "taken in" by liberal braintrusters whose only goal was GOP discord. Conservative Nebraska senator Carl Curtis exclaimed on the Senate floor that Rockefeller's Bastille Day statement typified the "self-serving tactics of a man desperately trying to retrieve his declining political fortunes."[41] Clearly, if Governor Rockefeller had gone "off the unity kick," the Republican Right had gone right along with him. Rocky's declaration of war on the Radical Right achieved few political gains for him and instead provoked already antagonistic GOP conservatives. His battle cry definitely placed him in the tradition of his New York predecessor and Right Wing *bête noire*, Tom Dewey. Like Tom Dewey before him, Rockefeller senselessly incited party conservatives, personalized the battle for the Republican party, and complicated his already formidable task of capturing the GOP nomination. Nevertheless, Rockefeller's declaration did point up Goldwater's and the Republican Right's vulnerability on the Radical Right issue.

Assessing future conservative chances shortly after the 1960 election, the *National Review*'s L. Brent Bozell warned the Republican Right against attaching too much importance to winning the Republican nomination under the "wrong circumstances"; party rivals might "set-up" Goldwater for a "we-told-you-so" defeat, Bozell wrote.[42] While such warnings overlooked the preference of party professionals for a popular presidential candidate who would help local candidates even if his cause were hopeless, periodic reports during the next few years stated that GOP chieftains would indeed "hand" Goldwater the nomination if JFK looked unbeatable.

Goldwater, for his part, remained both cautious and nonchalant about a possible run for the Republican presidential nomination. There was nothing paradoxical about this. Goldwater feared that a failed Goldwater presidential bid would damage the conservative cause. In addition, Goldwater displayed a "genuine reluctance" to become a presidential candidate. When asked to characterize his own activities regarding any presidential drive, Goldwater would merely say he was "just pooping around."[43]

Goldwater's easygoing approach was clearly not shared by the twenty-two Goldwater enthusiasts who met secretly at Chicago's Avenue Motel in October, 1961. This group (which included Steven Shadegg, manager of Goldwater's two Senate campaigns, F. Clifton White, a knowledgeable New York political pro, conservative congressman John Ashbrook of Ohio, and Donald Bruce of Indiana) would form the "nucleus" of the later draft-Goldwater movement. They unanimously wanted Goldwater atop the Republican ticket in 1964, but wisely—if somewhat fictitiously—dedicated themselves instead to building up a nationwide conservative force in the Republican party. The Avenue Motel participants chose F. Clifton White to head the operation, which took no name and operated inconspicuously out of Suite 3505 of the Chanin Building in New York.

For a time, the "3505 Project" struggled along, a virtual one-man show. White traveled through twenty-eight states in the spring of 1962 and attended all RNC meetings. He gathered Republican convention delegate lists back to 1948 and prepared a synopsis of laws governing delegate selection for the 1964 Republican convention. White also established ties with the Young Republicans and the National Federation of Republican Women. He even dipped into his own savings to keep the one-room operation afloat.

But this hush-hush movement was growing. A meeting at Chicago's Essex Inn Motel in early December, 1962, included fifty-five participants from almost every major state. Although the 1962 elections had proved disappointing for most conservatives, the mood of the Essex motel conferees was surprisingly upbeat. White, for instance, saw the fall election as a "stand-off," a fairly respectable GOP performance, considering it took place during the Cuban missile crisis.[44] The group believed that GOP troubles in California and New York demonstrated that the party's future depended on making a strong conservative bid in the South, the Midwest, and the mountain states. As for Project 3505, the leaders felt that the time had now come to mount a presidential campaign for standard-bearer Barry Goldwater—and the Essex Inn conclave immediately committed itself to his candidacy.

Project 3505 organizers had reason to be pleased. But then word of the Essex Inn meeting leaked to the press, and CBS television crews quickly descended on the Chicago meeting room. There was an instant outcry from the

New York Herald Tribune, which condemned the "bad timing, narrow motives and poor politics" of the Chicago conspirators. "Neither the plotting to promote Senator Goldwater for President," observed that voice of liberal Republicanism, "nor the conspiracy to block Governor Rockefeller contributes to the health or harmony of the party."[45] Perhaps the contemporary concern over the Radical Right made such a reaction understandable, but the *Tribune* was either naive or extremely cynical in its outrage. After all, the Chicago conservatives were hardly the first Republicans to lay plans for future political action.

But even Goldwater was furious. The Chicago revelations surprised and embarrassed him. Goldwater had long known—and approved—of Project 3505's existence. But he had assumed that the group was working solely to further GOP conservatism and he claimed to have no idea that Clifton White was a paid organizer. When White met with Goldwater in mid-January, 1963, the senator complained vehemently about those taking liberties with his "political neck." White returned from his appointment, according to *National Review* publisher William Rusher, "looking for a job."[46] Afterward, however, the Chicago "conspirators" tried to interest Goldwater in the organization they were developing. Their original purpose *had* been to develop general GOP conservatism, they assured him. But that phase of the operation had passed. It was now time to begin the 1964 Republican nomination race. Desperately trying to capture their candidate, Rusher and White portrayed Goldwater as the last great hope of the conservative cause. "I am profoundly convinced," Rusher wrote to Goldwater, "that the organization we have built is very probably the last one that will ever seek, in a serious and systematic way, to turn the GOP into more conservative channels."[47] Goldwater held firm. For the moment, he was *not* a candidate for the GOP presidential nomination and was opposed to any draft movement.

The mood was downcast when the executive committee of Project 3505 met on February 17, 1963, in Chicago. The group had to gamble. They decided to draft Goldwater without his consent. Their only hope was that Goldwater would not publicly repudiate them. To reduce that risk, the group named an important party figure, Texas state GOP boss Peter O'Donnell, as chairman of the new Draft Goldwater Committee. F. Clifton White would serve as executive director, and senators Curtis and Tower and Arizona congressman John Rhodes would round up support on Capitol Hill.

On April 8, 1963, the National Draft Goldwater Committee officially opened for business. There was no repudiation by Goldwater. But neither was there any encouragement, as Goldwater studiously avoided Draft Goldwater headquarters and its July Fourth rally in Washington, D.C. "Goldwater's not running the conservatives," the *New York Times*'s James Reston wrote in the fall of 1963, "the conservatives are running him."[48]

But Goldwater was ignoring neither the Draft Goldwater developments nor the larger Goldwater boom. Since early in 1963, Goldwater and other Republicans had come to believe that Kennedy could be defeated in 1964. As Rockefeller's appeal fell in national surveys, Goldwater's strength rose during the spring of 1963. Gallup polls indicated that no conservative Republican had measured higher since Robert Taft in 1952. Meanwhile, the Arizonan's hold on the GOP professionals grew tighter. "I'm a poker player," he remarked in the fall of 1963, "and I'm sitting with a pair and I don't know what the draw will be. If it's a good one I'll say yes."[49]

All political bets were off after the assassination of President John F. Kennedy on November 22, 1963. Among its many meanings for the nation, Kennedy's murder in Dallas was certainly a political development. Ironically, it set off a wave of anti-Radical Right sentiment. Moreover, although Republicans pledged to observe a moratorium on politicking, Kennedy's tragic departure only intensified speculation regarding the 1964 presidential sweepstakes.

Goldwater had lost more than a respected and friendly adversary in JFK; Kennedy's death drastically upset the senator's political plans. By late October, the Arizonan had determined to make the run. Now a "depressed" Goldwater immediately ordered the Draft Goldwater movement to suspend all activities. Meanwhile, polls registered a dramatic drop in Goldwater support. One state GOP boss from the Midwest best summed up this new anti-Goldwater sentiment: "He just doesn't look the same against Johnson that he did against Kennedy."[50] Goldwater's political strategy, of course, had rested on capturing the South. But with Lyndon Johnson, a Texan, sitting in the White House, the South was "up for grabs." LBJ could not be defeated, Goldwater confided to his wife.[51]

Goldwater, therefore, decided to "recognize reality" and skip the 1964 race. He met on December 8 with friends and advisors such as Arizona associate Dean Burch, Draft Goldwater chairman Peter O'Donnell, and senators Norris Cotton of New Hampshire and Carl Curtis of Nebraska. "Our cause is lost," said Goldwater, who then outlined his reasons for staying out of the 1964 Republican race. Senator Cotton protested. Nothing had really changed, he claimed. The issues were still the same. Cotton then appealed to Goldwater's sense of duty to both the conservative cause and the country.

Goldwater made no commitment on that December day, but Cotton's argument did it. Goldwater ultimately decided to run because of his feeling of responsibility to the conservative movement. Actually, Goldwater had little choice if he entertained any hopes of ever becoming president. An organization was in place, soldiers were ready to march, and there was the much-publicized "wave of conservatism" already sweeping through the country. So, although the specific political signs were far from favorable for Goldwater, he elected to take the plunge.

US News and World Report had good reason to state that "Barry Goldwater has climbed on his own bandwagon" after the senator formally announced his candidacy for the GOP presidential nomination on January 3, 1964. Standing on the patio of his hilltop home in Phoenix, this latest Right Wing Republican presidential aspirant promised to make his campaign "an engagement of principle." "I will not change my beliefs to win votes," Goldwater declared. "I will offer a choice, not an echo."[52]

10

Extremism in the Pursuit of Liberty Is No Vice

Senator Barry Goldwater's bid for the presidency in 1964 was in trouble from the very beginning.

Goldwater and his handlers, initially regarding the primaries as "political booby traps," had decided to stay out of all such 1964 contests except California's. But Goldwater was finally persuaded to enter the 1964 opener in New Hampshire, where his prospects seemed especially bright. Early private polls had Goldwater the overwhelming favorite in New Hampshire, and his forces had put together a star-studded delegate lineup that included moderate senator Norris Cotton and Doloris Bridges, widow of the Granite State's rock-ribbed Republican Styles Bridges. Goldwater also had the support of the state's leading newspaper, the ultra-conservative Manchester *Union-Leader*. As a result, the Goldwater camp anticipated a four-to-one New Hampshire triumph for their man.

But problems developed for the Goldwater team as the New Hampshire primary campaign got underway. Disappointed at failing to enlist former RNC chairman Leonard Hall—"the only real pro in the Republican Party"—to head his campaign, Goldwater called on Arizonan Denison Kitchel.[1] In doing so, Goldwater slighted such draft Goldwater organizers as F. Clifton White and Peter O'Donnell and opted for personal familiarity over professional competence. Kitchel sadly lacked national political experience and tended to rely only on former Arizona associates.

Furthermore, Goldwater's apparent advantages had a way of turning into political liabilities. The Goldwater camp quickly discovered the pitfalls inherent in the support of the vitriolic William Loeb, publisher of the Manchester *Union-Leader*. Loeb's paper so savaged Rockefeller—"the wife-swapper"—that Goldwater urged Loeb to soften his language. Conversely, when the senator attacked Teamster's Union boss Jimmy Hoffa, he ran up against Loeb, who had once received a loan from the union's Central State Pension Fund.

In another campaign twist, Goldwater's extreme candor, so disarming and helpful in his rise to power, now caused many embarrassments and contributed to the "shoot-from-the-hip" charge, a charge that dogged Goldwater throughout 1964. As early as mid-January, former Draft Goldwater chairman Peter O'Donnell urged Goldwater to "control the issues by only discussing those things which you have considered in advance."[2] Despite O'Donnell's advice, Goldwater gave few prepared speeches in New Hampshire and instead took questions from audiences, speaking in great detail on almost all issues and remaining staunchly conservative—and equally controversial. In the process, Goldwater came under intense fire for calling American missiles "undependable," for proposing that Social Security be made voluntary (which the press interpreted as a move to end the program), and for allegedly suggesting that NATO commanders control nuclear weapons. Sighed pro-Goldwater New Hampshire senator Cotton, "He seems to make a fetish of frankness."[3] Eventually, Goldwater handlers were forced to scale down their New Hampshire predictions to about a 40 percent share of the vote.

Was history repeating itself? Goldwater conservatives could well wonder as the New Hampshire returns came in. In the end, the Arizonan took 23 percent of the New Hampshire Republican vote to edge out New York governor Nelson Rockefeller at 20 percent. Just as in 1952, an attractive personality who was on overseas assignment and had waged no campaign in the Granite State won a stunning victory. Henry Cabot Lodge gained 35.4 percent of the New Hampshire Republican vote and complete control of the state's fourteen-member delegation with a write-in campaign spearheaded by some old 1952 Eisenhower backers.

Right Wing Republicans saw Lodge as the architect of Taft's 1952 defeat, the foremost apologist of Modern Republicanism, and a lazy campaigner as Nixon's vice-presidential runningmate in 1960. Moreover, in becoming the Kennedy administration's ambassador to South Vietnam, Lodge had implicated the GOP in a potential foreign policy disaster and thus lived up to the Republican Right's nickname for him—Henry Sabotage.

Conservative quarters brushed aside Lodge's New Hampshire victory and concentrated on the damage inflicted on Rockefeller. But Goldwater also came in for his share of criticism. The *National Review*'s Washington insider, "Quincy," wrote that the senator had "bumbled and fumbled," leaving New Hampshire voters unsure of his policy stands. Goldwater had to learn, "Quincy" added, the difference between leading the faithful and reaching out to undecided yet essentially like-minded voters. Goldwater, for his part, conceded he had "goofed up somewhere."[4]

Although Goldwater's New Hampshire loss heightened suspicions of Goldwater's nonelectability, Lodge's victory, coupled with his decision to remain in Saigon, benefited Goldwater by keeping moderate Republican, anti-Goldwater forces divided and off balance. The New Hampshire primary returns also prompted needed changes in the Goldwater nomination drive. The loss galvanized the Goldwater team and resulted in a more efficient organization in the future. Former Draft Goldwater director F. Clifton White was promoted to "co-ordinator of field operations." The candidate, too, began to accept advice more willingly. He made fewer campaign appearances and took greater care when he did speak. Moreover, the Goldwater organization began to rely more heavily on television and radio to bring the Goldwater message directly to the voter, thus by-passing, according to the *National Review*'s William S. Rickenbacker, the "Eastern Establishment" media that insisted on "distorting and quashing the Goldwater news."[5]

Primary wins followed. On April 13, Illinois Republicans gave Goldwater 64 percent of their vote compared with 26 percent for Maine's Senator Margaret Chase Smith. The Arizonan picked up about 40 of the 48 Illinois convention delegates at stake that day. A month later in the Nebraska primary, Goldwater triumphed over Ambassador Lodge and former Vice-President Nixon, both organized write-in candidates.

Although primary news monopolized newspaper headlines during the 1964 preconvention period, only sixteen states selected convention delegates this way. The vast majority of GOP delegates to the 1964 San Francisco convention were to be chosen in state caucuses and conventions, and Goldwater strategists had long concentrated their organizational efforts in these states. Here Goldwater had real strength.

The Goldwater organization, under F. Clifton White's direction, harnessed tireless Goldwater partisans, who inundated local organizations and eventually came to control state Republican parties. Consequently, Goldwater collected 47 convention delegates even before the New Hampshire polls opened. A week after his Granite State setback, South Carolina Republicans awarded the Arizonan its full sixteen-member delegation. By mid-May, after Goldwater victories in state conventions in Kansas, Nevada, Oklahoma, Wyoming, and Washington, the Goldwater camp was claiming over 290 delegates and had even more "sleepers" (secret pro-Goldwater delegates) in tactical reserve.[6]

Goldwater's overwhelmingly successful state convention tactics could not be used in California. Here success in a winner-take-all primary on June 3 remained crucial to the Goldwater nomination strategy. Although White calculated that Goldwater could still win a first-ballot nomination without California, the candidate himself stated publicly that a loss there would rule him out as the Republican nominee. The Arizonan's Illinois and Nebraska primary victories had failed to impress numerous party professionals and political pundits; his Nebraska primary performance had even disappointed

Goldwater himself. National opinion polls continued to show the senator with only second-rank support. Goldwater still had to prove himself as a popular vote-getter. Recognizing the importance of a California victory, Goldwater pulled out of the Oregon primary in order to devote full time to the campaign to the south, lifting Rocky's campaign with an Oregon victory and huge amounts of favorable publicity.

In California, Goldwater stuck with his post–New Hampshire campaign tactics. The Goldwater message mainly came to voters over the airwaves. Indeed, drastic cutbacks in the number of Goldwater campaign stops prompted William F. Knowland, the nominal head of Goldwater's California drive, to threaten twice to resign. Goldwater also watered down the content of his message. He assured California voters that he had no plans to make Social Security voluntary. Nor did he now advocate selling the entire TVA. Although Goldwater did get entangled on the issue of the use of low-yield atomic bombs in Vietnam, detailed policy proposals generally gave way to "Fourth of July Oratory."

While not as slick as the well-heeled Rockefeller operation, the Goldwater forces were well organized and had been hard at work since March—registering voters and marshalling Goldwater activists down to the precinct level. "Zeal" was the watchword of the Goldwater drive in California, especially in the ultra-conservative strongholds of Los Angeles. Another important factor in Goldwater's California crusade was "luck." On the weekend before the California vote, Nelson Rockefeller's wife gave birth to a son and this highlighted the Rockefeller divorce issue, an issue that some Goldwater partisans were exploiting with the slogan, "Do You Want a Leader or a Lover in the White House?"

"Do You Want a Leader or a Loner?" countered the Rockefeller camp, attempting to cast Rocky as the representative of mainstream Republicanism against Goldwater's extremism. Lodge partisans, having failed to get the ambassador's name on the ballot, were in fact openly supporting Rockefeller in California. Even so, attempts for a full-blown stop-Goldwater coalition ultimately failed in California. Responding to Rockefeller campaign literature picturing the New Yorker as their California stand-in, Nixon, Romney, and Governor William Scranton of Pennsylvania all publicly announced their neutrality in the California clash.

Nevertheless, stop-Goldwater talk persisted, with former President Dwight D. Eisenhower being at the center of such speculation. Goldwater-Eisenhower political differences were, of course, well known. Goldwater had earlier characterized Eisenhower's administration as little more than a "dime-store New Deal" and had met the possible presidential future of Ike's brother Milton with the remark, "one Eisenhower in a decade is enough." On the New Hampshire hustings in January, Goldwater had stated that he definitely included the Eisenhower administration in his charges regarding "30 years of fiscal irresponsibility."[7]

Eisenhower, for his part, distrusted Goldwater's "shoot-from-the-hip" approach. Still, Goldwater received an Eisenhower pat on the back upon entering the GOP nomination race, as did all other Republican presidential aspirants. Hibernating in Palm Springs, California, Ike seemed satisfied to play the benign, hands-off elder statesman and a lot of golf, activities encouraged by former administration associates like postmaster General Arthur Summerfield and treasury secretary George Humphrey, who were both Goldwater enthusiasts.

As the preconvention campaign heated up, however, Ike's anti-Goldwater associates—his brother Milton, former Minnesota governor Elmer Anderson, and Walter Thayer of the *New York Herald Tribune,* for example—urged him to take a more active role in the GOP nomination struggle. In the end they prevailed—to a degree. On May 25, almost a week before the California balloting, Ike described his "ideal" GOP presidential candidate for 1964 in an article in Thayer's paper. The *New York Herald Tribune,* in turn, released Ike's piece to the *New York Times* as well as to the national wire service.

While mentioning no names, Eisenhower stressed that his kind of candidate should support both the 1956 and 1960 GOP platforms. The former president underscored the importance of support for the United Nations and civil rights, and he especially praised the GOP congressional leadership for its support of President Johnson's civil rights bill then being debated on Capitol Hill. Goldwater, of couse, was known to oppose this legislation, and Eisenhower's profile generally seemed to rule out Goldwater as an Ike-approved standard-bearer in 1964. The *Tribune* left no doubt about this, running Eisenhower's piece along with an article by its national political correspondent Roscoe Drummond, who flatly made the point.

Out in California, Rockefeller rushed to stress his past support for the Eisenhower administration and the 1956 and 1960 GOP platforms. Already worried by Rockefeller's large and enthusiastic California crowds, the Goldwater camp was jolted by the news out of New York. Goldwater, himself, gamely noted the similarity between his foreign policy and the old Eisenhower-Dulles approach. Although Goldwater refused to say that Eisenhower's portrait was a planned anti-Goldwater attack, he did charge that a "mysterious clique in the East" had prevailed on Ike to write the portrait article. Further, the Arizonan subsequently appeared at one campaign stop with an arrow tucked under his arm, giving the profile appearance of having been shot in the back—a pose that would show "some of the problems I've had in the last few days."[8]

Meanwhile, Eisenhower, after a call from his pro-Goldwater friend

George Humphrey, professed to be startled by press interpretations that his portrait "read Goldwater out of the GOP." Whatever Ike intended, his portrait actually had little political impact. According to one survey, 76 percent of the California voters had no knowledge of Ike's profile, let alone the reasons behind it.

In the end, Goldwater won the important June 3 California primary and full control of the state's 86-member delegation. The Goldwater organization was jubilant. Yet Goldwater's slim victory margin—51.4 percent to Rockefeller's 48.6 percent—could be attributed mainly to the zeal of Goldwater's California workers. Doubts remained about Goldwater as a *national* vote-getter.

Although some GOP moderates now wnated to make peace with Goldwater in order to gain some say in the upcoming GOP campaign, the Republican party's nomination struggle was far from over. Stop-Goldwater forces were only regrouping after the California primary. Former Vice-President Richard M. Nixon emerged as their new champion by saying it would be a "tragedy" if Goldwater's views went unchallenged and unrepudiated within the Republican party. Goldwater thought Nixon sounded "more like Harold Stassen everyday," but other Republicans saw political doom in Goldwater's prospective nomination.

Any hopes of averting a GOP debacle, however, rested not with Nixon, but with Governor William W. Scranton of Pennsylvania. Here was a fresh political face. Elected congressman in 1960 and governor in 1962, Scranton had wide political appeal and impeccable GOP credentials. High among Scranton's accomplishments as Pennsylvania governor was the unification of the long-fractured Keystone State GOP. Politically, his dead-center Republicanism placed him closer to Ike than almost any other GOP figure. As Scranton himself said, "I am a liberal on civil rights, a conservative on fiscal policies and an internationalist on foreign affairs."[9] Like Ike, Scranton also lacked the all-consuming political lust of the normal presidential aspirant. Unlike Ike, however, Scranton needed this to get ahead.

Encouraged by Scranton's Harrisburg advisors, some GOP leaders had been expressing interest in Scranton since early 1963. But the governor himself had sidestepped all serious presidential talk by saying only that he would accept a "sincere and honest draft." Initially, no wide gulf separated Scranton and Goldwater. Scranton served in the Air Force Reserve under Goldwater, who considered Scranton his only "friend" among possible GOP presidential contenders. In fact, Goldwater wanted Scranton as his vice-presidential runningmate and even considered making some springtime arrangement with the Keystone State governor to lock up the nomination. Scranton, for his part, stated after the California primary that he could see no "basic differences" between Goldwater and himself, an admission that left the stop-Goldwater movement gasping, with the Republican national convention in San Francisco only weeks away. [10]

On June 6, however, the sagging stop-Goldwater movement temporarily revived when news broke of an Eisenhower-Scranton meeting in Gettysburg, Pennsylvania. Scranton claimed afterward that Ike had asked him to make himself "more available" for the GOP presidential nomination. At that same moment, Pennsylvania senator Hugh Scott also announced the formation of a Congressional Committee to Elect Scranton President.

The Eisenhower-Scranton parley, coming as it did on the weekend of the National Governors' Conference in Cleveland, fired speculation about possible anti-Goldwater maneuvers by GOP governors. Would Republican governors help torpedo Goldwater in 1964 as they had done to Taft in Houston in 1952? Goldwater partisans had reason to fear. Not only were liberal-moderate GOP governors trying to draft a progressive declaration of Republican principles, but Michigan's Governor George Romney was telling colleagues that he would battle Goldwater's "suicidal destruction of the Republican Party."

At the conference, Arizona governor Paul Fannin (one of the three outright Goldwater backers among the sixteen Republican governors) quickly stepped in to quash any statement of "progressive" principles, and Oregon governor Mark Hatfield, though no Goldwater backer, publicly ridiculed Romney's belated bravado before the other Republican chief executives. That left only Scranton. He had departed Gettysburg convinced that Ike was urging him to enter the GOP race and on Sunday arrived in Cleveland ready to announce his presidential candidacy on that morning's "Face the Nation" television broadcast.

Goldwater's handlers had feared that the Gettysburg meeting might spark a pro-Scranton move, and Clifton White had already called George Humphrey at his home in Cleveland. Humphrey, a strong Goldwater backer, was to be Eisenhower's host while the former president also visited Cleveland for the governor's conference. According to White, Humphrey telephoned Eisenhower on Saturday evening and bluntly told the former president that it would be embarrassing to entertain him at his home if Ike were simultaneously masterminding a dump-Goldwater campaign. When Ike later arrived in Cleveland, Humphrey never left his side.

One result of host Humphrey's careful shepherding of Eisenhower was the former president's speech to the Republican governors on Monday, which was seen as a call for GOP unity behind Barry Goldwater. An even more important Eisenhower call had taken place a day earlier. Two hours before Scranton's "Face the Nation" broadcast, Ike got in touch with Scranton and told the Pennsylvanian that he hoped that he (Ike) had not conveyed the wrong impression at Gettysburg the day before. Ike wanted Scranton to join no "cabal" against any other GOP contender. Scranton was devastated. He folded his announcement statement and put it in his coat pocket, where it remained. On "Face the Nation," Scranton gave a clumsy and confusing performance, even saying that Goldwater would be an accept-able and electable GOP nominee.

But Scranton, now labeled the "Hamlet of Harrisburg," and certain stop-Goldwater Republicans were not finished—or did not realize that they were finished. A few days after the Cleveland governors' conference, the Senate voted 71 to 29 to invoke cloture and end a 75-day filibuster on the currently pending Johnson civil rights legislation. Goldwater joined Repub-licans John Williams of Delaware and Carl Curtis of Nebraska in opposing cloture. In reality Goldwater had taken a stand against the civil rights bill. (Goldwater voted against the measure shortly thereafter.) In Harrisburg, Scranton, humiliated only days earlier, was "sick" over Goldwater's stand and gave up all hope of reasoning with the Arizonan. Despite the odds against nomination, Scranton decided that some Republican had to cham-pion the principles of Lincoln against Goldwater's conservatism.

On June 12, therefore, Pennsylvania governor William Scranton declared himself a candidate for the Republican presidential nomination, a "progressive Republican" who offered a "real choice," and not an "echo of fear and reaction." The Keystone State governor's chances in his battle against Goldwater's "easy answer" and "dimestore feudalism" were always extremely doubtful at best. But one result of the Scranton crusade was decidedly not. The Republican convention would be, predicted one top Re-publican, "the bloodiest damn convention you've seen in a long, long time."[11]

Goldwater perfunctorily welcomed Scranton to the GOP nomination race, but privately he seethed. Distressed by the possible harm of Scranton's "destructive attacks" and the "Goldwater can't win" arguments, the Arizo-nan blamed Scranton's late entry on the eastern "Republican Establish-ment," specifically Richard Nixon. The GOP's eastern wing did indeed rally around Scranton. Three days after Scranton's announcement, Rockefeller withdrew from the nomination race and threw his support to Scranton—"a candidate," said Rocky, "in the mainstream of American political thought and action."[12] The New York governor estimated that he could deliver over 85 of New York's 92 delegates to the Pennsylvanian, as well as his 18 Ore-gon supporters. The National Draft Lodge committee quickly got behind Scranton, and Lodge himself returned from Saigon at the end of June to command the Scranton forces.

Goldwater's actual vote against the civil rights bill made the clamor of anti-Goldwater Republicans all the more shrill. But no Scranton delegate boom ensued. It was too late for that, as most Republican leaders realized. Signs of Goldwater delegate strength abounded. Many former Rockefeller delegates were reportedly slipping into the Goldwater column. The New Jersey delegation, which was known to favor Scranton, refused to make an outright commitment to the Keystone State governor. And in spite of Scranton's personal pleas, Senator John Williams of Delaware dropped out as a favorite-son candidate and came out for Goldwater.

Throughout this maneuvering, the Goldwater force remained intact. Not only did Goldwater delegates hold solid for the Arizonan, but the senator's bandwagon kept rolling along. Scranton still hoped that Illinois senator Everett Dirksen would become a source of anti-Goldwater support. Dirksen, the GOP Senate minority leader, had lined up Republicans for the 1964 Civil Rights Act and had publicly ridiculed Goldwater's opposition to the measure. Now, Scranton urged Dirksen to stand as the "Land of Lincoln's" favorite son. But Dirksen gave Scranton no commitment. The rabid grassroots Goldwater sentiment in Illinois had definitely impressed the Senate minority leader.

Dirksen's deficiencies as a political kamikaze became apparent when the Illinois convention delegation met in Chicago on June 30. After a personal Scranton pitch to the delegation, Dirksen led the Illinois Republicans in voting unanimously to back Goldwater. A day later Dirksen confirmed that he would nominate Barry Goldwater at the GOP convention in San Francisco. The Republican party had ridden "the grey ghost of me-too" for too long, claimed Dirksen, who unlike Goldwater had often supported JFK and LBJ. "That old boy's got an antenna three feet long," said Goldwater.[13] Whatever the minority leader's reasons, Goldwater managers termed Dirksen's support the "clincher," and they now claimed 690 first-ballot votes, with only 655 needed to nominate.

As for Scranton, the real knockout blow came on the eve of the San Francisco gathering when Ohio governor James Rhodes, who now believed that Goldwater could win the presidency on the strength of an urban backlash vote in the North, urged the Pennsylvania governor to pull out of the race and join Goldwater on the Republican ticket. Then Rhodes freed the Ohio delegation from its favorite-son commitment to him and endorsed Goldwater. A Buckeye stampede to Goldwater at the convention appeared likely.

San Francisco proved a curious jumble of carnival and conflict. As the Republicans gathered in July, 1964, there was little of the outright physical hostility that had marked the Taft-Eisenhower political slugfest in 1952. While a seething subsurface bitterness existed, no factional tug-of-war was forecast. The Goldwater forces had the delegates—overwhelmingly—and this fact colored the atmosphere in the Cow Palace and in the city's hotel lobbies. Most Republicans had come to San Francisco anticipating the final triumph of Barry Goldwater and the Republican Right Wing.

San Francisco was Goldwater's during convention week. Clay busts of the Arizona senator sold for $65 at one local hotel. The city's jammed cable cars shared street space with muletrains, complete with little boys in ten-gallon hats and girls in sombreros and tasseled boots. At the senator's hospitality suite, grown-up Goldwater gals in cowboy outfits dispensed "Gold Water"—"the right drink for the conservative taste." But not all was convivial. On Sunday, 25,000 to 40,000 people demonstrated against Goldwater's stand on civil rights in a parade sponsored by the Congress on Racial Equality and attended by baseball star Jackie Robinson. All week long, civil rights demonstrators picketed outside the Cow Palace, while inside the flag-draped arena a silhouette of Lincoln hung.

Confidence and communications distinguished the Goldwater camp. A final preconvention Gallup poll that showed the senator trailing Scranton (60 percent to 34 percent among the nation's Republicans) worried Goldwater handlers not at all. Goldwater had the convention delegates, 730 to 800 of them, according to Goldwater advisors. Scranton's talk of stopping Goldwater on the first ballot was just convention gabble, as even Scranton had to know. Basically, all the Goldwater camp had to do was avoid making any major mistakes. To guarantee a smooth-running convention, the Goldwater organization installed a communications network of hitherto unmatched technological sophistication and expense. Years before, faulty organization had worked against Right Wing Republican Robert Taft's presidential drives. Goldwaterites would not make a similar mistake.

The 1964 Goldwater effort conjured up memories of Taft in yet another way. A memorandum circulated by the Goldwater high command entitled "Possible Opposition Tactics" showed that Right Wing Republicans still remembered the Eisenhower coup of 1952 with deep bitterness. Goldwater managers now dredged up all the machinations—"threats and cajolery," business and financial favors, blackmail, bullying and spying—that the Eisenhower camp had used "shamelessly" in Chicago to "rob" Taft of the nomination. "The Eastern wrecking crew of '52 is back in almost identical form," this Goldwater camp memo stated. "The 1952 violent tactics were successful against Bob Taft. . . . This time it will be much tougher." William F. Knowland publicly alerted Goldwater supporters to the probable "Super Madison Avenue Approach" of the Scranton operation.[14]

The first Scranton ploy was far less subtle. Desperately searching for some disruptive "incident" on the eve of the San Francisco parley, Scranton decided to challenge Goldwater to a debate before the entire convention. Written by a young aide, the "Scranton letter" characterized Goldwater delegates as "little more than chickens whose necks will be wrung at will." It went on to accuse Goldwater himself of "casually prescribing" nuclear warfare, "irresponsibility in the serious question of racial holocaust," and being the dupe of "radical elements." "In short," the Scranton letter concluded, "Goldwaterism has come to stand for a whole crazy-quilt collection of absurd and dangerous positions that would be soundly repudiated by the American people in November."[15]

Receiving Scranton's challenge on Sunday, the day before the GOP convention was to begin, Goldwater was "boiling mad," despite White's assurances that it would increase his first-ballot total to at least 1,000 votes. Having photocopied the letter for distribution to the convention delegates, Goldwater returned it to Scranton, saying he did not believe the governor had written it. Goldwater naturally declined Scranton's "ridiculous" invitation to debate. Scranton, for his part, had never seen the letter and said so the next day. The Pennsylvania governor also conceded that the challenge was too strongly worded. But Scranton accepted full responsibility for the letter and refused to apologize to Goldwater. In the end, Scranton's literary efforts proved not only to be a disaster for his own nomination, but also for Goldwater and the Republican party. No matter how much Scranton suffered, his broadside helped to fasten further a distorted image on Goldwater, the prospective Republican standard-bearer. Lyndon Johnson and the Democrats should have paid for such publicity.

Actually, the Scranton letter was the result of the failure of party moderates to create any "incident" in the Platform Committee procedures of the previous week. Scranton forces had hoped to nail down certain liberal platform planks that Goldwater would find unacceptable; some Goldwater delegates might then desert him for Scranton. Pursuing this strategy, Scranton had appeared before the Platform Committee and had delineated eleven major issues—civil rights, extremism, and Social Security—on which he differed dramatically with the Arizona senator.

Goldwater strategists, in turn, were determined not to hand the Scranton forces any real issue over the GOP platform, and the pro-Goldwater Platform Committee members expressed a willingness to make enough compromises so that continued squabbling by Scranton forces would look like nitpicking. The committee subsequently accepted moderate Scranton language on planks dealing with the United Nations, foreign aid, and Social Security but rejected Scranton planks on civil rights, extremism, presidential control of nuclear weapons, and a national right-to-work law.

Platform Committee moderates naturally complained about the Goldwater camp's "steamroller" and "Gestapo tactics," and proceeded to take their platform fight to the convention floor. On Tuesday evening, the long party platform was droned from the Cow Palace rostrum, as Goldwater managers got the convention through the peak television viewing hours in most of the nation without incident. Following the platform presentation, however, Scranton lieutenant Hugh Scott stepped forward to offer an "anti-extremism" plank that singled out the Ku Klux Klan and the John Birch Society. Not only were many Goldwater delegates offended that eastern Republicans regarded them as political extremists, but 100 of the 1,300 Republican delegates at San Francisco were bonafide Birchers, according to a society spokesman.[16]

Boos filled the Cow Palace as Scott made his proposal. Then, Governor Nelson Rockefeller came forward to speak for the plank against extremism. The Cow Palace erupted. Boos, hisses, catcalls, and cries of "We Want Barry" filled the hall as Rocky excoriated the infiltration and takeover of established political organizations by communist and Nazi methods. At points, Rocky could not go on—a martyrdom Goldwater managers thought he enjoyed.[17] Convention chairman Thruston Morton pounded the gavel in a futile attempt to maintain order.

In their command trailer, Goldwater managers ordered regional directors to stop the booing. But the dazzling Goldwater communications system proved useless. Except for some noise making in the Texas delegation, the major commotion came from the galleries, from rabble-rousers unknown to the Goldwater command. When this was determined, Goldwater operatives dispatched messengers to the galleries to try to stop the harmful racket.

The uproar ended, but not before the factional hostility was driven out into the open. When the convention voted, it gave a "thunderous no" to Scott's plank condemning the KKK and the Birch Society. Then, wanting no appearance of weakness, Goldwater convention managers directed their forces to vote down a mild proposal by Michigan's George Romney that decried extremism without singling out specific organizations. San Francisco Republicans also crushed other Scranton moves to broaden the platform's civil rights plank and to reaffirm presidential control over nuclear weapons. Finally, at 12:36 A.M., after eight hours of debate and contention, the convention adopted—without amendment—the Platform Committee's draft.

Goldwater remarked that the unamended platform merely reflected the Republican party's new "conservative majority."[18] The 1964 GOP platform did mark the changes in the Republican party since 1960, although it was hardly emphatic enough for some Goldwater zealots. On civil rights, for example, the 1960 platform had called for "vigorous enforcement" of existing civil rights statutes. The 1964 civil rights plank rather weakly pledged the "full implementation and faithful execution" of the Civil Rights Act of 1964 but stood against "inverse discrimination." The 1964 platform also backed away from the social-welfare and education commitments of the earlier document. The 1964 planks on defense and foreign policy betrayed a greater militance than Republicans had had in 1960. At that time, Republicans had termed military superiority an impossibility in the nuclear age. In 1964 Republicans pledged to achieve military supremacy. Further, the 1960 platform had expressed a faith in international negotiation that the 1964 document seemed to preclude. While not as nationalistic and aggressive as some earlier Goldwater foreign policy pronouncements, the 1964 Republican platform called for the "eventual liberation" of Communist-dominated regimes via peaceful means and for the recognition of a Cuban government in exile, as well as for aid for Cuban "freedom fighters." The aim of American foreign policy under the Republicans would be, declared the 1964 San Francisco statement, "victory."

If the 1964 Republican platform was no ringing right-wing manifesto, its calls for less government at home and victory abroad at least offered "A Choice Not an Echo." This fact was also underscored by the voting for the nomination on Wednesday evening which, at the completion of the first ballot, gave Goldwater 883 votes to Scranton's 214. Rockefeller held on to 114 votes and George Romney, 41. Scranton then came to the podium and asked all Republicans to rally round Goldwater. The Cow Palace throng whooped, shrieked, bellowed, and howled. A Right Wing Republican had captured the GOP nomination at last.

The Republican nominee still had to win over his entire party if there was any hope of driving Lyndon Johnson out of the White House. Goldwater lost no time in muffing every opportunity to do so. His first major blunder was his choice of a vice-presidential runningmate, Representative William E. Miller, who had taken over for Thruston Morton as RNC boss in June, 1961. A cocky, dapper little man given to grey homburgs and cigarette holders, this upstate New York congressman was sharp, even savage, in political debate—a perfect, low-roading "hatchet man" to complement Goldwater's high-road philosopher-king approach. Goldwater selected Miller, the GOP nominee told party state chairmen, because "he drives Johnson nuts." But Miller had other attributes. He came from the East, was a Roman Catholic, and some of Goldwater's advisors believed that the selection of RNC chairman Miller would help unite the GOP.

That notion proved badly mistaken. While hailing from New York, Miller was no "Eastern Republican," but an upstate conservative who had actually opposed Eisenhower policies more often than Goldwater. Moreover, Goldwater never even consulted with Eisenhower, Nixon, or other important party leaders on the choice. As a result, GOP moderates immediately complained about the Goldwater camp's "heavy-handed tactics" and "rubbing our faces in the dirt." But party moderates were themselves partly to blame. Their overblown anti-Goldwater rhetoric and last-ditch Scranton drive had gone far to tear apart the GOP and virtually rule out any GOP moderate for the second spot. The "Scranton letter" definitely shot down the most obvious vice-presidential selection—Scranton himself. Still, Goldwater remained responsible for his failure to try to reunite the party through consultation or creative compromise. In the fall, Goldwater would be asking the American people to make sweeping policy changes, and he needed a reassuring figure on the ticket. Miller was hardly that. Liberal and moderate Republicans in San Francisco viewed the Goldwater-Miller ticket as an ideal ticket—but only for the *Titanic*.

Goldwater's Thursday night acceptance speech provided him with another opportunity to bind the party, and again he failed. Thursday night got off to a promising start when Richard Nixon presented the new GOP standard-bearer to the convention in a masterful speech designed to gloss over party differences. The Cow Palace shook for fifteen minutes. Red, white, and gold balloons cascaded from the rafters. Delegates broke into the "Battle Hymn of the Republic" and, of course, the "We Want Barry" chant. This was Goldwater's moment. And Goldwater certainly gave Goldwater diehards some hard-line rhetoric to cheer about. But he offered moderate Republicans nothing at all. "Any who join us in all sincerity, we welcome," Goldwater declared in a flat, if not harsh, tone punctuated by popping balloons. "Those who do not care for our cause we do not expect to enter our ranks in any case." There was even more to disquiet moderate Republicans, as Goldwater added, "I would remind you that extremism in the defense of liberty is no vice. And let me remind you also that moderation in the pursuit of justice is no virtue."[19]

Although Goldwater partisans loved it, the GOP nominee had managed to make his acceptance speech a campaign issue for some of his own party brethren. His rhetorical indulgences regarding extremism and moderation left Republican moderates and liberals alike deeply troubled. That Goldwater's acceptance speech presaged further problems within the party could be seen by television viewers, who watched New York Senator Keating and several other delegates leave the convention floor as the Goldwater faithful went wild. Despite the New Yorker's later claim that he had left only to seek medical attention to a sore throat, Keating became something of a hero for Republican moderates and liberals. Not surprisingly, Rockefeller reacted the most vehemently, expressing his "amazement and shock" over Goldwater's "dangerous, irresponsible and frightening" address.

Eisenhower said he would campaign for Goldwater only after the senator cleared up these "confusing" remarks. Goldwater told Ike the next day that his historic Normandy landing had itself been an act of extremism. "I have never thought of it that way," the former president replied. Other Republicans, however, were not so easily appeased, and Goldwater initially made no real attempt to clarify his remarks.[20]

Conservatives, of course, delighted in Goldwater's nomination triumph as the upshot of past struggles and "the wave of the future." Conservative *Newsweek* columnist Raymond Moley saw the Goldwater nomination as the "culmination" of protest from within the party that had grown since 1948, and the *Chicago Tribune* hailed the victory of the "little guy" over the bankers and big city bosses of the GOP. "The 'liberals' and lachrymose elements of the crepe-hanging press," crowed the *Tribune,* "can't reconcile themselves to the fact that the people have at last taken over the Republican party."[21]

This Goldwater nomination also signaled certain other basic changes in American politics. The triumph of the Goldwater forces marked a political power shift both in the nation and in the Republican party from the East and Northeast to the South and West, the new American industrial frontier that would become known as the Sun Belt. The Goldwater nomination struggle had pitted the burgeoning power centers of the South and West against the eastern seaboard, with the Midwest now representing the crucial balance of power. Of course, this kind of regional conflict—primarily midwestern conservative Republicans against liberal "me-too" Republicans from the East—had long existed in the GOP. As previously noted, the *Chicago Tribune* and *Newsweek*'s Moley both placed the conflict in its historical context, and the Goldwater camp's "Possible Opposition Tactics" memo clearly established Goldwater as Taft's successor in the Republican Right's ongoing battle with eastern "kingmakers." Midwestern old-line Republicans could find much to exploit and enjoy in this transformation.

The organizational skill of the Goldwater forces had simply hastened this GOP power shift. In San Francisco, Goldwater controlled more delegates than any other contender even without delegates chosen in state primaries. This was not only a supreme tribute to the Goldwater organization, but also a comment on the opposition to Goldwater, belated, fragmented and ineffective. The general Republican belief that the Democrats were unbeatable in 1964 may have discouraged early organizational efforts by other Republican candidates. Unable to match the Goldwater organizational prowess, once the GOP nomination race got under way, moderate Republicans had to rely on creating an appealing and meaningful image in opposition to Goldwater Republicanism—a successful moderate approach in past battles with the Republican Right.

But this approach failed moderate Republicans in 1964. Far away in South Vietnam, Henry Cabot Lodge could offer little more than a faint echo of the GOP Camelot—Eisenhower Republicanism. Governor Nelson Rockefeller probably offered the clearest alternative, but he could not rise above his personal family and campaign problems. Scranton, for his part, consistently played down his differences with Senator Goldwater until the last moment of his noncandidacy, by which time it was too late.

Ultimately, Scranton's nomination bid was little more than a gesture to retain the "progressive image" of the Republican party. Powerless in San Francisco and knowing it, the Scranton forces could only whimper as the Goldwater camp wielded its hard-won convention power. Admittedly, the

Goldwater forces were unnecessarily and unwisely uncompromising in their convention control. But moderate Republicans often acted like spoilsports, and conservative Republicans had reason to complain about their "rule-or-ruin" tactics.

If GOP conservatives suspected their moderate brethren of rule-or-ruin tendencies, Republican moderates feared that Goldwater partisans were bent on a party purge after their nomination triumph. Goldwater's choice of Dean Burch, an obscure Arizonan with no national political stature, as the new national committee chairman suggested to party moderates—and even to some Goldwater loyalists—that certain Goldwater Republicans were more interested in ousting moderates from the GOP hierarchy than in ousting LBJ from the White House.

Goldwater men came to monopolize key spots in the national organization. They removed GOP national research director William B. Prenderghast and took RNC executive committee posts away from party moderates, leaving New York unrepresented for the first time in history. Moderate Republicans complained of getting little campaign aid from the national party organization. Furthermore, Republican middle-roaders now suspected the "Citizens for Goldwater" committee of being an apparatus for the "ruthless purge" of the GOP, as Old Guard Republicans had earlier eyed the "Citizens for Eisenhower." Reports that Burch deputy John Grenier had ordered the removal of all Lincoln and Eisenhower portraits from the walls of GOP headquarters said it all for anti-Goldwater Republicans.

Indeed, some postconvention personnel changes were only natural. Moderate Republicans under Dewey and Eisenhower had earlier done likewise. Reveling in the "completed occupation" of the Republican party apparatus and mocking the distress of GOP moderates, the *National Review* wondered, "What did they expect?"[22] Still, such callous attitudes certainly did not enhance GOP unity.

And that problem grew worse in the weeks following the San Francisco convention. Many businessmen who had traditionally been Republican were beginning to organize on behalf of Democrat Lyndon Johnson. Former Rockefeller delegates were steering clear of the Goldwater-Miller campaign efforts. In New York, Republican senators Keating and Javits and Representative John V. Lindsay of Manhattan's silk stocking district declared that they would not support the GOP nominee. Representatives James Fulton of Pennsylvania and Silvio Conte of Massachusetts joined other GOP moderates deserting Goldwater. Finally, governors Romney and Rockefeller continued to hold off on any endorsement. The Republican party was in disarray.

Belatedly, Goldwater tried to reassure factional rivals and patch up the GOP. In a publicized letter to Nixon, Goldwater tried to undo the damage of his San Francisco remarks on "extremism in the defense of liberty." He contended that these words "were examples of a quality of devotion to liberty and justice—'firmness in the right,' as Lincoln put it—for which no Republican, and, indeed, no American need apologize." Goldwater added, "It goes without saying that such devotion would not countenance illegal or improper means to achieve proper goals."[23]

Goldwater's major Republican harmony bid came shortly thereafter in Hershey, Pennsylvania. There, almost thirty GOP governors and gubernatorial candidates met with Goldwater, Miller, Eisenhower, and Nixon. Significantly, Pennsylvania governor William Scranton played host. At the Hershey session, Goldwater promised to continue the Eisenhower-Dulles foreign policy and to consult with Ike on key national security appointments. He also pledged to support Social Security and live up to his legally mandated civil rights responsibilities as president. Goldwater, moreover, repeated his repudiation of extremist groups and character assassins, singling out the KKK, but pointedly excluding the John Birch Society.

Goldwater also asked the Hershey Republicans for some straight talk of their own. They fully obliged. In fact, the Hershey conclave was marked by more candor on Goldwater's liabilities than political creativity on ways by which the Republicans could defeat LBJ and the Democrats. While some Hershey conferees lamented Goldwater's failure to spell out positions on specific issues, the consensus was that Goldwater's "shoot-from-the-hip" extremist image was continuing to bog down his campaign. Rockefeller, for his part, pressed Goldwater to make an emotional plea for civil rights that "fellows on the lower level" could grasp. Although the Hershey conference was generally amiable, Goldwater's own frustrations surfaced at one point. "I think it's time that we decide that you've got a candidate for the President and Vice President," he said. "You might not like us, but you're stuck with us. . . ."[24]

The Hershey conference ended with a superficial picture of GOP harmony. Although Goldwater proudly insisted that he had made no conciliations at all, political observers generally interpreted his Hershey performance as a peace offering to party moderates. One participant with a sense of history said that the Hershey gathering represented Ike's reclaiming of Morningside Heights, the site of the famous Taft-Eisenhower harmony conference in 1952.[25]

In the end, the Hershey conference triggered neither a rush of GOP endorsements nor an outpouring of popular support for Goldwater. While encouraged by Goldwater's Chocolate Town gestures, governors Romney and Rockefeller still refrained from outright endorsements and ruled out any pro-Goldwater stumping outside their respective states. Senators Javits, Keating, and Case all withheld their backing from Goldwater.

Goldwater had at least made a nod to Republican party moderates. But he was about a month too late. While the actual campaign time lost in that month was hardly crucial, the actions of Goldwater and his enthusiasts in those four weeks had reinforced the Goldwater image painted by his Democratic and Republican foes—that of a right-wing devil with hornrimmed glasses bent on the complete conservative takeover of the Republican party. Hershey, in turn, did not cause Goldwater to emerge as the leader of all Republicans. It did serve, however, as the final gavel of the Republican San Francisco convention. The Republicans were hardly happy and harmonious, but Goldwater could at last begin his campaign against Lyndon Johnson and the Democrats.

Since Goldwater had confounded political bettors who had counted him out several times before, the experts warily admitted as the fall canvass began that a Goldwater presidential victory was not impossible. True, Johnson had the powers of incumbency, the issue of peace and prosperity and, said Goldwater backers, the support of the national media. Johnson, moreover, enjoyed a wide lead in the popular opinion polls. But two new factors in American politics left observers unsure of potential Goldwater strength. The frantic political activity of super-patriot groups like the John Birch Society might disrupt standard voting patterns in California and Texas, and working-class resentment against black civil rights gains—white backlash—might cut into traditional Democratic majorities in northern cities. The Goldwater campaign organization also seemed extraordinarily designed to enhance Goldwater prospects.[26]

A few weeks into the 1964 campaign, Massachusetts senator Leverett Saltonstall introduced the GOP presidential nominee at a rally in Boston's Fenway Park. Goldwater, declared Saltonstall, was neither "trigger happy" nor "irresponsible."[27] This, after all, was *the* major issue of the 1964 campaign. Would Goldwater's foreign policy lead to the "disaster of nuclear war"? Would Goldwater's domestic prescriptions foster, as LBJ charged, an "atmosphere of hate and fear" and threaten "the whole course of American development"? That Republicans like Saltonstall had to address such questions indicated the nature of the troubles hounding the Goldwater crusade.

Goldwater, for his part, tried periodically to snuff out the "trigger-happy" issue. At his campaign kickoff, for instance, he contended that Republicans were "preoccupied with peace," and he pledged to end the military draft. But a split in the Goldwater camp hampered any sustained effort to moderate the Goldwater image. Conservative academicians and publicists such as the American Enterprise Institute's William Baroody and Karl Hess were elbowing out the conservative political technicians who had been largely responsible for Goldwater's nomination triumph.

One directive of the conservative think tank that proved especially disastrous stated that Goldwater would not stoop to discussing problems of local interest at campaign stops across the nation. Goldwater's campaign would be high-minded in principle and would not represent politics as usual. As a result, Goldwater passed up numerous opportunities to apply his conservative message to the legitimate special concerns of the voters—the public and private power problem in Idaho, for example. Thus, the Goldwater campaign took on a callous and sometimes downright comic quality, as the senator assailed the antipoverty program in poverty-stricken West Virginia or discussed crime in the streets in the peaceful retirement community of St. Petersburg, Florida, where, for some, the only crimes were Goldwater's opposition to Medicare and his various proposals to make Social Security voluntary.

Goldwater hoped for a presidential campaign that would amount to a broad debate of liberalism versus conservatism, a clear clash of philosophies. Goldwater declared at the beginning of the campaign, "I want to talk about freedom." And he often did, dealing with basic problems of American government and the contribution of liberal philosophy to the decline in American values, morals, and manners over the past thirty years. "You know in your hearts," Goldwater said repeatedly, "that something is wrong in our land. . . ."[28]

Star-spangled sloganeering that eschewed complicated issues, however, could not convince the American voter, enjoying both peace and prosperity, that there was indeed a threat to freedom or that the Goldwater way offered a better and brighter future. Throughout the fall of 1964, Goldwater groped futilely for a *winning* issue. Frequently, he hammered away at corruption in government, assailing the Johnson administration's "curious crew" and personally attacking the president as an "arm-twisting powergrabber" who only knew the art of "buying and bludgeoning votes." He once tarred the administration as being "soft on communism." In early October, hoping to ignite his campaign, Goldwater looked back to Eisenhower's 1952 "I shall go to Korea" crowd-pleaser and announced that as the next president he would ask Ike to head a military fact-finding expedition to Vietnam. However, the old 1952 magic was not there. The Goldwater campaign slogged on.

"In Your Heart You Know He's Right" ran the Republican campaign slogan. Yet the Goldwater campaign actually made no pitch to passions. Steering clear of the volatile civil rights issue, Goldwater denied himself any chance of directly cultivating the white backlash vote, although his remarks on "crime in the streets" and "law and order" were widely interpreted as code words in a racist appeal. Nor did he distinguish himself as a campaigner. His speeches, which usually followed no consistent theme and were delivered in an easy, colloquial manner, lacked punch. Goldwater seldom worked the crowds, avoiding the sidewalk tours and hand-pumping that are part of American presidential campaigns. Unfortunately, even Goldwater's approach to campaigning seemed to offer "A Choice Not an Echo." The

New Yorker's Richard Rovere summed up what political writers felt throughout the fall when he wrote, "The whole [Goldwater] enterprise has the air not of a great political campaign but of a great political caper—a series of pranks and calculated errors."[29]

Adding to the problems of the Goldwater campaign's ham-handedness were the wholesale desertions from the 1964 GOP cause. While political cartoonists and columnists savaged Goldwater, traditionally Republican newspapers and periodicals came out against the GOP nominee in record numbers, leading conservative Republicans to belabor the liberal bias of the communications media. While less partisan quarters also criticized the news media's "shabby" treatment of Goldwater, the GOP nominee and his staff were partly to blame, having made little effort to establish cordial relations with the working press.

Business also ran out on Goldwater, who grew bitter about "materially minded" corporate heads.[30] *Fortune* spoke for many Republican businessmen in chiding Goldwater Republicans for failing to consider the "great and subtle role" of fiscal policy.[31] The opening day of the Goldwater presidential campaign brought reports that a group of predominately Republican business leaders, led by Eisenhower's former cabinet officers Robert B. Anderson and Marion Folsom, had met at the White House with LBJ to form an independent business committee to support the Democratic ticket.

Even more damaging, numerous prominent Republican politicians joined the anti-Goldwater exodus, an exodus made all the easier by the Goldwater camp's failure to woo back liberal and moderate Republicans after the campaign got underway. In New York, neither Keating nor Javits endosed the GOP ticket. Nor did California's Senator Thomas Kuchel or Senator Clifford Case of New Jersey. Governor George Romney of Michigan pointedly stated that he only "accepted" the Goldwater candidacy. Certain disgruntled Republicans took positive action. Former Eisenhower aides Arthur Larson and Maxwell Rabb headed the National Citizens for Johnson and Humphrey organization. Robert Taft's brother Charles spearheaded the National Committee to Support Moderate Republicans, and some GOP middle-roaders launched *Project '68,* a magazine devoted to the anti-Goldwater Republican future. Indeed, the steady stream of GOP defectors prompted Washington humor columnist Art Buchwald to uncover the little-known political outfit of the 1964 campaign—"Republicans for Goldwater."[32]

Not that Johnson's campaign thrilled anti-Goldwaterites interested in any kind of meaningful debate of great national issues. The *New York Times,* for example, bemoaned LBJ's "pious platitudes" and "cloudy visions of the Great Society."[33] Nevertheless, Johnson's canvass was a masterpiece of American political campaigning—an effective blend of advertising (the famous daisy commercial), tub-thumping, and flesh-pressing in the grand style. "He could sell sand to a beachcomber," said one admirer of LBJ's "ya'll-come-to-the-speakin'" approach.[34] But Johnson would neither engage in Goldwater's hoped-for debate of liberalism versus conservatism nor respond recklessly to Goldwater-Miller barbs. Further, the incumbent never became an issue in the campaign. Instead, Johnson constantly placed Goldwater on the defensive, taking over where Rockefeller, Scranton, and other GOP moderates had left off. Goldwater and the nuclear issue— "Whose finger do you want on the nuclear button?"—became a major Democratic thrust of the 1964 campaign. Johnson succeeded, moreover, in making the election a referendum on "the whole course of American development." He established himself as the "safe candidate," the "true conservative." Conversely, public opinion surveys indicated that almost half the voters regarded Goldwater as a "radical."

Well before the end of the campaign, a deep gloom settled over Republican national headquarters. Despite Goldwater's victory claims to the end of his 80,000-mile political pilgrimage, there was no chance for a GOP presidential victory. The only question to be answered was the margin of a Goldwater defeat.

After the polls closed on election day 1964, the answer was not long in coming. President Lyndon Johnson, in fact, won an unprecedented landslide, racking up 43.1 million votes or 61 percent of the total electorate and gaining majorities in forty-four states, for 486 electoral votes. Goldwater trailed with 27.1 million popular tallies or 38.8 percent of the vote. He captured only six states, barely holding on to his home state of Arizona, for a total of 52 electoral votes.

Republicans of all kinds got caught in the Goldwater debacle. The electoral arithmetic was staggering. In the Senate, Democrats built up a powerful 68-to-32 majority by gaining two seats. The list of GOP survivors showed no special tilt, although moderate Republicans generally ran ahead of the Goldwater-Miller ticket. Goldwater hard-liners John J. Williams of Delaware and Roman Hruska of Nebraska turned in reelection victories, as did party middle-roaders Hugh Scott of Pennsylvania and Winston Prouty of Vermont. But conservative Edwin Mechem of New Mexico fell short in his reelection run against Democrat Joseph Montoya, while moderates J. Glenn Beall of Maryland lost to Joseph Tydings and Kenneth Keating of New York went down to defeat in his reelection bid against Robert F. Kennedy. Among Republicans seeking election to the Senate for the first time, Goldwater protégé Paul Fannin of Arizona won his race. And conservative former actor George Murphy defeated former Kennedy press secretary Pierre Salinger in California. But a strong Goldwater supporter, John S. Wold, lost to liberal Democrat Gale McGee in Montana. Moreover, traditional Right Wing Republicans such as Robert Taft, Jr., in Ohio and football coach Bud Wilkinson in Oklahoma also failed in their Senate bids.

In the House of Representatives, Republicans lost 38 seats, leaving the Democrats with a commanding 295-to-140 majority. Significantly, of the fifty-four Republican signers of a preconvention statement boosting Goldwater as a boon for GOP congressional candidates, seventeen retired *involuntarily*. Two House GOP conservative giants—Bruce Alger, a Texan seeking his sixth term, and Iowa's Ben Jensen, the ranking Republican on the House Appropriations Committee—also fell in the Goldwater massacre. In New York, right-wing stalwarts were especially hard hit, among them being Katharine St. George, John R. Pillion, and Steven Derounian. In Iowa, only one Republican remained in the state's seven-member congressional delegation, a delegation that had included only one Democrat before election day.

There was no GOP disaster relief at the state level. While Republicans lost one state house, leaving seventeen GOP governors in office, the party retained control of only six state legislatures after suffering losses in such strongholds as Iowa, Indiana, and Colorado. Republicans lost 62 seats in the Maine legislature, 35 in New Hampshire, 34 in North Dakota, and so on—this particular political body count rising to over 500 nationwide.

"I have every confidence that with all of you behind me, I could be another Alf Landon," Barry Goldwater had joked in accepting the Washington Alfalfa Club's mock presidential nomination in the lighter days of 1962.[35] Now, in 1964, Goldwater was not prepared to blame himself or the Republican Right for the Goldwater disaster that almost rivaled Landon's 1936 bust. Even in defeat, Goldwater managed to continue both the bumbling and bitterness of his campaign. The senator's belated concession statement conceded little to Johnson and contained no comfort for Republican losers. Explaining that Republicans would have fared better had they *wholeheartedly* supported the Goldwater-Miller ticket, he observed, "You cannot in this game of politics fight your own party. It just doesn't work."[36]

Here was irony—unintended irony.

Goldwater returned to Washington on the Friday after election day. The day was sunny yet brisk, and the landing strip at Dulles International Airport seemed perfect for one last campaign appearance. But there was no rally; the RNC had planned none, although RNC boss Dean Burch was at the airport along with vice-presidential nominee William Miller and Nebraska Senator Carl Curtis. About fifty other Goldwater diehards—most of them women—were also there to greet the defeated GOP standard-bearer. Some still sported their "Goldwater girl" straw hats and campaign buttons. Others held up placards—"Freedom: Born 1776 Died 1964" and "In Our Hearts We Still Know He's Right." When Goldwater alighted from his campaign jet, the meager assemblage began to chant "We want Barry." As he headed for a waiting automobile, some followers cried "Don't quit" and "See you in '68."

This modest Washington reception offered less welcome than welcome relief for Goldwater—relief from the postelection salvos already being directed against him and his Right Wing Republican allies. Moderate Republican senator Hugh Scott of Pennsylvania, whose connection to the failed 1948 Dewey White House bid made him something of an authority, charged that Goldwater's campaign was the worst run in presidential history. Idaho's Robert Smylie, an anti-Goldwater leader among Republican governors, claimed that the Republican nominee had come down on the "wrong side of every major issue." Anti-Goldwater Republicans had no doubts about 1964's electoral lessons. The campaign and its dreadful outcome, Rockefeller declared flatly, had answered all questions regarding Goldwater's role in the Republican future. Readers of the rabidly anti-Goldwater *New York Times* got a stern post–election day lecture on the folly of "right-wing extremists" in making a "revolutionary break" with the "centrist tradition" in American politics. "The great task for the G.O.P.," the *Times* pontificated, "will be to move back into the sunlight of modernism."[37]

Even Goldwater partisans were finding fault with the senator's run for the presidency. The *Los Angeles Times,* one of the few major newspapers to endorse the Arizonan, subsequently admonished Goldwater for his "poorly drawn issues, badly executed campaign and deliberate division within the minority party's ranks."[38] Conservative political scientist and Goldwater advisor Harry Jaffa of Claremont Men's College blamed unnamed Goldwater aides who failed to gauge the national mood and isolated the candidate. Numerous other conservative intellectuals believed that Goldwater, himself, had helped turn the campaign into an unenlightened personality contest.

Although such statements by GOP conservatives exceeded the usual postelection carping of a losing team and prompted William F. Buckley, Jr., to scold hard-line "backbiters," most Republican conservatives publicly remained downright bullish about the Goldwater bid and the GOP future.[39] The *Chicago Tribune* hailed the Goldwater tallies as an "impressive fact." Goldwater allies contended simplistically that November's GOP devastation paled in comparison with the party's earlier 1958 setback under Eisenhower. South Dakota senator Karl Mundt pointedly reminded Goldwater critics that GOP liberals and moderates had controlled "the circle of leadership for 29 of the last 30 years, and their string of successes is not very long." Right Wing Republicans simply countered GOP "gloom and doom" talk by pointing out, as did William F. Knowland, that "a party that pulls over 25 million votes is neither bankrupt nor on its deathbed."[40] Overall, GOP diehard sentiment was summed up best on the bright orange bumper stickers that began to appear shortly after election day: "Twenty-six Million Can't Be Wrong."

Goldwater, for his part, shared this hopeful sentiment and initially admitted to no major campaign mistakes. Indeed, he contended that his electoral showing and the million-dollar surplus remaining in the GOP coffers proved the success of his campaign. Goldwater flatly rejected the contention that his humiliation had damaged the conservative cause, despite his earlier remarks that an electoral share of less than 43 percent would do so.

Goldwater and the Republican Right had a ready—and in spots convincing—explanation for the Goldwater defeat. First and foremost, a Goldwater victory in 1964 was an impossibility after the Kennedy assassination. According to *Newsweek,* GOP vice-presidential candidate William Miller said with his characteristic tartness—or tactlessness, "The American people were just not in the mood to assassinate two Presidents in one year."[41]

Right Wing Republicans insisted further that any hope for even a respectable showing in this "no-win" situation was dashed well before the fall campaign began. Johnson and the Democrats had only to repeat the anti-Goldwater remarks of the senator's Republican rivals. Choosing to ignore independent polls that minimized the electoral impact of such GOP defections, many Goldwater Republicans held these "me-too" Republican mutineers mainly responsible for the Goldwater-Miller debacle. Ohio national committeewoman Katharine Kennedy Brown expressed vintage midwestern Republicanism in assailing the "Eastern seaboard financial interests" as a "forefront of defectors."[42]

Of course, Right Wing Republicans also gave Lyndon Johnson some credit for the rout of Goldwater and the GOP, though not for his statesmanship. Johnson not only benefited enormously from incumbency, being president in this fragile and difficult period following the assassination, but, claimed Goldwater and the conservative faithful, Johnson ruthlessly used the powers of the presidency to insure his election by politicizing the White House as no previous president had done and throwing the "full muscle and power of the federal government" against Goldwater.

Inevitably, Right Wing Republicans reserved a special resentment for the national media's role in Goldwater's demise. As far as Right Wing Republicans were concerned, the press's treatment of Goldwater in 1964 gave full and disturbing meaning to the term "adversary relationship." The "total collapse of press responsibility " was readily apparent to Right Wing Republicans during the 1964 campaign. The press, in branding Goldwater "irresponsible" and "trigger happy," had helped to keep him on the defensive from the outset. The report of CBS television newsman Daniel Shorr, in which he speculated wildly on Goldwater's "move to link up with" the German right-wing forces, was only the most glaring example of Goldwater's press problem. More generally, the media highlighted Goldwater campaign difficulties while ignoring such Johnson problems as the Bobby Baker influence scandal. Conservative media critics noted that the press gave banner coverage to GOP defections while downplaying anti-Johnson bolts by South Carolina senator Strom Thurmond and other southern Democrats.[43]

Even before the fall canvass, the candidate himself had complained bitterly about the "utter dishonesty" and "out-and-out" lies of the *New York Times* and the *San Francisco Chronicle*. He also had lashed out at political sages such as Walter Lippmann and Joseph Alsop. Goldwater was madder still after the election, telling columnist Westbrook Pegler that he had never realized how many "s.o.b.'s" there were in the press.[44] So vexed was one RNC member after election day that he came to the conclusion that Republican syndicates should buy control of all available media in order to "keep any Republican from being crucified."[45]

The November, 1964 humiliation of Goldwater, the GOP postelection party changes, and the advent of "one-party dominance" in the Eighty-ninth Congress, all prompted severe reactions of one kind or another. Conservative humorist Morris Ryskind, for example, was hardly laughing when he ordered "another round of hemlock on the rocks." Among the strong reactions were those of the *New York Times*'s James Reston and the *New York Herald Tribune*'s Roscoe Drummond. Reston concluded shortly after the polls closed, "Barry Goldwater not only lost the Presidential election . . . but the conservative cause as well." Drummond agreed, observing a few months later, "Goldwater is out. The Moderate Republicans are back in control. . . . Thus ends the party's experiment with extreme conservatism."[46]

What such pronouncements failed to consider, however, was the fact that the Republican Right had been entombed time and again since 1932, and—in whatever reincarnation—it had always returned to battle for control of the GOP. Political coroners failed once again to detect important Republican Right Wing vital signs. In fact, GOP conservatism was healthier in many respects in 1964–1965 than it had been since the 1920s. Although the presidency still remained, in Ambrose Bierce's phrase, "the greased pig of American politics," Right Wing Republicans had finally snared the Republican presidential nomination—a true triumph of will and organization. Of course, Goldwater's defeat was humiliating and harmful, inasmuch as it was commonly assumed to be the definitive test of the political appeal of Republicanism.

With opinion surveys showing, contrary to the statements of liberal political pundits, that conservative sentiment had apparently not suffered as a result of the Goldwater debacle, it was clear that in 1964–1965 conservatism remained as much a part of the American political mainstream as liberalism. It also became obvious—if it had not before this—that American political pundits should dispense with their biennial or quadrennial death notices of conservatism. In the case of Goldwater, the persistent feeling that he was not a bona fide conservative in 1964, but a "radical," showed that many considered him outside the mainstream even of the Republican Right. This assessment was as much a fault of the overblown reaction of Goldwater's enemies, partisan and otherwise, as it was the result of the inept Goldwater campaign. Indeed, in the end, Goldwater suffered the electoral setback, and not conservatism. As Goldwater organizer F. Clifton White saw it, "Conservatism was not defeated in this campaign, it was not even debated." [47]

Right Wing Republicans still firmly believed in the basic appeal or soundness of their credo. For them, external and nondoctrinal circumstances provided enough reason for the "unmaking" of Goldwater in November, 1964. They consoled themselves with the fact that only four years after Eisenhower and his Modern Republicanism, the Right Wing, party outlaws during most of the 1950s, had emerged again with vigor. In itself, this was a thrilling reaffirmation of the vitality of hard-line conservatism within the Republican party. Further, even in defeat, the Goldwater campaign had marshaled a record-breaking door-to-door canvass and an unprecedented number of financial contributions. Using direct mail and television appeals, the Goldwater Republicans had put together a far broader financial base than the Democrats. [48]

The organizational zeal of conservative-minded members of the GOP was not diminished by the 1964 defeat, and their continued dedication would be a significant factor in view of the gradual continued decline in the discipline of both American political parties. Hastened by the nonpartisan approaches of Willkie and later Eisenhower, this decline—ironically for liberal Republicans—left the GOP open to more issue-oriented conservatives who valued ideological purity over party victory. The Goldwater element within the GOP included numerous highly motivated, ideologically oriented political newcomers who by 1964 had captured control of many state organizations from the bottom up. Following Goldwater's electoral setback and failure to gain full control of the national party apparatus, Right Wing strength at the local and state level remained strong, and GOP office seekers thereafter had to take such strength into account. "As it is now," Goldwater himself wrote in early April, 1965, "the conservatives are still in control of the Republican Party and they will continue to be if they retain control of the state organizations." [49] Moreover, the Goldwater nomination signaled a shift of GOP intraparty power to the South and West. Regardless of the 1964 November returns, Goldwater's selection firmly established the Sun Belt region as a conservative challenger to the once dominant liberal "me-too" East within the GOP. The Republican party would never be the same again.

11
An Emerging
Republican Majority

The spirited charges and countercharges concerning the Goldwater debacle settled little as far as the GOP future was concerned. Goldwater and the Right Wing certainly gave no sign of factional retreat. Goldwater himself continued to talk of making the GOP a truly conservative party. Recent conservative Republican Strom Thurmond of South Carolina even invited Rockefeller and other Republican "radical leftists" to switch to the Democratic party. Right Wingers also brandished a November Harris survey showing that most Republicans favored continued conservative control of the party. Further, there was talk of new conservative prospects such as Texas senator John Tower, Colorado senator Peter Dominick, and Hollywood's Ronald Reagan. The Right Wing actor Reagan, who had set conservative hearts thumping during the 1964 campaign with a thrilling, pro-Goldwater speech over national television, kept up the courtship by commenting, "I don't think we should turn the high command over to leaders who were traitors during the battle just ended. The conservative philosophy was not repudiated." A day after the election, a group of Michigan conservatives formed "Republicans for Ronald Reagan" as the first step in pointing him toward the White House.[1]

Although Right Wing Republicans obviously had no intention of surrendering the GOP to their "me-too" rivals, Goldwater and his allies were aware that the electoral returns had made painfully clear that that day had not yet come. Despite their long-range goals, healing words were now a necessity. Under heavy fire for the Goldwater camp's "exclusive" fall campaign, RNC boss Burch urged party members to forge a consensus "which represents all elements of our party." Goldwater agreed, likening the GOP to a "tent" that had room enough for liberals and conservatives alike. Indeed, conservatives temporarily took up an old Eisenhower theme and called for an end to intra-party labeling that was only "misleading, divisive and stigmatic."[2]

Such chummy pronouncements could not long put off the power struggle within the party that was inevitable after the Goldwater defeat. And this came finally over the continuation of Goldwater ally Dean Burch as Republican national chairman. Hugh Scott, who had battled GOP hard-liners to remain as RNC boss after Dewey's 1948 defeat, now led the cry for Burch's gavel. Not long thereafter, Republican governors met in Denver and demanded Burch's departure, as well as a return to Republican "progressive" principles.[3]

Although Burch maintained, just as Scott had in 1948, that he possessed a four-year contract, Burch's retention was more than a simple contractual arrangement as far as Goldwater and his supporters were concerned. Goldwater wrote in a letter to all RNC members that the removal of Dean Burch now would be a "repudiation of a great segment of our party and a repudiation of me." Goldwater even suggested that Burch's dismissal might threaten the two-party system.[4]

Burch and Goldwater might have beaten down a simple challenge by Scott and by the Republican governors. But the anti-Burch drive ultimately enlisted several party powerhouses. Along with former president Eisenhower, important Goldwater backers such as F. Clifton White and George Humphrey gradually came to the conclusion that Burch had to go. So did Donald Ross of Nebraska, a Republican national committeeman and an erstwhile Goldwater backer who had become disgusted by Goldwater's inept 1964 campaign. After the election Ross secretly went to work with several like-minded midwestern colleagues to form an "Anti-Burch Society."

Hoping to replace Burch with Ohio state chairman Ray Bliss, Ross's society ultimately controlled enough RNC votes to embarrass Burch, at the very least. Goldwater had to back down. On January 12, 1965, he reluctantly announced that Burch would be replaced by Bliss on April 1. Later in January when the RNC ratified this arrangement, Goldwater kept up the harmonics—but on his own terms. Before the RNC, the Arizonan accepted full responsibility for all fall campaign mistakes and said that he was "sorry so many good men went down with me." Still, self-flagellation had never been the style of Goldwater or his allies, and the defeated standard-bearer mixed his mea culpas with declarations on "the false liabilities that were hung around my neck on July 15" and the LBJ-engineered opposition of the entire federal government. Despite the senator's claim that conservative Republicans were "not destroying our weapons," some hard-core Goldwaterites never reconciled themselves to their leader's "unnecessary" capitulation. Goldwater, in turn, resented the cries of "double-cross" from right wing ultras, but the *National Review* correctly noted that Goldwater's own initial intransigence made Burch's forced exit much more of an "embarrassment and a setback" than it had to be.[5]

Actually, the election of Ray Bliss helped Goldwater and most of his partisans to accept rather gracefully a change at national headquarters. Robert Taft himself had made Bliss chairman of the Ohio GOP after Truman's statewide victory over Dewey in 1948. Also, Bliss, whom Goldwater had wanted as national chairman in 1962, was known as a hard-working, "nuts-and-bolts" political manager who was not likely to try to lead Republicans along particular ideological lines. "If the Democratic Party is big enough for Harry Byrd and Hubert Humphrey," the new RNC head liked to say, "then the Republican Party is big enough for Jack Javits and Barry Goldwater."[6]

Bliss's live-and-let-live approach reflected the emerging Republican attitude of late January, 1965. So did the major postelection GOP change on Capitol Hill—the replacement of Indiana's Charles Halleck with Michigan's Gerald Ford as minority leader. Although Halleck blamed the GOP's fall defeat for his ouster, dump-Halleck talk had actually begun well before election day, and political observers generally regarded the Halleck-Ford duel as more of a "beauty contest" than an ideological showdown. Nevertheless, the attractive and energetic Ford was definitely no Right Wing Republican, and the election results had clearly impressed him. He subsequently proclaimed himself a "constructive moderate" and promised to recapture the "middle road of moderation"—a road most Republicans were happy to travel after the 1964 detour.[7]

Halleck's sack by House Republicans did highlight one of the major changes involving the Republican Right in the post–World War II period: the loss of a conservative-led Republican opposition on Capitol Hill. In 1945 and the immediate postwar years, Martin and Halleck in the House and Wherry, Taft, and Bridges in the Senate had commanded the GOP and its powerful Old Guard contingent. But the days of hard-line, anti–New Deal opposition were long gone. The consolidation of the New Deal programs and many of its fundamental assumptions under the Eisenhower administration enormously complicated Republican politics. Not only had former Old Guard stalwarts such as Martin and Halleck been compromised by their pro-Ike stands during the Republican 1950s, but Old Guard strength had suffered along with the Republican party, which had never prospered under Ike's Modern Republicanism. The dreadful GOP returns in the 1964 House and Senate races only capped the overall decline in Republican congressional strength since 1952.

The makeup of the new Senate GOP command also testified to reduced conservative influence. Illinois's Everett Dirksen remained as GOP minority leader. Despite the senator's nomination of Goldwater at San Francisco, Dirksen had actually dropped his Right Wing tag by the late 1950s. Indeed, the Right had often criticized Dirksen for his appeasement of JFK and LBJ. His nominating speech was significant mainly because it had signaled mainline GOP recognition of Goldwater's lock on the party nomination.

After the election, not only did Dirksen remain Senate GOP leader, but he reportedly urged Thruston Morton to stay on as Republican Senate campaign committee head, thus keeping Right Wing Peter Dominick out of the post that Goldwater had used as a stepping-stone to the GOP nomination.[8] Furthermore, Senate Right Wing Republicans mounted no challenge to minority whip Thomas Kuchel, despite the Californian's desertion of Goldwater in the fall campaign. Goldwater himself had never been a Senate GOP power by any means, but the fact that he would hold no seat in the Eighty-ninth Congress further illustrated the decline since the days of Wherry, Taft, and, even more recently, Bridges.

The scarcity of GOP conservative leaders and followers on Capitol Hill reflected the Republican Right's more general leadership problems following the 1964 elections. As far as national politics was concerned, Right Wing Republicans, unlike their factional rivals, had focused on a single leader in the postwar period. Taft had dominated the Republican Right when he was not dominating the entire Republican party. By the early 1960s, Goldwater had succeeded Taft as *the* spokesman of GOP conservatism. After Goldwater's November loss, however, the Republican Right had no strong, single leader. Repudiated at the polls, Goldwater remained largely a symbol of the Republican Right Wing, though it was still too early in 1965 to tell just what he symbolized—past failures or future prospects.

Despite hopeful hard-line talk regarding new conservative heroes, Tower of Texas and Dominick of Colorado were relative newcomers to the Senate, outside GOP leadership circles, and far from established political figures nationally. Ronald Reagan had potential, especially as Republicans proposed a new emphasis on television communication in the light of the Goldwater campaign's shortcomings in this area. Conceivably, Republican conservatives could move from supporting a candidate who looked like an actor to a candidate who was an actor. In 1965, however, Reagan appeared as little more than an accomplished television speechmaker with a deep interest in conservative politics. Consequently, the Goldwater defeat temporarily left Right Wing Republicans without effective, well-recognized national leadership in the face of the onslaught of Johnson's Great Society.

And the anticipated wave of liberal legislation came in a flood not seen since the high-water mark of the New Deal in the mid-1930s. Lyndon Johnson compensated for the lack of a crisis atmosphere with an overwhelming determination and a personal knowledge of Capitol Hill politics that went back to Roosevelt's prewar days. Like Roosevelt, LBJ benefited from an opposition in disarray—small, divided, intellectually and pragmatically unsure of itself. Before the 1964 election, Johnson had tried to establish his credentials as a friend of business and a sharp-eyed watchdog of government spending by, among other things, cutting back on lighting at the White House. But he had also set forth his abundance-for-all Great Society, and during the Eighty-ninth Congress the lights on Capitol Hill burned late into the night as legislators codified Johnson's visions of the Great Society.

Johnson succeeded in pushing Medicare, federal aid to education, the Voting Rights Act, housing legislation, and the enlargement of the antipoverty and Appalachian development programs through the Eighty-ninth Congress—a series of Great Society bills that read like an ADA dreamer's laundry list. Congress's failure to repeal the Taft-Hartley Act's right-to-work provision (section 14b) and its rejection of home rule for the District of Columbia stood as the lonely exceptions to LBJ's legislative wizardry. The 14(b) issue remained the single—if questionable—example for conservatives of what staunch opposition could still accomplish, although LBJ allegedly only made a halfhearted effort of this issue in exchange for Dirksen's support on the Voting Rights Act.[9] About the only other thing Right Wing Republicans could cheer was the end of each session of the Eighty-ninth Congress. As the *National Review*'s "Quincy" noted, at least the solons could then rest "the muscles of their hands wracked by cramps induced from the over-frequent use of the rubber stamp of Administration legislation."[10]

The Right Wing Republican reaction to LBJ's Great Society was surprisingly feeble, reflecting the weakened state of the Right in the immediate post-Goldwater years. Although a successful battle against the Great Society proposals was never a possibility anyway, the Republican Right's demoralized state on Capitol Hill manifested itself even more dramatically in its failure to wage a real intraparty struggle in the first congress after the Goldwater defeat.

Of course, conservative commentary bemoaned "liberal [GOP] complicity" in the Great Society victories. An American Conservative Union (ACU) brochure entitled "Democratic Majority for Victory" pointed out that the defection of a small but noisy "clique" of Republican liberals "allowed the Johnson Administration to whoosh through the Great Society." And Republican congressional leaders allowed these GOP rubber-stampers to go unpunished. Conservatives expected as much. Eschewing any antireform alliance with conservative southern democrats, the Republican Capitol Hill command was currently enamored of the concept of "constructive leadership," which provided that Republicans should not merely oppose Johnson initiatives, but supply "responsible" Republican alternatives instead. But such constructive leadership fell flat, as minority leader Gerald Ford quickly discovered when four of his poorly publicized legislative substitutes for Great Society proposals went down to defeat in the House. The *National Review*'s "Quincy" contended bitterly that the Republican leadership on Capitol Hill remained so afraid to upset "the Eastern liberal wing of the GOP that it does nothing."[11]

Soon, even cheerleaders of constructive leadership such as James Reston and the *New York Times* were conceding its failures, although blaming it mainly on the personal leadership of Ford and Dirksen.[12] Conservative M. Stanton Evans saw clearly that the "constructive leadership" was inherently flawed because it allowed any debate to proceed on terms favorable to the Democratic majority.[13] Even if Republican constructivists won the debate, Democratic self-interest made it unlikely that the victory would be repeated in congressional votes. Moreover, this approach implicated Republicans in any future programatic failures and, as Right Wing Republicans had claimed since 1933, made it difficult to convince voters that any real difference existed between the GOP and the Democratic party. Bereft of clear focus and animating intellectual drive, Ford and Dirksen's Republican congressional leadership during the Johnson years was bland, reactive, contradictory, when not incoherent. Republicans could only take heart there was a Democratic party.

Although Evans and other conservative commentators criticized this "constructive" approach, Representative John Ashbrook of Ohio, head of the ACU, was the only noteworthy GOP lawmaker who openly challenged the GOP leadership in this regard. The 1964 election returns may have made a deeper and far different impression on conservative Republicans on Capitol Hill than their defensive postelection comments initially indicated. It is also possible that these Right Wing Republicans remained mute as part of an altogether understandable effort to foster unity in the GOP after the internecine battles of 1964. But for now these are simply speculations. The precise reasons for Right Wing silence may only be known when historians can better piece together this period through manuscript collections that are not now available. Conservative Republicans saw no purpose in holding up the Great Society. They were convinced the Great Society "would choke on its own excesses." "There are lots of chickens that are going to start roosting on its doorstep when the costs of the Great Society are added," Dean Burch wrote in his chairman's report of early 1965.[14]

Needing no empirical evidence to oppose these programs, Right Wing Republicans certainly wasted no time in identifying the problems accompanying the Great Society. High taxes and the high cost of living (by 1960s standards), as well as the various problems in administering these new programs, simply confirmed the Right Wing Republicans' initial suspicions. "After reviewing the several programs on the Great Society," Wyoming senator Milward Simpson stated at the time, "and studying their excessive costs, tremendous wastes, and exorbitant salaries, I found that little was being accomplished other than the scandals, corruption and political shenanigans of the party in power." Furthermore, pollsters also soon began to chart the rise of the "big government" issue, especially among traditionally Democratic urban whites.[15] The latter were obviously coming to resent the pro-black tendency of Great Society legislation and the related intrusion of court-ordered school busing to achieve school desegregation. "White backlash," only speculated about in the 1964 election, became a definitive part of American political realities by early 1966.

Then there was Vietnam. "In 1964 I was told," a listener wrote to the right-wing radio commentator Fulton Lewis, "that if I voted for Barry Goldwater it would mean massive escalation of the war in Vietnam and defoliation of the jungles. Well, I did vote for Goldwater, and sure enough it happened."[16] Indeed, Right Wing Republicans took considerable satisfaction as Johnson ordered air strikes against North Vietnamese military installations and generally increased the American military commitment to South Vietnam. Unlike their liberal and moderate GOP brethren, Right Wing Republicans supported—unequivocally supported—the United States' role in Vietnam, and backed similar LBJ moves such as the dispatch of troops to Santo Domingo. For them, the conflict was the same—the global fight against Communist aggression. Although specific strategic reasons for an American presence in South Vietnam existed, Republican conservatives saw the fight in Southeast Asia mainly in its larger global context. South Vietnam—a sovereign anticommunist government in Right Wing eyes—could never be allowed to fall to the North Vietnamese.

GOP conservatives disagreed in the long run with the restraint of Johnson's Vietnam policy and with Johnson's failure to spell out the goals and objectives of his policy. Goldwater privately told LBJ that there could be no victory until the commander in chief "took off the hobbles" of the military in Vietnam. Defeat, remarked Goldwater, would be better than Johnson's halfway measures. As seen earlier, the Right's foreign policy had changed since the immediate post–World War II period. During the early Cold War years and the Korean War, the Republican Right had slowly shed its legacy of prewar isolationism. Taft biographer James Patterson notes that an undated paper on Taft's desk at his death read, "No Indo China—Except in case of emergency invasion by the Chinese," a message consistent with Taft's isolationist past. But there was no such feeling on the part of Right Wing Republicans by 1964. "Vietnam—without a question, Yes," was the message they would leave to history. Barry Goldwater bitterly attacked "dovish" Republicans such as Charles Percy and George Romney as "tired, tempting voices of appeasement and isolation." In another ironic twist, Right Wing Republicans now championed the war powers of the president against the one-time internationalist Senator William J. Fulbright, who, said M. Stanton Evans in the *National Review,* could now reintroduce what he had once so scorned—the Bricker Amendment.[17]

LBJ's foreign and domestic troubles had obvious political implications as the 1966 elections approached. The 1966 elections were crucial to Republicans of all shades, but they mattered most to GOP conservatives who had lost so much in 1964. The elections would demonstrate whether Republican conservatism—by now a more articulated and self-conscious movement than at any time since World War II—was sufficiently organized and in tune with the major trends of American life to bounce back after the Goldwater disaster. Polling data had already detected a drop in support for certain Great Society programs, particularly among traditionally Democratic groups, and if this trend could translate into votes then the Republican Right would acquire a crucial tool in its rehabilitation program. The year 1966—and not 1964—would thus become the key year in the post–World War II history of the Republican Right.

Republican and Republican Right prospects were naturally tied together in the immediate post-1964 years and the GOP as a whole depended heavily on the organizational genius of Ray Bliss. The new RNC chairman quickly set to rebuilding the party organization which he had described upon his arrival as a "second-echelon answering service." Hurriedly, Bliss not only built up the party structure, especially in reviving the party's urban outposts, but also guarded the party's institutional integrity by condemning the proliferation of Republican organizations or splinter groups. Conservatives often complained that the emphasis was on condemning rightist groups, although Bliss, according to approving observers, saw the future of the GOP in pragmatic rather than ideological terms. Such an emphasis prompted David Broder to write, on the first anniversary of the Goldwater nomination, "To all appearances the Goldwater era has ended."[18]

Appearances could deceive. The debacle of 1964 had taught and had changed Right Wing Republicans. But conservatism was still their creed. They had lost no faith in their objectives or in the ultimate willingness of the American people to choose conservative, limited government. The continued movement of the Young Republicans to the right both exemplified and enriched the power and persistence of conservative Republicanism. Political commentators were wrong in mistaking the Republican Right's growing political sophistication with abandonment of their conservative designs for the future of the GOP and the United States. Barry Goldwater and other conservatives joined Republicans such as Thruston Morton and Dirksen in "kicking the John Birch Society in the tail." Goldwater's refusal to repudiate the John Birch Society specifically became a symbol—and a costly symbol—of Goldwater's Radical Right problems in the 1964 campaign. Almost a year later, however, Goldwater himself urged Republicans to quit the Birch Society and finally admitted his error in blocking the anti-extremism plank at the San Francisco Republican convention. The distinctions involved in Birch Society "tail-kicking" were no doubt finer ones than those of 1964.[19] But they were made for chiefly tactical reasons.

When the Republican party roared back in 1966, the Republican Right roared back with it. GOP gains were the greatest in twenty years, as Republicans netted forty-seven House seats, three Senate seats, and eight governorships. In the state legislature races, Republicans more than recovered their 1964 losses in what Ray Bliss described as "victory in depth." If the 1966 elections presaged an emerging Republican majority, as Kevin Phillips later claimed, GOP conservatives focused on the conservative winners to explain what kind of Republicanism was triumphant. M. Stanton Evans cautioned that the eastern media, in highlighting the election of GOP Senate liberals—Mark Hatfield of Oregon, Charles Percy of Illinois, and Edward Brooke of Massachusetts—were ignoring the new conservative trend among the governors—Claude Kirk in Florida, Paul Laxalt in Nevada, John Williams in Arizona—and the new GOP congressmen from the South.

On balance, the 1966 elections represented a predictable return to the political center after the excesses of Johnson's Great Society. LBJ appeared to have been mistaken in reading the 1964 returns as anything more than a vote to preserve the status quo. The 1966 trend was conservative, but there was no conservative tide. In clear-cut liberal versus conservative clashes, Democrats Tom McIntyre in New Hampshire and Lee Metcalf in Montana were headed for the Senate after defeating conservative Republicans. Although John Tower won reelection to the Senate, even he had spent the years since 1964, as he put it, "accenting the more positive things, instead of constant opposition." The repeal of the Great Society was highly doubtful, but one thing was certain. As *US News and World Report* asserted, "The big bash is over."[20]

The eye-opening election of a Republican governor of California reaffirmed the proposition that the 1966 elections marked simply a rightward drift back to the political middle. "I've a feeling the people want a pause," was the decidedly moderate analysis of Ronald Reagan, the new hope of Right Wing Republicans after his election as governor of California. Former actor, former union activist, and former Democrat, Reagan had been on Right Wing minds since his sensational pro-Goldwater address in 1964. Handsome and telegenic, with an easy way that masked his consuming interest in politics, Reagan had all the attributes that the Republican Right needed in the wake of the Goldwater defeat. He had wisely concluded after the 1964 election that the Republican Right was in need of the "soft sell" in order "to prove our radicalism was an optical illusion."[21] F. Clifton White, the Goldwater political strategist, had in December, 1964, combined his efforts with those of California businessmen in urging Reagan to run for governor. Two years earlier, the popular Democratic incumbent Pat Brown and the deep and historic divisions of the California GOP had frustrated the veteran Richard Nixon in his ill-fated gubernatorial attempt. But, having moderated his essential conservatism during the campaign, Ronald Reagan—"citizen politician"—had managed to unite Republicans and in 1966 dispatched Brown with a surprising million-vote majority.

Reagan's political emergence, with all that it implied about conservative stands, political flexibility, and political communications, precisely met the needs of the Right Wing after 1964. Even more important, the election of a conservative as governor of California underscored the shift to the Sunbelt and to suburbia in American politics. California was, after all, the most western, most suburban state, and Reagan's election quickly became a rallying point for these new political forces. Significantly, on November 17, shortly after his California victory, Ronald Reagan and his inner circle gathered at his Pacific Palisades home to discuss his chances for the presidency.[22]

The successes, excesses, and distresses of the Democrats made Right Wing Republicans all the more confident that history and the future were on their side. The Democratic party, so triumphant in the 1964 elections and so successful in putting through the Great Society programs, was coming unglued by 1966 and would cannibalize itself by 1968. "War," "antiwar," "black," "white," "hawk," "dove," "protest," "reaction," "nonviolence," "violence," and above all, "change" were words that helped explain the reason. Unrelenting, even revolutionary, changes were shaking the structures of American society—structures that the Democratic party had done so much to shape since 1933. Northern white urban voters were joining southern Democrats in becoming more and more resentful of Great Society programs that favored Black America. In the Black community, moderate civil rights leadership had given way to Black Power advocates, apologists for the rioting that was becoming a summer ritual. "Law and order" rapidly ceased being a "code word" for racism and emerged as an issue in its own right among frightened whites. Meanwhile, the New Left scorned the assumptions of both Johnson's foreign and domestic programs. More traditional Democrats such as Richard Goodwin joined in blistering Johnson's Vietnam policy and, in a critique echoed by Robert F. Kennedy, attacked the Great Society's big-government domestic liberalism. Ultimately excommunicated from the liberal community because of his war escalation policy, LBJ decided not to stand for reelection. American liberalism, lamented Eric Goldman, the brilliant historian of the movement, had run out of fresh ideas and was in disarray. The *National Review* put it more bluntly: "The liberal approach to human problems has reached a dead end."[23]

Welcome as they were for conservatives, these developments first benefited Richard Nixon, not Ronald Reagan. Major Right Wing Republicans were responsible for this, having thrown their post-1964 support early to Nixon. Nixon had emerged from the 1964 campaign as both an astute judge and a beneficiary of Right Wing strength in the Republican party. A tireless campaigner for the Goldwater-Miller ticket, Nixon after the election applauded Goldwater's "very courageous campaign," called for a moratorium on "kicking Goldwater," and castigated Rockefeller and other "Eastern Republican dividers" as "spoilsports." Nixon obviously fancied "more than a backstage role" for himself in future GOP politics.[24]

Goldwater did too. Grateful for Nixon's support before and after the election and convinced that Nixon was the most conservative candidate that Right Wing Republicans could hope for in the near future, Goldwater announced in January, 1965, that the former vice-president was his choice for the 1968 Republican presidential nomination. Not that all doubts about Nixon's right-wing credentials had vanished. As Nixon himself commented on his new Right Wing backers, "They don't like me, but they tolerate me."[25]

Nixon saw to it that his Right Wing backers continued to be tolerant, emphasizing conservative domestic themes and never wavering in his commitment to a free South Vietnam. Not only did Nixon court the conservatives, but he also built up solid organizational support by traveling ceaselessly on behalf of GOP congressional candidates in 1966. Perhaps a few GOP conservatives actually believed that the much-publicized "New Nixon" embraced a new-found ideological conservatism that set him apart from the earlier pragmatic Nixon. In any case, most Right Wing Republicans, all too familiar with Nixonian pragmatism, believed that he would always respond to popular political pressures and that these were now mainly conservative and would remain so. Moreover, a successful Nixon candidacy would keep the Republican nomination from a liberal Republican such as Romney or Rockefeller. Nixon thus became the "conservative" candidate. Former Goldwater backers such as John Ashbrook, William F. Buckley, and senators Strom Thurmond and John Tower followed Goldwater's example and backed Nixon. Richard Kleindienst, using his earlier Goldwater experience, even served as Nixon's director of field operations in the 1968 primaries. This was not the first time that GOP conservatives had allowed personal and practical political considerations to overrule strict ideological constraints, yet the *National Review*'s William H. Rusher later wrote that conservatives who opted for Nixon in 1969 owed history an accounting for this "uncharacteristic but unavoidable streak of opportunistic calculation."[26]

The early endorsements of Nixon by these conservatives mortally wounded a Reagan bid for the GOP nomination in 1968. But there were also other factors. A homosexual scandal in Reagan's administration in the summer of 1967 hampered an early all-out Reagan drive. And, ironically, Robert Kennedy's assassination in a California hotel hall eliminated what F. Clifton White, one of the foremost political strategists in the Republican Right, claimed was Ronald Reagan's strongest argument. The California governor would be the perfect GOP candidate—image for image—if the Democrats selected Kennedy. Pursuing the nomination right up to the Miami convention, Reagan also ran headlong into Nixon's solid conservative support in the South, held firm by South Carolina senator Strom Thurmond. Nixon won on the first ballot, garnering 692 votes compared with Rockefeller's 277 and Reagan's 182 (other candidates divided up the remaining 182 delegates) before the convention made the decision unanimous. Reagan supporters congratulated themselves on coming so close; White later maintained not too convincingly that the change of six votes in certain unit-rule states would have opened up the convention for a third-ballot Reagan victory.[27]

The loss was Reagan's, not GOP conservatives'. If anything, Reagan's unsuccessful bid presaged bountiful conservative tomorrows. In the meantime, the autumn of 1968 disappointed neither Nixon's nor Reagan's conservative backers. From his Miami acceptance through the final campaign stop, the Nixon message was solidly conservative. A hard line on law and order, warnings against the decline of national prestige and military might, attacks on an increasingly impersonal bureaucracy, and paeans to voluntary solutions for the nation's economic and social problems—these Nixon themes encouraged conservatives. The nation's mood was conservative, wrote James J. Kilpatrick, but it was not as much a reactionary impulse as a national desire to "sit still for a while."[28] Nixon's final victory in November tasted all the sweeter to Republican conservatives when Wallace's totals were added in—votes which they figured as largely conservative votes.

Keven Phillips, a lawyer in Nixon's justice department and a careful student of American electoral patterns who had served as a campaign strategist in 1968, believed that the 1968 electoral results signaled nothing less than "an emerging Republican majority." It would be a distinctly conservative majority. As set forth in a book entitled *The Emerging Republican Majority*, Phillips claimed that the New Deal era of a Democratic majority was coming to a close; the 1966 elections had foreshadowed and the 1968 election confirmed that the GOP was hovering at the brink of majority party status. Conceivably, Goldwater's 1964 electoral debacle would be to the forthcoming Republican political revolution what Al Smith's 1928 defeat had been to Roosevelt's Democratic Revolution.[29] That would depend chiefly on bringing the bulk of the Wallace vote into the Republican fold. This "emerging Republican majority" was being built in middle-class suburbs whose growth now exceeded that of urban areas, and in the booming new areas of the Sun Belt and the new industrial frontiers of the South and Southwest. Even in the older urban areas of the Northeast and Midwest, where the vote was falling off, Wallace and Nixon had made gains among blue-collar workers, white ethnics, and Catholics, traditionally Democratic voters. Although the Negro problem, according to Phillips, was mainly responsible for the Democratic coalition's demise, the Republican emergence would depend upon a slowing down of government spending, taxes, and social experimentation, as well as administration support for positive economic programs such as aid to parochial schools.[30]

Quickly branded the "Southern Strategy," Phillips's "emerging Republican majority" thesis delighted GOP conservatives, but it required some political artistry on Nixon's part. No doubt mindful of Goldwater's earlier difficulties in publicly mulling over political strategies, Nixon explained to reporters in 1969 that he had not read Phillips's work, although he instantly rejected its conclusions as "writing off" certain sections of the country.[31] Other Nixon moves, however, showed that the president fully comprehended the political forces Phillips had delineated in such detail. The nominations of Clement F. Haynsworth and G. Harold Carswell to the Supreme Court, repudiated by the Senate, remained important thrusts in Nixon's so-called "Southern Strategy" that included administration opposition to busing school children to achieve racial desegregation and recommendations for weakening amendments to the extension of the Voting Rights Act of 1965.

If Phillips's "emerging Republican majority" with its southern-strategy implications was too controversial to find a place on Nixon's reading list, *The Real Majority* by Ben Wattenburg and Richard Scammon was not. Indeed, the president had reportedly read an advance copy of what William Rusher later described as little more than a "pallid rewrite" of Phillips's "emerging Republican majority." Scammon and Wattenberg explained in their book that the "Social Issue"—the concerns of the average person—was the *main* political issue for Democrats and Republicans alike. A successful American political party must move to the "center," and at this time that meant addressing the "Social Issue"—presumed voter resentment over violence, crime, drugs, pornography, and permissiveness.[32]

In Nixon, Scammon and Wattenberg had found an ardent disciple. In the 1970 congressional campaign, Nixon sent out Vice-President Spiro Agnew, an ethnic and a Catholic, to lay claim to the "Social Issue" by using conservative rhetoric and warnings against "radical liberalism." The administration was in electoral pursuit of the "Silent Majority." The White House targeted Democratic Senate incumbents Joseph Tydings of Maryland and Albert Gore of Tennessee for defeat. In the end, Gore lost to Republican William Brock, identified as a "moderate conservative," and Tydings fell to J. Glenn Beall, Jr., a pro-administration moderate. In the process, Democrats were not the only targets of the Nixon-Agnew gambit, as Republican senator Charles Goodell ruefully discovered in his New York election race. Exasperated by Goodell's "dovish" attacks on the president's Vietnam policy, the White House endorsed Conservative party candidate James Buckley (brother of William) over the "rad-lib" Goodell. Calling to mind Goodell's political about-face since Rockefeller had selected him to fill Robert Kennedy's Senate seat, Agnew dubbed him the Christine Jorgensen of American politics—a reference to a British call girl who had undergone a sex change operation.[33]

Although Goodell's defeat stood as one of the White House's more significant victories, the dramatic party realignment prophesied by Phillips did not occur. White House favorite George Bush, a second-term congressman from Houston, came up short in his Texas Senate race against Democrat Lloyd Bentsen. And the Senate, where Republicans gained only two seats, remained in Democratic hands. Republicans suffered nine net losses in the House, small only when one failed to consider that Nixon was the first modern president to begin his presidency with the opposition in control of Congress. Further White House disappointment came when not even a bipartisan conservative majority materialized in the variegated 1970 congressional election returns. *New York Times* correspondent R.W. Apple wrily suggested that 1970 therefore be called, "the year of the non-emerging Republican majority."[34]

Indeed, by 1971, a potential but as yet unrealized Republican majority and Agnew's alliterative attacks were about all that Right Wing Republicans could actually call their own. Conservatives, to be sure, appreciated both Nixon's unsuccessful and successful appointments to the Supreme Court. Chief Justice Warren Burger and Justices William H. Rehnquist and Harry Blackman moved the court away from the liberal activism and criminal rights emphasis of the Warren court.[35] But what about the executive branch? Hugh Scott, elected Senate Majority leader after the death of Everett Dirksen in 1969, reportedly said, "The conservatives get the rhetoric, we (liberals) get the action." The words of this Right Wing *bête noire* stung because they were true.[36]

Many top administration appointments did go to suspicious Republicans and Democrats. Nixon's appointments of James E. Allen as U.S. Commissioner of Education and Henry Kissinger, a Harvard University professor and former Kennedy advisor, as National Security Advisor annoyed Right Wing Republicans. One writer counted fourteen Kissinger staffers who had earlier advised Kennedy and Johnson. F. Clifton White later wrote that conservatives remained political outcasts during the Nixon years.[37] What could GOP conservatives conclude when Nixon made Daniel Patrick Moynihan, Harvard professor and former advisor to Kennedy and Johnson, his domestic affairs advisor? Right Wing Republicans would later read the press reports detailing Moynihan's White House musings on the similarities between Nixon and "conservative reformer" Benjamin Disraeli. They were not surprised—even if they were horrified—when the latter-day Tory reformer accepted such Great Society programs as model cities and rent subsidies, and embraced Moynihan's own Family Assistance Plan, which conservatives believed would make welfare more comfortable and increase the number of welfare recipients.

Early in 1969 Barry Goldwater privately warned Nixon of the power of LBJ holdovers in the bureaucracy to frustrate any effort to take charge of his own administration.[38] Ultimately, Great Society agencies and programs not only survived, but new bureaucratic impositions such as wide-ranging Environmental Protection Agency regulations and racial quotas in the form of the Philadelphia Plan actually took root.

Even Nixon himself became highly suspect once again. In 1971 he proposed an unbalanced budget, a new health plan, and reportedly announced, "I am now a Keynesian." Furthermore, his New Economic Plan (NEP) embraced wage, price, and credit controls. For those who needed reminding or documentation, a brace of books—Evans and Novak's *Nixon in the White House* and Richard J. Whalen's *Catch the Falling Flag*—appeared in the fall of 1971. These volumes spelled out Nixon's themeless pragmatism. Whalen, a highly regarded conservative who had quit as a Nixon speech writer just before the 1968 GOP convention, bemoaned Nixon's amorality and absence of "ideology or central commitment."[39]

In foreign affairs and defense policy, conservative theoreticians were far less pleased with Nixon, despite their stalwart support of his Vietnam policy. The administration's policy of detente with the Soviet Union posed a theoretical dilemma for Right Wing Republicans, whose hard-line anticommunism had persisted since before 1945. Conservatives believed that accommodation with the Soviets and U.S. acceptance of the post–World War II map of eastern Europe might be interpreted as approval of the Soviet system and its foreign policy of aggression and intimidation. Further, conservative intellectuals doubted the practical benefits of detente. While the Soviets gained American technology, grain, and a strategic arms agreement that left them with more missiles, the United States was left only with the warm feelings brought on by big power summitry and the release of Soviet Jews, as Patrick Buchanan later wrote.[40] According to conservative critics, Nixonian detente was "a one-way street" that masked simple business greed and the absence of a coherent foreign policy.

The administration's position on detente was all the more perilous because of what the *National Review* saw as Nixon's "approximation of the Liberal Left" on matters of national defense.[41] Indeed, the coincidental deterioration of American defenses and the buildup of Soviet weaponry prompted conservative Republican lawmakers such as James Buckley, Gordon Allot, Peter Dominick, and others to call on the administration to strengthen the American military and naval position. This represented a rare public criticism of the Nixon administration by conservatives who were *not* intellectuals or commentators.

The distinction between conservative politicians and conservative intellectuals and commentators continued to hold up when in July, 1971, President Nixon announced his forthcoming trip to Communist China. This trip heralded a new era in Sino-American relations, as did the subsequent decision of the United States not to oppose Communist China's admission to the United Nations, These developments struck at the very center of

Nixon–Republican Right accommodation—a hard-line anticommunist foreign policy. No matter how wayward the domestic policies had been and continued to be over the years, conservatives could count on his unstinting anticommunism. A young Nixon had once savaged the Truman administration's Asian policy and, along with conservatives and the "China Lobby," had made recognition of the Communist Chinese out of the question. Now, the bedrock of Nixon's relationship with the Republican Right and the basis of U.S. Asian policy were both jeopardized.

Yet the reaction on Nixon's Right was mild indeed, as major conservative Republican political figures left it to a few conservative pundits to rail against the president's planned foreign policy odyssey. Although Goldwater maintained his opposition to mainland China's admission to the United Nations, his major concern was the safe future of Taiwan. Assured by the administration, the senator from Arizona gave his approval to Nixon's effort to improve the dialogue between the United States and the Communist Chinese. Nor was there any outcry from the other political leader of Right Wing Republicans, Governor Ronald Reagan of California. Having been notified in advance of Nixon's China announcement, Reagan hailed the "bold and decisive move" and assured conservatives that Nixon was going to China "only to talk." Newspaper reporters in search of political revolt sparked by Nixon's foreign policy departure had to settle for a story on Nixon's own congressman, John Schmitz of Orange County, who "disestablished relations with the White House."[42]

But Right Wing pundits and publicists reacted to Nixon's China initiative with shock and anger. William Loeb of the Manchester *Union Leader,* whose strident rhetoric often served as a measure of the intensity of conservative feeling, railed against the China initiative as being "immoral, indecent, insane and frought with danger." Up until mid-March, 1971, the *National Review* had found in favor of the Nixon administration, but by the end of that summer that was no longer the case. Nixon's China policy taxed its patience to the breakpoint. William F. Buckley described the China trip as a "real blow to American Anti-Communism." Likening it to the Soviet-Nazi pact of 1939, an angry and betrayed Buckley retained little hope that a popular reaction would force a reconsideration on the administration's part, because "the public is hell bent on appeasement."[43]

But, despite the rather mild reaction of the Republican Right to Nixon's China sortie, there were still some political repercussions. "The China thing was a major shock," the ACU's director, Jeffrey Bell, remarked at the time. "It crystallized a lot of things already in the docket." The upshot of this crystallization came in July, 1971, when the so-called "Manhattan 12"—a prominent group of *National Review* intellectuals that included William F. Buckley, William Rusher, and William Burnham—resolved to "suspend support for Nixon." Kevin Phillips subsequently claimed that the Manhattan 12's break with Nixon was not a trivial act, and, indeed, the suspension of support by this cadre of conservative intellectuals soon led to the emergence of a bona fide conservative candidate for the GOP nomination, John Ashbrook. Ashbrook's ACU had complained within weeks after Nixon's inauguration in 1969 of the president's "suspected" liberal tendencies. The passing of time merely confirmed early ACU fears. By early 1972 Ashbrook was asking, "What major conservative tenet do we have that hasn't undergone reversal?"[44]

The Ashbrook candidacy had no intention or hope of taking the 1972 Republican nomination away from Nixon. Ashbrook's supporters only wanted to scare Nixon into a more conservative stance. In the end, campaigning without organization, without funds, without even a campaign manager after the New Hampshire primary, Ashbrook waged little more than a protest, and a weak one at that. Ashbrook garnered only 11 percent of the New Hampshire vote and 10 percent of the Florida vote, thereby inconspicuously taking his campaign right into the GOP convention in Miami. Indeed, Ashbrook's dismal effort convinced one future New Right leader, Richard A. Viguerie, that the conservative movement badly lacked effective political leadership.[45]

In January, 1972, the *New York Times* could coo that President Nixon during the past several years had abandoned "outmoded conservative doctrine." "The old issues have faded," continued the *Times,* "and the old controversies collapsed."[46]

Significantly, the same actions that elicited such praise from the *Times* brought no public shrieks of anger from the Right Wing politicians. Earlier, in the face of Eisenhower's much more modest transgressions, conservative commentators *and* conservative GOP solons alike had complained regularly and loudly. Even Taft, committed to cooperation with Ike, had not hesitated to chide the administration openly. Yet, as Nixon decreed wage and price controls and tripped off to China, the Republican Right *politicians* remained publicly mute, reserving their grumbling for one another in private. In so doing, Republican Right Wing politicians were continuing a public silence regarding any intraparty differences that dated back to 1965. Later, conservatives would blame themselves for not exerting more leverage on this Republican president during his first term. Evans and Novak would single out Barry Goldwater as the primary culprit. Perhaps Goldwater and other conservative Republicans deliberately refrained from criticizing a Republican president who was under fire on too many other fronts. In any case, only future examination of the manuscript collections of current prominent Right Wing political figures will yield clues to their private doubts or an explanation for their virtual silence during this period. Whatever their motivations, Right Wing Republicans such as Barry Goldwater and Ronald Reagan remained Nixon supporters. Goldwater, for his part, met murmurings of conservative dissension by asking for patience from his former follow-ers.[47] Nixon, in turn, shrewdly realized that an occasional invitation to the Oval Office or a cross-country telephone consultation was enough to keep most Right Wing Republicans quiet. Practicing conservative politicians such as James Buckley and Ronald Reagan remained behind the president and Barry Goldwater, trying to discourage dissension.

Yet Ashbrook and other GOP conservatives could afford a few sincere smiles in the months after his protest campaign. Vice-President Spiro Agnew, a hero to many GOP conservatives, was retained on the Republican ticket. And the whole tenor of the Miami convention restirred conservative hopes in Richard Nixon and the GOP. The *National Review* remarked after-ward that the convention of 1972 "may turn out to have been one of the great turning points in American politics."[48] The Republican party was shown to be a "center right" party, and its rank and file were generally con-servative. Moreover, Nixon himself subsequently campaigned mainly on conservative issues—antibusing and a slowdown in social spending. Mean-while, George McGovern, Nixon's Democratic opponent, would have made any Republican from Wendell Willkie to Nelson Rockefeller look like a straitlaced Old Guardsman or Goldwaterite.

The November election results proved beyond doubt that the president had put together a bipartisan conservative majority. Significantly, Philadel-phia's Democratic mayor, Frank Rizzo, had supported the president, and the AFL-CIO's George Meany, unable to go quite that far, had denied McGovern his endorsement. Conservatives saw the Nixon landslide as less a McGovern-induced Democratic defeat than an indication of their longed-for emerging Republican majority. More thrilling for conservatves, Nixon evi-dently did too. Beginning his second term, President Nixon immediately set out to cut down the size of the federal government. As the *New York Times* was forced to admit only two years after its claims of Nixon's abandonment of outmoded conservative doctrine, "the tide of reaction that is sweeping across America is more than a Republican effort to cancel out the remnants of Johnsonian egalitarianism. It is rather a break with more than 40 years of essentially liberal momentum."[49]

Nixon's efforts to turn the nation to the right, along with conservative dreams of a bright political future, were quickly overwhelmed as Watergate and related scandals began to unravel in early 1973. Only months after McGovern's defeat, and only weeks after Nixon had set a conservative domestic course, the administration began to lose the capacity to govern as Watergate consumed all. Ironically, Watergate represented Nixon's final sell-out of the Republican Right. Frustrated and disappointed during the first term, conservatives had regained hope with Nixon's new conservative initiatives. From 1969 to 1972, conservatives had gotten only the rhetoric; now it seemed they were about to get both the rhetoric *and* the action. But just as Nixon was obviously moving toward the right, he fell into increasing legal and political trouble over Watergate.

Watergate thus presented a special dilemma for Right Wing Republicans. Before the seamy details of the scandal became clear, the *National Review,* for example, dismissed Watergate as merely a "power struggle," a media storm aimed at undoing the results of the 1968 and 1972 elections. The ultimate target of Nixon's enemies was the "emerging new majority." As Nixon's tactics and misdeeds came to merit censure, conservatives held that the character flaws in Nixon and his associates must be distinguished from the administration's conservative rhetoric and proposals. Even so, breaking with Nixon was no easy decision for Right Wing Republicans. It meant opposing a Republican president and, according to William F. Buckley, agreeing at least on one issue with the *New York Times,* "an abject form of capitulation."[50]

Conservatives nevertheless finally condemned Nixon's Watergate behavior. And their words carried added weight, because of the unspoken belief that conservatives made up the bulk of Nixon and GOP support. Early on, columnist James J. Kilpatrick urged Nixon to disclose more information. When the president refused, Kilpatrick recommended in October, 1973, that he resign. Goldwater, in turn, was unprepared to go so far so fast. However, his bluntly stated disgust with White House tactics during the Watergate investigation received much popular attention. "It's beginning to smell like Teapot Dome," said Goldwater in April, 1973. Consequently, anti-Nixon liberals embraced Goldwater as their favorite conservative by late 1973.[51] Other prominent Right Wing figures also spoke out. Worried about the popular, if mistaken, impression that Nixon was a true conservative, John Ashbrook asked Nixon to step down in the spring of 1974. Senator James Buckley of New York did the same.

Nixon's troubles were one thing; Vice-President Spiro Agnew's were another. Nixon's ties to the Republican Right although significant, had always been tentative, temporary, and suspect. But Agnew's criticisms of the media and the liberal community had made him the conservative darling in the administration from the beginning. In many eyes, in fact, Agnew had eclipsed California governor Ronald Reagan as *the* conservative candidate for the GOP nomination in 1976. Thus, when Agnew resigned in October, 1973 for accepting bribes while Maryland's governor, conservatives were devastated. "It is a terrible irony," William F. Buckley told the New York Conservative party on the night of Agnew's departure, "that at the moment of history when liberalism is sputtering in confusion, we should be plagued by weak and devious men."[52]

Nixon's own subsequent resignation in August, 1974, was met by Republican conservatives with ambivalence. Never fully sold on Nixon, the Republican Right realized that his destiny and theirs were inextricably linked.

His demise was therefore no cause for joy. On the other hand, Watergate had transformed him into an unalloyed embarrassment. Thus it was that the *National Review,* striving to put the best face on the matter, gamely wrote after the resignation, "The future is filled with hope."[53]

Nixon's resignation was all the more difficult for conservatives because of the known tendencies of his successor, Gerald Ford. At the time of the election of Ford as vice-president, GOP conservatives recalled without fondness his dubious "constructive leadership" as House minority leader during the Johnson years. Although Ford's popularity on Capitol Hill had assured his easy confirmation as vice-president, his first appointments and actions as president rekindled conservative fears. Former Pennsylvania governor William Scranton moved into the White House as a transition advisor. Ford's proposal for amnesty for Vietnam draft resisters incurred Right Wing displeasure, which was further intensified when he selected former New York senator Charles Goodell to head the program.

But nothing embittered Right Wing Republicans as much as Ford's selection of Nelson Rockefeller as his vice-president. Although Rockefeller's recent moves to the right may have been enough to earn editorial rebukes from the *New York Times,* the Right had never approved of Rockefeller. William Rusher claimed that the selection of the New Yorker revealed the new president's "profound ignorance of the basic forces dominating the Republican party." Richard Viguerie later attributed the birth of the New Right to Rockefeller's nomination. Still, there was no open Right Wing fight against the Rockefeller nomination; such internecine party strife was unthinkable in the aftermath of Watergate. Goldwater, for his part, decided instead to concentrate his efforts on blocking Rockefeller's vice-presidential nomination in 1976.[54] Ultimately but belatedly, Ford acknowledged the dominant forces at work in the party when he agreed to Rocky's replacement on the ticket in 1976.

Conceivably, some political observers might wonder whether the White House were in Republican hands if there was no Right Wing Republican squawking about administration appointments. But Ford's subsequent performance as president was no more confidence-inspiring for many Right Wing Republicans. His support of the Equal Rights Amendment (ERA) and a budget that included a $52 billion deficit set him apart from the Right Wing of his party. Even when Ford moved in the proper direction, such as his response to the North Vietnamese invasion of South Vietnam, he did so too late for some conservatives. Actually, the final Communist takeover of South Vietnam underscored for all conservatives the utter futility of the Nixon and current Ford policy of detente, not only in Southeast Asia, but everywhere else in the world. Conservative concerns multiplied when Ford fired Secretary of Defense James Schlesinger, who openly disagreed with the primary architect of detente, Henry Kissinger, and who persistently warned against the shifting power balance in favor of the Soviet Union. Finally, Ford's refusal to see Russian émigré Alexandr Solzhenitsyn, who represented for the Right the greatest moral voice against Soviet communism, demonstrated again that the policy of detente was bereft of moral and logical meaning.

By 1974–1975, a frustration that had been growing among the GOP Right Wing since before the first Nixon administration burst into the open. What, conservatives asked themselves, had over six years of Republican governance accomplished? South Vietnam had gone under, Red China had been recognized, detente had become the entrenched foreign policy, and the military balance of power was shifting in the Soviets' favor. More school children were being bused than ever before, and a Republican administration had even established racial quotas. One Republican president had declared himself a Keynesian and surrendered to wage and price controls, while his successor had proposed huge budgets with huge deficits. All the while, Great Society programs survived and grew. And, despite the Republican electoral victories of 1968 and 1972, the party had reached by mid-1974 its lowest voter-identification level since the Gallup poll began asking such questions in 1937.[55] In the November election, moreover, Republicans watched as Democrats gained forty-nine House seats and four governorships.

"Has the Republican vessel been so severely damaged in the Watergate battering that it is no longer seaworthy?" asked Patrick Buchanan, former Nixon speech writer and now conservative columnist. He was not alone in posing this particular question. A series of books, including Buchanan's own *Conservative Votes, Liberal Victories,* proclaimed that now was the time for a conservative third party. *National Review* publisher William Rusher presented the most comprehensive proposal along this line, even recommending that it be named the Independence party. Rusher's new party would try to reclaim Nixon's old "new majority" by joining the social conservatism of Catholics, ethnics, blue-collar workers, and independents to more traditional conservative economic and foreign policies. The Independence party would simply replace the GOP as the Republican party had long ago supplanted the moribund Whig party.[56]

A new party of their own was indeed the main talk when conservatives convened in Washington in February, 1975. The result of this meeting was the establishment of a Committee on Conservative Alternatives. Practicing GOP politicians, however, stayed aloof from this venture, fearing its impact on their political futures. Yet, they were intrigued with the idea and especially with the prospect that it might force changes within the GOP as it existed. According to Evans and Novak, former governor Reagan publicly broached the idea only to dismiss it after a talk with Holmes Tuttle, a friend, advisor, and influential California Republican.[57] Although also rejecting a third-party move, some Right Wing Republicans, meeting at the invitation of James Buckley, ominously issued President Ford a warning that conservative Republican support should not be taken for granted.[58]

As Ford prepared to seek the Republican presidential nomination in 1976, he made a number of moves to secure support on his right. Dean Burch, former RNC chairman during the Goldwater campaign, was made a prominent advisor in the Ford political organization. As his campaign chairman, Ford selected Secretary of the Army Howard Calloway, a prominent southern conservative who immediately began talk that helped to encourage Rockefeller's subsequent withdrawal as Ford's 1976 runningmate. In addition, Ford vetoed more and more congressional spending bills. He was proving educable if not entirely accceptable. Yet these attentions and presidential actions merely kept the Right's frustrations from spilling over, but only partly accounted for Ford's success in securing the endorsements of several Right Wing powers. Ford was, after all, a Republican presidential incumbent seeking his party's nomination. Goldwater was convinced that the party needed continuity above all else after Watergate and therefore endorsed Ford.[59] Along with Goldwater, the president could count on the support of GOP Capitol Hill and organization leaders, and the vast majority of governors, including such Republican conservatives as minority leader John Rhodes of Arizona and Texas senator John Tower.

But again, as in 1968 and 1972, the Republican Right remained split. Before Nixon's resignation, the demise of Spiro Agnew had projected Reagan into the front-runner position among all Republican presidential possibilities. Indeed, in one poll, Reagan claimed 29 percent support, compared with Rockefeller's 19 percent and former treasury secretary and Democrat John Connally's 16 percent. Ford's elevation to the presidency naturally altered the equation for Reagan, who became a syndicated radio commentator after the end of his second term as California governor. Reagan advisor John Sears, however, believed that Ford was far from a typical incumbent. His claims to the Republican nomination were illegitimate and therefore vulnerable. In addition, personal reasons were tempting Reagan to take on Ford. Unlike Nixon, Ford failed to consult with Reagan, especially on appointments. And Evans and Novak have written that Reagan quite simply considered himself a better man than Ford.[60]

Ford and Reagan also differed on foreign policy and in their political styles. Reagan spoke a blunt conservative rhetoric, while Ford had compromised and accommodated far too often on Capitol Hill not to have acquired a flatulent verbiage. Reagan consistently moved audiences with emotional calls for a new national sense of mission and greatness. The Republican party, he declared, must "raise a banner of no pale pastels, but bold colors which makes it unmistakably clear where we stand on all the issues troubling the people." Ford's well-established nice-guy reputation and feckless mono-tones allowed no such fervent appeals. Conservative George Will found Reagan only "marginally" more conservative than Ford. Their major differ-ences lay in Reagan's superior rhetorical skills, but Will held this as a "very important" difference in modern American politics. Significantly, this dis-tinction was crucial to the Reagan Right's political approach, as North Caro-lina senator Jesse Helms later demonstrated in saying of the Right's hopes, "What we're talking about is a conservatism that leaves absolutely no doubt."[61]

Pledged to a balanced budget, tough law-and-order policies, and a strong national defense, Ronald Reagan ultimately decided on a second bid for the Republican presidential nomination. He would run as an outsider—outside the "Washington buddy system" that he claimed was insensitive to the American taxpayer. He enlisted the aid of less established Capitol Hill figures such as Idaho senator James McClure, Jesse Helms of North Carolina, and Illinois congressman Phillip Crane. The two Reagan backers among GOP governors were South Carolina's James Edwards and New Hampshire's Meldrim Thomson. Reagan did have the endorsement of major conservative periodicals and theoreticians, as well as the benefit of armies of hard-line workers. Even Ford later conceded, "We had most of the generals on our side, but Reagan had most of the troops."[62]

The Reagan strategy called for a few quick primary wins that would force Ford out of the race early. Yet Reagan was immediately placed on the defensive by his earlier suggestion that $90 billion could be cut out of the federal budget by returning certain federal programs to the states. This widely criticized proposal highlighted Reagan's more general difficulty in exploiting domestic issues in his struggle against Ford. Jules Witcover, in his book on the 1976 presidential race, regarded the $90 billion speech as "the ultimate undoing" of Reagan's political fortunes.[63]

As in 1952 and 1964, New Hampshire Republicans once again disap-pointed the conservative candidate. Reagan lost to Ford by only 1,317 out of 108,000 votes, but publicly stated expectations of some prominent Reagan supporters had been higher. What Reagan gamely called his "moral victory" in New Hampshire was followed by unmitigated defeat in Florida, where Ford claimed 53 percent of the vote to Reagan's 47 percent. In both New Hampshire and Florida, Reagan was placed on the defensive by his own dis-cussion of the problems of the Social Security system. Again, the so-called Goldwater problem resurfaced, as it would do once more when Reagan, dur-ing the Tennessee primary campaign, said that selling the TVA "would be something to look at." Philosophically, of course, Reagan had no objection to being compared with Goldwater. The Californian believed that Goldwater was "ahead of his time" and unfairly portrayed by his foes. In 1976, however, Reagan observed that Goldwater's 1964 campaign taught him the value of placing his qualifiers *before* any policy declaration.[64]

Reagan advisors, who obviously were not totally impressed by emerging Republican majority theses and the electoral data of 1968 and 1972, had failed to contest Ford in big northeastern states, and losses here added even greater pressure on Reagan to pull out of the race midway into the primary season. But a dramatic turnaround started suddenly in North Carolina after Reagan began hammering away at Ford's and Kissinger's policy of detente. He restated his earlier promise to replace Kissinger upon taking office. In addition, North Carolina television viewers saw new Reagan advertisements that were bold and unabashedly conservative in contrast with his earlier bland spots. In subsequent appearances, Reagan continued to lambast Ford's foreign policy, especially the alleged surrender of the Panama Canal. Indeed, so sharp did Reagan's assaults become that, according to Evans and Novak, even some conservatives grew alarmed at his aggressiveness. Goldwater himself criticized Reagan's Panama Canal position as "irresponsible."[65] Nevertheless, after his North Carolina victory, Reagan went on to defeat Ford in the important Texas primary, followed three nights later by wins in Indiana, Alabama, and Georgia.

Dramatic as this late spring comeback was, Reagan could not claim the GOP nomination. But with the formal selection of the delegates over, neither could President Ford. The Ford-Reagan nomination struggle therefore became a tug-of-war for groups of uncommitted delegates—and even single uncommitted delegates. And the president had an obvious advantage on this front. Reagan's top advisor, John Sears, believed that Reagan had to gamble in order to stay alive until the GOP convention in Kansas City.

Sears had a well-deserved reputation as a political tactician. When but thirty-four years old, he had helped to mastermind the political comeback of Richard Nixon. Sears's current presence in the Reagan camp attested to Reagan's own tactical pragmatism, as well as indicating that such sentiment now also dominated the Reagan camp. Sears knew that in the end Reagan had to secure delegates from the North and East if he was to have a chance. The crucial Mississippi delegation was reportedly tilting to Ford. In a fateful eleventh-hour gamble Sears recommended, and Reagan agreed, that Pennsylvania senator Richard Schweiker, a certified liberal Republican with ADA and AFL-CIO approval, be designated as his vice-presidential runningmate. Sprung upon an incredulous party just before the convention opened, the Schweiker selection also created doubts about Reagan among certain party conservatives. Howard Phillips of the Conservative Caucus declared that Reagan had "betrayed the trust of those who look to him for leadership." Mississippi GOP chairman Clark Reed found the Schweiker pick "wrong and dumb." George Will sneered, "Their caper is another subtraction from the dignity of the political vocation. Neither Reagan nor Schweiker understands how to broaden a political base without cracking political foundations."[66]

What is astonishing is that Reagan's naming of Schweiker never sparked a full-fledged rebellion among a significant number of Reagan followers. Not that Reagan delegates were delighted by the Schweiker choice; they certainly were not. Yet considering the Right's abhorrence of Schweiker's political outlook and the earlier Right Wing Republican anger over Ford's selection of Rockefeller, the Reagan Right's relative quiescence remains noteworthy. Either they realized the early selection of Schweiker was a last-ditch effort on Reagan's part or were demonstrating the political flexibility and understanding that Reagan possessed naturally. The move failed to break off the Pennsylvania delegation from Ford, although Jules Witcover later wrote that it did "buy time" by putting Mississippi in a "holding pattern." Ultimately Sears's gambit was credited with keeping Reagan's candidacy alive when Ford appeared on the brink of victory.[67]

Unwilling to break open the convention with a serious fight over substantive issues, Reagan aides John Sears and Martin Anderson instead proposed a change in the convention rules. Their proposed rule (16-C)—labeled the "misery loves company amendment" by Ford people—would require candidates to name their vice-presidential runningmates before the presidential balloting.[68] It was on this issue that the Reagan forces would test their strength at the Kansas City convention. Although the Reagan camp's strategy was all too obvious, and all too contrary to political tradition, they came remarkably close to winning this punchless issue. On rule 16-C, Reagan garnered 1,069 votes to Ford's 1,180. Afterward, Ford's managers allowed the more catalytic plank reaffirming "morality in foreign policy" (an anti-Kissinger, anti-detente statement) to pass.

The subsequent and unsurprising nomination of Gerald Ford proved to be no more than a minor defeat for those conservative Republicans who had lined up with Ronald Reagan. First, Reagan had clearly made his point by coming so close to denying Ford the GOP nomination. Conservative backers of both Ford and Reagan had reason to be pleased at the conclusion of the convention. Reagan conservatives, led by Jesse Helms, had redrafted much of the original White House platform draft, and Ford's convention managers conceded to Reagan forces on almost all foreign policy planks. Further, there was the Reagan-approved selection of Ford's vice-presidential runningmate, conservative Kansas senator Robert Dole. The former RNC chairman was no factional heavyweight, but his place on the November ticket was enough to leave the GOP united at the close of the Kansas City convention. The Ford-Reagan struggle amounted to little more than a "family argument," according to F. Clifton White, himself a Ford aide in 1976.[69]

Still, Ford was not entirely satisfactory and never had been for many conservatives. Although he promised to campaign on the issues of free enterprise and a strong national defense, his conservatism remained the milder conservatism of the older Republican party of the Midwest and Northeast. It was moderate on such social issues as the ERA, busing, and abortion. Ford Republicans—as contrasted with numerous GOP conservatives who were simply backing the president—entertained a greater faith in detente and a lesser concern over the shifting strategic balance. Reagan Republicanism, with its greater aggressiveness, sharper ideological focus, and growing Sun Belt flavor, certainly differed in degree, if not in kind. "Kansas City was a watershed," the *National Review* correctly noted after the 1976 election; "it was a conservative convention, almost entirely so, but its conservatism was incompletely defined."[70]

12

Our Time Has Come

On January 20, 1981—a brief four and one-half years after the Kansas City convention—Washington was preparing for the inauguration of Ronald Wilson Reagan as the fortieth president of the United States. Reagan Republicans had captured Washington by election on November 4, 1980, by invasion in the weeks following, and by extravaganza in the days immediately preceding inauguration day.

President-elect Reagan had, as the phase went, "played" the capital in the weeks after his electoral landslide. Proving that his anti-Washington rhetoric would apply only to policy matters and not the social and cultural affairs or the political courtesies of the nation's capital, Reagan dropped in on the Supreme Court justices, called on both houses of Congress, and conferred with Republican and Democratic leaders alike in mid-November. "Tip" O'Neill, Speaker of the House, warned ex-Governor Reagan that he had now come up to the big leagues, after only minor league experience in California. The recently repudiated presidency of Georgia's Jimmy Carter gave O'Neill's blunt words added weight.[1]

But this was a time of Republican—Right Wing Republican—celebration. At a dinner for Republican senators and the president-elect hosted by Senator Howard Baker, Reagan paid tribute to the first Right Wing Republican candidate for president, Barry Goldwater. "If he hadn't walked that lonely road," Reagan said, "some of us wouldn't be here tonight." In all, there was wide agreement that Reagan was off to an excellent start. Even in the Georgetown salons, where Nixon and Carter had always remained outsiders, Reagan hobnobbed with Washington high society at a December party given by *Washington Post* chairman Katharine Graham. Even Graham's newspaper praised the "special sensitivity and class" demonstrated by the president-elect during his November visit.[2] Reagan's high style encouraged the belief that class and elegance would now quickly replace Carter's Dogpatch on the Potomac, as observers of these matters unfairly portrayed Washington's recent social atmosphere.

The days immediately preceding the inauguration showed clearly what a change Reagan's Washington would mark from Carter's ascetic reign. The much-maligned "three-martini lunch" of the Carter years became a symbol of the underclass by comparison with the private jets, limousines, and diamonds that dazzled Washington in the preinaugural whirl of concerts, receptions, parties, and fireworks. It was "Hollywood East," sneered the critics. Following a candlelight dinner on Sunday, January 18, came Monday evening's night club entertainment at the Capital Center, a Frank Sinatra production with Johnny Carson as emcee. Although critics universally panned the show, the Reagans, seated in purple stuffed chairs, seemed to enjoy the occasion. Many words—both serious and silly—would be written on the new age of media politics and Ronald Reagan's crucial place in it. Still, the Reagans' enjoying the Sinatra spectacular certainly symbolized one important change in the Republican Right Wing since 1945—could one possibly imagine Robert Taft, the Dagwood Bumstead of American politics, uncomfortably seated in one of the purple chairs, presiding over such a spectacle? Indeed, even Barry Goldwater's "conscience of a conservative" compelled him to protest the garishness of the inaugural week at a time when many Americans were undergoing economic difficulties.[3] It was significant itself that neither Goldwater nor Taft arrived at such a day of triumph.

On the balmy Washington morning of Tuesday, January 20, the first of an estimated crowd of 150,000 was filling up the Capitol grounds to see the inauguration of Right Wing Republican Ronald Reagan. The ceremonies would take place for the first time on the Capitol's West Front, and commentators made much of the symbolism of this break with tradition. Promising his own new departures, former California governor Ronald Reagan, who represented the rise of the Sun Belt, would face west in taking the oath of office. It was indeed the signal for a new political day.

Working through the night and into the dawn of that new day was President Jimmy Carter. His final hours in the White House were devoted to winning the freedom of fifty-two Americans who were suffering through their 444th day of captivity in Iran. Their plight had been a central focus of the previous year's presidential campaign, and at 8:30 A.M., Carter would call President-elect Reagan and inform him of the final agreement that secured their release. Even Jimmy Carter was helping to make Ronald Reagan's inauguration truly a "new beginning."

The hostage release was the coda of a troubled presidency. Someday, historians may look back at the Carter administration as some now view Herbert Hoover's presidency. Both of these engineers headed administrations that preceded precedent-shattering administrations. Both Carter and Hoover were driven from office by the inadequacy of their halfway measures, their own political ineptitude, and the unrelenting pressure of external forces. F. Clifton White has written that Carter came across in 1976 as something of a conservative. Well into his administration, a Gallup poll showed that 45 percent of the American people believed Carter to be a "conservative," while 36 percent regarded him as being "liberal."[4] Clearly Carter was conservative in many respects. A balanced budget remained an unrealized Carter goal, but deregulation, civil service reform, cuts in the growth of domestic spending, and a belated increase in military spending made up part of the Carter record. There was then some measure of validity in Senator Kennedy's fevered assertion that Carter was a "Reagan clone."

Whatever historians conclude, Kennedy's charge did point up Carter's center-right position in the Democratic party. By 1976 the party reforms of 1968 and the failed "new politics" of George McGovern in 1972 had left the Democratic party a wrangling mass of ethnic and interest groups. The story of the "emerging Republican majority" had been little more than an account of the breakup of Franklin Roosevelt's Democratic coalition. The 1972 Democratic condition illustrated, Theodore White observed, how the party's "liberal idea of progress of a previous half-century had hardened into liberal theology which terrified millions of old clients."[5] Yet Nixon's 1972 inroads into the Democratic coalition quickly disappeared in the wake of the Watergate tragedy.

Mildly conservative southerner Jimmy Carter came out of nowhere to capture the much-coveted Democratic presidential nomination of 1976. Claiming the support of a Democratic South that had outgrown George Wallace's manifestos and gaining a reputation as a supreme political contortionist, Carter reunited FDR's Democratic party for perhaps its final time. In reclaiming the South for the Democrats, however, Jimmy Carter did for southerners what John Kennedy had done for Catholics—freed them of any future automatic loyalty to group or sectional candidate. Nevertheless, on election day 1976, this majority party candidate's talents as the "Great Homogenizer" proved only a secondary reason for his slim victory over Gerald Ford, as polls indicated that Watergate—specifically Ford's pardon of Nixon—primarily explained the election results.[6]

The uncertainty of President Carter's hold on the Democratic party became apparent even before domestic or foreign crisis tested his administration. His relations with the Democratic Congress were generally awful. In the face of high inflation and unemployment, the Soviet invasion of Afghanistan, and the American hostage crisis in Iran, Carter watched as party liberals deserted him for Teddy Kennedy. Kennedy's bid for the Democratic nomination failed miserably, but it forced Carter to accept a series of liberal platform amendments, including a proposal for a $12 billion jobs program.

Among the many ironies of the Carter presidency was that his personal unpopularity by 1980 forced him to dwell upon his place in the tradition of the Democratic party in his fall campaign against Ronald Reagan. Yet even if Carter could have claimed that tradition, which Kennedy followers had said he never could, the utility of that tradition had become questionable indeed some time before. Jimmy Carter had helped reconstitute the Roosevelt coalition in 1976, but he was a spent force by 1980—in and out of the Democratic party. One final indication of Carter's strained relationship with his party came when he conceded to Reagan hours before the polls had closed on the West Coast. This last, selfish act of a political leader, whose party leadership had been under attack for some time, especially hurt the prospects of congressional Democrats who had worked earlier in the fall to dissociate themselves from the Carter ticket.

Neither Carter nor the Democratic party was strong enough in 1980. Exit polling revealed the vote to be an overwhelming personal rejection of Carter. A *New York Times*-CBS News poll showed 38 percent of Reagan's supporters voted for the Republican because of their dissatisfaction with Carter. A *Washington Star* editorial best summed up the widely accepted anti-Carter interpretation of the election: "Whatever the American people want from a president, they weren't getting it from Jimmy Carter." Carter himself naturally rejected the contention that the American people had turned against him personally. Meeting with reporters on the day after the election, he blamed his downfall on a number of factors that were beyond his control—the hostage crisis, for example, and OPEC oil price hikes and inflation. Also responsible for his defeat, Carter maintained, was the post-Watergate mood of skepticism toward political leaders (a sentiment that had favored him four years earlier), and the natural tendency of the American voter to turn out incumbent presidents.[7]

After the November defeat, Democrats alternately debated overhauling the party structure, exploiting the latest political technologies, and redefining the party philosophy—the same things the GOP had done in response to the Roosevelt revolution. Carter, for his part, finished out his sad presidency working to assure "the best transition ever" and laboring right up to the end for the release of the American hostages in Iran. Indeed, after two virtually sleepless nights, the haggard and worn president rushed to meet his successor at the north portico of the White House for their ride to Capitol Hill and the inaugural ceremonies.

At the inaugural ceremonies on the West Front of the Capitol, majority leader Howard Baker led the Senate to its place. Vice-President-elect George Bush followed. The roles of Baker and Bush on this day pointed up crucial changes in the Republican party and the Republican Right over the preceding fifteen years.

Not in twenty-eight years had the GOP controlled the Congress, but Ronald Reagan would at least begin his presidency with a Republican Senate. And this Republican majority was a conservative Republican majority at that. Indeed, young GOP conservatives from the West had established themselves by the late 1970s as "the virtual leaders of the Republican opposition in the Senate." GOP conservative senators such as Orrin Hatch and Jake Garn of Utah, Harrison Schmitt of New Mexico, James McClure of Idaho, and Paul Laxalt of Nevada quite consciously stood apart from older GOP conservatives like Barry Goldwater, Strom Thurmond, and John Tower. Not only were they far more at home with the media, but they prided themselves on their practical effectiveness. Considering the latter, it was no wonder that Robert A. Taft was mentioned on their list of heroes.[8]

Operating through their Senate Steering Committee, they quickly made a difference on Capitol Hill, helping to kill a Carter labor reform bill, working relentlessly to stop Medicare payments for abortions, and almost preventing the ratification of the Panama Canal treaties. Indeed, Laxalt took the minority leader's desk to direct the Republican opposition to the treaties after Baker decided to support them. (An indication of the power and sophistication of this new group became apparent when Baker relinquished the minority leader's desk to Laxalt for the Panama Canal treaties debate, and Laxalt wisely refrained from attacking Baker for his apostasy on such a charged issue.) Their strong opposition to abortion (*the* unifying element of the group) indicated the emergence of new issues of legislative concern, but their agenda also included more traditional Right Wing Republican stands. In delineating the goal of the "new" Senate Republicans in 1979, Nevada's Paul Laxalt was simply reiterating the age-old conservative Republican hope when he said that the Republican party msut be made "to stand for something."

The election to the Senate in 1978 of such Right Wing Republicans as William Armstrong of Colorado, Roger Jepsen of Iowa, and Gordon Humphrey of New Hampshire added to this "new" conservative block, and Laxalt reportedly now had enough votes to further his goal of standing for something by ousting Howard Baker as minority leader. Laxalt, however, was thinking about 1980 politics. Then, he would be running for reelection and, he hoped, directing another Reagan presidential bid. Laxalt therefore decided not to challenge Baker in 1979.[9]

Baker, for his part, relied on his "statesmanlike" moderate Republicanism in his campaign for the Republican nomination in 1980. But tied down by Senate business, Baker never waged an effective campaign and withdrew early in the race. After the Republicans captured the Senate in November, Baker was assured of his unanimous election as majority leader only after Reagan backed and Laxalt nominated him in the interest of party unity. Baker publicly promised to help the new president carry out his campaign commitments. Laxalt, moreover, hardly needed the title. Like Taft in the Eightieth Congress, he had all the influence he needed as the new president's "eyes and ears" in the Senate.[10] Moreover, Laxalt's western conservative colleagues, who had come to Washington in the Republican-poor post-Watergate days, would now take over the major posts and committee chairmanships in the Senate.

Vice-President George Bush would be presiding over the new Republican Senate. His role on January 20, 1981, also helped to illustrate the great changes in Republican politics since 1964. In 1964, Houston businessman George Bush, an energetic young conservative, had won praise even as he lost his race for the Senate. In the intervening years, Bush had built a solid record as a congressman from Houston (1967–1971) and as Republican national chairman, ambassador to the United Nations, U.S. Representative to mainland China, and CIA director. As ex-Governor Carter floundered in Washington and ex-Governor Reagan tried to convince voters that California was simply a microcosm of the United States, Bush tried to parlay his experience into the Republican presidential nomination.

Bush's impressive résumé was only one of his strengths as he stalked the GOP nomination in 1980. His age—fifty-six—was initially believed to be important in the contest against the sixty-nine-year-old Ronald Reagan. Bush's daily jogs while on the campaign trail silently made the distinction— a crucial distinction. Reflecting the rightward trend in the GOP that had gained force beginning in the early 1960s, Ronald Reagan's principal rival for the Republican nomination in 1980 was initially content to be cast basically as a younger Reagan. Bush's foreign and domestic policies—gas and oil decontrol, less taxation, and opposition to the SALT II, the latest strategic arms limitation treaty—placed him safely within the conservative mainstream of the GOP. Only on the post-1964 social issues—his opposition to a constitutional ban on abortion and his support of the ERA—did Bush differ greatly from Reagan. And Bush had no desire to make these latter issues the basis for his campaign for the nomination. Indeed, early in the race, Bush reportedly feared being pinned with a "moderate" label.[11] Considering both the Baker and Bush candidacies for the 1980 GOP presidential nomination, even the *National Review* found good things to say about political trends within the Republican party: "In the year 1979, be it noted, 'moderate Republicanism' is represented by . . . a) a former CIA director, and b) a Border State hawk—both of whom favor deep tax cuts and a tough foreign policy. Things aren't that bad." As the *National Review* concluded, "Ronald Reagan had already won the principal policy issues within the Republican Party."[12]

It was largely Bush's ceaseless campaigning paired with Reagan's light campaigning that brought Bush a victory in Iowa caucuses. Bush now had what he called "Big Mo" (momentum) for the primary battles beginning in New Hampshire. After Iowa, with Reagan now fully engaged in the contest and retiring the age issue, Bush had to set himself apart from Reagan. Although favoring tax cuts, Bush rejected the Kemp-Roth plan to slash tax rates by 30 percent in three years. Reagan, of course, had endorsed this approach for some time, and Bush now characterized it as "voodoo economics," a nifty campaign phrase that boomeranged when the Democrats began using it during and after the fall campaign. Reagan supporters especially opposed Bush's stands on the ERA and abortion. Many also found the buttoned-down Bush—a Yale "preppy" and son of former Connecticut senator Prescott Bush—to be too much of the "Northeastern establishment." His membership in the much-maligned Trilateral Commission, a group of worldwide businessmen, scholars, and public officials concerned with economic and foreign policy issues—could provoke bitter charges of "internationalism" and "elitism" in certain Right Wing quarters. Here was an old yet still strong prejudice of Right Wing Republicans.

Bush lost "Big Mo" forever after Reagan's victory in the New Hampshire primary. Despite his primary victories in Massachusetts, Connecticut, Pennsylvania, and Michigan, Bush never challenged Reagan in any Republican stronghold. Reluctantly, Reagan's final and foremost opponent withdrew at the end of May.

The selection of George Bush as Ronald Reagan's vice-presidential runningmate will long intrigue historians, especially as new information becomes available on the unsuccessful negotiation to put together a "dream ticket" of Reagan and former President Ford. The impetus behind the failed and the final selections contrasts sharply with the intraparty dynamics of the GOP in 1964. First, Reagan showed a flexibility and an imagination in finding a ticketmate that Barry Goldwater never evidenced. Conservatives had taken some valuable lessons from 1964. For his part, Ronald Reagan demonstrated again his own political shrewdness. Still, Reagan had far more room to operate than Goldwater had in 1964. Detroit in 1980 was a lovefeast compared with the San Francisco slugfest in 1964. Ford and Bush were much closer to Reagan philosophically than Rockefeller was to Goldwater; and Bush's "voodoo economics" or Ford's publicly expressed doubts about Reagan's electability hardly compared with the notorious "Scranton letter" or other anti-Goldwater statements uttered by Republicans in 1964. Republicans in 1980 were more generally agreed than at any time since 1945. And this agreement was on essentially conservative positions. Reagan did not have to reach too far left on the GOP spectrum to tap Bush for the second spot in 1980.

Having agreed to support the platform fully, Bush told reporters, "I'm not going to be nickled and dimed to death. I'm not permitting myself to accent differences we've had during the campaign." Bush's reference to the slight differences was appropriate. Of course, ideological fights are relative; doctrinal disputes can be the most vicious. There was plenty of muttering over the Bush selection. Howard Phillips snarled, "Governor Reagan sounded like Winston Churchill but behaved like Neville Chamberlain."

But these Republicans smelled victory, too. Bush's pledge to support the *entire* platform was enough to prevent North Carolina Senator Jesse Helms from having himself nominated as an alternative to Bush. Paul Weyrich of the National Committee for the Survival of a Free Congress was alone among prominent conservatives in refusing to work for the Reagan-Bush ticket. [13]

At 11:34 A.M., Ronald Reagan stepped to the podium on the West Front of the Capitol. Half a world away, the fifty-two American hostages traveled by bus in the Iranian night to Teheran's Mehrabad Airport, where they would board an Algerian airliner that would take them to freedom. Back in Washington, Reagan, dressed in a charcoal gray club coat, striped pants, and a gray vest and tie, stepped forward at 11:57 A.M. to take the oath of office. As the fifty-two Americans inched toward the end of their captivity, Chief Justice Warren Burger administered the oath to Ronald Reagan, the fortieth president of the United States. It was, *Time* wrote, an "extraordinary conjuncture of events." [14]

The new challenges of governance—fundamentally different governance—awaited. The long crusade of Ronald Reagan and the longer crusade of the Republican Right to control the Republican party and the White House had succeeded—magnificently. But how secure, how conclusive was the triumph of the Republican Right? There were claims that Reagan was *the indispensable* figure in the Republican Right. And what about Reagan himself? There remained memories of his pragmatism and flexibility as governor of California and questions about his commitment to certain Right Wing positions.

"Our time has come," Maryland representative Robert Bauman had said back in early 1979, referring to the prospects of conservative Right Wing Republicans. The chairman of the ACU had few doubters since a widely discussed conservative surge had occurred during the Carter years. More Americans were calling themselves "conservative," even if these conservatives often simultaneously took "liberal" positions on specific issues—positions favoring increased funds for medical care, schooling, the elderly, and the unemployed. One Gallup poll reported that 47 percent of the American people now considered themselves to be "conservative," while 32 percent claimed to be "liberals" and 10 percent, "middle roaders." In 1964 self-styled conservatives made up 30 percent of the American populace. National magazines in 1977 featured cover stories on the rising conservative mood in the United States. In explanation, Alaska's Republican senator Ted Stevens speculated that Republican conservatives "simply had to watch as the Democrats tried to prove that government could do everything in order to show it could not." Columnist George Will explained that inflation—which jumped to a double-digit rate during the Carter years—was the great "conservatizing agent." The growing influence and financial well-being of the conservative think tanks such as the Hoover Institute, the American Enterprise Institute, and the Heritage Foundation demonstrated that American conservatism had become a dynamic force of many components.[16]

Not even the Republican Right could claim sole political proprietorship of the new conservative trend. Indeed, political developments in 1978 proved that at least fiscal conservatism had become fashionable across the political spectrum. It had been the year of the American tax revolt. In June of that year, the passage of Proposition 13 in California sparked similar movements across the nation to limit government taxing directly and government spending indirectly. Reagan's successor, California governor Jerry Brown, a Democrat, secured his reputation as a political maverick by leading the drive for a balanced budget amendment. Across the country in Massachusetts, Democrat Edward King used conservative fiscal and social policies to upset incumbent Governor Michael Dukakis in the Democratic primary, going on to be elected governor in November. Indeed, Democrats as a whole began to present themselves in the fall of 1978 as born-again fiscal conservatives. Conceivably, their success in doing so prevented further party defeats. But postelection analysts also had to conclude that the days of brave new Democratic social programs were gone. Carter's cutbacks in domestic programs would face far less opposition from his own party.[17]

Republican conservatives could hardly revel as Democrats turned conservative policies to their own advantage. But the signs of a significant conservative trend were present in the emergence at this same time of the New Right. Right Wing Republicans assumed that the GOP, with the Right in control, would be in the best position to capitalize on this particular movement. Political observer Kevin Phillips had first used the term "New Right" to describe "social conservatives" such as Paul Weyrich, Howard Phillips, and Terry Dolan. By 1977 "New Right" had become synonymous with a growing coalition of single-issue and multi-issue grassroots groups and individuals working against everything from gun control to drugs, high taxes to abortion—and the "liberal" candidates who supported these policies. Essentially, New Right politics involved "organizing discontent" against the liberal social policies of the past fifteen years.[18]

Led by Phyllis Schlafly, who organized the Eagle Forum and Stop-ERA, the New Right had helped prevent by 1980 what had once been considered a foregone conclusion upon its passage by Congress in 1972—the final ratification of the Equal Rights Amendment. Even though it successfully battled to end federal financing of abortions, the New Right made a constitutional ban on abortion its ultimate goal. Besides opposing gun control, relaxation of drug laws, and homosexual rights legislation, the New Right embraced an issue that earlier conservatives such as Barry Goldwater had championed—a constitutional amendment to overturn the Supreme Court ruling against public school prayer. Critics charged that these New Right constitutional initiatives contradicted traditional conservative opposition to government regulation and interference. New Right theorists, on the other hand, countered that far-reaching government social programs and Supreme Court rulings had interfered already; a counteroffensive in behalf of traditional values was now needed. For example, the intrusion of federal programs into the affairs of the American family led Senator Paul Laxalt to introduce the family protection bill in 1979. Such New Right initiatives demonstrated the movement's conscious dissimilarity to the earlier conservatism of the Republican Right. New Right activist Paul Weyrich, organizer of the Committee for the Survival of a Free Congress, made the point succinctly: "We are radicals who want to change the existing power structure. We are not conservative in the sense that conservative means accepting the status quo."[19]

New Right activists saw themselves as different from the old Right in yet another way. The New Right got things done. Richard Viguerie contended that conservatism had long been primarily an intellectual movement; Old Right lawmakers were content to make their speeches in opposition to the latest liberal proposal and keep their constituents happy. Viguerie noted that New Right leaders were indebted to the 1964 Goldwater campaign for giving them their initiation in practical politics. Since then, however, the New Right single- and multi-issue organizations had pioneered in the application of high technology to politics. Viguerie himself had learned direct mail techniques in the 1950s and 1960s under the tutelage of Marvin Liebman, an organizer of Right Wing causes, including the fabled "China Lobby." With a list of about 12,000 Goldwater campaign contributors, Viguerie started his own direct mail company in 1965. Almost a decade later, as Viguerie tells it, the conservative *non*reaction to Gerald Ford's selection of Nelson Rockefeller as vice-president convinced him that the Right needed not more intellectuals, but marketers. Viguerie soon became identified with the use by the conservative cause of direct mail, which, he claimed, had the advantage of "bypassing the Left's monopoly of national news media." Direct mail, computers, telephone marketing, and cable television were soon bringing the New Right's messages directly to the gamut of discontented groups. Before long, the New Right had identified an estimated 4 million contributors and counted 15 million people on its computer tapes.[20]

The New Right's expanding political reach translated into legislative victories. The consumer protection agency, federal financing of congressional elections, post-card voter registration—the New Right gained credit for the defeat of these Carter proposals. The New Right's opposition to the Panama Canal treaties reportedly made the Senate ratification vote as slim as it was. Later, in 1978, the New Right turned from contesting issues to trying to swing elections. The first news of New Right electoral prowess came out of New Jersey, where conservative Jeffrey Bell edged out liberal Republican fixture Senator Clifford Case in the GOP primary. That fall, a New Right organization—the National Conservative Political Action Committee (NCPAC), directed by Terry Dolan, won national notoriety. NCPAC targeted for defeat liberal Senator Dick Clark of Iowa and Senator Thomas McIntyre of New Hampshire and went about publicizing—critics charged, distorting— their "liberal" voting records for the voters at home. When Roger Jepsen in Iowa and Gordon Humphrey in New Hampshire beat those liberal warhorses, the New Right established itself as a major electoral force. Subsequently, Terry Dolan and his NCPAC marked six major liberal senators for electoral extinction in 1980.

The Moral Majority represented another element of the amorphous New Right. Actually, Moral Majority was the name of the organization founded in 1979 by television preacher Jerry Falwell, but the term itself came to apply generally to present-day political activism of fundamentalists and evangelists. Weyrich had undertaken to enlist television ministers such as James Robinson, Pat Robertson, and Jerry Falwell in the conservative cause. The importance of the "born agains" in American politics had become apparent in 1976 when Democrat Jimmy Carter corralled their vote by virtue of his much-publicized religious conversion. Not since William Jennings Bryan and the 1920s had religious fundamentalism taken on such importance in American politics. Unfortunately, however, Carter's personal rebirth could not compensate for the liberal policies of his administration. Thus the religious right, with Weyrich's aid, took on a Republican identification. "In the last several years," Falwell contended, "Americans have literally stood by and watched as godless, spineless leaders have brought our nation floundering to the brink of death."[21] But now Falwell appealed to his flock to vote only for candidates who supported the Bible. According to his reading of scripture, that meant candidates pledged to such things as increased defense spending, a balanced budget, and a constitutional ban on abortion.

Of course, the early 1960s had witnessed the emergence of the Christian Right. Preachers such as Billy Hargis and Dr. Fred Schwarz had earlier called the multitudes to the banner of Barry Goldwater. But these precursors of the Moral Majority were old-fashioned in their medium and message. Where Hargis and Schwarz were preoccupied with the communist threat, the Moral Majority concentrated on the evils of liberal humanism and the welfare state. The radio evangelists and big-top crusaders of the earlier Christian Right had little of the technological sophistication of the Falwells—and nowhere near the political influence of the contemporary Religious Right in combination with the larger New Right.

The New Right and the Moral Majority were natural allies of the Republican Right Wing as 1980 approached—but it was only an alliance. New Right leaders remained loyal to the "movement," and not to the Republican party—or even to the Republican Right. As they saw it, the goals of each were not the same, even if their interests might run parallel. New Right organizations such as NCPAC not only aided Democratic candidates, but wanted to become even more bipartisan. Indeed, New Right leaders disparaged the Republican party as both an institution and a marketing vehicle. "The Republican Party is a fraud," NCPAC's Dolan declared. "It's a social club where rich people go to pick their noses."[22]

New Right leaders further believed it would be "crazy" to tie the movement to the patently unappealing Republican label. "I don't believe that in my lifetime you will ever again be able to market the word 'Republican,'" said the New Right's marketing genius, Richard Viguerie. "You could as easily sell the Edsel or Typhoid Mary."[23] This lack of commitment to the GOP—an attitude symptomatic of the general weakening of both major political parties in the post–World War II era—raised a number of problems for Right Wing Republicans who retained their allegiance to the Republican party and who hoped to include the New Right in their winning Republican presidential coalition.

"I cannot remember a time," James J. Kilpatrick wrote in December, 1978, "not even in the heyday of Barry Goldwater 14 years ago, when there has been so much interest in conservatism." Unlike its posture in that earlier period, however, the Republican party stood essentially united—united on conservative fundamentals. The ideological gap between the GOP's right and left wings had narrowed since 1976, when, as seen previously, it was not that great. The *National Review*'s marked tolerance of the candidacies of moderate Republicans Bush and Baker illustrated the change. At the other end of the Republican spectrum, the Ripon Society, once the guardian of liberal Republican virtue, was now bestowing favorable ratings to one-time Republican foes like Barry Goldwater and Jesse Helms. As economic issues became more important, Ripon Republicans were moving away from their earlier assumption that government should play an active role in the economy. John C. Topping, society president, now believed the time had come for conservatives and "progressives" to work together for the "good of the GOP." Shifts like this gave weight to Ronald Reagan's statement of early 1979, "Never has the Republican Party been more unified."[24]

Reagan was one Republican who could capitalize on both the recent conservative upsurge and GOP unity. He had assured his supporters at Kansas City that, despite his failed bid for the Republican nomination, "the cause" would go on. Shortly after the November election, Reagan's transformation of his "Citizens for Reagan" campaign organization into "Citizens for the Republic" convinced F. Clifton White, for one, that Reagan himself would see to it that "the cause" went on by again running for the presidency. On November 13, 1979, Reagan formally announced his candidacy for the nomination. Since 1976, he had worked to woo party moderates by proving that he was, in Laxalt's words, a "responsible conservative" and "not a right-wing nut with horns coming out of his ears."[25] Still, there were doubts about Reagan's ability to overcome the age issue; he would be sixty-nine in 1980. But Ronald Reagan quickly disposed of this and six major Republican opponents in the spring of 1980. In beating Bush in New Hampshire, John Connally in South Carolina, and John Anderson in Illinois, Reagan demonstrated he could draw support from Republicans and Democrats alike. Yet all of this contrary contemporary evidence was not enough to keep former President Gerald Ford from repeating the conventional wisdom of the last half-century. Ford, who privately still resented what he regarded as Reagan's halfhearted fall campaign effort in 1976, publicly declared in mid-March that Reagan was "unelectable." A flurry of meetings—one between Ford and John Sears, who had been fired the day of the New Hampshire primary as Reagan's campaign director—and press reports centered on a possible Ford bid for the GOP nomination. In the end, however, Ford stayed out of the race after finding little support from Capitol Hill Republicans for such a last-minute effort.[26] Indeed, the Republican nomination race was over well before Bush's withdrawal in late May.

Ronald Reagan had persevered to become the second bona fide Right Wing Republican in sixteen years to win the GOP presidential nomination. Unlike Goldwater, however, Reagan had firm control over the party—and worked to keep it that way. The Republican convention in Detroit was more on the order of a coronation, with the unprecedented "dream ticket" negotiations precluding the usual lifelessness of such affairs.

Although the Republican platform agreed to in Detroit was vintage Right Wing Republicanism, some Old Guard Republicans might not have recognized some of its planks. Detroit Republicans remained the guardians of the private sector and the enemies of government interference in the marketplace. The platform proposed cutbacks in the twin scourges of government spending and government regulation. However, both Reagan and the platform were vague about which programs would be cut; only the education and energy departments were ticketed for extinction. Both were Carter creations. Reagan's and the Republican party's general laissez faire approach could best be seen in the platform's call for the decontrol of oil and gas prices. There were also planks opposing gun control, school busing for the purposes of racial desegregation, and affirmative action or racial quotas. In addition, Republicans advocated a tougher foreign policy and a buildup of conventional and strategic forces.

Well into the spring, Reagan admitted that his 1980 campaign speeches were a rehash of what he had been saying for the last twenty-five years. The 1980 Republican platform confirmed this fact, but it also outlined some changes in programs and new concerns. As Evans and Novak pointed out in their book on the Reagan revolution, Reagan broke with the Republican tradition of austerity economics. He did so as early as 1978 by embracing the

Kemp-Roth proposal to cut marginal tax rates by 30 percent over three years. "Supply-side" theorists maintained that such a cut would precipitate a burst of economic activity which high marginal tax rates had long held back. Theoretically, government revenues would climb because of increased taxable earnings. This would allow for the increased military spending and the balanced budget promised in the GOP platform. Indeed, some supply-siders— Representative Jack Kemp of Buffalo, for instance—rejected any spending cuts, and Reagan talked vaguely of making savings by eliminating fraud and abuse. Of course, cutting taxes had long been part of the conservative creed. Traditional wisdom, however, said that tax cuts would require attendant cuts in government spending. In this way GOP conservatives would achieve their *sine qua non*, what Howard Buffet in 1945 called the "all-American goal"—the balanced budget. The fact that the term "voodoo economics" originated with Republicans underscored the break that Ronald Reagan, Kemp, and the supply-siders had made with traditional Republicans.

The social issue planks of the Republican platform and Reagan's questioned commitment to them reflected the changes in the post–1964 Republican Right and in American political issues. In 1964 Goldwater had introduced "quality of life" issues—crime in the street, school prayer, and the larger question of America's moral tone—into political debate. But Goldwater's major themes centered on traditional conservative concerns of big government growth and foreign policy weakness. The New Right insured that the Republican platform of 1980 would have to address or finesse a series of social issues that since the mid-1970s had noisily taken their place on the American agenda.

The New Right had two possible candidates in the GOP—Philip Crane and Ronald Reagan. Having enlisted the services of Richard Viguerie, Illinois congressman Philip Crane, a forty-eight-year-old who faintly resembled John Kennedy, became the first announced candidate in August, 1978. Former chairman of the ACU, Crane matched Reagan's conservatism on traditional economic and foreign policy issues and spoke out more strongly on such social issues as abortion and school prayer. Although Crane's candidacy reflected the vigor and variety of Republican conservatism, his competition was not universally viewed as healthy. In a tight race, he could harm the major conservative candidate, Ronald Reagan. But Crane simply could not contend with the electoral force of Reagan. He withdrew quietly midway through the primary season, having won no convention delegates. He had won, however, the resentment of Reagan supporters upset by Crane's dangerous pretentions.[27]

But Reagan's New Right bona fides were suspect and remained so. As California governor he had signed the nation's most liberal abortion law. Also, Reagan had initially supported the ERA (a cause Taft had supported). But these earlier Reagan positions changed. He later explained away the dra-

matic increase in California abortions as the result of an unanticipated loop-
hole in the statute and ultimately endorsed a constitutional ban on abortions. He had also reversed his position on the ERA.

Overall, however, Reagan treated the New Right as simply one constituency—a potentially troublesome constituency—of the Republican Right and
the Republican party. He could woo or steer clear of them as the situation
dictated. Evans and Novak have concluded that New Right social issues were
of secondary importance to Reagan. When these forces put through a platform plank advocating the appointment of judges who respected family
values and the sanctity of human life, the Reagan camp reportedly regretted
its failure to exert enough control over the platform writing. Reagan's later
trip to Dallas, where he spoke before 14,000 fundamentalist preachers and
praised the awakening of religious America, was but the wedding ceremony
in what Evans and Novak characterized as a risky "marriage of convenience."[28]

The New Right and the Religious Right were simply elements of a Republican party that assembled in Detroit in July, 1980. Yet, even as political
observers dissected the Republican party and its now dominant Right into
different components, unity and intraparty goodwill distinguished this second triumph of conservative Republicanism. Colorado senator William
Armstrong, a hard-liner on *all* conservative issues, said unabashedly that differences on social issues were no longer that important.[29] Obviously, Right
Wing Republicans could have quarreled with their rivals within the party or
even among themselves. But the likely prospects of unseating the disastrous
Carter encouraged Republicans of all kinds to temper their hostilities.

Further evidence of this came when after the primaries certain Right
Wing Republicans made a move to dump Bill Brock as the Republican
national chairman. Since 1977, after taking over a party that was described
as an "emptying shell" and a small shell at that, Brock had won wide praise
for his efforts to "bring about the emerging Republican majority from the
bottom up" by utilizing direct mail solicitation and reaching out to urban,
female, and black constituencies. His successful effort to hold the 1980
Republican national convention in Detroit symbolized this new Republican
commitment. Nevertheless, conservatives—Senator Laxalt, for example—
still burned over Brock's refusal to bankroll their fight against the Panama
Canal treaties. Reportedly, Laxalt and other Reagan intimates such as Lyn
Nofziger and Edwin Meese wanted the campaign strictly in Reaganite
hands. Brock had to go. F. Clifton White, however, had witnessed in 1964
Goldwater's manifold difficulties stemming from Republican organization
changes—"purges," said his critics—ranging from RNC research positions
to the chairmanship itself. White joined with House GOP minority leader
John Rhodes, Jack Kemp, and Reagan campaign advisors like William Casey
in urging Reagan to keep Brock at his current post. The prominently

reported Brock issue came to be regarded as an important indicator of the Reagan organization's relation to all factions of the Republican party.[30] Ultimately, Reagan's decision to keep Brock as RNC boss presaged the candidate's wise leadership at the Detroit convention, where he successfully mollified black and female Republicans who were unhappy with certain platform planks.

Reagan's masterful Detroit performance, which included his selection of Bush, as well as his moves after the convention to incorporate establishment Republicans into his campaign (and later into his administration) demonstrated that Reagan had profited from the lessons of sixteen years earlier. He was not alone. "Back in the Goldwater convention we disagreed viciously," remarked one California delegate to both the San Francisco and Detroit triumphs. "Maybe I'd like some of that old excitement here, but this time we sense that the odds are better with Reagan, and while our conservative views haven't changed we've mellowed."[31]

The 1980 fall presidential campaign recalled the 1964 contest between Goldwater and Johnson in several major ways. Indeed, the struggle of sixteen years before served as a history lesson for both Carter and Reagan—unavailing for Carter and invaluable for Reagan.

President Carter campaigned against a Right Wing Republican under far less favorable circumstances than had President Johnson. The same conditions that sustained Senator Kennedy's challenge would continue to plague Carter throughout the fall. Unlike Johnson, Carter had no fully united party behind him and had to scramble desperately to reunite the Democrats and also to reclaim the Democratic tradition. Unlike Johnson, Carter could not take credit for economic prosperity and could capitalize on peace only if the maddening humiliation of the Iranian hostage crisis and renewed Soviet adventurism were forgotten. Perhaps Carter's achievements were every bit as respectable as LBJ's by 1964, but Carter had much more to be defensive about and could never indulge in anything similar to Johnson's 1964 campaign promises of the Great Society.

But Jimmy Carter seemed to plagiarize the attacks on the GOP candidates of the 1964 campaign. Johnson had called the 1964 election a referendum on "the whole course of American development"; Carter correctly emphasized the "profound difference" between himself and Reagan. Johnson had scored against Goldwater by asking voters, "Whose finger do you want on the nuclear button?" Carter, in turn, flatly stated that Reagan's election could lead to war and that the election was a choice between "peace or war." "I'm not insinuating that he's a war monger," Carter insisted lamely in mid-October.[32] There were other Carter insinuations and accusations during the campaign, and these too, made use of rhetoric that had proved so telling against Goldwater sixteen years earlier. Reagan, Carter charged, had injected "racism" and "hatred" into the campaign by his use of "code words" such as states' rights. Reagan's election, Carter went on, would be "divisive" to the country by separating people of different races and religions. Unlike 1964, however, the Democratic and not the Republican Right Wing candidate became the issue as the mean-spirited negativism of the incumbent's campaign tactics drew widespread admonition. Carter himself acknowledged that he had gotten "carried away" in several of his attacks on Reagan, although no one accused him of "shoot-from-the-hip" tendencies.[33]

The shoot-from-the-hip charge, which had so bedeviled Goldwater, briefly plagued Reagan when he made some damaging gaffes early in the fall. He drew sharp criticism for, among other things, claiming that Carter had opened his campaign "in the city that gave birth to and is the present body of the Ku Klux Klan," and for calling the Vietnam War "a noble cause." But Reagan's managers moved quickly and effectively to kill this potential issue, limiting the press's access to the candidate.[34] Thus, only briefly did Reagan's fall campaign effort repeat one of the many Goldwater mistakes of 1964. As he showed at various times since 1964, Reagan had learned valuable lessons from the Goldwater experience; they helped him to avoid making mistakes that campaign observers were only too ready to see another Right Wing Republican presidential candidate make. Reagan would not be a 1980 Goldwater. There were many reasons for this, but Ronald Reagan's cheerful smile and campaign style, even as he articulated Goldwater-like policies, were major factors. Carter's full realization of this came when he gave viewers of his televised debate with Reagan the opportunity to compare his own harsh characterizations with the affability and thoughtful demeanor of the Republican candidate before them.

Actually, Reagan's fall campaign amounted to much more than avoiding the mistakes of or comparisons with a defeated standard-bearer of the Republican Right Wing. Indeed, against a Democratic candidate who was ostentatiously attempting to associate himself with the Democratic tradition, Right Wing Republican Reagan made claims to the heritage of John Kennedy, Harry Truman, and even Franklin D. Roosevelt. Reagan, with the aid of his upbeat supply-side economic assumptions, worked to become this election's master of coalition or consensus politics. In a splendid acceptance speech in Detroit, Reagan occasionally spoke of fascism in the New Deal, quoting Franklin Roosevelt with approval—although he cited FDR's 1932 platform promises of a balanced budget and cuts in government spending, a longstanding GOP tactic. After Detroit, Reagan maintained that he, not Carter, represented the traditional Democratic values of John Kennedy and Harry Truman. Supply-side Republicans were now using John Kennedy as an authority in their pitch for tax cuts, and both Truman and John Kennedy quotations could bolster the arguments of foreign policy hard-liners.

As if Reagan's exploiting the words of departed party heroes were not galling enough for Democrats, he was also aggressively pursuing longtime vulnerable constituencies. Notions of an emerging Republican majority resurfaced. Reagan's states' rights pronouncements had obvious appeal in Carter's own back yard, the South. The Republican candidate's stands in favor of tuition tax credits and a constitutional ban on abortion were designed to appeal to Democratic Roman Catholics and white ethnics in the northeastern and midwestern industrial states. Furthermore, Reagan's tenure as president of the Screen Actors Guild made his moves to appeal to rank-and-file workers all the more credible. If Right Wing positions had changed little since 1945, the rhetoric of the Right as represented by Reagan had undergone some astonishing alterations.

"Mr. Carter Must Go!" shouted the Republican party platform of 1980. Ultimately, making and keeping Jimmy Carter as *the* issue in the 1980 campaign stood as Reagan's major campaign accomplishment. Reagan resurrected the "misery index," a combined measure of inflation and unemployment that Carter had used successfully against Ford in 1976. The "misery index" had shot up under Carter, and Reagan now asked Americans if they were better off than they were four years ago. The answer was obvious, and renewed Soviet adventurism in Afghanistan and the "galling metaphor" of the American hostages in Iran suggested a similar response to any such foreign policy question.[35] The question still remained: could high disapproval ratings of Carter and doubts about his competence be turned into Reagan votes in a year when neither candidate was said to be eliciting very positive support from the American voter?

The 1980 presidential campaign resembled the one of sixteen years earlier in one other crucial respect. It culminated in an electoral landslide triggered in part by the overwhelming personal rejection of the loser. But the similarities ended there, for it was the Right Wing Republican challenger who triumphed over the Democratic incumbent president. The extent of Ronald Reagan's victory surprised not only the pollsters but Reagan's most ardent supporters. Reagan claimed 51 percent of the popular vote and won 44 states to collect 489 electoral votes. President Carter's 42 percent of the popular vote allowed him to capture six states and the District of Columbia for 49 electoral votes. Moreover, even in the unlikely event that all of independent candidate John Anderson's support (7.8 percent of the popular vote) had gone to Carter, Reagan still would have won the presidency. The American people had elected a Right Wing Republican as their president.

In the end, Reagan further upset the conventional wisdom by demonstrating considerable coattail pull for congressional Republicans. Not since 1928 had Republicans won control of the Senate, but they did on November 4, 1980. Also, the GOP gained 46 additional seats in the House of Representatives on election day, although it would still remain in the minority.

The many and varied electoral postmortems began immediately. Some

pundits scurried back to their notes on the "emerging Republican majority." Former Nixon speech writer and current resident conservative columnist at the *New York Times,* William Safire, wrote the most colorful comment on the Reagan victory. "Like a great soaking wet shaggy dog," Safire
wrote, "the Silent Majority—banished from the house during the Watergate
storms—romped back into the nation's parlor and shook itself vigorously."
"Emerging Republican majority" notions only became more firmly entrenched upon inspection of Reagan's raid on traditional Democratic constituencies. This Right Wing Republican had left Carter with only his home
state of Georgia in the South and had attracted significant numbers of blue-
collar workers, ethnics, Roman Catholics, and Jews. Republicans stuck with
Reagan in landslide-making numbers. RNC chairman Bill Brock caught the
GOP mood by saying, "We have brought together the elements of a new coalition." He quickly added, however, "The cementing of that depends on
our performance in office."[36]

Obviously, the Reagan administration's performance in office would affect the Republican party future. But there was considerable reason to doubt
that even a sterling Reagan performance would usher in a new partisan
realignment and a Republican era. Political scientists and political observers
had documented the declining influence of American political parties. Six
years after his *Emerging Republican Majority,* Kevin Phillips himself had
meditated on the media's role in weakening American political parties—
and particularly the Republican party of postindustrial America.[37] The 1980
elections offered up evidence that called into question the possibility of an
era of GOP national party dominance. First, exit polling attested that much
of the Reagan vote was a personal rejection of Jimmy Carter and his feckless
presidency. Pollsters blamed their astonishing failure to divine the winner
on the belated choice of the many American voters who lacked strong commitment to either candidate or party.[38] However limited, the showing of
John Anderson made a similar point, and the appalling 52 percent voter
turnout—the lowest in thirty-two years—had implications beyond partisan
political realignment.

A cause and an expression of the decline of American political parties
could be seen during and immediately after the presidential campaign in
the form of the New Right. Single-issue and ideologically oriented political
action groups had in recent years pushed their way into the political process.
The NCPAC had targeted six Democratic liberal senators for defeat in 1980.
Four of the hunted—Birch Bayh of Indiana, Frank Church of Idaho, George
McGovern of South Dakota, and John Culver of Iowa—fell on election day.
NCPAC's Terry Dolan, calling the election "a massive conservative man-
date," issued a new "tentative" hit list for 1982 that included such liberal
Democrats as Senator Ted Kennedy and even liberal Republican senators
Robert T. Stafford of Vermont, John Chafee of Rhode Island, and Lowell

Weicker of Connecticut. Dolan warned, "Liberals ought to be very intimidated by the mood of the American public."[39] The Reverend Jerry Falwell of the Moral Majority claimed to have registered 4 million voters and brought out 10 million voters to the polls. Falwell hailed the Religious Right as being "the primary factor" in the election of a conservative Senate.[40] Without deep allegiance to the Republican party, these new ward heelers of the media age wanted their share of the credit for the election of Ronald Reagan and others.

Other quarters on the Right quarreled with the style and substance of this New Right analysis. Senator-elect Dan Quayle, who had beaten New Right target Birch Bayh in Indiana, charged that the New Right political organizations actually helped their intended victims by causing a backlash against their negative advertising and bully-boy image. Vice-President elect George Bush, already being warned to step in line by the New Right, declared defiantly that Ronald Reagan owed his victory to no one group, and columnist George Will admonished the "banty roosters" of the New Right for their "unpleasant crowing." Wrote Will, the outcome "does not mean that the meanies won."[41]

Will argued that Reagan had "forced and won a national referendum on alternative economic and defense policies." Clearly, there was a widespread disenchantment with the economic and foreign policies of Carter and the Democratic party. They had failed. End inflation and shore up America's global stature were the twin messages of the 1980 election. President-elect Reagan had won an opportunity to try his conservative approach, but there remained much evidence to call into question Reagan voters' commitment to the full conservatism of Reagan and the Republican Right. Americans were still, as they had been since their beginning, a pragmatic people. Results counted. Carter had surrendered millions of voters to Reagan because of his general lack of competence and his specific inability to dampen inflation.

The overwhelming personal rejection of Carter does nothing to diminish the fundamental importance of Reagan's triumph. Reagan had demonstrated an ability to capitalize on anti-Carter sentiment, and anti-Carter Reagan voters had still selected a candidate who promised the most fundamental shift in national policies since Barry Goldwater promised to become the most conservative president after Calvin Coolidge. The anti-Carter vote therefore underscored the growing conservative sentiment in the nation since the mid-1960s.

But the pragmatism of the American voter was also clearly demonstrated in the 1980 election. Earlier national surveys showed that self-described conservatives were taking decidedly unconservative positions on specific issues. Self-described "liberals," likewise, reportedly made up 27 percent of the Reagan vote.[42] These realities, combined with the many diverse elements in and out of the Republican Right that constituted the Reagan majority, made the ultimate triumph of Ronald Reagan and the Republican Right all the more questionable. For some time columnist James J. Kilpatrick had perceptively pointed out that the recent conservative boom still was far from ideologically grounded. After election day 1980, Kilpatrick penned the most punchy *and* prudent message for the now many-shaded Republican Right Wing: Reagan "won a glorious victory. The millennium, it ain't."[42]

Whether such a millennium ever arrived would be determined over the next decade—in the White House, in the Congress, and in voting booths across the United States. On inauguration day 1981, however, two things were clear. One of the great political clichés of the post-New Deal age was now a fatality of history—the long-held belief that a Right Wing or Old Guard Republican could win the Republican presidential nomination, but never the presidency. Second, Ronald Reagan and the Republican Right were interpreting his 1980 victory as an unmistakable mandate for the policies Reagan had preached on his long road to the presidency. And one of the ironies of American history remained: election "mandates" are more matters of will and skill after an election than of vote tallies, as the presidencies of Polk, Lincoln, and Wilson demonstrated.

Upon completing the oath of office, Ronald Reagan, fortieth president of the United States, delivered an inaugural address that simultaneously restated familiar themes and signaled new national policies for the coming years. Calling for an "era of National renewal," Reagan promised swift and bold action to confront the problems of inflation and unemployment. But Reagan, who was already being called the "Roosevelt of the Right," outlined an approach that differed fundamentally from that of the New Deal. "In the present crisis," he declared, "government is not the solution to our problem; government is the problem." Reagan promised to curb the size and influence of the federal establishment and restore the balance between the various levels of government.[44] The new president's twenty-minute address was not without its stirring moments, but it was chiefly a simple and upbeat call for action—conservative action—to solve the nation's problems.

As Reagan reached the end of his inaugural address, an Algerian plane full of Americans in their first moments of freedom left the runway in Iran. Yet this was not the only happy coincidence shining on the first moments of the Reagan presidency. In 1933 reporters had made much of the symbolism of the sun's emergence at the dramatic point in Franklin Roosevelt's inaugural address. On January 20, 1981, reporters would do likewise when the sun peeked through to spotlight Reagan—"the Roosevelt of the Right"—as he reached peroration of his inaugural message.[45] The Reagan presidency had begun.

Notes

Abbreviations Used in Notes

DDE   Dwight David Eisenhower
DDEL   Dwight David Eisenhower Library
DDEP   Dwight David Eisenhower Papers
NYT   *New York Times*
PPI   Post-Presidential Papers, Individual Correspondence Files, Herbert Hoover Papers
RG   Record Group
RT   Robert Taft
RTP   Robert Taft Papers

Chapter 1

1. Allen Drury, *A Senate Journal, 1943-1945* (New York: McGraw-Hill, 1963), p. 293.

2. RT to Julius Klein, Nov. 22, 1944, Box 46, Robert Taft Papers, Library of Congress (hereafter cited as RTP).

3. *Cong. Record,* 79 Cong., 1 Sess., p. 10391; ibid., 2 Sess., p. A4025.

4. *Milwaukee Sentinel,* Oct. 23, 1946.

5. *Cong. Record,* 79 Cong., 2 Sess., p. 4056.

6. Ibid., p. 2355.

7. Malcolm Moos, *The Republicans: A History of Their Party* (New York: Random, 1956), p. 323.

8. *Cong. Record,* 79 Cong., 1 Sess., p. 2020.

9. Athan G. Theoharis, *The Yalta Myths: An Issue in U.S. Politics, 1945-1955* (Columbia: University of Missouri Press, 1970), pp. 32, 222.

10. *Cong. Record,* 79 Cong., 2 Sess., p. A1048.

11. Milton Lehman, "Salesman in the Senate," *Collier's* 117 (Dec. 14, 1946); 78.

12. Walter S. Poole, "The Quest for a Republican Foreign Policy: 1941-1951" (Ph.D. diss., University of Pennsylvania, 1968), p. 308; *Cong. Record,* 79 Cong., 1 Sess., p. 6256.

13. Poole, "The Quest for a Republican Foreign Policy," p. 140; *Cong. Record,* 80 Cong., 1 Sess., p. 735.

14. James T. Patterson, *Mr. Republican: A Biography of Robert A. Taft* (Boston: Houghton Mifflin, 1972), p. 197.

15. *Milwaukee Sentinel,* Nov. 5, 1947, p. 10.

16. James M. Burns, *Roosevelt: The Lion and the Fox* (New York: Harcourt, Brace and World, 1956), p. 271.

17. *Newsweek,* Jan. 22, 1945, p. 44; Burns, *Roosevelt: The Lion and the Fox,* p. 447.

18. RT to Tom L. Gibson, Apr. 3, 1945, Box 42, RTP.

19. Edward R. Martin, *Always Be On Time* (Harrisburg, Pa.: Telegraph Press, 1959), p. 169; Daniel Reed to Leonard Hall, Dec. 10, 1948, Box 44, Daniel R. Reed Papers, Olin Library, Cornell University, Ithaca, N.Y.

20. George H. Mayer, *The Republican Party, 1854-1966* 2nd ed. (New York: Oxford University Press, 1962), p. 448.

21. Moos, *The Republicans,* p. 415.

22. RT to B.P. Hickenlooper, Aug. 19, 1944, Box 199, RTP; RT to Roger Flaherty, July 25, 1944, Box 193, RTP.

23. Bernard Devoto, "The Easy Chair," *Harper's* 190, no. 136 (Jan., 1945): 135.

24. John W. Bricker to Eric F. Goldman, Jan. 24, 1955, Box 116, Bricker Papers, Ohio Historical Society Library, Columbus, Ohio.

25. Donald R. McCoy, *Landon of Kansas* (Lincoln: University of Nebraska Press, 1966), p. 260; Donald B. Johnson, *The Republican Party and Wendell Willkie,* Illinois Studies in the Social Sciences, vol. 66 (Urbana: University of Illinois Press, 1960), p. 13; *Newsweek,* Nov. 11, 1936, p. 14: and Devoto, "The Easy Chair," p. 136.

26. Harrison Spangler to RT, Jan. 22, 1945, Box 42, RTP.

27. *New York Times* (hereafter abbreviated *NYT*), Dec. 6, 1945, p. 18; RT to Harrison Spangler, Dec. 7, 1945, Box 953, RTP.

28. *NYT,* Dec. 6, 1945, p. 38; *Chicago Tribune,* Dec. 7, 1945, p. 10 and December 8, 1945, pp. 1, 9.

29. *Chicago Tribune,* Jan. 25, 1946, p. 22; *Nation* 16 (Dec. 22, 1945): 675.

30. RT to Wallace Townsend, Apr. 3, 1946, Box 954, RTP: R.R. McCormick to B.C. Reece, May 5, 1946, File 65.5.3, B. Carroll Reece Papers, B. Carroll Reece Museum, East Tennessee State University, Johnson City, Tenn.; *Chicago Tribune,* Apr. 28, 1946, p. 18.

31. *Philadelphia Record,* Apr. 3, 1946; *US News,* Apr. 12, 1946, p. 65.

32. RT to J.C. Argentsinger, Apr. 8, 1946, Box 1297, RTP; RT to Wallace Townsend, Apr. 3, 1946, Box 954, RTP.

33. Alonzo L. Hamby, *Beyond the New Deal: Harry S. Truman and American Liberalism* (New York: Columbia University Press, 1973), p. 41.

34. Homer Capehart to Herbert Hoover, May 26, 1945, Post Presidential Papers, Individual Correspondence File (PPI), Herbert Hoover Presidential Library, West Branch, Iowa.

35. Hamby, *Beyond the New Deal,* p. xix.

36. RT to R.J. Ingalls, May 12, 1945, RTP, Box 42.

37. RT to Henry W. Taft, May 25, 1945, Box 3, RTP.

38. Patterson, *Mr. Republican,* p. 313.

39. Alf M. Landon to Harold B. Johnson, Jan. 23, 1946, Alf M. Landon Papers, Box 10.123, Kansas State Historical Society, Topeka, Kan.

Chapter 2

1. Daniel Reed to Clarence L. Lathrop, Nov. 22, 1946, Box 45, Reed Papers; *Cong. Record,* 80 Cong., 1 Sess., p. 2215; *NYT,* Nov. 18, 1946, p. 2; *US News,* Nov. 15, 1946, p. 13; *Chicago Tribune,* Nov. 7, 1946, p. 22.

2. *Time,* Mar. 11, 1946, p. 24; ibid., Oct. 28, 1946, p. 27; *US News,* Nov. 15, 1946, p. 70.

3. *Time,* Mar. 29, 1943, p. 13.

4. William S. White, *The Taft Story* (New York: Harper and Row, 1954), p. 56.

5. *US News,* Nov. 15, 1946, pp. 26, 28.

6. Louis H. Bean, "The Republican 'Mandate' of '48," *New York Times Magazine,* Jan. 19, 1947, p. 16.

7. *Life,* Oct. 28, 1946, p. 36.

8. *Human Events* 3 (Nov. 6, 1946): 5; *Time,* Nov. 18, 1946, p. 24; *Milwaukee Sentinel,* Nov. 6, 1946, p. 10.

9. *Time,* Nov. 18, 1946, p. 24.

10. Ibid.

11. "Old Guard Supreme," *New Republic* 116 (Jan. 13, 1947): 8.

12. Paul F. Healy, "Big Noise from Nebraska," *Collier's* 126 (Aug. 5, 1950): 22.

13. RT to Walter S. Hallanan, Mar. 12, 1947, Box 959, RTP.

14. *Cong. Record.,* 80 Cong., 1 Sess., p. A458.

15. Ibid., p. 3022.

16. Raymond E. Baldwin, "Where the GOP has Failed," *American Magazine* 164 (Sept. 1947): 25.

17. *Cong. Record,* 80 Cong., 1 Sess., p. 1164; George D. Aiken, "Senator Aiken Warns His Party," *New York Times Magazine,* Mar. 23, 1947, pp. 71, 10.

18. *NYT,* Mar. 3, 1947, p. 9; *Newsweek,* Mar. 17, 1947, p. 30.

19. *NYT,* Mar. 18, 1947, p. 3.

20. Baldwin, "Where the GOP has Failed," pp. 131, 133; "Rumblings," *New Republic* 116 (Mar. 17, 1947),: 9.

21. "Had Enough?" *Nation* 164 (Mar. 22, 1947): 319; *Newsweek,* Mar. 17, 1947, p. 30; *US News,* Mar. 14, 1947, p. 23.

22. *Saturday Evening Post,* Apr. 12, 1947, p. 152.

23. R. Alton Lee, *Truman and Taft-Hartley: A Question of Mandate* (Lexington: University of Kentucky Press, 1966), pp. 52, 62.

24. Patterson, *Mr. Republican,* p. 359.

25. Herbert Hoover to RT, July 24, 1947, PPI, Box 529, Folder 3885, Hoover Papers.

26. Patterson, *Mr. Republican,* p. 319.

27. Ibid., p. 391.

28. Susan Hartmann, *Truman and the 80th Congress* (Columbia: University of Missouri Press, 1971), p. 8.

29. Patterson, *Mr. Republican,* p. 319.

30. Ibid., pp. 259, 333; RT to Hugh Butler, Nov. 21, 1947, Box 980, RTP; RT to E. Kendall Gillett, Mar. 22, 1949, Box 980, RTP.

31. John Taber to Louis H. Fulmer, Nov. 25, 1946, Box 56, John Taber Papers, Olin Library, Cornell University, Ithaca, N.Y.; Marvin E. Stromer, *The Making of a Political Leader: Kenneth S. Wherry and the United States Senate* (Lincoln: University of Nebraska Press, 1969), p. 164.

32. *Cong. Record,* 80 Cong., 1 Sess., p. 2215.

33. White, *The Taft Story,* p. 143; RT to Roy D. Moore, Mar. 26, 1948, Box 968, RTP.

34. Arthur Vandenberg, Jr., ed., *The Private Papers of Senator Vandenberg* (Boston: Houghton Mifflin, 1952), p. 334.

35. Herbert Hoover to John O'Laughlin, June 23, 1947, Box 459, Folder 3460, Hoover Papers.

36. RT to Dorothy Thompson, May 31, 1947, Box 961, RTP.

37. Robert R. McCormick to Robert E. Wood, Feb. 19, 1947, Box 11, Robert E. Wood Papers, Herbert Hoover Library, West Branch, Iowa.

38. *Cong. Record,* 80 Cong., 1 Sess., p. 2215.

39. John Lewis Gaddis, *The United States and the Origins of the Cold War, 1941-1947* (New York: Columbia University Press, 1973), p. 351.

40. Forrest [?] to RT, March 16, 1947, Box 42, Taber Papers; John Taber to William Athawes, Mar. 24, 1947, Box 42, Taber Papers.

41. Michael P. Poder, "The Senatorial Career of William E. Jenner" (Ph.D. diss., University of Notre Dame, 1976), p. 106.

42. Mary Welek Atwell, "Congressional Opponents of Early Cold War Legislation" (Ph.D.

diss., Saint Louis University, 1973), pp. 17, 45; *Cong. Record,* 80 Cong., 1 Sess., pp. 4606-7.

43. H. Bradford Westerfield, *Foreign Policy and Party Politics: Pearl Harbor to Korea* (New Haven, Conn.: Yale University Press, 1955), p. 224; H.H. Harris, "Crustiest Crusader: John Taber, King of the Shining Meat Ax," *Reporter* 8 (May 26, 1953): 27.

44. *Life,* June 21, 1954, p. 130.

45. RT to Herbert Hoover, July 11, 1947, Herbert Hoover to RT, July 16, 1947, and RT to Herbert Hoover, August 13, 1947, PPI, Box 529, Folder 3885, Hoover Papers.

46. RT to Frank Gannett, Dec. 26, 1947, Box 966, RTP.

47. RT to Henry P. Luce, Feb. 2, 1949, Box 968, RTP.

48. RT to Charles M. White, Dec. 31, 1947, Box 48, RTP.

49. John Taber to Edgar C. Spaven, Nov. 28, 1947, Box 42, Taber Papers.

50. *Chicago Tribune,* June 21, 1948, p. 20.

51. Eric F. Goldman, *The Crucial Decade—and After: America, 1945-1960* (New York: Alfred A. Knopf, 1971), p. 56.

52. Hartmann, *Truman and the 80th Congress,* p. 132.

53. Daniel Reed to Clarence L. Lathrop, Nov. 22, 1946, Box 45, Reed Papers.

Chapter 3

1. *Philadelphia Inquirer,* June 22, 1948, p. 1.

2. *NYT,* Dec. 18, 1946, pp. 1, 3, and Nov. 16, 1947, VII-7.

3. *NYT,* Dec. 18, 1946, IV-3.

4. E.H. Taylor to Alf M. Landon, Nov. 29, 1946, Box 10.124, Landon Papers.

5. Patterson, *Mr. Republican,* pp. 267-69; RT to R.A. Forster, Mar. 21, 1946, Box 953, RTP.

6. RT to John B. Hollister, Jan. 7, 1947, Box 46, RTP; RT to Burrell Wright, Dec. 26, 1946, Box 953, RTP; and *NYT,* Mar. 6, 1947, p. 17.

7. Patterson, *Mr. Republican,* p. 391; and B.E. Tate to RT, Dec. 24, 1947, Box 285, RTP.

8. Patterson, *Mr. Republican,* p. 165.

9. B.E. Tate to RT, Dec. 24, 1947, Box 285, RTP; RT to Richard B. Scandrett, Dec. 31, 1947, Box 48, RTP.

10. *Time,* Jan. 20, 1947, p. 26; Richard Rovere, "Taft: Is This the Best We've Got?" *Harper's* 207 (Apr. 1948): 289-92; Patterson, *Mr. Republican,* p. 395.

11. RT to John J. Williams, June 30, 1948, Box 48, RTP.

12. Sterling Morton to Alf M. Landon, Jan. 3, 1947, Box 40, Sterling Morton Papers, Chicago Historical Society, Chicago, Ill.

13. Bonner Fellers Oral History Interview, Box 11, Herbert Hoover Presidential Library.

14. *NYT,* July 6, 1947, IV-8.

15. *Human Events* 4 (Sept. 3, 1947).

16. Howard B. Schonberger, "The General and the Presidency: Douglas MacArthur and the Election of 1948," *Wisconsin Magazine of History* 57 (Spring 1974): 208.

17. Douglas MacArthur to R.E. Wood, Oct. 15, 1947, RG 10, Douglas MacArthur Papers, MacArthur Memorial Library, Norfolk, Va.

18. Eastwood to Hanford MacNider, Oct. 14, 1947, Box 73, Hanford MacNider Papers, Herbert Hoover Presidential Library, West Branch, Iowa.

19. Ibid.

20. Carolyn Mattern, "The Man on the Dark Horse: The Presidential Campaigns for General Douglas MacArthur, 1944 and 1948" (Ph.D. diss., University of Wisconsin, 1976), pp. 210, 209.

21. R.E. Wood to Douglas MacArthur, Dec. 4, 1947, Box 42, Wood Papers; Douglas MacArthur to R.E. Wood, Nov. 16, 1947, RG 10, MacArthur Papers; R.E. Wood to Douglas MacArthur, Dec. 12, 1947, Box 42, Wood Papers.

22. Mattern, "The Man on the Dark Horse," p. 216; *NYT,* Mar. 14, 1948, IV-7.

23. R.E. Wood to Douglas MacArthur, Apr. 9, 1948, Box 42, Wood Papers; *NYT,* Apr. 8, 1948, p. 1; Mattern, "The Man on the Dark Horse," pp. 228-29.

24. R.E. Wood to Gen. Douglas MacArthur, Apr. 15, 1948, Box 10, Wood Papers.

25. *NYT,* Apr. 18, 1948, IV-3; Apr. 25, 1948, IV-7; May 2, 1948, p. 62.

26. *NYT,* Jan. 26, 1948, p. 1.

27. Patterson, *Mr. Republican,* pp. 407, 406.

28. *Washington Post,* June 21, 1948, p. 9.

29. Schonberger, "The General and the Presidency," p. 208; *Human Events* 5 (May 12, 1948).

30. Alf M. Landon to Felix Morley, Dec. 31, 1946, Box 3, Felix Morley Papers, Herbert Hoover Presidential Library, West Branch, Iowa.

31. *Time,* Mar. 16, 1947, p. 20.

32. Edward E. Martin Diary, July 15, 1948, Joseph Martin Papers, Cushing-Martin Library, Stonehill College, Easton, Mass.; *Newsweek,* July 5, 1948, p. 14.

33. *NYT,* June 24, 1948, p. 7; Edward Martin to Cecil B. Highland, Nov. 27, 1948, Campaign Material, Box 3, Edward Martin Papers, Pennsylvania State Archives, Harrisburg, Pa.; J. Glenn Beall to Edward Martin, July 14, 1948, General Correspondence, Box 1, Edward Martin Papers.

34. James P. Kem to Graham Mozealous, July 13, 1948, Folder 03980, James P. Kem Papers, University of Missouri, Columbia.

35. *Chicago Tribune,* June 25, 1948, p. 2.

36. *Newsweek,* July 7, 1948, p. 16.

37. Ibid.; Henry Z. Scheele, *Charlie A. Halleck: A Political Biography* (New York: Exposition Press, 1966), p. 120.

38. Ibid., p. 121.

39. Vandenberg, *Private Papers of Senator Vandenberg,* p. 438; RT to Dwight H. Green, June 29, 1948, Box 48, RTP.

40. Interview with John W. Bricker, Nov. 2, 1978.

41. C.A. Halleck to Faye Hollman, July 26, 1948, Correspondence 1948, June-July, Charles A. Halleck Papers, Lilly Library, Indiana University, Bloomington; *NYT,* June 25, 1948, p. 22; Phyllis Schlafly, *A Choice Not an Echo,* (Alton, Ill.: Marquette Press, 1964), p. 48.

42. Vandenberg, *Private Papers of Senator Vandenberg,* p. 428.

43. Wayne Morse, "Liberal Hopes Under Dewey," *Nation* 167 (Oct. 23, 1948): 459.

44. *NYT,* June 22, 1948, p. 6, and June 24, 1948, p. 6.

45. White, *The Taft Story,* p. 118.

46. RT to Oscar Solbert, June 30, 1948, Box 48, RTP; RT to Alfred A. Dustin, Dec. 29, 1948, Box 907, RTP.

47. RT to Sinclair Weeks, July 1, 1948, Box 48, RTP; RT to John D. Hartigan, July 1, 1948, Box 46, RTP.

48. RT to Oscar Solbert, July 30, 1948, Box 48, RTP.

49. Robert J. Donovan, *Conflict and Crisis: The Presidency of Harry S. Truman, 1945-48* (New York: W.W. Norton, 1977), p. 408.

50. *Philadelphia Inquirer,* July 16, 1948, p. 2; Irvin Ross, *The Loneliest Campaign: The Truman Victory of 1948* (New York: New American Library, 1968), p. 137; Charles A. Halleck to Ellsworth B. Buck, July 31, 1948, Correspondence 1948, June, July, Halleck Papers.

51. Robert A. Divine, *Foreign Policy and U.S. Presidential Elections, 1940-1948* (New York: Franklin Watts, 1974), pp. 225-26.

52. Ross, *The Loneliest Campaign,* p. 167; Donovan, *Conflict and Crisis,* pp. 426, 423.

53. *NYT,* Oct. 31, 1948, p. 62.

54. *Baltimore Sun,* Nov. 7, 1948.

Chapter 4

1. *NYT,* Nov. 12, 1948, p. 22; White, *The Taft Story,* p. 82; B.C. Reece to Edward Martin, n.d. and Walter S. Hallanan to Edward Martin, Nov. 10, 1948, Campaign Material, Box 3, Edward Martin Papers.

2. Walter S. Hallanan to Edward Martin, Nov. 10, 1948, Campaign Material, Box 3, Edward Martin Papers; Homer B. Mann to RT, Dec. 22, 1948, and RT to Alfred A. Dustin, Dec. 29, 1948, Box 970, RTP.

3. John Sherman Cooper to Joseph Alsop, Nov. 8, 1948, Box 4, Joseph and Stewart Alsop Papers, Library of Congress; Henry Cabot Lodge, Jr., "Does the Republican Party Have a Future?" *Saturday Evening Post* 221 (Jan. 29, 1949): 23, 82.

4. Clarence Budington Kelland to B. Carroll Reece, Nov. 5, 1948, Box 288, RTP; C.B. Kelland, "Why the Republicans Lost," *American Mercury* 144 (Feb. 1949): 181.

5. Walter S. Hallanan to Edward Martin, Nov. 13, 1948, Campaign Material, Box 3, Edward Martin Papers; James P. Kem to Walter H. Baird, Dec. 14, 1948, Folder 03974, Kem Papers; RT to Alfred A. Dustin, Dec. 29, 1948, Box 970, RTP.

6. Kelland, "Why the Republicans Lost," p. 182.

7. Mayer, *The Republican Party,* p. 472; B.C. Reece to Edward Martin, n.d., Campaign Material, Box 3, Edward Martin Papers.

8. *US News and World Report,* Feb. 4, 1949, p. 22.

9. *Time,* Nov. 29, 1948, p. 22.

10. Alf M. Landon to RT, Dec. 29, 1948, Box 980, RTP; *NYT,* Jan. 25, 1949, p. 1.

11. RT to Carroll Reece, June 2, 1950, Box 990, RTP; RT to Col. R.B. Creager, Jan. 5, 1949, Box 980, RTP.

12. C.B. Kelland to Herbert Hoover, Feb. 1, 1949 and Feb. 26, 1949, PPI, Box 386, Hoover Papers.

13. *Newsweek,* Aug. 15, 1949, p. 24.

14. RT to A.R. Knight, Aug. 6, 1949, and RT to George Gunderson, Aug. 6, 1949, Box 980, RTP; RT to Ralph F. Gates, Sept. 2, 1949, Box 318, RTP; RT to Chester K. Gillespie, Aug. 27, 1948, Box 982, RTP.

15. *NYT,* Jan. 2, 1949, IV-3.

16. *NYT,* Jan. 4, 1949, p. 3.

17. *Time,* Jan. 10, 1949, p. 15; *New Republic* 120 (Jan. 17, 1949): 8; *Saturday Evening Post* 220 (Mar. 12, 1949): 10; RT to Basil Brewer, Jan. 7, 1949, Box 288, RTP; John Chamberlain, "The Condition of the Republicans," *Yale Review* 38 (Mar. 1949): 385, 398, 396.

18. C.B. Kelland, to Herbert Hoover, Feb. 26, 149, PPI, Box 386, Hoover Papers.

19. Sterling Morton to Alf M. Landon, Nov. 25, 1949, Box 10.127, Landon Papers.

20. *Newsweek,* Dec. 26, 1949, p. 14.

21. *Chicago Tribune,* Feb. 8, 1950, p. 20.

22. *Newsweek,* Feb. 20, 1950, p. 38; Henry Cabot Lodge, Jr., "Modernize the GOP," *Atlantic Monthly* 175 (Mar. 29, 1950): 28.

23. *NYT,* Feb. 12, 1950, IV-7.

24. Richard Rovere, *Senator Joe McCarthy* (Cleveland: World Publishing, 1970), p. 125.

25. Michael O'Brien, *McCarthy and McCarthyism in Wisconsin* (Columbia: University of Missouri Press, 1980), pp. 97-98; Robert Griffith, *The Politics of Fear: Joseph R. McCarthy and the Senate* (Lexington: University Press of Kentucky, 1970), pp. 10-20.

26. *Newsweek,* July 31, 1950, p. 25; Stromer, *The Making of a Political Leader,* p. 19.

27. RT to Joseph McCarthy, May 2, 1950, Box 983, RTP; Patterson, *Mr. Republican,* pp. 446-48; RT to Walter E. Balterson, Aug. 28, 1951, Box 1094, RTP; Rovere, *Senator Joe McCarthy,* p. 65.

28. R.E. Wood to Margaret Chase Smith, June 21, 1950, Box 16, Wood Papers.

29. Griffith, *Politics of Fear,* pp. 100-101; Richard M. Fried, *Men Against McCarthy* (New York: Columbia University Press, 1976), pp. 75-88; *Newsweek,* July 31, 1950, p. 12.

30. "Conservative Revival," *Life* 28 (May 15, 1950): 38; "A Trend is Running Toward an Enlightened Conservatism," *Life* 29 (July 3, 1950): 18.

31. *Time,* Sept. 11, 1950, p. 25; "A Trend is Running Toward an Enlightened Conservatism," p. 18.

32. RT to David A. Hillstrom, Apr. 29, 1950, and Apr. 18, 1950, Box 989, RTP.

33. *NYT,* May 18, 1950, p. 28; Frederick Nelson, "New Challenger Arises to Plague G.O.P. Old Guard," *Saturday Evening Post* 222 (June 25, 1950): 10; *US News and World Report,* June 9, 1950, p. 14.

34. *NYT,* Nov. 9, 1950, p. 32.

35. *Chicago Tribune,* Nov. 9, 1950, p. 16.

36. Robert E. Wood to Douglas MacArthur, Nov. 17, 1950, Box 43, Wood Papers.

37. RT to Styles Bridges, Nov. 11, 1950, Box 991, RTP.

38. *Chicago Tribune,* Nov. 9, 1950, p. 16; Robert R. McCormick to RT, Nov. 8, 1950, Box 990, RTP; Sterling Morton to RT, Nov. 29, 1950, Box 319, RTP; RT to Harry Zweifel, Nov. 21, 1950, Box 990, RTP.

39. James P. Kem to J. John Gillis, Dec. 5, 1950, Folder 06676, Kem Papers.

40. *NYT,* Oct. 31, 1950, p. 22, and Nov. 4, 1950, p. 7; *US News and World Report,* Nov. 17, 1950, p. 34; Ronald J. Caridi, *The Korean War and American Politics: The Republican Party as a Case Study* (Philadelphia: University of Pennsylvania Press, 1968), p. 94; *NYT,* Nov. 4, 1950, p. 7; Fried, *Men Against McCarthy,* pp. 109-21; Griffith, *The Politics of Fear,* pp. 122-31; Joe McCarthy to Robert E. Wood, December 13, 1950, Box 11, Wood Papers.

41. William F. Knowland Oral History Interview, No. 333, Dwight D. Eisenhower Library, Abilene, Kan. (hereafter DDEP and DDEL).

42. Caridi, *Korean War and American Politics,* p. 9; Poole, "The Quest for a Republican Foreign Policy," pp. 355-56.

43. Daniel Reed to Mary W. Mulholland, Nov. 21, 1949, Box 20, Reed Papers.

44. Caridi, *Korean War and American Politics,* pp. 33, 36, 45, 71-3, 55; Stromer, *The Making of a Political Leader, p. 64; Cong. Record,* 81 Cong., 2 Sess., p. 14214.

45. Caridi, *Korean War and American Politics,* p. 75.

46. Ibid., pp. 116, 119, 93.

47. Poder, "Senatorial Career of William Jenner," p. 90; Goldman, *The Crucial Decade—And After,* p. 203.

48. William Manchester, *American Caesar: Douglas MacArthur, 1880-1964* (Boston: Little, Brown, 1978), p. 661.

49. Vandenberg, *Private Papers of Senator Vandenberg,* p. 548; Cecil W. Crabb, Jr., *Bipartisan Foreign Policy: Myth or Reality?* (Evanston, Ill.: Row, Patterson, 1957), p. 200.

50. *Cong. Record,* 81 Cong., 1 Sess., pp. 33449, 4514.

51. *Newsweek,* Aug. 25, 1950, p. 28.

52. *NYT,* Nov. 4, 1950, p. 7.

53. *Chicago Tribune,* Nov. 9, 1950, p. 16; *Theoharis,* The Yalta Myths, pp. 102-04.

54. Daniel Reed to Bertrand Snell, Feb. 20, 1951, Box 49, Reed Papers.

55. Herbert Hoover, "Our National Policies in This Crisis," *Vital Speeches* 17 (Jan. 1, 1951): 165-67.

56. RT to Robert H. Dent, Apr. 6, 1951, Box 1094, RTP; and *Cong. Record,* 82 Cong., 1 Sess., pp. 58, 56, 61.

57. Stromer, *The Making of a Political Leader,* p. 131.

58. *Cong. Record,* 82 Cong., 1 Sess., pp. 1719, 686, 1711, 1582.

59. RT to Herbert Bayard Swope, Jan. 13, 1951, Box 1045, RTP; *Cong. Record,* 82 Cong., 1 Sess., p. 1122; Poole, "The Quest for a Republican Foreign Policy," p. 378.

60. Robert Taft, *A Foreign Policy for Americans* (Garden City, N.Y.: Doubleday, 1951),

p. 36; Arthur M. Schlesinger, Jr., *The Imperial Presidency* (Boston: Houghton Mifflin, 1973), p. 140.

61. Hamby, *Beyond the New Deal*, p. 241.

62. White, *The Taft Story*, p. 80.

63. *NYT*, Feb. 18, 1951, IV-3.

Chapter 5

1. Dwight D. Eisenhower, *At Ease: Stories I Tell to My Friends* (Garden City, N.Y.: Doubleday, 1967), pp. 370-71; Dwight D. Eisenhower, *Mandate for Change, 1953-1956* (Garden City, N.Y.: Doubleday, 1963), pp. 13-14.

2. L. Richard Guylay Oral History Interview, DDEL.

3. George W. Malone to Ben Tate, Mar. 15, 1951, Box 534, RTP; David S. Ingalls to RT, Nov. 15, 1951, Box 532, RTP.

4. George Creel to Karl E. Mundt, Mar. 7, 1952, and Karl E. Mundt to George Creel, Mar. 11, 1952, George Creel Papers, Library of Congress.

5. George Creel to Karl E. Mundt, March 7, 1952, Box 4, Creel Papers; John Hamilton to Julius Klein, Mar. 28, 1952, and Julius Klein to John Hamilton, Mar. 17, 1952, Box 380, RTP.

6. George Creel to Herbert Hoover, Dec. 11, 1951, Box 4, Creel Papers.

7. Ben E. Tate to RT, Dec. 16, 1951, Box 1120, RTP; Tom E. Coleman to RT, Dec. 26, 1951, Box 1052, RTP; RT to Herbert Hoover, Dec. 27, 1951, Box 484, RTP.

8. Frank E. Gannett to Douglas MacArthur, Jan. 22, 1952, Box 43, Wood Papers.

9. Karl E. Mundt to R.E. Wood, February 16, 1952, Box 12, Wood Papers.

10. *NYT*, Sept. 7, 1951, p. 11; John Marshall to David S. Ingalls, Sept. 10, 1951, Box 533, RTP.

11. J.D. Hamilton to Douglas MacArthur, Oct. 10, 1951, RG 5, MacArthur Papers.

12. John D.M. Hamilton to Roy Dunn, Dec. 10, 1951, Box 532, RTP.

13. John B. Hollister to RT, Dec. 18, 1951, Box 532, RTP.

14. *NYT*, Feb. 24, 1952, IV-3.

15. Douglas MacArthur to Col. Earl H. Blaik, Jan. 31, 1952, RG 10, MacArthur Papers.

16. Clarence J. Brown to Walter C. Plouser, Mar. 26, 1952, Box 18, Clarence J. Brown Papers, Ohio Historical Society, Columbus; *NYT*, Jan. 18, 1952, p. 19.

17. Albert Wedemeyer to RT, Nov. 8, 1952, PPI, Box 543, Hoover Papers.

18. John Taber to George B. Williams, Feb. 5, 1952, Box 69, Taber Papers.

19. James P. Selvage to L. Richard Guylay, Feb. 11, 1952, Box 531, RTP.

20. William Loeb to Douglas MacArthur, Jan. 17, 1952, RG 10, MacArthur Papers; John B. Hollister, "Memorandum of Trip to New Hampshire," Apr. 6, 1951, Box 491, RTP.

21. Clarence J. Brown to Walter C. Plouser, Mar. 26, 1952, Box 18, Brown Papers.

22. Ibid.

23. Paul T. David, Malcolm Moos, and Ralph M. Goldman, *Presidential Nominating Politics in 1952,* Vol I: *The National Story* (Baltimore: Johns Hopkins University Press, 1954), p. 50; Tom E. Coleman to David S. Ingalls, Sept. 25, 1951, Box 531, RTP.

24. David, Moos, and Goldman, *Presidential Nominating Politics in 1952,* Vol III: *The South*, pp. 325-26; *NYT*, June 22, 1952, IV-1.

25. *NYT*, June 6, 1952, p. 12; David, Moos, and Goldman, *Presidential Nominating Politics in 1952,* Vol. I: *The National Story*, p. 52.

26. *NYT*, June 7, 1952, p. 1.

27. *Chicago Tribune*, July 8, 1952, p. 16.

28. *Philadelphia Inquirer*, July 7, 1952, p. 2.

29. *Chicago Tribune*, July 8, 1952, p. 16.

30. *NYT*, July 6, 1952, IV-3.

31. Tom Coleman to Clarence Brown, July 14, 1952, Box 531, RTP.

32. L. Richard Guylay Oral History Interview, DDEL.

33. Manchester, *American Caesar,* p. 689.

34. RT, "Analysis of the Results of the Chicago Convention," Box 488, RTP.

35. Interview with John W. Bricker, Nov. 2, 1978.

36. R.E. Wood to R.R. McCormick, May 2, 1952, Box 11, Wood Papers.

37. Wedemeyer Oral History Interview, Herbert Hoover Library; RT, "Analysis of the Results of the Chicago Convention," Box 488, RTP.

38. David, Moos, and Goldman, *Presidential Nominating Politics in 1952,* Vol. I: *The National Story,* p. 97.

39. Richard M. Nixon, *RN: The Memoirs of Richard Nixon* (New York: Grosset and Dunlap, 1978), p. 190.

40. Bernard DeVoto, "The End of the Stalwarts," *Harper's* 204 (Sept. 1952): 78-81.

41. Richard Rovere, "Letter from Chicago," *New Yorker* 28 (July 19, 1952): 75.

42. Wayne Morse, "The G.O.P. Platform," *New Republic* 127 (Aug. 4, 1952): 12.

43. RT, "Analysis of the Results of the Chicago Convention," Box 488, RTP.

44. Walter S. Hallanan to Ben E. Tate, Aug. 4, 1952, Box 463, RTP; Herbert Hoover to Victor Emanuel, July 22, 1952, PPI, Box 325, Hoover Papers; A.C. Wedemeyer to Douglas MacArthur, Aug. 11, 1952, RG 10, MacArthur Papers.

45. *US News and World Report,* Aug. 1, 1952, p. 40.

46. *NYT,* Aug, 1, 1952, p. 1; B.C. Reece to RT, Aug. 22, 1952, File 62.12.134, Reece Papers; John Taber to Paul Taber, July 13, 1952, Box 69, RTP; A.C. Wedemeyer to Douglas MacArthur, Aug. 11, 1952, RG 10, MacArthur Papers.

47. DDE to Paul G. Hoffman, July 17, 1952, Box 10, ACW Administrative File, DDEP, DDEL.

48. Richard H. Rovere, *Affairs of State: The Eisenhower Years* (New York: Farrar, Straus and Cudahy, 1956), p. 40; Robert Humphreys to Sherman Adams, Jan. 30, 1959, Box 3, Arthur Summerfield Papers, DDEL.

49. *NYT,* Aug. 26, 1952, p. 8.

50. *Time,* Sept. 22, 1952, p. 24.

51. Rovere, *Affairs of State,* p. 105.

52. RT to Cole J. Younger, Aug. 7, 1952, Box 484, RTP.

53. RT to John D.M. Hamilton, Sept. 4, 1952, Box 533, RTP; RT to B. Carroll Reece, Aug. 14, 1952, File 62.12.431, Reece Papers.

54. RT to Everett Dirksen, Aug. 14, 1952, Box 1225, RTP; RT to Thomas E. Coleman, Aug. 14, 1952, Box 483, RTP.

55. RT to Albert Hawkes, Sept. 18, 1952, Box 483, RTP; L. Richard Guylay Oral History Interview, DDEL; Patterson, *Mr. Republican,* p. 578.

56. Howard Buffett to Douglas MacArthur, Sept. 18, 1952, RG 10, Box 2, MacArthur Papers.

57. *NYT,* Oct. 11, 1952, p. 13; RT to W.G. Skelly, Nov. 15, 1952, Box 484, RTP; A.C. Wedemeyer to Douglas MacArthur, Sept. 18, 1952, and Oct. 21, 1952, RG 10, Box 10, MacArthur Papers; James H. Rand to R.E. Wood, Oct. 8, 1952, Box 10, Wood Papers.

58. Sherman Adams to Walter J. Kohler, Sept. 9, 1952, Official File 138-c-4, Republican Presidential Campaign (1), Box 711, DDEP; O'Brien, *McCarthy and McCarthyism in Wisconsin,* p. 139.

59. *NYT,* Nov. 2, 1952, IV-1 and Oct. 11, 1952, p. 8; Norman A. Graebner, *The New Isolationism: A Study in Politics and Foreign Policy Since 1950* (New York: Ronald Press, 1956), p. 99.

60. *NYT,* Oct. 26, 1952, p. 72.

61. A.C. Wedemeyer to Herbert Hoover, Oct. 6, 1952, PPI, Box 549, Hoover Papers.

62. Schlafly, *A Choice Not an Echo,* p. 65.

63. *NYT,* Oct. 26, 1952, p. 72.

64. *NYT,* Nov. 6, 1952, p. 1.

65. "Perhaps the G.O.P. Worried Too Much," *Saturday Evening Post* 221 (Dec. 3, 1955): 10; Patterson, *Mr. Republican,* p. 580; Louis Harris, *Is There a Republican Majority? Political Trends, 1952-1956* (New York: Harper, 1954), pp. 56-57.

66. Herbert Hoover to Joseph N. Pew, Jr., Nov. 10, 1952, PPI, Box 466, Hoover Papers.

67. RT to Frank Whetstone, Dec. 1, 1952, Box 373, RTP; RT to Edward W. Allen, Nov. 13, 1952, Box 483, RTP.

68. Harris, *Is There a Republican Majority?,* p. 204.

Chapter 6

1. *NYT,* Nov. 8, 1952, IV-2.

2. RT to John T. Graves, Dec. 24, 1952, Box 52, RTP.

3. RT to Gen. A.C. Wedemeyer, Dec. 6, 1952, Box 483, RTP.

4. RT to James R. Clark, Dec. 6, 1952, Box 483, RTP.

5. *US News and World Report,* Dec. 12, 1952, p. 19; *NYT,* Dec. 3, 1952, p. 1.

6. RT to Kendall M. Gillette, Jan. 27, 1953, Box 1297, RTP: RT to Richard S. Wilcox, Dec. 27, 1952, Box 404, RTP.

7. RT to R.B. Snowden, Dec. 6, 1952 and RT to Wallace D. Malone, Dec. 6, 1952, Box 1206, RTP.

8. RT to Vernon Romney, Dec. 5, 1952, Box 484, RTP; RT to John Temple Graves, Dec. 2, 1952, Box 1205, RTP.

9. Henry C. Dworshak to RT, Dec. 1, 1952, Box 1225, RTP.

10. RT to Walter S. Hallanan, Dec. 27, 1952, Box 1165, RTP.

11. *NYT,* Dec. 13, 1952, p. 12.

12. RT to William Loeb, Dec. 19, 1952, Box 483, RTP.

14. E.D. Millikin to Frank Carlson, Nov. 13, 1952, Box 92.9, Frank Carlson Papers, Kansas Historical Society, Topeka.

15. Joseph Martin, *My First Fifty Years in Politics* (New York: McGraw-Hill, 1960), p. 232.

16. *NYT,* Jan. 21, 1953, p. 20.

17. *Washington Post,* Feb. 3, 1953, pp. 1, 9.

18. Herbert S. Parmet, *Eisenhower and the American Crusades* (New York: Macmillan, 1972), p. 218.

19. Daniel Reed to Roy E. Brownell, Jan. 19, 1953, Box 47, Reed Papers.

20. Robert J. Donovan, *Eisenhower: The Inside Story* (New York: Harper, 1956), p. 60.

21. RT to Walter Harnischfeger, Nov. 17, 1953, Box 1249, RTP; RT to Edmond E. Lincoln, Feb. 12, 1953, RTP, Box 1316.

22. Donovan, *Eisenhower,* p. 111.

23. DDE Diaries, May 1, 1953, Box 1, DDEP.

24. John Taber to Daniel A. Reed, June 29, 1953, and Daniel A. Reed to John Taber, June 27, 1953, Box 155, Taber Papers.

25. *NYT,* July 12, 1953, IV-2; DDE to Daniel Reed, Aug. 8, 1953, Box 22, Reed Papers.

26. *Cong. Record,* 83 Cong., 1 Sess., p. 2285.

27. RT to Don Rowley, Apr. 15, 1953, Box 123, RTP.

28. *US News and World Report,* Apr. 3, 1953, p. 89; White, *The Taft Story,* p. 239; Graebner, *The New Isolationism,* p. 134.

29. *Human Events* 10 (Apr. 1, 1953).

30. White, *The Taft Story,* p. 248.

31. Donovan, *Eisenhower,* pp. 136-37.

32. *US News and World Report,* June 5, 1953, pp. 37-38.

33. RT to Herbert Hoover, June 5, 1953, PPI, Box 529, Herbert Hoover Papers; RT to Eustace Seligman, June 5, 1953, Box 1264, RTP.

34. RT to A.G. Spieker, Apr. 8, 1953, Box 1264, RTP; RT to Homer T. Bone, July 1953, Box 98, RTP.

35. Eisenhower, *Mandate for Change,* p. 219.

36. DDE Diary, Apr. 1, 1953, Box 1, DDEP.

37. RT to Col. Cecil B. Highland, Feb. 12, 1953, Box 1299, RTP; RT to French Jenkins, Apr. 8, 1953, Box 1298, RTP; RT to Felix Morley, June 29, 1953, Box 5, Morley Papers.

38. *NYT,* May 13, 1953, IV-3 and July 19, 1953, IV-3.

39. *Human Events* 10 (Aug. 12, 1953).

40. DDE Diary, June 1, 1953, Box 1, DDEP.

41. *Washington Post,* July 20, 1953, p. 6.

42. Rovere, "Letter from Chicago," *New Yorker* 28 (July 18, 1952): 74.

43. Victor Emanuel to Herbert Hoover, Aug. 1, 1958, PPI, Box 325, Herbert Hoover Papers.

44. *NYT,* July 19, 1953, IV-3.

45. White, *The Taft Story,* p. 273.

Chapter 7

1. DDE Diary, July 24, 1953, Box 1, DDEP; Sherman Adams, *First Hand Report: The Story of the Eisenhower Administration* (New York: Harper, 1961), p. 104; John W. Bricker to Jack Kuhn, Aug. 20, 1954, and John W. Bricker to Mr. and Mrs. Frank Hoycross, Aug. 11, 1954, Box 113, Bricker Papers.

2. DDE Diary, July 24, 1953, Box 1, DDEP.

3. Donovan, *Eisenhower,* p. 105.

4. DDE to William Robinson, Mar. 12, 1954, DDE Diary, Box 3, DDEP; Theoharis, *The Yalta Myths,* p. 185.

5. Rovere, *Senator Joe McCarthy,* p. 188; Griffith, *The Politics of Fear,* p. 210.

6. RT to Don Rowley, Apr. 15, 1953, Box 2141, RTP.

7. Griffith, *The Politics of Fear,* p. 200; Donovan, *Eisenhower,* p. 257; DDE to William Robinson, Mar. 12, 1954, DDE Diary, Box 3, DDEP.

8. Griffith, *The Politics of Fear,* p. 219; Karl E. Mundt to Len Hall, Thanksgiving Day, 1953, and Karl E. Mundt to Len Hall, Dec. 13, Box 3, Leonard Hall Papers, DDEL.

9. *Chicago Tribune,* Feb. 25, 1954, p. 14.

10. Griffith, *The Politics of Fear,* p. 247.

11. John Taber to Mrs. John D. Anderson, Apr. 19, 1954, John Taber to G.W. Briggs, Mar. 18, 1954, John Taber to Miss Jean W. Miller, June 9, 1954, Box 108, Taber Papers.

12. Griffith, *The Politics of Fear,* p. 271.

13. Donovan, *Eisenhower,* p. 249; *Human Events* 10 (Aug. 12, 1953).

14. *US News and World Report,* Mar. 5, 1954, pp. 71, 73.

15. James L. McConaughy, Jr., "While Eisenhower Proposes the Old Guard Disposes," *Life* 36 (June 21, 1954): 121.

16. Clare E. Hoffman to Len Hall, Sept. 8, 1953, Box 80, Hall Papers.

17. Robert K. Bingham, "Westbrook Pegler and that Man in the White House," *The Reporter* 11 (Aug. 17, 1954): 35-36; *Newsweek,* Mar. 8, 1954, p. 74.

18. DDE Diaries, Apr. 1, 1953, Box 1, DDEP; *Time,* May 17, 1954, p. 24.

19. McConaughy, "While Eisenhower Proposes the Old Guard Disposes," p. 139.

20. Theodore H. White, "Pivotal Campaign in Illinois: Joe Meek vs. Paul Douglas," *The Reporter* 11 (Oct. 17, 1954): 35-36; "Interview between the President, Joseph T. Meek and Senator Dirksen," Apr. 28, 1954, Ann Whitman Administration Diary, Box 2, DDEP; Joseph T. Meek to Robert Humphreys, Dec. 3, 1954, Box 3, Joseph T. Meek Papers, Chicago Historical Society, Chicago.

21. *NYT,* Nov. 21, 1954, IV-3, and Nov. 14, 1954, IV-5.

22. DDE to William E. Robinson, Mar. 12, 1954, DDE Diary, Box 3, DDEP.

23. Bricker Oral History Interview, DDEL; *Cong. Record,* 83 Cong., 2 Sess., pp. 16284, 16010, 5610; Interview with John W. Bricker, Nov. 2, 1978.

24. *Cong. Record,* 83 Cong., 2 Sess., p. 16005.

25. Ibid., pp. 16001, 12737, 16000.

26. Ibid., p. 16001; Griffith, *The Politics of Fear,* p. 310.

27. *NYT,* Dec. 3, 1954, p. 14.

28. *Milwaukee Sentinel,* Nov. 16, 1954, p. 8; Poder, "The Senatorial Career of William E. Jenner," p. 271; Edward A. Keller Oral History Interview, Box 11, HHL.

29. *Cong. Record,* 83 Cong., 2 Sess., p. 16030; *NYT,* Dec. 21, 1954, p. 1 and Nov. 5, 1954, Box 2, DDEP.

30. DDE Diary, Jan. 18, 1954, Box 23, DDEP; DDE to William E. Robinson, Mar. 12, 1954, DDE Diary, Box 2, DDEP; DDE Diary, June 15, 1954, Box 2, DDEP.

31. DDE to Alfred M. Gruenther, July 7, 1954, DDE Diary, Box 4, DDEP.

32. *NYT,* Dec. 5, 1954, p. 1.

33. *Time,* Dec. 13, 1955, p. 1.

34. *Chicago Tribune,* Feb. 18, 1955, p. 1.

35. *NYT,* Feb. 18, 1955, p. 7, and Feb. 15, 1955, p. 16; Henry Cabot Lodge to DDE, Feb. 14, 1955, Ann C. Whitman Administration Series, Box 27, DDEP.

36. DDE to Joseph W. Martin, Aug. 11, 1955, Box 38, Joseph Martin Papers.

37. L. Brent Bozell, "National Trends," *National Review* 1 (Nov. 19, 1955): 12; *NYT,* Nov. 6, 1955, p. 67.

38. *Time,* Sept. 19, 1955, p. 20.

39. *NYT,* Mar. 2, 1956, p. 15.

40. Nixon, *RN,* p. 170; Ann Whitman Diary, Feb. 9, 1956, Box 8, DDEP.

41. *NYT,* Aug. 21, 1956, p. 15.

42. Selig Harrison, "A Talk with Arthur Larson," *New Republic* 145 (Sept. 3, 1956): 6; *National Review* 2 (June 27, 1956): 5.

43. Arthur Larson, *A Republican Looks at His Party* (New York: Harper, 1956): 5.

44. *National Review,* 2 (Sept. 8, 1956): 9; Stewart Alsop, "Just What is Modern Republicanism," *Saturday Evening Post* 230 (July 27, 1957): 89; Willmore Kendall, "Case Dismissed," *National Review* 2 (July 25, 1956): 19.

45. Merlo Pusey, "The New Republicanism," *Saturday Review* 39 (July 14, 1956): 12; *Newsweek,* Sept 3, 1956, p. 33; *NYT,* Aug. 24, 1956, p. 32.

46. *Life* 41 (Sept. 3, 1956): 32.

47. John R. Schmidhauser, "Eisenhower Republicans," *The Reporter* 15 (Sept. 20, 1956): p. 27.

48. William F. Buckley, Jr., "Mr. Eisenhower and the Eisenhower Program," *National Review* 1 (Mar. 21, 1956): 10; Robert Bendiner, "All Aboard the Coattail Express," *The Reporter* 14 (June 20, 1956): 25.

49. *National Review* 2 (Oct. 27, 1956): 5.

50. B.C. Reece to Leonard Hall, Oct. 10, 1956, Box 93, Hall Papers; Katharine Kennedy Brown to Len Hall, Oct. 10, 1956, Box 92, Hall Papers.

51. Paul G. Hoffman, "How Eisenhower Saved the Republican Party," *Collier's* 138 (Oct. 26, 1956): 44, 45, 17; Martin, *My First Fifty Years in Politics,* p. 235. Ike's meditations on a possible independent candidacy were revealed months earlier in Donovan, *Eisenhower,* p. 152.

52. William F. Knowland to Len Hall, Oct. 16, 1956, Box 93, Hall Papers; John W. Bricker to Mrs. William M. Ahlstrom, Oct. 29, 1956, Box 124, Bricker Papers; Barry Goldwater to Sherman Adams, Oct. 12, 1956, and Sherman Adams to Barry Goldwater, Oct. 16, 1956, Official File C-4, Box 712, DDEP.

53. Revilo Oliver, "Chicago: The Opposition Speaks," *National Review* 3 (Feb. 23, 1957): 181; *NYT,* Oct. 13, 1956, p. 31, and Nov. 27, 1956, p. 26.

54. Wilton B. Persons, "Memorandum for the Record," Apr. 15, 1957, Ann C. Whitman Diary, Box 8, DDEP; "Diary Staff Notes," Apr. 1957, DDE Diary, Box 13, DDEP.

55. Richard Rovere, "Letter from Washington," *New Yorker* 32 (Nov. 7, 1956): 96.

56. John W. Bricker to T.K. Harris, June 22, 1954, Box 106, Bricker Papers.

57. *NYT,* Nov. 7, 1956, pp. 30, 12.

58. Herman Welker to R.E. Wood, Feb. 26, 1957, Box 20, Wood Papers.

59. *NYT,* Nov. 11, 1956, IV-5.

Chapter 8

1. Maurice Klain, "The Disarming of President Eisenhower," *The Reporter* 15 (Sept. 20, 1956): 26.

2. *NYT,* Aug. 20, 1956, p. 8; *US News and World Report,* Jan. 11, 1957, p. 71; Klain, "The Disarming of President Eisenhower," p. 26.

3. L. Brent Bozell, ". . . To See Where Sits the Wind," *National Review* 3 (May 25, 1957): 493; *NYT,* Feb. 10, 1957, p. 67.

4. C. Budington Kelland, "Has the Republican Party A Future?" *Vital Speeches of the Day* 23 (Apr. 15, 1957): 399; *Time,* May 20, 1957, p. 20; *NYT,* Feb. 17, 1957, IV-10.

5. *NYT,* Feb. 13, 1957, p. 25; *Cong. Record,* 85 Cong., 1 Sess., p. 1946.

6. *Newsweek,* Feb. 4, 1957, p. 24.

7. *US News and World Report,* May 3, 1957, pp. 126, 132; *NYT,* Mar. 13, 1957, p. 39.

8. Richard Rovere, "Letter from Washington," *New Yorker* 33 (Apr. 27, 1957): 70; *Time,* June 23, 1961, p. 15.

9. *Time,* Apr. 22, 1957, pp. 25-26; *Cong. Record,* 85 Cong., 1 Sess., p. 5262.

10. *Time,* May 20, 1957, p. 26.

11. L. Brent Bozell, ". . . To See Where Sits the Wind," p. 495.

12. L. Brent Bozell, "Wait Till Next Year: Some Notes on the 85th Congress," *National Review* 4 (Sept. 1, 1957): 362.

13. Herbert Hoover to David Lawrence, Sept. 3, 1957, PPI, Box 402, Herbert Hoover Papers; *Meet The Press* 1 (Sept. 1, 1957): 362.

14. *Business Week* No. 1462 (Sept. 7, 1957): 27; L. Brent Bozell, "The Groggy Old Party," *National Review* 4 (Nov. 23, 1957): 464.

15. *US News and World Report,* Aug. 18, 1957, p. 48; interview with John W. Bricker, Nov. 2, 1978.

16. Emmet John Hughes, *The Ordeal of Power: A Political Memoir of the Eisenhower Years* (New York: Atheneum, 1963), p. 249.

17. *Newsweek,* Aug. 5, 1957, p. 27; *National Review* 6 (Sept. 13, 1958): 173.

18. *National Review* 4 (Nov. 16, 1957): 440.

19. *Newsweek,* Apr. 19, 1958, p. 124.

20. B.C. Reece to Sterling Morton, Apr. 14, 1958, File 62.12.15, Reece Papers.

21. *Newsweek,* Sept. 22, 1958, p. 28.

22. B.C. Reece to Joseph N. Pew, Jr., June 24, 1958, File 62.12.15, Reece Papers.

23. Hughes, *Ordeal of Power,* p. 269; "Why Must Republicans Always Clobber One Another?" *Saturday Evening Post* 231 (Aug. 9, 1958): 10.

24. John W. Bricker to Walter Trohan, Dec. 3, 1958, Box 32, Trohan Papers.

25. Clarence Brown to Meade Alcorn, Nov. 10, 1958, Box 15, Brown Papers; *US News and World Report,* Mar. 16, 1959, p. 54.

26. *Wall Street Journal,* Nov. 21, 1958, p. 8.

27. *Time,* Nov. 17, 1958, p. 58.

28. John W. Bricker to Walter Trohan, Dec. 3, 1958, Box 32, Trohan Papers.

29. *NYT,* July 19, 1959, IV-11.

30. *Newsweek,* Nov. 17, 1958, p. 30.

31. L. Brent Bozell, "The 1958 Elections: Coroner's Report," *National Review* 6 (Nov. 12, 1958): 333.

32. "Happy Pair," *New Republic* 130 (Dec. 29, 1958): 2; Neil MacNeil, *Dirksen: Portrait of a Public Man* (New York: World Publishing, 1970), pp. 146-48.

33. *Time,* Jan. 19, 1959, p. 17; Martin, *My First Fifty Years in Politics,* pp. 23, 1, 5, 3.

34. Scheele, *Charlie Halleck,* p. 16; Martin, *My First Fifty Years in Politics,* p. 14; Charles Halleck Oral History Interview, DDEL.

35. *Time,* Jan. 19, 1959, p. 17.

36. *NYT,* Jan. 7, 1959, p. 25; Joseph W. Martin to A.J. Kearnes, Jan. 19, 1959, and Joseph W. Martin to Isabelle J. Jones, Jan. 9, 1959, Folder 47, Joseph Martin Papers.

37. *Newsweek,* Feb. 2, 1959, p. 21.

38. *Time,* Feb. 9, 1959, p. 14.

39. Daniel Reed to Charles Stewart Mott, Feb. 2, 1959, Box 48, Reed Papers.

40. Bryce Harlow Oral History Interview, DDEL.

41. *NYT,* Dec. 27, 1959, p. 1.

42. L. Brent Bozell, "Goldwater on the First Ballot," *National Review* 8 (June 18, 1960): 388.

43. William S. White, "Nixon: What Kind of President?" *Harper's* 214 (Jan. 1958): 30.

44. Barry M. Goldwater, *With No Apologies: The Personal and Political Memoirs of United States Senator Barry M. Goldwater* (New York: William Morrow, 1979), p. 110; *US News and World Report,* Apr. 25, 1960, p. 81.

45. *National Review* 8 (Apr. 30, 1960): 1.

46. *Time,* Aug. 1, 1960, pp. 12, 9.

47. *NYT,* July 24, 1960, pp. 1, 38; *Time,* Aug. 1, 1960, p. 12; L. Brent Bozell, "Checkmate," *National Review* 9 (Aug. 6, 1960): 3.

48. Stephen Shadegg, *What Happened to Goldwater? The Inside History of the 1964 Republican Campaign* (New York: Holt, Rinehart and Winston, 1965), p. 32.

49. *NYT,* July 28, 1960, p. 14.

50. Mayer, *The Republican Party,* p. 508.

51. L. Brent Bozell, "Goldwater's Leadership: An Assessment," *National Review* 9 (Aug. 13, 1960): 75.

52. *US News and World Report,* Nov. 21, 1960, p. 49.

53. L. Brent Bozell, "The Challenge to Conservatism, I," *National Review* 9 (Dec. 3, 1960): 343.

54. Len Hall to DDE, Nov. 11, 1960, Official File-138-C-4, Box 714, DDEP.

55. Adams, *First Hand Report,* p. 19.

56. Gary W. Reichard, *Reaffirmation of Republicanism: Eisenhower and the Eighty-third Congress* (Knoxville: University of Tennessee Press, 1975), pp. 118, 236-37.

57. Fred I. Greenstein, "Eisenhower as an Activist President: A Look at New Evidence," *Political Science Quarterly* 94 (Winter, 1979-80): 575-99; Further scholarly reevaluation is reviewed in Victor De Santis, "Eisenhower Revisionism," *Review of Politics* 38 (Apr. 1976): 190-207; and Gary W. Reichard, "Eisenhower as President: The Changing View," *South Atlantic Quarterly* 77 (Summer 1978): 265-81. Popular accounts appeared in Murray Kempton, "The Underestimation of Dwight D. Eisenhower, *Esquire* (Sept. 1967): 108; Garry Wills, *Nixon Agonistes: The Crisis of the Self-Made Man* (Boston: Houghton Mifflin, 1969).

Chapter 9

1. *Newsweek,* Nov. 14, 1960, p. 9.

2. *NYT,* Oct. 28, 1961, p. 22; *Time,* June 23, 1961, p. 12.

3. Ralph DeToledano, *The Winning Side: The Case for Goldwater Republicanism* (New York: Putnam, 1963), p. 19.

4. *Time*, Sept. 29, 1958, p. 15.

5. *Newsweek*, July 4, 1960, p. 26.

6. Barry Goldwater, *The Conscience of a Conservative* (Shepherdsville, Ky.: Victor Publishing, 1960), n.p.

7. Barry Goldwater, "A Conservative Sets Out His Credo," *New York Times Magazine*, July 31, 1961, p. 20; *US News and World Report*, Sept. 2, 1963, p. 40.

8. Goldwater, *Conscience of a Conservative*, pp. 61-62; Robert Sheehan, "Arizona Fundamentalist," *Fortune* 12 (May 1961): 139.

9. Goldwater, *Conscience of a Conservative*, p. 89; *Newsweek*, Aug. 7, 1961, p. 18.

10. Barry Goldwater, "How to Win the Cold War," *New York Times Magazine*, Sept. 17, 1961, p. 100.

11. "Blurred Image," *Commonwealth* 74 (Apr. 21, 1961): 93.

12. *New York Herald Tribune*, July 1, 1962, p. 1.

13. *Newsweek*, July 16, 1962, p. 19.

14. *NYT*, Nov. 6, 1962, p. 21 and Nov. 8, 1962, p. 21.

15. F. Clifton White, *Suite 3505: The Story of the Draft Goldwater Movement* (New Rochelle, N.Y.: Arlington House, 1967), p. 82; William Rusher, "Crossroads for the GOP," *National Review* 14 (Feb. 12, 1963): 109.

16. *NYT*, Nov. 27, 1962, p. 33; "And Don't Look," *National Review* 13 (Nov. 20, 1962): 377.

17. *Newsweek*, Nov. 19, 1962, p. 42.

18. *NYT*, Nov. 9, 1962, p. 39.

19. Virginius Dabney, "What the GOP is Doing in the South," *Harper's* 226 (May 1963): 92.

20. Ibid., Nov. 19, 1961, p. 72, and Nov. 29, 1961, p. 29; *Time*, Nov. 10, 1961, p. 53.

21. Meade C. Alcorn Oral History Interview, DDEL.

22. Ward S. Just, "'This Schizophrenia Business' Comes to the GOP," *The Reporter* 27 (Dec. 20, 1962): 24; Goldwater, "The GOP Invades the South," pp. 10, 12; *National Review* 14 (Apr. 9, 1963): 282; Ibid. 13 (Jan. 23, 1962): 4.

23. Dean Smith, *Conservatism: A Guide to its Past, Present and Future in American Politics* (New York: Avon Books, 1963): 15.

24. T. George Harris, "The Rampant Right Invades the GOP," *Look* 27 (July 16, 1963): 25.

25. George H. Nash, *The Conservative Intellectual Movement in America: Since 1945* (New York: Basic Books, 1976), pp. 58, 67, 69, 256-57.

26. Chamberlain, "The Condition of the Republicans," p. 398; RT to St. Clair Archer, July 16, 1947, Box 959, RTP; George R. Leighton to RT, Aug. 27, 1952, Box 801, RTP.

27. Nash, *The Conservative Intellectual Movement in America*, p. 157.

28. Patterson, *Mr. Republican*, p. 330.

29. M. Stanton Evans, *Revolt on the Campus* (Chicago: McGraw-Hill, 1963), p. 96.

30. *Time*, Feb. 10, 1961, p. 34; *NYT*, May 13, 1962, p. 34; Evans, *Revolt on the Campus*, p. 8.

31. *Time*, Feb. 10, 1961, p. 37.

32. Evans, *Revolt on the Campus*, pp. 39, 54.

33. Patterson, *Mr. Republican*, p. 329; William H. White, "The New Irresponsibles," *Harper's* 223 (Nov. 1961): 107; Harris, "The Rampant Right Invades the GOP," p. 20; and "Bidding for the Right-Wing Dollar," *Nation* 194 (Jan. 20, 1962): 42-43.

34. *NYT*, Feb. 7, 1962, p. 36.

35. *Newsweek*, Apr. 10, 1961, p. 30; DeToledano, *The Winning Side*, p. 12.

36. Henry C. Dworshak to RT, Dec. 1, 1952, Box 1225, RTP.

37. Goldwater, *With No Apologies*, p. 158; White, *Suite 3505*, p. 86.

38. *US News and World Report,* Mar. 18, 1963, p. 43, and Dec. 4, 1961, p. 36; Goldwater, *With No Apologies,* p. 158; White, *Suite 3505,* p. 145.

39. *Newsweek,* July 22, 1963, p. 19.

40. *NYT,* July 15, 1963, p. 23.

41. Ibid., July 17, 1963, p. 17, July 15, 1963, p. 23, July 19, 1963, p. 54; *Newsweek,* July 29, 1963, p. 19.

42. L. Brent Bozell, "The Challenge to Conservatives, II," *National Review* 10 (Jan. 14, 1961): 12.

43. Robert D. Novak, *The Agony of the G.O.P. 1964* (New York: MacMillan, 1965), pp. 236-37.

44. White, *Suite 3505,* p. 82.

45. *New York Herald Tribune,* Dec. 5, 1962, p. 62.

46. Barry Goldwater to William A. Rusher, Jan. 22, 1963, Box 18, F. Clifton White Papers, Olin Library, Cornell University, Ithaca, N.Y.; Rusher, "Suite 3505," *National Review* 16 (Aug. 11, 1964): 685.

47. F. Clifton White to Barry Goldwater, Jan. 31, 1963, and William Rusher to Barry Goldwater, Jan. 23, 1963, Box 18, F. Clifton White Papers.

48. *NYT,* Sept. 27, 1963, p. 28; *New York Herald Tribune,* May 26, 1963, p. 16; White, *Suite 3505,* pp. 148, 215.

49. *NYT,* Oct. 25, 1963, p. 18.

50. White, *Suite 3505,* p. 253; Shadegg, *What Happened to Goldwater?* pp. 73, 74; *US News and World Report,* Dec. 21, 1964, p. 56; *NYT,* Dec. 20, 1963, IV-5, and Oct. 10, 1964, p. 14.

51. *US News and World Report,* Dec. 21, 1964, p. 56.

52. Ibid., Jan. 13, 1964, p. 19.

Chapter 10

1. Barry Goldwater to Arthur Summerfield, Feb. 14, 1964, Box 13, Robert Humphreys Papers, DDEL.

2. Peter O'Donnell to Barry Goldwater, Jan. 12, 1964, Box 9, F. Clifton White Papers.

3. Charles Mohr, "Close Look at a Puzzled Candidate," *New York Times Magazine,* May 17, 1964, p. 11.

4. *National Review* 16 (Mar. 12, 1964): 218; *National Review Bulletin* 16 (Mar. 31, 1964): 5; *NYT,* Mar. 11, 1964, p. 1.

5. William F. Rickenbacker, "Looking Up: A Visit to GHQ," *National Review* 16 (May 5, 1964): 354.

6. White, *Suite 3505,* p. 370.

7. *Time,* May 25, 1963, p. 24; *NYT,* Feb. 20, 1964, p. 18.

8. *NYT,* May 26, 1964, p. 23; *Time,* June 5, 1964, p. 20.

9. *Time,* June 19, 1964, p. 15.

10. Novak, *The Agony of the GOP, 1964,* p. 272; Mohr, "Close Look at a Puzzled Candidate," p. 102; Steven Shadegg to Richard D. Kleindienst, Mar. 3, 1964, Box 8, F. Clifton White Papers.

11. *Newsweek,* June 22, 1964, p. 25.

12. *NYT,* June 16, 1964, p. 1.

13. Rowland Evans and Robert Novak, "The Men Around Goldwater," *Saturday Evening Post* 237 (Oct. 24, 1964): 34; *NYT,* Feb. 2, 1964, p. 1; *Chicago Tribune,* July 1, 1964, p. 1.

14. "Memo to Goldwater Chairmen: Possible Opposition Tactics," July 1, 1964 Box 7, F. Clifton White Papers; *Los Angeles Times,* July 12, 1964, p. 3.

15. *NYT,* July 14, 1964, p. 22.

16. *NYT,* Oct. 24, 1964, IV-6.

17. Shadegg, *What Happened to Goldwater?,* p. 160.

18. *NYT,* July 15, 1964, p. 1, and July 16, 1964, p. 1.

19. *NYT,* July 17, 1964, p. 10.

20. *NYT,* July 18, 1964, p. 6, and July 17, 1964, p. 1; Richard H. Rovere, *The Goldwater Caper* (New York: Harcourt, Brace and World, 1965), p. 95.

21. *Chicago Tribune,* July 16, 1964, p. 16.

22. "Focus on Nov. 3," *National Review* 16 (Aug. 25, 1964): 711.

23. *US News and World Report,* Aug. 24, 1964, p. 34.

24. *Newsweek,* Dec. 14, 1964, pp. 26-27.

25. *NYT,* Aug. 16, 1964, IV-4; *Newsweek,* Aug. 24, 1964, p. 20.

26. Theodore H. White, *The Making of a President 1964* (New York: Atheneum, 1965), p. 316; *NYT,* July 19, 1964, IV-3; *Washington Post,* Nov. 12, 1964, p. 1.

27. *Washington Post,* Sept. 25, 1964, p. 1.

28. Ibid., July 28, 1964, p. 26 and Sept. 13, 1964, p. 5.

29. Rovere, *The Goldwater Caper,* p. 148.

30. Barry Goldwater to Walter Thayer, Nov. 16, 1964, Box 39, Walter Trohan Papers, Herbert Hoover Presidential Library.

31. *Fortune* 70 (Aug. 1964): 100.

32. *Washington Post,* Sept. 24, 1964, A-21.

33. *NYT,* Nov. 1, 1964, p. 10.

34. *Washington Post,* Nov. 3, 1964, p. 13.

35. *US News and World Report,* Feb. 21, 1963, p. 68.

36. *NYT,* Nov. 5, 1964, p. 20.

37. Ibid., Nov. 1964, p. 38.

38. *Los Angeles Times,* Nov. 8, 1964, E-6.

39. William F. Buckley, Jr., "Senator Goldwater and the Backbiters," *National Review* 17 (Jan. 12, 1965): 16.

40. *Chicago Tribune,* Nov. 5, 1964, p. 20; *Washington Post,* Nov. 5, 1964, p. 5; "The Election," *National Review* 16 (Nov. 17, 1964): 1000; *US News and World Report,* Nov. 16, 1964, p. 77.

41. *Newsweek,* Feb. 1, 1964, p. 21.

42. Katharine Kennedy Brown to Barry Goldwater, Jan. 7, 1965, Barry Goldwater Papers, Reel No. 1 of microfilm copies available at Olin Library, Cornell University, Ithaca, N.Y.

43. M. Stanton Evans, *The Future of Conservatism: From Taft to Reagan and Beyond* (New York: Holt, Rinehart and Winston, 1968), p. 199; Karl Hess, *In a Cause that Will Triumph: The Goldwater Campaign and the Future of Conservatism* (New York: Doubleday, 1967), pp. 102-32.

44. *Newsweek,* July 27, 1964, p. 84; Barry Goldwater to Westbrook Pegler, June 9, 1964, Box 37, James Westbrook Pegler Papers, Herbert Hoover Presidential Library.

45. Albert B. Fay to Barry Goldwater, Dec. 29, 1964, Reel No. 1, Goldwater Papers.

46. *Los Angeles Times,* Nov. 6, 1964, II-5; *NYT,* Nov. 4, 1964, p. 23; *New York Herald Tribune,* Jan. 15, 1965, p. 33.

47. *NYT,* Nov. 23, 1964, p. 42.

48. Karl A. Lamb, "Under One Roof: Barry Goldwater's Campaign Staff" in *Republican Politics: The 1964 Campaign and its Aftermath for the Party,* ed. by Bernard Cosman and Robert J. Huckshorn (New York: Frederick A. Praeger, 1968), p. 42; Herbert E. Alexander, "Money and Votes: Party Finance, 1964," ibid., pp. 116, 117, 149; "The Election," *National Review* 16 (Nov. 17, 1964): 1001.

49. Barry Goldwater to Gladys Kelleher, April 15, 1965, Reel No. 4, Goldwater Papers.

Chapter 11

1. *NYT,* Nov. 15, 1964, p. 1, Nov. 11, 1964, p. 1; *Newsweek,* Nov. 16, 1964, p. 25, Nov. 9, 1964, p. 32; David S. Broder and Stephen Hess, *The Republican Establishment: The Present and Future of the GOP* (New York: Harper and Row, 1967), pp. 254, 277.

2. *US News and World Report,* Nov. 23, 1964, p. 42, Dec. 21, 1964, p. 47; Mrs. Elmer M. Smith to Barry Goldwater, Dec. 26, 1964, Reel No. 1, Goldwater Papers.

3. *Newsweek,* Nov. 30, 1964, p. 106.

4. *NYT,* Nov. 29, 1964, IV-5; *Time,* Jan. 8, 1965, p. 18; "Realignment," *National Review* 21 (Dec. 1, 1964): 1047.

5. *Cong. Record,* 89 Cong., 1 Sess., pp. 1421-23; *NYT,* Jan. 13, 1965, p. 38; *Newsweek,* Jan. 25, 1965, p. 23; "GOP Shuffle," *National Review* 17 (Jan. 26, 1965): 49.

6. *Time,* Jan. 22, 1965, p. 20.

7. Charles A. Halleck to Samuel M. Lehman, Jan. 13, 1965, Halleck Papers; Scheele, *Charlie Halleck,* pp. 243, 258; "House Republicans Drop the Old Guard," *Business Week* 1845 (Jan. 9, 1965): 22; *US News and World Report,* Jan. 18, 1965, p. 36; Gerald R. Ford, "What Can Save the G.O.P.?" *Fortune* 71 (Jan. 1965): 140.

8. Broder and Hess, *The Republican Establishment,* p. 396; "Focus on Washington," *National Review* 17 (Mar. 9, 1965): 17.

9. M. Stanton Evans, "Why 14(b) Wasn't Repealed," *National Review* 18 (Mar. 8, 1966): 10; Alonzo L. Hamby, *The Imperial Years: The United States Since 1939* (New York: Weybright and Talley, 1976), p. 310.

10. *National Review Bulletin* 17 (Nov. 9, 1965): 4.

11. "Focus on Washington," *National Review* 20 (Jan. 16, 1966): 18; *National Review Bulletin* 22 (Apr. 13, 1965): 5.

12. *NYT,* Apr. 17, 1966, IV-14; Sept. 11, 1966, p. 42; Feb. 5, 1968, IV-5; May 22, 1967, p. 42.

13. M. Stanton Evans, *The Future of Conservatism,* p. 239.

14. *NYT,* Feb. 15, 1965, p. 1.

15. *Cong. Record,* 89 Cong., 2 Sess., p. 14113; *National Review Bulletin* 18 (Jan. 18, 1966): 1.

16. *National Review Bulletin* 18 (Mar. 29, 1966): 23.

17. Goldwater, *With No Apologies,* p. 210; Patterson, *Mr. Republican,* p. 611; *NYT,* Oct. 29, 1967, p. 43; M. Stanton Evans, "At Home," *National Review Bulletin* 23 (June 8, 1971): 86.

18. David S. Broder, "Bliss Rules the Elephant," *New York Times Magazine,* Mar. 25, 1965, p. 54; *NYT,* July 7, 1965, p. 9.

19. *Newsweek,* Nov. 21, 1966, p. 32; M. Stanton Evans, "From New York to California," *National Review Bulletin* 63 (Dec. 6, 1966): 5.

20. Broder and Hess, *The Republican Establishment,* p. 347; *US News and World Report,* Nov. 21, 1966, p. 41.

21. *Newsweek,* Nov. 21, 1966, p. 32; Ronald Reagan, "The Republican Party and the Conservative Movement," *National Review* 16 (Dec. 1, 1964): 1055.

22. F. Clifton White and William J. Gill, *Why Reagan Won: A Narrative History of the Conservative Movement, 1964-1981* (Chicago: Regnery Gateway, 1981), p. 87.

23. Eric Goldman, "The Liberals, the Blacks and the War," *New York Times Magazine,* Nov. 30, 1969, p. 40; "1968," *National Review* 20 (Aug. 13, 1968): 793.

24. *Newsweek,* Nov. 16, 1964, pp. 26, 31, and Nov. 9, 1964, p. 31; *NYT,* Nov. 6, 1964, pp. 1, 21.

25. Broder and Hess, *The Republican Establishment,* p. 176.

26. William Rusher, *The Making of a New Majority Party* (New York: Sheed and Ward, 1975), pp. 64-65.

27. White and Gill, *Why Reagan Won*, pp. 92, 37.

28. James J. Kilpatrick, "Random Notes from the Campaign Trail," *National Review* 20 (Dec. 3, 1968): 1212.

29. Kevin Phillips, *The Emerging Republican Majority* (New Rochelle, N.Y.: Arlington House, 1970), pp. 435, 32, 36, 57.

30. Ibid., pp. 38, 441, 180, 186.

31. *NYT,* Sept. 27, 1969, p. 14.

32. Ibid., Oct. 23, 1970, p. 46; Rusher, *The Making of a New Majority Party,* p. 71; Richard M. Scammon and Ben J. Wattenberg, *The Real Majority* (New York: Coward-McCann, 1970), pp. 20-21, 39, 73-76.

33. *NYT,* Oct. 9, 1970, p. 49.

34. Ibid., Nov. 8, 1970, IV-1.

35. Rusher, *The Making of a New Majority Party,* p. 75.

36. Patrick J. Buchanan, *Conservative Votes—Liberal Victories: Why the Right Has Failed* (New York: New York Times Book Company, 1975), p. 3.

37. White and Gill, *Why Reagan Won,* p. 132.

38. Goldwater, *With No Apologies,* p. 213.

39. *NYT,* Oct. 7, 1971, VII-5; Rowland Evans and Robert D. Novak, *Nixon in the White House: The Frustrations of Power* (New York: Random, 1971); Richard J. Whalen, *Catch the Falling Flag: A Republican's Challenge to His Party* (Boston: Houghton Mifflin, 1972), p. viii.

40. Buchanan, *Conservative Votes—Liberal Victories,* p. 147.

41. *National Review Bulletin* 23 (Nov. 26, 1971): 182.

42. Goldwater, *With No Apologies,* p. 234; *NYT,* Sept. 6, 1971, p. 8.

43. Bill Kovack, "Nixon's Top Left-Wing for William Loeb," *New York Times Magazine,* Dec. 12, 1971, p. 14; "Are the Elephant and the Donkey Twins?" *National Review* 23 (Mar. 23, 1971): 303; *Washington Star,* July 24, 1971, A-5; *National Review Bulletin* 213, (Aug. 3, 1971): 113.

44. *Washington Post,* Aug. 1, 1971, A-2; *NYT,* Mar. 3, 1969, p. 15, and Jan. 11, 1972, p. 75.

45. Anthony R. Dolan, "Scaring Mr. Nixon," ibid., Mar. 4, 1972, p. 27; Richard A. Viguerie, *The New Right: We're Ready to Lead* (Falls Church, Va.: The Viguerie Company, 1981), p. 36.

46. *NYT,* Jan. 31, 1972, p. 40.

47. Rowland Evans and Robert Novak, *The Reagan Revolution* (New York: E.P. Dutton, 1981), p. 126; *NYT,* Mar. 14, 1969, p. 14.

48. "Convention Notes," *National Review* 24 (Sept. 15, 1972), p. 991.

49. *NYT,* Jan. 15, 1973, p. 28.

50. *National Review* 25 (July 4, 1973): 721; William F. Buckley, "Understanding Conservatives," ibid. 26 (Apr. 26, 1974), p. 17.

51. Goldwater, *With No Apologies,* p. 251; *NYT,* Jan. 9, 1974, p. 1.

52. William F. Buckley, "Envoi, Spiro Agnew," *National Review* 25 (Nov. 9, 1973): 1227.

53. "The GOP and the Future," ibid, 25 (Aug. 30, 1974): 966.

54. Rusher, *The Making of a New Majority Party,* p. 93; Viguerie, *The New Right,* pp. 50-51; Goldwater, *With No Apologies,* p. 275.

55. *NYT,* July 18, 1974, p. 24.

56. Buchanan, *Conservative Votes—Liberal Victories,* p. 8; Kevin P. Phillips, *Mediacracy: American Parties and Politics in the Communications Age* (Garden City, N.Y.: Doubleday, 1975), p. 198; Rusher, *The Making of a New Majority Party,* pp. 96, 113.

57. Evans and Novak, *The Reagan Revolution,* p. 44.

58. *NYT,* Mar. 2, 1975, p. 42, and Mar. 3, 1975, p. 11.

59. Goldwater, *With No Apologies,* pp. 275-76.

60. Jules Witcover, *Marathon: The Pursuit of the Presidency, 1972-1976* (New York: Viking, 1977), p. 46.

61. George F. Will, *The Pursuit of Happiness and Other Sobering Thoughts* (New York: Harper and Row, 1978), pp. 164-65; *NYT*, Aug. 13, 1976, A-11.

62. Gerald Ford, *A Time to Heal* (New York: Harper and Row, 1979), p. 334.

63. Witcover, *Marathon*, p. 373.

64. Ibid., pp. 393, 394, 427-28, 96-98.

65. Evans and Novak, *The Reagan Revolution*, p. 58; *NYT*, May 10, 1976, p. 20.

66. Witcover, *Marathon*, p. 463; Will, *The Pursuit of Happiness and Other Sobering Thoughts*, p. 169.

67. Witcover, *Marathon*, pp. 469, 477; *NYT*, Aug. 5, 1976, p. 24.

68. Ford, *A Time to Heal*, p. 396.

69. White and Gill, *Why Reagan Won*, p. 162.

70. "Ford or Reagan?" *National Review* 28 (July 23, 1976): 768; "Republicans: 1976," ibid. 28 (Sept. 3, 1976): 938; "And the GOP," ibid. 28 (Nov. 26, 1976): 1277.

Chapter 12

1. *Newsweek*, Dec. 1, 1980, p. 30.

2. *Washington Post*, Nov. 20, 180, F-1; ibid., A-18.

3. *Newsweek*, Feb. 2, 1981, p. 55.

4. White and Gill, *Why Reagan Won*, p. 194; *Newsweek*, Nov. 7, 1977, p. 36.

5. Theodore H. White, *The Making of the President 1972* (New York: Atheneum, 1973), p. 33.

6. *National Review* 28 (Mar. 19, 1976): 9; Witcover, *Marathon*, p. 643.

7. *Newsweek*, Nov. 10, 1980, p. 28; *NYT*, Nov. 9, 1980, p. 28; *Washington Star*, Nov. 6, 1980, A-16; *Washington Post*, Nov. 6, 1980, A-21.

8. Sanford Unger, "Washington: The New Conservatives," *Atlantic* 243 (Feb. 1979): 20, 22.

9. Ibid., p. 24.

10. *Washington Post*, Dec. 3, 1980, A-2; *Newsweek*, Dec. 15, 1980, p. 30.

11. Ibid., Jan. 21, 1980, p. 39.

12. "Republicans," *National Review* 31 (Nov. 23, 1979): 1476.

13. *Washington Post*, July 17, 1980, p. 1, and July 18, 1980, A-9.

14. *Time*, Feb. 2, 1981, p. 9.

15. Evans and Novak, *The Reagan Revolution*, pp. xii, 212.

16. *US News and World Report*, May 5, 1979, p. 11, and Jan. 23, 1978, p. 25; *NYT*, Jan. 22, 1978, p. 1; *Newsweek*, Apr. 2, 1979, p. 32, and Nov. 7, 1977, p. 36.

17. *US News and World Report*, Nov. 20, 1978, pp. 20-21.

18. Viguerie, *The New Right*, p. 53; Phillips, *Mediacracy*, p. 205; Nick Kotz, "King Midas of the New Right," *Atlantic* 242 (Apr. 1978): 53.

19. Viguerie, *The New Right*, p. 56; Kotz, "King Midas of the New Right," pp. 52, 56.

20. Viguerie, *The New Right*, pp. 50, 90.

21. Ibid., n.p.

22. Ibid., p. 87; *Time*, Aug. 20, 1977, p. 20; "The Sorry State of the GOP," *New Republic* 176 (Dec. 10, 1977): 14.

23. J. Brian Smith, "The Cause vs. the Party," *Nation* 227 (Sept. 9, 1978): 208.

24. James J. Kilpatrick, "The Good Old Tide of Conservatism," *Nation's Business* 66 (Dec. 1978): 14; Alan Crawford, "A Mid-Life Crisis: Ripon Agonistes," *National Review* 26 (Sept. 14, 1978): 1154-1155; *Newsweek*, Feb. 5, 1979, p. 31.

25. White and Gill, *Why Reagan Won*, pp. 191, 203.

26. Ibid., p. 216.

27. Neal B. Freeman, "There are Losers and Losers," *National Review* 32 (Apr. 4, 1980): 318.

28. Evans and Novak, *The Reagan Revolution,* 210.

29. Richard E. Cohen, "Republican Senators Flex Their Muscles," *National Journal* 20 (Sept. 20, 1980): 1549.

30. *NYT,* June 11, 1980, A-28; White and Gill, *Why Reagan Won,* p. 282; *NYT,* June 14, 1980, A-14.

31. *NYT,* July 15, 1980, p. 8.

32. Ibid., Oct. 13, 1980, p. 19.

33. Ibid., Oct. 9, 1980, p. 8.

34. *Washington Post,* Sept. 5, 1980, p. 1, and Sept. 9, 1980, A-1.

35. *Newsweek,* Feb. 2, 1981, p. 52.

36. *NYT,* Nov. 6, 1980, A-35; *Washington Post,* Nov. 5, 1980, p. 1; *NYT,* Jan. 21, 1981, B-2.

37. Everett C. Ladd, Jr., and Charles D. Hadley, *Transformations of the American Party System: Political Coalitions from the New Deal to the 1970's* (New York: W.W. Norton, 1975), pp. 24, 334-35, 339, 344; Samuel Lubell, *The Hidden Crisis in American Politics* (New York: W.W. Norton, 1971), p. 278; Walter D. Burnham, *Critical Elections and the Mainspring of American Politics* (New York: W.W. Norton, 1970), p. 82.

38. *NYT,* Nov. 6, 1980, p. 33.

39. *Washington Post,* Nov. 12, 1980, A-10.

40. *Washington Star,* Nov. 8, 1980, A-3.

41. *Washington Post,* Nov. 9, 1980, D-7.

42. *NYT,* Nov. 9, 1980, p. 28.

43. James J. Kilpatrick, "How Real is That Trend Toward Conservatism," *Nation's Business* 66 (Apr. 1978): 13; James J. Kilpatrick, "The Good Old Tide of Conservatism," ibid. 66, (Dec. 1978): 14; *Washington Star,* Nov. 8, 1980, A-15.

44. *NYT,* Jan. 21, 1981, B-1.

45. Ibid., p. 4.

Bibliography

UNPUBLISHED SOURCES

Manuscript Collections

Alsop, Joseph and Stewart. Papers. Manuscripts Division, Library of Congress.

Bricker, John W. Papers. Ohio Historical Society, Columbus, Ohio.

Bridges, Styles. Papers. Danforth Library. New England College, Hennicker, New Hampshire.

Brown, Clarence. Papers. Ohio Historical Society, Columbus, Ohio.

Carlson, Frank. Papers. Kansas State Historical Society, Topeka, Kansas.

Creel, George. Papers. Manuscripts Division. Library of Congress.

Dirksen, Everett M. Papers (opened sections only). The Everett McKinley Dirksen Leadership Research Center, Pekin, Illinois.

Eisenhower, Dwight D. Papers. Dwight D. Eisenhower Library, Abilene, Kansas.

Gannett, Frank E. Papers. Olin Library. Cornell University, Ithaca, New York.

Goldwater, Barry Morris. Papers (microfilmed copies). Olin Library, Cornell University, Ithaca, New York.

Hall, Leonard W. Papers. Dwight D. Eisenhower Library, Abilene, Kansas.

Halleck, Charles A. Papers. Lilly Library, Indiana University, Bloomington, Indiana.

Hickenlooper, Bourke P. Papers. Herbert Hoover Presidential Library, West Branch, Iowa.

Hoover, Herbert. Papers. Herbert Hoover Presidential Library, West Branch, Iowa.

Humphreys, Robert. Papers. Dwight D. Eisenhower Library, Abilene, Kansas.

Kem, James P. Papers. University of Missouri, Columbia, Missouri.

Landon, Alfred. Papers. Kansas Historical Society, Topeka, Kansas.

MacArthur, Douglas. Papers. MacArthur Memorial Library, Norfolk, Virginia.

MacNider, Hanford. Papers. Herbert Hoover Presidential Library, West Branch, Iowa.

Manion, Clarence. Papers. Chicago Historical Society, Chicago, Illinois.

Martin, Edward. Papers. Pennsylvania State Archives, Harrisburg, Pennsylvania.

Martin, Joseph. Papers. Cushing-Martin Library, Stonehill, College Easton, Massachusetts.

Meek, Joseph T. Papers. Chicago Historical Society, Chicago, Illinois.

Miller, William E. Papers. Olin Library. Cornell University, Ithaca, New York.

Morley, Felix. Papers. Herbert Hoover Presidential Library, West Branch, Iowa.

Morton, Sterling. Papers. Chicago Historical Society, Chicago, Illinois.

Pegler, James Westbrook. Papers. Herbert Hoover Presidential Library, West Branch, Iowa.

Reece, B. Carroll. Papers. Carroll Reece Museum, East Tennessee State University, Johnson City, Tennessee.

Reed, Daniel. Papers. Olin Library, Cornell University, Ithaca, New York.

Republican National Committee. Papers. Olin Library, Cornell University, Ithaca, New York.

St. George, Katharine. Papers. Olin Library, Cornell University, Ithaca, New York.

Schoeppel, Andrew. Papers. Kansas State Historical Society, Topeka, Kansas.

Summerfield, Arthur E. Papers. Dwight D. Eisenhower Library, Abilene, Kansas.

Taber, John. Papers. Olin Library, Cornell University, Ithaca, New York.

Taft, Robert A. Papers. Manuscripts Division. Library of Congress.

Trohan, Walter. Papers. Herbert Hoover Presidential Library, West Branch, Iowa.

Veide, Harold. Papers. The Everett McKinley Dirksen Leadership Research Center, Pekin, Illinois.

White, F. Clifton. Papers. Olin Library, Cornell University, Ithaca, New York.

White, Wallace. Papers. Manuscripts Division, Library of Congress.

Wood, Robert E. Papers. Herbert Hoover Presidential Library, West Branch, Iowa.

Dissertations

Atwell, Mary Welek. "Congressional Opponents of Early Cold War Legislation." Ph.D. dissertation, Saint Louis University, 1973.

Mattern, Carolyn. "The Man on the Dark Horse: The Presidential Campaigns for General Douglas MacArthur, 1944 and 1948." Ph.D. dissertation, University of Wisconsin, 1976.

Poder, Michael P. "The Senatorial Career of William E. Jenner." Ph.D. dissertation, University of Notre Dame, 1976.

Poole, Walter S. "The Quest for a Republican Foreign Policy: 1941-1951." Ph.D. dissertation, University of Pennsylvania, 1968.

PUBLISHED SOURCES

Newspapers and periodicals proved indispensable to this work. The accounts and interpretations in the *New York Times*, the *Chicago Tribune*, *Time*, *Newsweek*, *U.S. News and World Report*, *Human Events*, and the *National Review* inform the whole book, but were especially valuable in researching the period since 1965. These newspapers and periodicals are not listed in the bibliography. However, readers will find specific citations in the notes to each chapter.

Books

Adams, Sherman. *First Hand Report: The Story of the Eisenhower Administration*. New York: Harper, 1961.

Alder, Selig. *The Isolationist Impulse: Its Twentieth Century Reaction*. New York: Aberlard-Schuman, 1957.

Alexander, Charles C. *Holding the Line: The Eisenhower Era, 1952-1961*. Bloomington: Indiana University Press, 1976.

Bachrack, Stanley D. *The Committee of One Million: "China Lobby" Politics, 1953-1971*. New York: Columbia University Press, 1976.

Bell, Daniel, ed. *The Radical Right: The New American Right*. New York: Criterion Books, 1955.

Binkley, Wilfred E. *American Political Parties: Their Natural History*. 4th ed. New York: Alfred A. Knopf, 1963.

Broder, David S., and Hess, Stephen. *The Republican Establishment: The Present and Future of the GOP*. New York: Harper and Row, 1967.

Browles, J. Allen. *The John Birch Society: Anatomy of a Protest*. Boston: Beacon Press, 1964.

Buchanan, Patrick J. *Conservative Votes—Liberal Victories: Why the Right Has Failed*. New York: New York Times Book Company (Quadrangle Books), 1975.

Buckley, William F., Jr., ed. *Odyssey of a Friend: Whittaker Chambers' Letters to William F. Buckley, Jr., 1954-1961*. New York: Putnam's, 1969.

Burnham, Walter D. *Critical Elections and the Mainspring of American Politics*. New York: W.W. Norton, 1970.

Burns, James M. *The Deadlock of Democracy: Four Party Politics in America*. Englewood Cliffs, N.J.: Prentice-Hall, 1963.

————. *Roosevelt: The Lion and the Fox*. New York: Harcourt, Brace and World, Harvest Books, 1956.

Caridi, Ronald J. *The Korean War and American Politics: The Republican Party as a Case Study*. Philadelphia: University of Pennsylvania Press, 1968.

Childs, Marquis. *Eisenhower: Captive Hero—A Critical Study of the General and the President*. New York: Harcourt, Brace and World, 1958.

Cotton, Norris. *In the Senate Amidst the Conflict and the Turmoil*. New York: Dodd, Mead, 1978.

Crabb, Cecil W., Jr. *Bipartisan Foreign Policy: Myth and Reality?* Evanston, Ill.: Row, Patterson, 1957.

Crawford, Alan. *Thunder on the Right: The "New Right" and the Politics of Resentment*. New York: Pantheon Books, 1980.

Dale, Edwin, Jr. *Conservatives in Power: A Study in Frustration*. Garden City, N.Y.: Doubleday, 1960.

David, Paul T., Malcolm Moos, and Ralph M. Goldman. *Presidential Nominating Politics in 1952*. Vol. 1: *The National Story*. Baltimore: Johns Hopkins University Press, 1954.

DeToledano, Ralph. *The Winning Side: The Case for Goldwater Republicanism*. New York: Putnam's, 1963.

Doenecke, Justus D. *Not to the Swift: The Old Isolationists in the Cold War Era*. Lewisburg, Pa.: Bucknell University Press, 1979.

Divine, Robert A. *Foreign Policy and U.S. Presidential Elections, 1940-1948*. New York: Franklin Watts, 1974.

————. *Second Chance: The Triumph of Internationalism in American During World War II*. New York: Harcourt, Brace, Jovanovich, 1970.

Donovan, Robert J. *Conflict and Crisis: The Presidency of Harry S. Truman, 1945-1948*. New York: W.W. Norton, 1977.

————. *Eisenhower: The Inside Story*. New York: Harper, 1956.

Drury, Allen. *A Senate Journal, 1943-1945*. New York: McGraw-Hill, 1963.

Eisenhower, Dwight D. *At Ease: Stories I Tell to My Friends*. Garden City, N.Y.: Doubleday, 1967.

———. *Mandate for Change, 1953-1956*. Garden City, N.Y.: Doubleday, 1963.

———. *Waging Peace, 1956-1961*. Garden City, N.Y.: Doubleday, 1965.

Epstein, Benjamin R., and Arnold Forster. *The Radical Right: Report on the John Birch Society and Its Allies*. New York: Random, 1967.

Evans, M. Stanton. *The Future of Conservatism: From Taft to Reagan and Beyond*. New York: Holt, Rinehart and Winston, 1968.

———. *Revolt on the Campus*. Chicago: McGraw-Hill, 1963.

Evans, Rowland, and Robert D. Novak. *Nixon in the White House: The Frustrations of Power*. New York: Random, 1971.

Evans, Rowland, and Robert Novak. *The Reagan Revolution*. New York: E.P. Dutton, 1981.

Feis, Herbert. *From Trust to Terror: The Onset of the Cold War, 1945-1950*. New York: W.W. Norton, 1970.

Ford, Gerald R. *A Time to Heal*. New York: Harper and Row, 1979.

Fried, Richard M. *Men Against McCarthy*. New York: Columbia University Press, 1976.

Gaddis, John Lewis. *The United States and the Origins of the Cold War, 1941-1947*. New York: Columbia University Press, 1973.

Goldman, Eric F. *The Crucial Decade—and After: America, 1945-1960*. New York: Alfred A. Knopf, 1971.

Goldwater, Barry. *The Conscience of a Conservative*. Shepherdsville, Ky.: Victor Publishing, 1960.

———. *Why Not Victory*. New York: McGraw-Hill, 1962.

———. *With No Apologies: The Personal and Political Memoirs of United States Senator Barry M. Goldwater*. New York: William Morrow, 1979.

Graebner, Norman A. *The New Isolationism: A Study in Politics and Foreign Policy since 1950*. New York: Ronald Press, 1956.

Griffith, Robert. *Politics of Fear: Joseph R. McCarthy and the Senate*. Lexington: University Press of Kentucky, 1970.

Hamby, Alonzo L. *Beyond the New Deal: Harry S. Truman and American Liberalism*. New York: Columbia University Press, 1973.

———. *The Imperial Years: The United States Since 1939*. New York: Weybright and Talley, 1976.

Harris, Louis. *Is There a Republican Majority? Political Trends, 1952-1956*. New York: Harper, 1954.

Harrison, Gordon. *Road to the Right: The Tradition and Hope of American Conservatism*. New York: William Morrow, 1954.

Hartmann, Susan. *Truman and the 80th Congress*. Columbia: University of Missouri Press, 1971.

Hess, Karl. *In a Cause that Will Triumph: The Goldwater Campaign and the Future of Conservatism*. New York: Doubleday, 1967.

Hughes, Emmet John. *The Ordeal of Power: A Political Memoir of the Eisenhower Years*. New York: Atheneum, 1963.

Johnson, Donald E. *The Republican Party and Wendell Willkie.* Illinois Studies in the Social Sciences, vol. 66. Urbana: University of Illinois Press, 1960.

Joyner, Conrad. *The Republican Dilemma: Conservatism or Progressivism.* Tucson, Ariz.: University of Arizona Press, 1963.

Kahn, E.J., Jr. *The China Hands: America's Foreign Service Officers and What Befell Them.* New York: Viking Press, 1975.

Kemp, Jack. *An American Renaissance: A Strategy for the 1980's.* New York: Harper and Row, 1979.

Kessel, John J. *The Goldwater Coalition: Republican Strategies in 1964.* New York: Bobbs-Merrill, 1968.

Ladd, Everett C., Jr., and Charles D. Hadley. *Transformation of the American Party System: Political Coalitions from the New Deal to the 1970's.* New York: W.W. Norton, 1975.

Larson, Arthur. *Eisenhower: The President Nobody Knew.* New York: Scribner's, 1968.

————. *A Republican Looks at His Party.* New York: Harper, 1956.

Lee, R. Alton. *Truman and Taft-Hartley: A Question of Mandate.* Lexington: University Press of Kentucky, 1966.

Lipset, Seymour Martin, and Earl Raab. *The Politics of Unreason: Right-Wing Extremism in America.* New York: Harper and Row, 1970.

Lodge, Henry Cabot, Jr. *As It Was: An Inside View of Politics and Power in the 50's and 60's.* New York: W.W. Norton, 1976.

Lubell, Samuel. *The Future of American Politics.* 3rd ed. New York: Harper and Row, 1965.

————. *The Hidden Crisis in American Politics.* New York: W.W. Norton, 1971.

————. *Revolt of the Moderates.* New York: Harper, 1956.

MacNeil, Neil. *Dirksen: Portrait of a Public Man.* New York: World Publishing, 1970.

McCoy, Donald R. *Landon of Kansas.* Lincoln: University of Nebraska Press, 1966.

Manchester, William. *American Caesar: Douglas MacArthur, 1880-1964.* Boston: Little, Brown, 1978.

Martin, Edward R. *Always Be On Time.* Harrisburg, Pa.: Telegraph Press, 1959.

Martin, Joseph. *My First Fifty Years in Politics.* New York: McGraw-Hill, 1960.

Mayer, George H. *The Republican Party, 1854-1966.* 2nd ed. New York: Oxford University Press, 1962.

Miles, Michael W. *The Odyssey of the American Right.* New York: Oxford University Press, 1980.

Moley, Raymond. *The Republican Opportunity.* New York: Duell, Sloan and Pearce, 1962.

Moos, Malcolm. *The Republicans: A History of Their Party.* New York: Random, 1956.

Nash, George H. *The Conservative Intellectual Movement in America: Since 1945.* New York: Basic Books, 1976.

Neal, Steve. *The Eisenhowers: Reluctant Dynasty.* New York: Doubleday, 1978.

Nixon, Richard M. *RN: The Memoirs of Richard Nixon.* New York: Grosset and Dunlap, 1978.

————. *Six Crises.* Garden City, N.Y.: Doubleday, 1962.

Novak, Robert. *The Agony of the GOP.* New York: MacMillan, 1965.

O'Brien, Michael. *McCarthy and McCarthyism in Wisconsin.* Columbia: University of Missouri Press, 1980.

Parmet, Herbert S. *Eisenhower and the American Crusades.* New York: Macmillan, 1972.

Patterson, James T. *Congressional Conservatism and the New Deal: The Growth of the Conservative Coalition in Congress, 1933-1939.* Lexington: University Press of Kentucky, 1967.

————. *Mr. Republican: A Biography of Robert A. Taft.* Boston: Houghton Mifflin, 1972.

Phillips, Cabell B. *The 1940's: Decade of Triumph and Trouble.* New York: Macmillan, 1975.

Phillips, Kevin. *The Emerging Republican Majority.* New Rochelle, N.Y.: Arlington House, 1969.

————. *Mediacracy: American Parties and Politics in the Communications Age.* Garden City, N.Y.: Doubleday, 1975.

Reichard, Gary W. *The Reaffirmation of Republicanism: Eisenhower and the Eighty-Third Congress.* Knoxville: University of Tennessee Press, 1975.

Ross, Irvin. *The Loneliest Campaign: The Truman Victory of 1948.* New York: New American Library, 1968.

Rossiter, Clinton. *Conservatism in America: The Thankless Persuasion.* 2nd ed. New York: Alfred A. Knopf, 1964.

Rovere, Richard H. *Affairs of State: The Eisenhower Years.* New York: Farrar, Straus and Cudahy, 1956.

————. *The Goldwater Caper.* New York: Harcourt, Brace and World, 1965.

————. *Senator Joe McCarthy.* Cleveland: World Publishing, Meridian Books, 1970.

Rusher, William A. *The Making of the New Majority Party.* New York: Sheed and Ward, 1975.

Safire, William. *Before the Fall: An Insider's View of the Pre-Watergate White House.* Garden City, N.Y.: Doubleday, 1975.

Scammon, Richard M., and Ben. J. Wattenberg. *The Real Majority.* New York: Coward-McCann, 1970.

Scheele, Henry Z. *Charlie A. Halleck: A Political Biography.* New York: Exposition Press, 1966.

Schlafly, Phyllis. *A Choice Not an Echo.* Alton, Ill.: Pere Marquette Press, 1964.

Schlesinger, Arthur M., Jr. *The Age of Roosevelt: The Politics of Upheaval.* Boston: Houghton Mifflin, 1960.

————, ed. *History of U.S. Political Parties.* 4 vols. New York: Chelsea House, 1973.

————. *The Imperial Presidency.* Boston: Houghton Mifflin, 1973.

Scott, Hugh. *Come to the Party.* Englewood-Cliffs, N.J.: Prentice-Hall, 1968.

Shadegg, Steven. *What Happened to Goldwater? The Inside Story of the 1964 Republican Campaign.* New York: Holt, Rinehart and Winston, 1965.

Sherwin, Mark. *The Extremists.* New York: St. Martin's Press, 1963.

Smith, Dean. *Conservatism: A Guide to Its Past, Present and Future in American Politics.* New York: Avon Books, 1963.

Stein, Herbert. *The Fiscal Revolution in America.* Chicago: University of Chicago Press, 1969.

Stromer, Marvin E. *The Making of a Political Leader: Kenneth S. Wherry and the United States Senate.* Lincoln: University of Nebraska Press, 1969.

Taft, Robert A. *A Foreign Policy for Americans.* Garden City, N.Y.: Doubleday, 1951.

Thayer, George. *The Farther Shores of Politics: The American Political Fringe Today.* New York: Simon and Schuster, 1967.

Theoharis, Athan G. *The Yalta Myths: An Issue in U.S. Politics, 1945-1955.* Columbia: University of Missouri Press, 1970.

Tompkins, C. David. *Senator Arthur H. Vandenberg: The Evolution of a Modern Republican, 1884-1945.* East Lansing: Michigan State University Press, 1970.

Vandenberg, Arthur, Jr., ed. *The Private Papers of Senator Vandenberg.* Boston: Houghton Mifflin, 1952.

Viguerie, Richard A. *The New Right: We're Ready to Lead.* Falls Church, Va.: The Viguerie Co., 1981.

Westerfield, H. Bradford. *Foreign Policy and Party Politics Pearl Harbor to Korea.* New Haven, Conn.: Yale University Press, 1955.

Whalen, Richard J. *Catch the Falling Flag: A Republican's Challenge to his Party.* Boston: Houghton Mifflin, 1972.

White, F. Clifton. *Suite 3505: The Story of the Draft Goldwater Movement.* New Rochelle, N.Y.: Arlington House, 1967.

White, F. Clifton and William J. Gill. *Why Reagan Won: The Conservative Movement, 1964-1981.* Chicago: Regnery Gateway, 1981.

White, Theodore H. *America in Search of Itself: The Making of the President, 1956-1980.* New York: Harper and Row, 1982.

———. *The Making of a President 1960.* New York: Atheneum, 1961.

———. *The Making of a President 1964.* New York: Atheneum, 1965.

———. *The Making of the President 1968.* New York: Atheneum, 1969.

———. *The Making of the President 1972.* New York: Atheneum, 1973.

White, William S. *The Taft Story.* New York: Harper and Row, 1954.

Will, George F. *The Pursuit of Happiness and Other Sobering Thoughts.* New York: Harper and Row, 1978.

Witcover, Jules. *Marathon: The Pursuit of the Presidency, 1972-1976.* New York: Viking, 1977.

Wolfskill, George. *The Revolt of the Conservatives: A History of the American Liberty League, 1934-1940.* Boston: Houghton Mifflin, 1962.

Articles

Annunziata, Frank. "The Progressive as Conservative: George Creel's Quarrel with New Deal Liberalism." *Wisconsin Magazine of History* 57 (Spring, 1974): 220-33.

Chamberlain, John. "The Condition of the Republicans." *Yale Review* 38 (March, 1949): 385-98.

Goldbloom, Maurice J. "What is the 'Right' Up To?" *Commentary* 16 (September, 1953): 207-213.

Greenstein, Fred J. "Eisenhower as an Activist President: A Look at New Evidence." *Political Science Quarterly* 90 (Winter, 1979-1980): 575-99.

Griffith, Robert. "Dwight D. Eisenhower and the Corporate Commonwealth." *American Historical Review* 87 (February, 1982): 87-122.

Moore, John. "The Conservative Coalition in the U.S. Senate." *Journal of Southern History* 33 (August 1967): 368-76.

Palermo, Patrick J. "The Midwestern Republican Tradition." *Capitol Studies* 5 (Spring, 1977): 43-56.

Reichard, Gary. "Eisenhower and the Bricker Amendment." *Prologue* 6 (Summer, 1974): 88-98.

Rudolf, Frederick. "The American Liberty League." *American Historical Review* 56 (October, 1950): 19-33.

Schonberger, Howard B. "The General and the Presidency: Douglas MacArthur and the Election of 1948." *Wisconsin Magazine of History* 57 (Spring, 1974): 201-19.

Smith, George H.E. "Bipartisan Foreign Policy in Partisan Politics." *American Perspective* 4 (Spring, 1950): 157-69.

Smuckler, Ralph H. "The Region of Isolationism." *American Political Science Review* 67 (Spring, 1950): 157-69.

Westin, Alan. "The John Birch Society." *Commentary* 32 (August, 1961): 93-104.

Index